Jim Scriv
Celia Bingham
Adrian Tennant
Steve Wasserman

Straightforward

Advanced Teacher's Book

MACMILLAN

Macmillan Education
Between Towns Road, Oxford OX4 3PP
A division of Macmillan Publishers Limited
Companies and representatives throughout the world

ISBN 978-1-4050-1084-9

First published 2008

Designed by eMC Design Ltd; www.emcdesign.org.uk

Illustrated by Asa Andersson, Rowan Barnes-Murphy, Fred Blunt, Anne Cakebread, Paul Collicutt, Chris Ede, Celia Hart, Tim Kahane, Joanna Kerr, Darren Lingard, Bill Piggins, Eric Smith.

Cover design by Macmillan Publishers Limited

Cover photography: Top line (left to right) **Bananastock**, **Photolibrary**, + (br), **Getty**/Greg Wood, **Getty**/Taxi, **Alamy**/CW Images x 2. Bottom line (left to right) **Getty**/ Photographers Choice, **Corbis**/Micha Pawlitzki/Zefa, **Corbis**/Darren Gulin, **Corbis**/A&J Verkaik, **Corbis**/Randy Faris.

Authors' acknowledgements
The authors would like to thank Julie Penn and Nick Sheard for all their support and guidance in writing this book. Thanks also to Katie Stephens for design management.

The authors and publishers would like to thank the following for permission to reproduce their photographs: **Bananastock** p236 (m, b); **BRAND X** p245; **Corbis**/ Xiaoyang Liu p243; **Getty Images** p237; **Photoalto** p236 (t); **Superstock** p222; **The Daily Telegraph**/Andrew Crowley p233

The author and publishers are grateful for permission to reprint the following copyright material:
Bicycle – lyrics and original recording by Livingston Taylor and Maggie Taylor, copyright © 1996 Morgan Creek Music, reproduced with permission. All Rights Reserved.
Housework – lyrics by Robert Palmer and Stephen Fellows, copyright © 1991 Chelsea Music Publishing and Another Planet Music, reproduced with permission. All Rights Reserved.
Housework – original recording composed by Robert Palmer/Stephen Fellows published by Heavy Nova Music/Zomba Enterprises Inc (P) 1990 the copyright in this sound recording is owned by Remlap Co. Inc under exclusive licence to EMI Records. Licensed courtesy of EMI Commercial Markets.
Jamaica Farewell – words and music by Irving Burgie, copyright © 1955; Renewed 1983 Cherry Lane Music Publishing Company, Inc. (ASCAP), Lord Burgess Music Publishing Company (ASCAP) and Dimensional Music Of 1091 (ASCAP). Worldwide Rights for Lord Burgess Music Publishing Company and Dimensional Music of 1091 Administered by Cherry Lane Music Publishing Company, Inc. International Copyright Secured. All Rights Reserved.
These Foolish Things – lyrics by Strachey/Maschwitz copyright © Lafleur Music Ltd. 1936. Reproduced by permission of Boosey & Hawkes Music Publishers Ltd.
These Foolish Things – original recording composed by Jack Strachey & Eric Maschwitz copyright © Strachey/ Maschwitz. Reproduced courtesy of EMI Records.

Extract from 'Abandoned by mother. Father unknown. Instead I have a wonderful life in England' by Elizabeth Grive copyright © Elizabeth Grive 2004, first published in The Daily Telegraph 20/09/04, reprinted by permission of the publisher.

Material 'Lonely Planet Guide to Experimental Travel' from website www.accesstoexcellence.co.uk, reprinted by permission of the publisher; Material on 'Presentation Skills' from website www.curved-vision.co.uk, reprinted by permission of the publisher; Extract from 'Letters: Waste campaign' by Sian Berry and Richard Gregory copyright © Sian Berry & Richard Gregory 2007, first published in The Independent 2/2/07, reprinted by permission of the authors; Extract from 'Stricken Atlantic rowers rescued' by Caroline Gammell, copyright © Press Association 2006, first printed in The Independent 23/1/06, reprinted by permission of Press Association; Extract from 'Squatters seize home of ill pensioner' news article copyright © The Daily Mail 2004, first published by The Daily Mail 21/7/04, reprinted by permission of Solo. Syndication; Extract from 'Young, successful – and hitting the Quarterlife Crisis' by Neil Sears copyright © 2001, first published by The Daily Mail 24/5/01, reprinted by permission of Solo Syndication; Extract from ''Blade Runner' tough to judge' by Michael Johnson copyright © Telegraph Group Limited 2007, first published in The Telegraph online 25/7/07, reprinted by permission of the publisher; Extract from 'Your business blog' by Richard Tyler copyright © Telegraph Group Limited 2007, first published in The Telegraph online 28/6/07, reprinted by permission of the publisher; Adapted *CEF* material used with kind permission from Council of Europe.

Printed and bound in Hong Kong

2012 2011 2010 2009 2008
10 9 8 7 6 5 4 3 2

Contents

		Reading & Listening	Speaking	Writing: Student's Book	Writing: Workbook
7A	**R**	*A new broom*	Talking about misbehaviour at school	A narrative p 132	Writing a narrative: using narrative tenses, linking events, describing emotion
7B	**L**	Conversation about rudeness	Discussing good and bad behaviour Selecting posters for a national campaign		
7C	**R**	*A missing person*	Ranking and comparing books		
7D	**L**	Radio news reports	Discussing law breaking ***Did you know?*** Canadian Mounties		
8A	**R**	Mr Hilditch & Robert and Lizzie	Describing people's personality and appearance		Writing a description: the five senses, participle phrases, writing a description of a visit
8B	**L**	Conversation about birth order	Discussing quotations about sisterhood ***Did you know?*** Famous American siblings		
8C	**R**	*End of a friendship*	Discussing relationships		
8D	**L**	Six people talk about being single	Discussing compatibility		
9A	**R**	*The city of tomorrow*	Submitting and presenting a plan for a new town	A letter of complaint p 134	Writing a letter of complaint: explaining the results of problems, articles
9B	**L**	Radio programme about squatting	Roleplay: viewing a property ***Did you know?*** Listed buildings		
9C	**R**	*A happy marriage*	Selecting holiday activities		
9D	**L**	Conversation about experimental travel	Ranking travel options		
10A	**R**	*Made it!*	Discussing endurance races		Writing a letter of thanks: expressions of thanks, explaining why you are grateful, writing a letter of thanks
10B	**L**	Six people talk about success	Discussing views about success		
10C	**R**	*The Wrong Guy*	Talking about problematic situations ***Did you know?*** BBC		
10D	**L**	A stabbing incident	Ordering and describing a picture story		
11A	**R**	*I wandered lonely as a cloud*	Romanticism ***Did you know?*** Romanticism	An essay p 136	Writing an essay (1): expressing a viewpoint, arguing against a viewpoint
11B	**L**	Interview with Will Ramsay	Selecting artworks for buildings		
11C	**R**	*The quietest place on earth*	Describing the thoughts of people in photos		
11D	**L**	Five people talk about the New Music Award	Presenting a music device		
12A	**L**	Twelve scientific explanations	Discussing science questions ***Did you know?*** Science in schools		Writing an essay (2): result clauses, writing an essay
12B	**R**	*Wearable electronics*	Submitting and presenting a project for a competition		
12C	**L**	Radio discussion about technology in sport	Debating technology in the home		
12D			Ranking and selecting photos ***Did you know?*** Revision quiz		

Introduction

A straightforward approach

Approaches to language teaching come and go. When I first taught English, over twenty years ago in a Moroccan high school, I and most of my colleagues used a grammar-translation approach. Since then, in a variety of institutions in many different countries, I have used audiolingual techniques in a Direct Method school, a functional-situational approach, 'hard' and 'soft' versions of the communicative approach, a lexical approach, a task-based approach and a number of combinations of all of these. Over the years, it became increasingly clear that the grail of the 'perfect' approach was elusive and unobtainable. Different things work with different students in different educational contexts. We live, as the US-based educationalist Kumaravadivelu has put it, in a 'post-method condition'. The best approach to any language teaching situation will be eclectic, drawing on a multitude of approaches and techniques, choosing and shaping them in ways that are appropriate to our own particular classrooms. The approach in *Straightforward*, therefore, is eclectic and seeks to incorporate elements from many different approaches to language teaching.

Coursebooks, of course, reflect changing fashions and in recent years we have seen examples that follow a task-based approach, a lexical approach or approaches that are driven by an analysis of computer databases. With *Straightforward*, we did not want to be restricted in this way. As students develop their language competence and their autonomy as learners, their needs will change and our approach to teaching will need to change, too. Because of this, our approach to syllabus and task design changes through the levels of the course. All of the levels share the same basic design, but the approaches to the teaching of grammar and the assumptions about students' independence, for example, are not exactly the same from one level to the next.

The features of *Straightforward* that are common to all the levels include the following:

- All lessons include a balance of language learning and language using (language work and skills work).
- There is a stronger than usual focus on vocabulary development. This involves both the learning of words and phrases and attention to how these items are used (i.e. the grammar of vocabulary). For our research, we have used the same database as the *Macmillan English Dictionary*.
- The grammatical syllabus will be familiar but it is also contemporary, reflecting insights from the analysis of language corpora.
- In every lesson, language is contextualized and presented in either a spoken or written text, and every lesson includes opportunities for either reading or listening. Word lists are provided at the end of every unit in the *Language reference* sections.
- There is a wide variety of types of text, both in terms of content and source (articles, newspaper cuttings, brochures, websites, emails, etc.). The topics are varied and the approaches to them are lively.
- Many of the texts focus on aspects of culture in the English-speaking world and encourage intercultural comparison. This work is reinforced by regular *Did you know?* sections that contain further cultural information.
- Every lesson contains opportunities for communicative practice. There are a wide variety of these speaking tasks, so that students have the opportunity to develop a range of communicative skills.

As teachers, we face many challenges in our working lives and finding the time for all that we have to do, let alone what we would like to do, is often difficult. *Straightforward* sets out to make life for teachers as easy as possible. Each lesson is presented on a double page in a clear, easy-to-use way, with each section labelled so that students know exactly what they should be focussing on. The exercises and activities are designed and written so that teachers may go into their classrooms with a minimum of preparation and come out at the end without having encountered any unpleasant surprises along the way. They do not need to spend valuable time figuring out in advance what a particular activity involves.

It would be wrong, however, to pretend that a coursebook can provide all of the answers all of the time. Particular students, particular classrooms and particular schools vary too greatly for it to be possible to provide one 'route map' that will be appropriate to everybody. For this reason, the *Straightforward Teacher's Book* provides a wealth of suggestions for ways of adapting, extending and abridging the material in the Student's Book. Even when things work very well, we still need to vary our approach from time to time so that we keep fresh, so that we keep experimenting and learning, and so that we continue to develop ourselves. So even though it won't matter if you forget to bring the Teacher's Book into class with you, I am sure that you will come to value the Teacher's Book highly as a tool for professional development.

Series authors

Philip Kerr

Roy Norris

The Common European Framework

The *Common European Framework of Reference for Languages: Learning, teaching, assessment* (CEF) of the Council of Europe is a long and commonly misunderstood document. The *CEF* is being used in many different ways in many different educational contexts around the world, but it was never intended to tell teachers what to do or how to do it. As the authors of the *CEF* point out, its objective is to raise questions, not to answer them. It is intended to describe, rather than to prescribe or proscribe. It is, in other words, exactly what it says: a document for reference. It was devised and written so that users could adapt its scaling system and descriptors critically, adapting them to the needs of their own educational contexts. Indeed, it is such a long and unwieldy document that it would be impractical and unrealistic to attempt to apply it to any educational context without adaptation and modification.

The most well-known part of the *CEF* is the scale which describes a learner's language proficiency. There are six points on this scale (A1, A2, B1, B2, C1 and C2) and these range from a very low-level beginner to a very sophisticated language user with a level that is approximately equivalent to the Cambridge Proficiency examination, for example.

These levels do not correspond to years of language learning or academic study, nor are they intended to. The vast majority of learners never reach level C2 and they do not need to either, whether it is for work or examination purposes. This majority can expect to reach the fourth or the fifth level (B2 or C1), but it will typically take them more than four or five years of school study to get there. What is more, progress in language learning does not proceed in an orderly, predictable year-by-year fashion: improvements will be more marked at some stages of learning than at others. For these reasons, it is not possible or desirable for a coursebook (which represents a year's study in most educational contexts) to correspond exactly to the Council of Europe's levels – whatever some books may claim to the contrary! Having said that, it is possible to establish broad equivalences between the levels of *Straightforward* and the Common European Framework.

Straightforward level	Common European Framework
Beginner	A1
Elementary	A1–A2
Pre-intermediate	A2–B1
Intermediate	B1
Upper Intermediate	B2
Advanced	C1

The levels in the *CEF* are described in terms of competences – what learners *can do* with the language. These *can-do* statements are extremely useful in determining course objectives, and we kept these closely in mind when we planned and wrote *Straightforward*. There are, however, two important points to bear in mind. The *can-do* statements are too numerous and too detailed for a course to attempt to work towards all of them. Some selection and modification is necessary and inevitable. Secondly, the organization of the syllabus cannot only be informed by descriptions of what a student should be able to do. The *can-do* statements are intended to describe and help in evaluation, not to determine the structure of a learning programme.

Although there can be no exact correspondence between the *can-do* lists and the organization of a coursebook, *Straightforward* reflects both the detail and the philosophy of the *CEF* in many ways. Here are a few examples:

- In line with the *CEF*, *Straightforward* takes an approach to language learning that balances the importance of knowing about the language with the need to do things with it.
- The situational activities (e.g. roleplay) directly reflect the communicative needs that are outlined in the *CEF*.
- Grammar and vocabulary are always presented and practised in such a way that the communicative value of this language is transparent to the student.
- Students are encouraged to develop their sub-skills and strategies in using the four language skills of reading, writing, speaking and listening in ways that also directly reflect the *can-do* statements in the *CEF*.
- Learning tasks that provide opportunities for students to practise the four skills, reflect the variety of text-types and interactions that are outlined in the *CEF*.
- Self-assessment checklists for each unit of the Student's Book encourage students to reflect on their language learning and language needs.

Besides the scales and the descriptions of competences, the *CEF* emphasizes the aims of language learning. Among these is the need to become independent and autonomous as a learner, and the recognition that language learning can encourage cooperation and other social values.
Our approach in *Straightforward* to the development of autonomy is a gradual one and recognizes that, at lower levels especially, many students actually want or need to be dependent for a time. We believe that independence cannot be imposed on anyone: it must be acquired. However, from the very start, we encourage students to work cooperatively in pairs and groups. In our selection of topics, texts and tasks, we have attempted to promote a knowledge of other cultures, to encourage open-mindedness and to foster respect for others.

The complete text of the *CEF* is available in print in at least eighteen languages. It is also freely available online in English and a number of other languages. For further information, go to the Council of Europe's website at www.coe.int

Methodology advances
The Common European Framework – What can an Advanced student do?

- *The Common European Framework (CEF) describes two 'Advanced' levels. These are named C1 ('Effective Operational Proficiency') and C2 ('Mastery'). The* Straightforward Advanced *Student's Book takes students through C1 level. Here is the CEF overview description of a C1 level student:*
  - Can understand a wide range of demanding, longer texts, and recognize implicit meaning.
  - Can express him/herself fluently and spontaneously without much obvious searching for expressions.
  - Can use language flexibly and effectively for social, academic and professional purposes.
  - Can produce clear, well-structured, detailed text on complex subjects, showing controlled use of organizational patterns, connectors and cohesive devices.

material from Council of Europe

- *There are some important things to understand about these. Firstly, as with all CEF descriptions, the focus is on what a student* **can do** *as opposed to simply describing 'in-the-head' language knowledge. The second important point is that these descriptions are of an effective C1 level user (but remember that this is the target that most of your students are aiming to reach) rather than where they are at the moment when they begin the course. So don't worry too much if your class doesn't seem to fully meet these criteria yet. In fact, it's also worth noting that some native speakers wouldn't meet these descriptions! At C1 level, we are talking not just about someone who can use English, but someone trained and experienced at using English skilfully to achieve specific things in some quite demanding contexts.*
- *The CEF descriptions are helpful, but, of course, quite generalized. Later in this book we'll look at some of the more detailed descriptions for specific skills.*
- *Having seen the C1 descriptions, you may be wondering what extra abilities a C2 user might have. So here, to help give you that perspective, is the equivalent description of a C2 user:*
  - Can understand with ease virtually everything heard or read.
  - Can summarize information from different spoken and written sources, reconstructing arguments and accounts in a coherent presentation.
  - Can express him/herself spontaneously, very fluently and precisely, differentiating finer shades of meaning even in more complex situations.

material from Council of Europe

Straightforward Advanced – a summary

Straightforward is a general English course aimed at adults and young adults. The Student's Book contains material for approximately 90 hours of classroom study. Extra material for practice, revision, homework and tests are found in the other components (see below).

Student's Book

There are twelve units in the Student's Book, each of which contains four lessons (A, B, C and D) and two pages of language reference. Each double-page is designed for approximately 90 minutes of classroom study.

Each unit contains:

- two to three grammar sections
- two to four vocabulary sections
- one pronunciation or speech feature section
- four to seven speaking skills sections
- two reading skills sections
- two listening skills sections
- one *Did you know?* section

The Student's Book also contains six double-page writing lessons in a separate section. The writing lessons focus on six core text types and are linked in topic to the odd-numbered units in the main body of the Student's Book. Each writing lesson includes a sample text and a focus on key language leading towards a final writing task. The writing section is designed to develop students' abilities to deal with a variety of written genres.

At the back of the Student's Book, there is one page of review exercises for each of the twelve units. Material for the communication activities and tapescripts for some of the listening exercises are found at the end of the book.

Class CDs

The three CDs contain recordings of all the listening, pronunciation and speech feature exercises in the Student's Book. The track listings are shown in the instructions for exercises in the Student's Book.

CD-ROM

The CD-ROM contains practice activities that are closely linked to the Student's Book. There are 120 activities, ten for each unit in the Student's Book. The activities practise the grammar, vocabulary and pronunciation that feature in the Student's Book. There are also additional *Listening* and *Reading* texts.

The CD-ROM has a comprehensive *Vocabulary* reference section with *Macmillan English Dictionary* definitions of all the vocabulary from the Student's Book. It also features a *Grammar* reference section with example sentences and explanations of all the grammar in the Student's Book.

The *Results* section allows students to keep a record of their score, as well as the number of times activities have been done. The CD-ROM also contains a useful *Help* section.

Portfolio

The *Straightforward* Portfolio is like a diary. In it students find:

- a place to keep their own personal record of work they do during their course.
- a place to write down their thoughts and feelings about the work they do.
- questions to encourage them to think about their English and their studies.
- some puzzles, cartoons, jokes and interesting quotations.

The Portfolio is in three sections:

1 Before the course

The introductory pages help students to analyze what they can already do in English and to set targets for the future.

2 During the course

The diary sections give students the opportunity to record their thoughts as they work through their Student's Book. There is one diary page for each lesson in the Student's Book.

3 After the course

At the end of the Portfolio there are some pages to help students analyze the progress they have made and to help them assess their English at the end of the course.

The *Straightforward* Portfolios are based on ideas in the Common European Framework (see page ix). Using the Portfolio will help your students to think more deeply about their learning and to become clearer about the progress they are making in English. Completing the diary sections in the Portfolio can help your students to learn the language better. They not only give them writing practice, but also encourage them to reflect on what they have learnt and how they have learnt it. By reflecting on the language, they are likely to understand things in more detail and to remember them better. The Portfolio is designed for students to use on their own as a personal book and diary. However, some teachers may like to include a weekly Portfolio slot in class time.

Workbook (includes audio CD)

For each lesson in the Student's Book, there is one page of exercises to provide further practice of the grammar and vocabulary.

The Workbook includes twelve additional pages of writing practice. These consolidate and extend the work of the writing lessons in the Student's Book.

The Workbook also contains supplementary reading material. There is a reading skills double-page for each of the twelve Student's Book units. There is also an excerpt from John Banville's Booker Prize winning novel, *The Sea*, which provides an opportunity for extensive reading skills practice.

The Workbook audio CD contains recordings of all the Workbook reading texts. Students are encouraged to listen and read simultaneously. In the process, they gain self-confidence and develop their ability to tackle longer texts. Dictation exercises from the Workbook are also included on this CD.

The Workbook is available with or without the answer key.

Teacher's Book (includes two resource CDs)

The Teacher's Book provides step-by-step notes for each lesson. These include:

- short lesson summaries
- answers to all exercises and explanatory language notes
- suggestions for alternative procedures
- suggestions for supplementary activities and extra discussion questions
- advice for different class types (stronger/weaker students, older/younger students, etc.)
- supplementary cultural notes
- ideas for homework and further study

The Teacher's Book also includes one photocopiable worksheet for each of the 48 lessons (including four songs). These provide further communicative practice of the language from the lesson.

Throughout the Teacher's Book, there are *Methodology Advances* sections. See page xiii for further information.

The two resource CDs contain:

- twelve unit tests
- four progress tests
- twelve self-assessment checklists
- original recordings of the four songs
- listening material for the tests

The two resource CDs are at the back of the Teacher's Book. CD 1 contains the test and self-assessment checklists, both of which can be adapted and customized to suit teachers' particular needs. CD 2 contains the audio material for the tests and recordings of the four songs from the photocopiable worksheets.

There is a test for each of the twelve units in the Student's Book. These unit tests focus on the grammar and vocabulary that has been presented in the unit.

The four progress tests (after every three units) contain separate sections to test the four skills as well as a section that focuses on language.

CD 1 also includes twelve self-assessment checklists, one for each of the Student's Book units. After they have completed a unit, the students can use the checklist to assess themselves on how well they think they can do specific things in English.

Grammar

The approach to the presentation of grammar in *Straightforward* varies, depending on a number of factors. Generally speaking, students are shown the grammatical rules and patterns before being asked to practise them. However, when the language can be considered to be 'revision', rather than 'new', a guided discovery approach is taken. Sometimes, these approaches are combined when a grammar section contains both 'revision' and 'new' language. As students progress through the levels of the course, a guided discovery approach is used more and more often. We recognize that the choice of appropriate methodology will be informed by many considerations. For this reason, the Teacher's Book contains suggestions for alternative approaches.

Every lesson with a grammar focus includes a *Grammar box*, which shows the basic rules and patterns. More detailed explanations can be found in the *Language reference* pages at the end of each unit. The Teacher's Book contains further useful language notes for the teacher.

A sequence of grammar practice exercises always follows the presentation. These include mechanical manipulation of grammatical forms and patterns, as well as more communicative practice. There are plenty of opportunities for students to personalize their use of this language. Many teachers will want to provide further practice. This can be found in the review pages, in the corresponding pages of the Workbook and in the suggestions and photocopiable pages in the Teacher's Book.

Vocabulary

We believe that vocabulary development is probably the most important task that language learners face, and, for this reason, there are more vocabulary sections in *Straightforward* than in most other coursebooks.

It is not always easy to say whether a particular language item is grammar or vocabulary. Most people would probably agree, for example, that a set of phrasal verbs should come under the heading of 'vocabulary'. But when we want students to understand how these verbs work in context (e.g. are they transitive or intransitive? are they separable or inseparable?), we seem to be moving into an area that is more grammatical. The vocabulary sections in *Straightforward* fall into two broad areas: groups of words that are related in terms of meaning, and groups of words that are related in terms of how they are used with other words (collocation, associated patterns, dependent prepositions, etc.).

In the same way that students are always asked to do something with the grammar that they have studied, vocabulary sections always include exercises that require students to use the new words. New vocabulary items are also recycled in texts, other exercises and in the Workbook material.

In the *Language reference* sections at the end of each unit, you will find a word list that contains the vocabulary items that have appeared in the unit. The red words use a simple coding system indicates how common, and therefore how useful to learn, the words are. This system is based on the *Macmillan English Dictionary*. *** words are the most common and basic words, ** words are very common words, * words are fairly common words. Both students and teachers will find the word lists useful for revision purposes.

Pronunciation & Speech feature

Each unit of *Straightforward Advanced* contains one pronunciation or speech feature section. There is no general agreement in the world of English language teaching about the best order in which to teach the various features of English pronunciation, and even at advanced level students can have problems making themselves understood. The aim of these sections is to raise students' awareness of aspects of English pronunciation that may be affecting their intelligibility and to give them some opportunities to produce English sounds, stress and intonation patterns. The speech feature sections raise awareness of grammatical as well as phonological aspects of native-speaker speech.

In addition to the time that is spent on pronunciation work in these sections, many teachers will want to integrate work on pronunciation at other times during the course. The Teacher's Book offers many suggestions for how to go about this.

Reading & listening

Language is best understood when it is seen or heard in context and every lesson in *Straightforward* contains either a reading or a listening text. The tasks that accompany these texts encourage students to get to grips with the meaning of the text before they focus on the details of the language that the texts contain. In their mother tongue, students use a range of strategies and techniques when reading or listening, and the tasks in *Straightforward* are intended to encourage students to transfer these strategies and techniques to English.

The tasks are designed so that they can be achieved without the students understanding every word of what they read or hear. It is important that students learn to tolerate *not* understanding everything they come across. Having said that, some of the tasks in *Straightforward Advanced* require a very detailed understanding of the text.

Scripts for some of the listening texts can be found at the back of the book, and these can be used to direct the students' attention to particular language items once the sequence of comprehension tasks has been completed. The scripts can also be useful in some mixed ability classes. But, as far as possible, students should be encouraged to approach the listening exercises without referring to the written version.

Speaking

A language is learnt, at least in part, through the student's attempts to use it. When students attempt to communicate meanings in English, they have the chance to practise what they have learnt and to experiment with what they have not learnt (or only partially learnt). The many speaking sections in *Straightforward* are intended to provide opportunities for students to do both these things.

We know from research that different kinds of speaking tasks make different requirements on the learners. So it is important that students are given a variety of speaking tasks in order to be challenged in different ways. Some tasks encourage students to work together towards finding a solution to a problem (convergent tasks), others allow for a greater divergence of views and opinions and do not have any fixed 'end point'. Some tasks require students to say quite a lot in one go (extended turns), others require more frequent shorter turns in dialogues and conversations. Some tasks require students to work in groups, some in pairs, and some to make individual presentations. In order to provide opportunities for this variety, *Straightforward* contains a great variety of task types: solving problems, discussing and arguing, brainstorming and putting things in order, telling stories and personal anecdotes, describing and evaluating, roleplays and conversations, and so on.

Writing

Students benefit from written consolidation and practice of the language that they have studied, but they also need to develop their ability to communicate in English in written form. The writing syllabus for *Straightforward Advanced* is divided between the Student's Book and the Workbook. At the back of the Student's Book, there are six double-page writing lessons. These relate in topic to the six odd-numbered units in the main body of the Student's Book and the lessons can be used either in the classroom or for self-study. The Workbook provides further practice and extension of the work in the writing lessons of the Student's Book.

The writing lessons begin by showing students a model of a particular genre. Before producing a similar piece of writing, the students will look at a range of features of written English: linking events, formal and informal style, arguing against a viewpoint etc. In addition, there is a bank of useful phrases for written English at the back of the Workbook.

Did you know?

Every unit contains one *Did you know?* section. These are short texts that contain cultural information about the English-speaking world. Besides being informative and interesting, these sections are designed to encourage cross-cultural comparison and to provide further opportunities for speaking.

Further study (including homework, web research, extensive reading)

It would be wonderful if we could reach a high level of language proficiency just by attending a few hours of lessons every week. Sadly, this is not the case and our students must be encouraged to do everything possible to extend their learning opportunities outside the classroom.

The Workbook provides further practice of language that has been presented in the lessons and, although this can be used in the classroom, many teachers will prefer to set this as homework.

It is well known that regular extensive reading is also of enormous help. The workbook contains an excerpt from a novel that can be used for this purpose, but the students who make the fastest progress will be those who use their own initiative to find and read material that interests them.

For many students nowadays, the easiest and cheapest source of material is online. The Teacher's Book contains *Web research tasks* that will encourage students to become more autonomous in their learning. Students can do these individually, in pairs or in small groups. One way of organizing these activities is by giving students a time limit (e.g. ten minutes), during which they have to find out as much as possible about a particular topic. They then share the information they have gathered in this way (they could also be asked to write short reports as a follow-up).

Methodology guidelines

As well as containing basic advice on how to use the lesson material in the Student's Book, this Teacher's Book has a wide range of other useful methodological help, to give you creative ideas and help your teaching develop. These two pages provide a brief introduction to each of these sections.

Methodology advances

This Teacher's Book includes a number of sections called *Methodology advances*. These sections include ideas and suggestions that may encourage you to try some experimental steps in your own teaching, perhaps to take a few risks, to try out some new ideas or to think a little more about what lies behind the work you and your students are doing.

These *Methodology advances* sections link to specific items in the Student's Book lesson, but are also intended to have a wider, more generalized use and I hope you will consider trying out ideas from them at other places in the course. With any luck, you will find that your teaching improves as the range of your methodological choices gain depth.

The Students

Skills

Vocabulary

Grammar

Teaching

Methodology guidelines: Discussion starters

Many lessons in this Teacher's Book include a number of suggestions for *Discussion starters*. These usually take the form of questions, provocative comments, etc. intended to get students to start thinking and talking, often at the start of a new lesson, when a new topic or theme is being introduced. This section suggests a range of possible ideas for using these in class.

N.B. There are often a lot of ideas for *Discussion starters* in the lessons. Remember that you are definitely not intended to use them all! The idea is to offer you a range of possible ideas – so that you can pick ones that you like or which might appeal to your class.

Typical use: working in whole-class mode.

- Ask the questions randomly around the class.
- Make sure you pay more attention to the *meaning* of what students say rather than focussing too much on *accuracy*.
- Respond to the ideas and views students state. As far as possible, turn it into a conversation. Get them interested and involved.

Pairs/Groups: Choose one question or statement that you think is particularly interesting and write it on the board. Put students into pairs or small groups to say what they think about it. After a few minutes a spokesperson from each pair/group reports back to the whole room.

Starting with individuals: Choose a number of the questions and write them on the board (or prepare handouts with them printed on). Ask students to work on their own and write two or three sentence in response to each question/statement. After sufficient thinking and writing time, gather students together in small groups to compare.

Methodology guidelines: Test before you teach

At the start of many lessons the Teacher's Book suggests some optional *Test before you teach* tasks. Although it may feel strange to set tasks that are specifically designed to allow students to use language items that will only be 'taught' later in the Student's Book lesson, these tasks have a number of purposes.

Firstly, they are *diagnostic* – i.e. they allow you to get an idea of how much the students can do with the items you plan to teach. This may lead you to change what you do later in some ways. Secondly, they are *motivational*, i.e. they help students to realize for themselves what they can or can't do.

Methodology guidelines: Web research tasks

This Teacher's Book includes many ideas for extension tasks using the internet. Where appropriate, a list of web search key words is suggested.

All *Web research tasks* provide work on relevant reading skills work, scanning search engine results, as well as reading the final web pages. Web research tasks may also lead to a lot speaking and negotiation between students working together.

Setting up *Web research tasks*

To allow all students to work simultaneously, you will ideally need to have enough internet-connected computers so that a maximum of three students work per computer. If this is not possible you will need to allow some students to work on the task while others do other work, e.g. allowing a six-minute time slot at the computer for each pair of students.

Running *Web research tasks*

The tasks usually give suggestions of useful *web search key words*. We have given these (rather than actual internet addresses) because web addresses tend to change suddenly – but these search words are likely to produce good results at any time.

Methodology guidelines: Grammar boxes

In every lesson of the Students' Book in which new grammar is introduced you will find a *Grammar box*. These boxes summarize information about the new language being studied. In most cases no methodological instructions or exercises are offered, so the teacher has many options about how to use them. This section suggests a number of typical ideas for using these as well as a few more unusual possibilities. In every case you can mix and match ideas to suit your class.

- Ask students to quietly read through the information to themselves.
- Ask one or two students to read the information aloud to the rest of the class.
- Ask students to work in pairs and read the information aloud to each other.
- Books closed: before students look at the *Grammar box*, read it aloud to them. At various key points pause and elicit what the next word or words might be. Clearly confirm right answers. When you have finished allow students to open books and read the information through quietly.
- Books closed: write the information from the grammar box on the board trying to keep the same layout as the book. Leave gaps at key places. Ask students to either copy the diagram and fill it in or come to the board and fill in the information there. Allow students to discuss the suggested answers before they check with the printed version.
- Books closed: use the information in the grammar box to inform your own question-making. Elicit the information item by item, example by example, from students and note it on the board. When the information is complete, allow students to open their books and find the same content printed there.

Introducing the coursebook

When students first get their new Student's Book, allow them time to browse through it for a minute or two rather than leaping straight into lesson 1A. You could structure this by calling out specific tasks which students then complete and compare in pairs before you call out the next task. Tasks might include: (a) find out how many lessons there are; (b) find out how many pages long each lesson is; (c) what can you find in the sections at the back of the book?; (d) where can you find the language reference sections?; (e) look at the index. Which lesson name sounds most interesting to you?; (f) find a picture you like.

1A | A fresh start

What the lesson is about

Theme	South Africa & change
Speaking	Groupwork: writing and asking questions from a fact file on South Africa
Reading	Three texts about change and South Africa: changing your appearance – cosmetic surgery in South Africa; lifestyle change – emigrating to South Africa; changes in South African society post-apartheid
Vocabulary	Change

Speaking

If you want a lead-in ...

Discussion starters

➋ *Methodology guidelines: Discussion starters, page xiv*

- Write the following on the board and ask students to think about what they mean and the connection between them:
  Nelson Mandela   Cape Town   Apartheid   Springboks
  Johannesburg
- Discuss what students know about these people, places and things.
- Answers: The connection is South Africa. Nelson Mandela is a former political prisoner and ex-president of South Africa; Cape Town is the country's legislative capital; Apartheid is the name given to the policy of racial segregation that used to be in place in South Africa; Springboks is the national rugby team (named after the native antelope) and Johannesburg is South Africa's largest city.

Pre-teach key words: change

- Write the following words and phrases from the texts on the board: *a fresh start, liberation, cosmetic surgery, a break with the past, transition, a new life abroad.*
- Ask students to check the meanings of the words in their dictionaries. Then put students in pairs or small groups to discuss what the words and phrases might refer to, and how they relate to change. Have a brief class feedback session.

Introducing the theme: change

- Brainstorm reasons why people go to live abroad. Elicit and write on the board some or all of the following: *a new job, improving employment prospects, a better standard of living, a new boyfriend or girlfriend, wanting to see the world, running away from bad times or failed relationships at home, wanting better weather, wanting to learn a new language, for political or economic reasons (refugees).*
- Ask students if they would like to go and live abroad, and, if so, where and why.

Methodology advances
What does Advanced really mean?

- *In language teaching, all level names are likely to be something of a generalization. The students that you meet in class are always going to have a disparate range of levels in terms of their knowledge and skills – so the saying that 'every class is a mixed level class' is invariably true. However, an Advanced class is often more mixed than any other. This reflects the many different ways that students become 'advanced' (see Methodology advances: Different types of Advanced students, page 10).*
- *But before we look in more detail at these differences, let's start by seeing if there are any useful generalizations we can make about some (or most) of our students. Bearing in mind the warning that none of this is going to be true for everyone in your class, we can still define a typical student starting work at Advanced level.*

  He/She ...
  - *is familiar with, and can use, all the tenses and main structures of English (and has probably studied them formally in class).*
  - *still makes mistakes, but these rarely interfere with successful communication.*
  - *is more likely to have significant problems in the area of vocabulary (e.g. with collocations and chunks) than with grammar.*
  - *may still have some noticeable oddities in pronunciation (sounds, word stress, intonation, connected fluent speech).*
  - *can read almost any kind of everyday authentic material (or listen to most everyday conversations) and follow most of the content, though specialized vocabulary, accent, cultural references and colloquial language may prove to be stumbling blocks.*
  - *may have become very good at overview / gist / general meaning comprehension tasks in listening and reading and at extracting specific details but this can cover up significant problems in understanding fine points of meaning in texts. He/She may be unaware that they have such blind spots.*
  - *is often weaker at writing than at the other skills.*
  - *has some fossilized errors (i.e. ones that seem to be fixed and unshiftable).*
- *Note that this is a description a typical student starting a C1 Advanced level course – which isn't the same as someone who has successfully met all the criteria for a C1 level language user (see Methodology advances: The Common European Framework – What can an Advanced student do?, page x).*

1

- Groupwork. Ask students to look at the photos of South Africa. They use the ideas in the box as prompts to tell each other what they know about the country.

Cultural notes: Images of South Africa

- The photographs on pages 6 and 7 show, from left to right, a springbok, (a type of antelope which is the national animal of South Africa), grapes growing in Cape province (a major wine-producing area), the South African Cape coastline, and the iconic picture of Nelson Mandela in a rugby jersey shaking hands with Francois Pienaar, who was captain of the South African national rugby team when they won the final of the 1995 Rugby World Cup in South Africa. South Africa also won the World Cup in 2007.

2

Communication activities: Student's Book pages 138 & 155

- Pairwork. Put students from different groups into A and B pairs. Ask them to turn to their respective pages at the back of the book and to read the fact file on South Africa.
- They then work on their own and use the fact file to write five questions for their partner to answer. Remind them that they should write questions that they think their partner will be able to answer.

3

- Students take it in turns to ask each other their questions.
- At the end of the activity, you could ask if any of the students have been to South Africa and for their impressions of the country.

Extra task: quiz

- Follow up the speaking activity with a class quiz called 'Name Four'. Allow students to study their partners' fact files for a few minutes. Then ask them to close their books. Ask the following questions.
  1 *Can you name four official South African languages?*
  2 *Can you name four neighbouring countries?*
  3 *Can you name four major cities?*
  4 *Can you name four historical events?*
- Possible answers: 1 English, Afrikaans, Swazi, Zulu; 2 Namibia, Botswana, Zimbabwe, Mozambique; 3 Johannesburg, Cape Town, Durban, Pretoria; 4 The Boer War, the gaining of independence, the policy of Apartheid becoming/ceasing to become law, Nelson Mandela becoming president.

Language notes: reading

- Note the English pronunciation of the following countries, cities and languages in the communication activities texts:
- **Namibia** /nəˈmɪbɪə/; **Botswana** /bɒtˈswɑːnə/; **Zimbabwe** /zɪmˈbɑːbweɪ/; **Mozambique** /məʊzæmˈbiːk/; **Lesotho** /leˈsuːtuː/; **Swaziland** /ˈswɑːzɪlænd/
- **Johannesburg** /dʒəʊˈhænəzbɜː(r)g/; **Pretoria** /prəˈtɔːrɪə/
- **Swazi** /ˈswɑːzi/; **Zulu** /ˈzuːluː/; **Xhosa** /ˈkəʊzə/ (In the Xhosa language, the first sound of this word is a 'clicking' noise made by pressing the tongue against the palate.)

Cultural notes: South Africa

- Nelson Mandela /mænˈdelə/ was born in 1918. He was the son of a Xhosa chief and grew up in a mud hut. After qualifying as a lawyer, he helped form the military wing of the ANC (African National Congress) and was captured and imprisoned for treason by the South African authorities in 1964. He wasn't released until 1990. In 1991, he became the first black president of South Africa, a position he held until 1997. Mandela's leadership and humanity have been essential in reconciling and unifying the people of South Africa since the end of the Apartheid regime.
- Apartheid /əˈpɑː(r)teɪt, əˈpɑː(r)taɪt/ was a system of racial segregation instituted by the National Party following its rise to power in 1948. It aimed to keep black and white people apart. Black people were obliged to live in the 'homelands' (the less prosperous rural areas), mixed marriages were illegal, and black and white people were prohibited from sharing the same amenities, such as beaches, buses and hospitals. The system wasn't abolished until 1990.
- Afrikaaners /ˌæfrɪˈkɑːnə(r)z/ (called Boers /bəʊə(r)s/ in the nineteenth and early twentieth century) are white South Africans who first arrived in the country in the eighteenth century. They were protestant farmers of Dutch heritage who settled the hinterland of South Africa. Their first language is Afrikaans /ˌæfrɪˈkɑːns/, which derives from the Dutch language.
- Today, South Africa is a democratic country which prides itself on being a 'rainbow nation' with many people of different ethnic origin and many languages. It is ruled by the ANC in coalition with other parties. Its president is Thabo Mbeki /ˈtɑːbəʊ mˈbegi/. Its biggest problems are economic inequality and the rise of HIV/AIDS. Information correct at time of publishing.

Reading

The reading is three texts about the topic of change connected with South Africa. The first text is about changing your appearance and the growing popularity of travelling to South Africa to undergo cosmetic surgery. The second text is about a British woman who wants to change her life by emigrating to South Africa. The third text is about the change in South African society since the end of apartheid.

1

- Students read the texts and answer the questions.
- They could then compare their answers with a partner before you check with the class.

1
A change of appearance
B change of country
C political change

2
A newspaper article
B novel
C history book

2

- Students read the texts again and answer the questions.
- They could then compare their answers with a partner before you check with the class.

Text A
1 Cosmetic surgery is cheaper in South Africa than in Britain.
2 Not to expect too much from the operation. The change won't necessarily make them happy.
Text B
1 She had recently divorced. She wanted to put the past behind her and start a new life abroad.
2 They did not think it was a good idea. It's a long way from Britain and she knew nobody there.
Text C
1 South Africa was going through a period of change from a strict regime to a more liberated society. An increase in crime was a consequence of this change.
2 The black leader putting on the colours of a mainly white team symbolized a move towards a united, egalitarian society and a mood of reconciliation.

Alternative procedure: jigsaw reading

- You could exploit these texts as a jigsaw reading activity. Divide the class into groups of three. Each student reads one of the texts (A, B or C). Make sure each student reads a different text from the other members of their group. Students then have to interview each other to find the answers to the questions in exercise 2.

3

- Students match the highlighted words in the text to the definitions.

a	concurred	f	hail
b	divided up	g	setting up
c	reverberated	h	ruled out
d	comes to	i	shuttled
e	donned		

Language notes: reading

- Note the following idiomatic vocabulary from the texts:
- To ***yearn for*** something means to long for/want it very much.
- ***Swanky*** means very luxurious.
- If you experience ***raised eyebrows***, you cause a lot of surprise or (in some contexts) disapproval.
- ***Forced smiles*** are smiles that are not genuine.
- To ***keep in touch*** with someone means that you maintain contact with them, usually by writing and phoning.
- You ***roots*** are the friends, family and background that tie you to a place.
- A ***failed marriage*** is a marriage that ended in separation or divorce.
- To ***bury the past*** is to forget about the past and move on with your life.
- ***Car-hijacking*** refers to the practice of stopping cars on the road with weapons and stealing them.
- ***Diehard*** means resistant to change or new ideas.
- You may wish to check these phrases by writing the words from the text on one side of the board, and the synonymous phrases given on the other side of the board, and asking different students to explain them.

4

- Pairwork. Students discuss the questions with a partner.

Cultural notes: plastic surgery

- Cosmetic or plastic surgery describes surgical procedures which improve someone's appearance. Once the reserve of the rich and famous, cosmetic surgery is becoming increasingly mainstream. The most common procedures are breast augmentation (changing the size or shape of the breasts), rhinoplasty (reshaping the nose) and liposuction (removal of fat).

VOCABULARY & SPEAKING: change

- Pairwork. Students discuss the questions with a partner.

2

- Students complete the sentences with the correct form of the verbs in the box.
- They could then compare their answers with a partner before you check with the class.

1	converting	5	alter
2	vary	6	transformed / altered
3	switching	7	transfers / is transferred
4	adapt	8	shift / be shifted

3

- Pairwork. Students discuss the sentences in exercise 2 with a partner, and say which ones are true for them.

Web research task

➲ *Methodology guidelines: Web research tasks, page xiv*

- Ask students to research one area of knowledge about South Africa on the internet. This could be cities, history, sports, etc. Ask students to write a short extract for a holiday brochure or website based on their findings. If students have researched the same area, you could pair them up to write the extract in class.
- Ask students to make a class poster by sticking their extracts on a large sheet of paper, ideally with some photos, and putting it on the classroom wall.

Web research key words

- South Africa; cities/history/sport

IF YOU WANT SOMETHING EXTRA ...

➲ *Photocopiable activity, page 211*
➲ *Teacher's notes, page 192*

1B | First day

What the lesson is about

Theme	Starting at a new school
Speaking	Groupwork: discussing the first day of a new experience
Listening	Radio interview about how to reduce the anxiety of moving to a new school
Grammar	Simple & continuous verb forms
Speech feature	Approximation

If you want a lead-in …

Test before you teach

Methodology guidelines: Test before you teach, page xiv

- Write the following on the board:
  What / do / weekend?
  What / do / next weekend?
  How long / study / English?
  What / have / for breakfast this morning?
  What / do / last Sunday?
  Where / live / five years from now?
- Ask students to prepare questions to ask a partner. Then put students in pairs to ask and answer.
- During feedback, ask students which tenses they chose to use for each question. Make a note of the problems your students have encountered, and make sure you deal with them when the students study the Grammar section on page 9.

Pre-teach key words: first day feelings

- By way of lead-in, and to prepare students for the Speaking activity on page 7, revise adjectives of feeling.
- Write *First day feelings* on the board, and ask students how people feel on different 'first days'. Try to elicit *nervous, anxious, excited, shy, sensitive, keen, confused, emotional*, etc.

Introducing the theme: first days

- Ask students to imagine a new student is about to join your English class. Put students in pairs to think of three or four pieces of advice to give that student to help him or her through the first day.
- Ask for advice from around the class, and decide which pieces of advice are the best.

Speaking

1

- Groupwork. Students discuss in small groups how they might feel on their first day in each of the situations.
- Go round monitoring and give help where needed.

2

- Students discuss the question in their groups and give reasons why they felt the way they did.

Listening

The listening is a radio interview with an educational psychologist and former teacher about how to help schoolchildren cope with the anxiety and stress of changing schools at the age of eleven, when they move from primary to secondary school.

1

- Explain that students are going to listen to part of a radio interview about starting a new school. Before they listen, ask them to read the questions in exercise 2 and predict what type of information might go in each gap. They can then discuss their ideas with a partner.

Extra task: vocabulary

- Prepare students for the Listening by selecting and writing on the board key phrases from the text, checking their meaning, and asking students how they relate to the idea of a first day at school. Write up the following:
  a rite of passage = a major change in a person's life (e.g. getting married)
  a huge leap = a big move
  alleviate anxiety = make someone feel calmer
  a smooth transition = a gentle and easy change from one thing to another

2 1.1

- Students listen to the interview and complete the sentences.

1	a teacher	5	ask lots of questions
2	childhood	6	(regular) routine
3	a dozen	7	separated; divorced
4	talk; listen to	8	make as many friends

1.1

JH = Jackie Haylett P = Presenter

JH: … and all of this can help make the transition from the safe, cosy environment of home to the new and unfamiliar world of school that much smoother. It's a huge leap, an enormous change, but one which young children generally adapt to reasonably quickly.

P: That's good to hear. It's coming up to half past eleven here on *Roundabout* and with me this morning is educational psychologist and former teacher, Jackie Haylett. Up and down the country, schools have opened their doors once again and Jackie's here to give us advice on how to help our children who have just started back. Now Jackie, we've just been talking about children's very first day at school, but how about the move up into secondary education? That's another big leap, isn't it?

JH: Yes, indeed. The change from primary to secondary school is very much a rite of passage – it marks the beginning of the move from childhood into adolescence and brings with it some major changes in the lives of children. For the previous year or so they've been the oldest and biggest in the school, and now, once again, they're the youngest. They no longer have just one single teacher for all subjects; now there are anything up to a dozen of them, all unfamiliar and all with different personalities. The building is new, the books are new, everything's new and like all major changes this creates a certain amount of anxiety.

P: So what can parents do to help alleviate this anxiety, to ease the transition for their children?
JH: A number of things. Perhaps the most important is that they should take time to talk and listen to their child after each schoolday to check how things are going. Sounds obvious, but far too many fail to do it. Showing interest in this way can help a child feel supported and more confident. Resist the temptation to ask lots of questions though – like an adult coming home from work, a child will probably be tired, hungry and maybe a little short-tempered from having to cope with so many changes all at once. Just chatting naturally should encourage him or her to open up and talk.
P: And how about before the schoolday starts? What should parents be doing then?
JH: Well, another very important way of reducing anxiety is by making the effort to establish a regular routine – making sure, for example, that the child gets up in time each day to have a decent breakfast. But the routine and preparation for school should really begin the night before. Children generally need a lot of help organizing themselves, so it's a good idea to make a checklist together of all the equipment and books needed for each day's classes. Then get your child to pack the schoolbag before he or she goes off to bed – nice and early of course, about eight thirtyish is a good time for an eleven-year-old. And if parents are separated or divorced, make two checklists – one for each household.
P: Excellent idea. Now I know from when I was bringing up my own children that the two or three times we moved house and they had to change schools, one of their main fears was that they weren't going to know anybody. They were worried they'd have no friends. Can we as parents do anything in that area?
JH: Yes, we can.
P: I thought you'd say that.
JH: Well, I can't guarantee it will work in all cases, but I think the least we can do is encourage our children to make as many friends as possible. Help them in the process by telling them that they're welcome to invite their friends round after school or at weekends. At the same time, though, it's important to reassure them that friendships take time and effort and sometimes they don't work out.
P: … as my two girls know only too well. Now let's move on if we may to another major change. Later this month something like 60,000 school leavers will be starting their first year at a university in the UK. Some parents are probably wondering what on earth they can do to help their son or daughter, now that they are almost adults. What would you say to them, Jackie?
JH: Well, you know, school leavers share many of the same anxieties as the eleven-year-olds we've just been talking about …

Alternative procedure: listen before writing

- When students have to write whole words into a text, they can sometimes spend all their time writing, and forget to listen. To avoid this, ask students to listen and not write on first playing. When the recording has finished, ask students to write their answers, then check with a partner. If necessary, play the recording again, and be prepared to pause the recording to give students time to write in words.

Extra task: roleplay

- Put students in pairs. Tell student A they are about to go to university and live away from home. Tell student B that they are A's parent. Student A must think of aspects of the change that worry a new student (e.g. *I might not like the course*). Student B must think of what worries a parent (e.g. *He/She might never phone home*). Once students have thought of a few ideas, tell them to share their concerns, and try to provide support and advice for each other.
- At the end, have a brief feedback session, and find out who gave the best advice.

Cultural notes: British state school system

- In the British state school system, children go to primary school from the age of four or five to eleven. They then go on to secondary school. Students may leave school at sixteen but the majority stay on until they are eighteen before going on to work or university.
- Primary school children are generally called 'pupils'. At secondary school, they may be called 'pupils' or 'students'. At university, they are 'students' or 'undergraduates'.

Methodology advances
Advanced students are successful learners

- *An Advanced student, by definition, has gone beyond the Intermediate plateau – whether through their own choice or that of their parents, teachers or the education system they are a part of. The fact that many Advanced level students seem particularly focussed, persevering, demanding or driven may reflect that often they actually are different in motivation and personality from the average Elementary or Pre-intermediate student, and the proof is that they have got so far. They have the mind-set, skills and personality that have enabled them to be successful at a very difficult task, namely, learning a foreign language well. They represent only a tiny percentage of a much wider range of people who originally started out learning English.*
- *So, Advanced students are successful learners. They have done something right to get this far. However, they do not always recognize that themselves, and some of the students in your class may, in these first few lessons, be doubting their ability to cope with the level of difficulty of the material in this book. Here are two ideas for drawing their attention to their own achievements. Simple activities like these can have a surprisingly positive effect on an individual's self-esteem and on a whole class's sense of purpose.*

My English history

- *Ask students to write a brief history of their subjective experience of learning English – not the teachers, dates, schools and other facts, but focussing on their own changing attitudes and feelings. Use some of these starter questions to get students going:*
  When you started learning English, how good did you think it was possible for you to get?
  Were you successful at English from the start – or did success only come slowly?
  How has your own progress compared with other students you have worked with?
  Think of the other people you started learning with. Do you still know any of them? How many of them do you think might have become as good at English as you are?
  What things have motivated you most in your learning? What have been the biggest road blocks?

Best moments in English

- *Ask students to take a minute or two to think back and choose two or three times when they have been really pleased with their ability to use English or it has proved particularly useful.*
- *Hand out a sheet of A3 paper to each student and request that they draw a sketch of those occasions. Convince them not to be concerned about their artistic ability (or lack of it) – stick people are fine! They should just do their best to capture the moments as images rather than in words.*
- *When pictures are ready, invite students to meet up and look at each other's work. After a few possible giggles, encourage students to talk more seriously. Each student can say what their picture shows and why this was an important moment for them.*
- *The activity may help some students to realize that their English learning has been for a purpose and that they have achieved something quite positive from it.*

SPEECH FEATURE: approximation

1

- Students complete the sentences taken from the listening with the approximating expressions in the box.

1 up
2 so
3 anything
4 About
5 something

2

- Students use the approximating expressions in the box to express the items 1–6 in two different ways.

Possible answers:
1 about 20 days; around 20 days or something like that
2 It's coming up to 6pm; about 6pm
3 just over / roughly / somewhere in the region of £21; £21 something
4 around five hours or something like that; just over / roughly five hours
5 about / something like / just over / roughly / in the region of 230 kilometres
6 about / something like / roughly 7,000 light years away; 7,000 odd light years away

Language notes: approximation

- Here are the exact meanings of these 'approximating' expressions:
- ***About/around/roughly/some/somewhere in the region of/something like*** mean *approximately*.
- ***Over/upwards of*** means more than.
- ***Under*** means less than.
- ***Up to 20*** means no more than 20; ***nearly 20*** means perhaps eighteen or nineteen but not quite 20; ***20 odd, 20 something and 20 or so*** mean a few more than 20, but the number is inexact or unknown.
- We use ***-ish*** as an affix on an adjective to mean *approximately* (e.g. *thirtyish*) or *tallish* (e.g. *quite tall*).

3

- Pairwork. Students talk about themselves using approximating expressions. They can use the ideas from the box if they want.

Extra task: approximation

- Prepare some questions to ask students, which require approximate answers. For example:
  How many students are there in this school? How many people are there in the country? How far is it from here to the capital city/nearest major city? How many copies of this Student's Book are there in this classroom?
- Ask the questions (or write them on the board) and ask students to give you approximate answers.

GRAMMAR: simple & continuous verb forms

➲ *Language reference, Student's Book page 14*
➲ *Methodology guidelines: Grammar boxes, page xiv*

1

- Students name the tenses used in the sentences from the recording.

1 past continuous; past simple
2 present simple
3 present continuous
4 present perfect
5 present perfect continuous
6 future simple
7 future continuous

2

- Students could work with a partner to discuss why the simple or continuous form is used in the sentences before you check the answers with the class.

1 past continuous – an action in progress in the past; past simple – a repeated action in the past
2 present simple – a state in the present
3 present continuous – a continued state
4 present perfect – a recently completed action
5 present perfect continuous – a recent continued action
6 future simple – future action
7 future continuous – a continued future action

Language notes: simple & continuous verb forms

- The simple aspect describes an action that is seen to be complete. This encompasses single, completed actions, e.g. *I broke my leg/I've read this book*, habits and routines, e.g. *I get up at 9*, and states, e.g. *I like chips*.
- The continuous aspect describes actions that are temporary not permanent, and have duration. The action isn't seen to be complete – we are viewing it at some point between when it starts and when it ends. This encompasses temporary activities, e.g. *I'm staying with friends at the moment*, activities that are interrupted, e.g. *He was sleeping when I arrived*, incomplete actions, e.g. *I've been reading a book*, and activities that are incomplete and have duration, e.g. *I've been studying English for ages*.
- A good way to help students who have problems here is to ask check questions about the examples. *Is it complete? Is it temporary? Is it happening/Did it happen over a period of time?*

3

- Students choose the correct form of the verbs to complete the texts. Remind them that in some cases both forms can be used.
- They could then compare their answers with a partner before you check with the class.

1 know; 'm having; hired; agreed; 'll come / be coming
2 is being; aren't; is growing; wants; feels / is feeling
3 lives / is living; was taken; appears; fell; broke; was having; been phoning; aren't answering; think; phoned

4

- Students think of an example for each situation. They then compare and discuss each one with their partner.

Extra task

- Write the following time phrases on the board:
  often *for a week* *these days* *last Saturday*
  later *between six and seven* *this time last year*
  in 2012 *recently* *hardly ever* *after*
  in a few minutes *since June* *while*
- Divide students into teams of four, five or six, and ask the students to sit in a circle if possible. Student 1 must make a sentence with 'often'. Student 2 makes a sentence with *for a week*, and so on. Check that students are using the correct aspect. If a student makes an inaccurate sentence (or can't think of one) they are out. Keep playing until only one student is left.

IF YOU WANT SOMETHING EXTRA ...

Photocopiable activity, page 212
Teacher's notes, page 192

1c | Growing up

What the lesson is about

Theme	Reflections on becoming older
Speaking	Talking about different ages
Reading	*Growing up on television*: a text about a TV programme following the lives of fourteen people every seven years
Vocabulary	Age
Grammar	Reference & substitution

If you want a lead-in ...

Discussion starters

➋ *Methodology guidelines: Discussion starters, page xiv*

- *What age would you like to be? Why?*
- *What are the most typical interests, activities and preoccupations of people in their twenties/thirties/forties/fifties/sixties?*
- *In your opinion, what is the best age to do the following?*
  a get married b have children c go to university
  d travel round the world e retire

Pre-teach key words: growing up

- Write the following phrases, which are near opposites on the board.
  1 *privileged background/humble beginnings*
  2 *calm and composed/ill-at-ease*
  3 *have ups and downs/feel happy in your own skin*
  (Meanings: 1 rich, supportive background/poor start in life; 2 relaxed/uncomfortable; 3 have good days and bad days/feel happy about yourself)
- Ask students to say what they think the phrases mean. Then ask, *What sort of people come from a privileged background? At what age do you tend to feel more calm and composed or more ill-at-ease?*

Vocabulary & speaking: age

1

- Students work on their own and arrange the terms to describe age in chronological order from youngest to oldest.

> a newborn; a toddler; a preteen; a teenager; a twentysomething; a 30-year-old; a middle-aged man / woman; a senior citizen

2

- Students read the sentences and decide how old the people are.
- They could then compare their answers with a partner before you check with the class.

> 1 18 (when she legally becomes an adult, though clearly this depends on the country)
> 2 30 (he's just become 30)
> 3 over 40
> 4 middle-aged
> 5 near the age of retirement (the exact age depends on the country. In Britain it is 60 for a woman and 65 for a man.)
> 6 approaching the age of 70

Cultural & language notes

- A ***toddler*** is a baby who can walk. It comes from the verb 'toddle' which describes the ungainly walk of a small child.
- ***Preteen*** is a relatively new expression used to describe a child of ten, eleven or twelve who has not reached adolescence, but is starting to show all the signs of wanting to be a teenager!
- A ***senior citizen*** is a person who has reached the statutory retirement age of 65 (or 60 for a woman). An alternative, slightly less sensitive expression is OAP or (Old Age) Pensioner.
- Being described as ***middle-aged*** is something most people try to put off for as long as possible, so it's difficult to pinpoint exactly when it starts and finishes. Young people would probably say that it starts around 40, but people of about 40 would probably say it starts at 45 or later.
- In Britain, legally, people ***come of age*** when they reach eighteen. At this age, the law considers people to be adult, and they can vote, buy a house and buy alcohol only when they reach this age. Previously the age was 21, and many people still consider the 21st birthday to be the beginning of adulthood.
- The expression ***on the wrong side of 40*** is an amusing way of saying 'over 40'.
- A ***midlife crisis*** describes the feelings of worry and doubt that some people experience when they reach middle age.
- ***Coming up to*** and ***getting on for*** both mean 'approaching'. ***Getting on*** also implies 'getting old'.

3

- Students look at the people in the photos and use the words and expressions from exercises 1 and 2 to say how old they think they are.

4

- Pairwork. Students take it in turns to talk about the people in the photos without actually mentioning their age. Tell them to use the three discussion points about age when they are talking about each person. Their partner guesses the person/people they are talking about.

Alternative procedure: advantages & disadvantages

- With weaker classes, prepare students for this activity by brainstorming on to the board advantages, disadvantages and concerns people have at the ages in the photos before doing the pairwork. Or refer students to the ideas generated in the Discussion starters lead-in activity (if you did it).

Extra task: discussion

- If you have mixed ages in your class, and you feel students will be comfortable with revealing their age, have a discussion about what the advantages and disadvantages are of being the age your students have reached.

Reading

The reading text is about *7-Up*, a 1960s British television documentary which set out to follow the lives of fourteen seven-year-olds, with an update on their progress broadcast on television every seven years. The text focuses on the lives of three of the participants and what has happened to them, and talks about why the programme has been so successful.

1
- Students read the title of the text and the introduction, then discuss the question with a partner.

2
- Students read the text to find out which of the areas they discussed in exercise 1 were mentioned in the text.

Examples of general areas mentioned:
- happiness
- work and careers
- changes in physical appearance
- education
- houses
- relationships and families (brief mention in penultimate paragraph)

3
- Students read the text again and choose the correct alternative to complete the sentences.
- They could then compare their answers with a partner before you check with the class.

1 how they feel about their lives
2 past is reflected in his face
3 was carefully planned for him
4 has been no obstacle to success
5 taxi driver
6 less than enthusiastic about appearing in the series

4
- Pairwork. Students discuss the questions with a partner.
- Ask students if they found out anything interesting from their partner in their discussion.

Extra task: discussion

- Extend the pairwork activity in exercise 4, and recycle vocabulary from the text, by writing the following questions on the board for discussion:
  Do you feel happier in your skin now than you used to? In what ways?
  Do you have a strong sense of purpose in life?
  Do you feel you life is mapped out? In what ways?
  Do you feel your background has helped or hindered you?

Language notes: reading

- The text is rich in vocabulary. If you chose not to pre-teach the words suggested in the **Pre-teach key words section**, then you may wish to look at these words in context.
- Alternatively, you may wish to get students to find some of the idiomatic phrasal verbs in the text:
  To ***turn out*** is to develop in a particular way e.g. *He was a quiet child but he turned out to be an extrovert.*
  To ***map out*** something (or to ***map*** something ***out***) is to plan it.
  In the context of the reading text, to ***get on***, is to become successful in life.
  If things ***work out***, they happen as planned.
  To ***set up*** a company or organization is to start it.
  If something is ***held up to scrutiny***, it is inspected or examined.

Cultural note: 7-Up

- Granada Television is an independent television company that provides programmes for the ITV network in Britain. Producer Michael Apted's programme was groundbreaking in 1964 and each seven-yearly update is eagerly awaited and discussed.

GRAMMAR: reference & substitution

➋ *Language reference, Student's Book page 14*
➋ *Methodology guidelines: Grammar boxes, page xiv*

1
- Students look back at the highlighted words in the text and explain what the words refer to.
- They could then compare their answers with a partner before you check with the class.

then – 1964
these individuals – fourteen seven-year-olds
this – the fact that they have all had their ups and downs
not – he was (not) going to be an astronaut
that – the profession
one – route to financial wellbeing
that – training to be or becoming a jockey
does – drive a London cab
it – the programme / the *7-Up* series
do – come back on the programme
one – instalment

2
- Students complete the sentences with the words in the box.
- They could then compare their answers with a partner before you check with the class.

1	ones; one	5	do; there
2	nor	6	not
3	That	7	so
4	does	8	those

3
- Ask students to look back at the sentences in exercises 2. For each of the sentences, they have to write a sentence to precede it.
- Go through the example with the class to make sure students know what to do. Then ask them to work on their own to write the initial sentence of the dialogues.

4
- Pairwork. Students take it in turns to read out their sentences in random order for their partner to reply using an appropriate response from the sentences in exercise 2.

Language notes: reference & substitution

Reference
- ***This, that, these*** and ***those*** are used as determiners, e.g. *this news, those days* or pronouns, e.g. *This is great.* They refer back to previously stated ideas and are often used to avoid repetition.

Substitution
- Auxiliary verbs such as ***do*** or ***did*** are used to avoid repeating the verb, e.g. *Joe came but Sue didn't.*
- Similarly, ***so/neither/nor*** + auxiliary verb + subject is used to avoid repetition when saying two things are similar, e.g. *John likes chips and so do I* or *Sarah doesn't go to university and neither does Paul.*

- ***So/not*** are used in place of a *that* clause e.g. *I hope not/I think so* or a conditional clause, e.g. *If not, let me know.*
- ***One/ones*** replace countable nouns, e.g. *I don't want one.*
- ***Then*** and ***there*** replace times and places, e.g. *He wasn't there.*

Methodology advances
Different types of Advanced students

- *We can identify quite a number of different kinds of Advanced student. Here are a few you might meet:*

The 'only-just' advanced student
In some schools, the majority of students in an Advanced class will be at the lower end of the Advanced description. They will be starting on the Advanced course, perhaps after having just passed a lower level exam. These students, while they should be fully capable of successfully studying an Advanced course, will have the most new things to learn and the most errors to make.

The student at the top of the escalator
Some students who arrive in Advanced classes are quite clearly not Advanced. They have simply arrived at the top of the school's level structure. This may be for a number of reasons:

- *They have repeatedly moved up a level automatically at the end of every school year.*
- *Other factors than level have determined which class they go to (e.g. the wish to keep a group of friends together).*
- *They have been a weak student who should have stayed in a certain level but (for purely logistical reasons, such as the fact that they have already studied the Student's Book at a certain level) the school has promoted them above their actual level. These promotions can happen repeatedly, level after level, until a student somehow arrives at the highest level, way above their real level.*

For whatever reason a student arrives at 'the top of the escalator' this kind of student may prove to be a problem for both teacher and other students. The teacher will need to decide how to deal with the weaker language knowledge and the lower skills level of the student.

The mixed-ability advanced student
Some advanced students have marked differences in ability in particular language or skills areas. I once taught an advanced class with a Japanese student whose grammatical knowledge and writing ability was very advanced, but whose speaking skills were little more than intermediate.

The non-native native speaker
When you meet someone whose English seems particularly natural and impressive it is worth enquiring about their life story and personal background. There is sometimes a very good explanation as to how their English has become good. Here are some example stories:

- *The student has spent a year or more living (and going to school) in an English-speaking country, e.g. while travelling with parents who were posted to work overseas.*
- *Although the student lives in a non-English speaking country, one of their parents (or another relative or carer) is a native English speaker who often uses English with them. Similarly, the parents may come from different cultures and use English as a lingua franca within the family.*
- *The student has been brought up in a home where the parents have made a decision to use English themselves some of the time (in order to help their children learn the language). I have been surprised by how many non-native parents I have met that read their child a bedtime story in English, or show English children's TV programmes on DVD.*
- *The student works in an English-speaking environment, e.g. in a multi-national company.*

The very advanced student
Some students are simply very Advanced. For a variety of reasons, often to do with natural aptitude, they have somehow become extremely knowledgeable and skilful. Luckily, these students often also seem to have a high degree of motivation and are keen to keep practising and expanding their knowledge, even though they may be in a class that is actually working at a lower level than their own. Finding ways to keep challenging them can prove demanding to the teacher.

IF YOU WANT SOMETHING EXTRA …

- *Photocopiable activity, page 213*
- *Teacher's notes, page 192*

1D | The quarterlife crisis

What the lesson is about

Theme	Problems with being 18–35
Speaking	Roleplay: people making changes
Listening	Five people talking about expectations of what life should be like at certain ages
Vocabulary	Noun suffixes
Did you know?	UK charity: *Help the Aged*

If you want a lead-in ...

Discussion starters

➋ *Methodology guidelines: Discussion starters, page xiv*

- *What are the most difficult and stressful change of life situations that we have to face in our lives? In what ways are they stressful? What's the most difficult change of life situation you have faced? Why was it difficult? How did you deal with it?*

Test before you teach

➋ *Methodology guidelines: Test before you teach, page xiv*

- Write the following suffixes on the board:
  -ence -ment -al -ure -ence -ness -cy -ity -hood
- Put students in pairs or small teams. Tell students they have four minutes to write as many nouns using these suffixes as they can think of.
- During feedback, ask the pair or team who claim to have written the most nouns to read them out to the class. Correct any errors.

Introducing the theme: the quarterlife crisis

- Discuss with students what is meant by a 'quarterlife crisis.' Brainstorm life events or issues that could contribute to a quarterlife crisis (i.e. problems faced by 18 to 35 year olds) onto the board. Try to elicit: getting a new job, going to university, leaving home, going to live abroad, moving house, getting married.
- Ask students to describe their personal experience of any of the above to the class.

Listening

The listening is five people talking about the problems of being twentysomething in 21st-century Britain: the unrealistically high expectations some people have for their lives, the difficulty of becoming independent from parents because of lack of money and the overwhelming feelings of insecurity and disappointment.

1

- Pairwork. Ask students to look at the pairs of photos and talk about the changes we have to make and the different responsibilities we have when we become adults.

2

➋ *Communication activities, Student's Book page 138*

- Students read the extract and discuss the questions.
- When students have finished their discussion, ask them to turn to page 138 to check their ideas.

3 1.2–1.6

- Explain that students are going to listen to five people talking about the problems of being twentysomething. For each speaker, they should decide whether this person believes twentysomethings have a good reason to complain about their situation or not.
- Students listen to the recording. They can then check their answers with a partner before you check with the class.

1 ✓ 2 ✓ 3 ✗ 4 ✓ 5 ✓

1.2–1.6

Speaker 1
A lot of people my age are talking about this quarterlife crisis thing. There seems to be this idea that a lack of stability is a bad thing, that it gives us an overwhelming feeling of insecurity, that we somehow have too much choice, too many decisions to make. Is it OK, for example, to switch jobs every year or so or is it better to stick with one company? Do I really enjoy the single life or should I be thinking about marriage? Is it cool to live close to my parents or should I go to the other end of the country to show how independent I really am? And so on. But I honestly can't see how having choice can be a problem. Surely being able to decide what we do is a good thing – adds a bit of spice to life. Wouldn't it be dull if we had it all mapped out?!

Speaker 2
I have this incredible feeling of dissatisfaction and disillusionment with adult life. When I was at college I always thought I'd have everything sorted out by my late twenties – I'd be married, living in my own home and leading a comfortable life on a decent salary. Instead of which, what have I got? A one-year contract with no job security, long working hours and a boyfriend I hardly ever see because we're both so busy. And there's no way I can afford to buy my own place – property prices are far too high – so at the age of 28, I'm still sharing a rented flat just like I was ten years ago. We all seem to be just treading water, going nowhere fast. They say that young people have more choice than previous generations, but what's the good of choice if you can't afford to do anything?

Speaker 3
The problem with young people nowadays is that many of them have unrealistically high expectations, which are subsequently not met. They only have themselves to blame for this. They are too easily influenced by the media and the whole culture of celebrity. In the TV series *Friends*, for example, there is a group of twentysomethings sharing this enormous and impossibly expensive flat in New York, and young people watching think 'That's what I want.' And they want it now. And when the realization hits them that they can't have it, they feel cheated, angry somehow, as if they have been sold a lie. There seems to be a failure among youngsters to grasp the reality of adult life, to understand that there is a limit to what they can realistically hope to achieve in their twenties. They lack maturity, or, to put it another way, they just need to grow up.

Speaker 4
Jane, my granddaughter, is 24, but in some respects she's just like a teenager. Still living at home, still having to depend on her mother and father, still bringing home boyfriends, just like she did when she was sixteen. She has no choice, really. And then, on the other hand, there she is working up in London, in an adult job with adult responsibilities. No wonder she's feeling a bit confused. It was all so much more clear-cut in my day – we got married, had children and knew exactly where we were going and what we had to do. That was just the way it was. Poor Jane seems to be in crisis at the moment – she wants her independence, but can't afford to buy a place on her own; she'd like to settle down and have kids, but she also wants to focus on her career. Not easy – I don't envy these youngsters nowadays, you know.

Speaker 5
I enjoyed my time at university – my life had structure and I loved the subject I was studying. But it didn't prepare me very well for the outside world – we were all a bit cocooned, overprotected from the harsh realities of life. I soon discovered when I graduated that having a degree nowadays is absolutely no guarantee of a decent job – everyone seems to go to university these days. So now I'm doing something I don't enjoy and which has very little to do with what I studied, in the hope that something better will come along later. The uncertainty of it all has caused me to doubt my own abilities, and feel very anxious about the future. It really is a difficult time for graduates like myself. Fortunately, there are others out there with the same kind of worries and I often get help and advice from fellow sufferers on the message board at quarterlifecrisis dot com.

4
- Students match one of the statements to each speaker.
- They can then check their answers with a partner before you check with the class.

1 h 2 d 3 c 4 f 5 a

5
- Pairwork. Students discuss the questions with a partner.
- Go round monitoring and give help where needed. Then students discuss the questions as a whole class.

Language notes: reading
- You may wish to check some of the more colloquial and idiomatic language in the text.
- To ***switch jobs*** is to change jobs.
- If you ***stick with*** something or someone, you stay with them.
- If something ***adds a bit of spice***, it makes things more interesting.
- To ***tread water*** is to stay where you are, without making any progress. Literally, it means to move your arms and legs in water in a way that keeps you afloat without moving.
- When ***realization (of something) hits you***, you suddenly become aware of the situation.
- To ***grasp the reality*** of something is to see the situation as it really is.
- If you are ***cocooned*** from something, you are protected from it; a cocoon is a covering that allows certain insects to be protected while changing form, e.g. from a caterpillar to a moth or butterfly.

Extra task: discussion
- Ask students *What do you think are the most serious problems facing young people in this age group?*
- Ask them what advice they would give to the people in the listening texts who have problems?

VOCABULARY: noun suffixes

1a
- Students write the adjectives formed from the nouns listed.

1	insecure	4	mature
2	responsible	5	uncertain
3	real		

b
- Students then write the verbs formed from the nouns listed.

decide; dissatisfy; expect; realize

2a
- Students use the suffixes in the box to form nouns for each group of verbs.
- They can then check their answers with a partner before you check with the class.

1 burial; denial; survival
2 disappointment; achievement; involvement
3 failure; departure; procedure
4 existence; occurrence; obedience

b
- Students then use the suffixes in the box to form nouns for each group of adjectives.
- They can then check their answers with a partner before you check with the class.

1 sincerity; flexibility; generosity
2 sadness; tiredness; seriousness
3 pregnancy; urgency; accuracy
4 absence; patience; intelligence

3a
- Students complete the text with the correct noun form of the words in brackets.
- They can then check their answers with a partner before you check with the class.

1	fondness	6	wisdom
2	freedom	7	truth
3	innocence	8	Ignorance
4	inhibitions	9	enthusiasm
5	confidence	10	retirement

b
- Students say whether they share the same feelings as the speaker in exercise 3a.

Extra task: adjectives to verbs

- Put students in pairs. Tell the Student A in each pair to write down ten adjectives from the lesson, (*insecure, real, mature, generous*, etc). Tell the Student B in each pair to write down ten verbs from the lesson, (*decide, expect, bury, occur,* etc). Each A reads out his or her adjectives and tests B's ability to turn them into nouns. Then each B reads out his or her verbs and tests A's ability to turn them into verbs. Find out which student gets most right.

Extra task: describe the word

- Write the following words on a piece of paper: *demonstrator, politician, newsreader, consultant, employee, environmentalist*. On a different piece of paper, write *novelist, researcher, participant, spectator, historian, referee*. Stick the first piece of paper to a wall at the front of the class, and the second to a wall at the back. Ask half the class to walk and copy the words at the front on to a piece of paper. The other half of the class copy the words on the back wall. Pair students with someone who has different words. Students must then take it in turns to describe their words without using any part of the word given, and their partner must guess the word. Find out which pair finishes first.

Language notes: noun suffixes

- There are no real rules here for changing adjectives and verbs to nouns, just tendencies. For example, ***-ible*** generally changes to ***-ibility***. However, as ***-ent*** might change to ***-ence*** (e.g. *patient/patience*) or ***-ency*** (e.g. *fluent/fluency*) or even add ***-ment***, (e.g. *content/contentment*) it is probably best to merely point out that these suffix endings need learning.
- There may be a change in pronunciation or shift in stress when a word is changed from verb/adjective to noun. For example:

real /rɪəl/	*reality* /ri'æləti/
occur /ə'kɜː(r)/	*occurrence* /ə'kʌrəns/
sincere /sɪn'sɪə(r)/	*sincerity* /sɪn'serəti/
responsible /rɪ'spɒnsəb(ə)l/	*responsibility* /rɪˌspɒnsə'bɪləti/

- Notice: *burial* /'beriəl/ but *denial* /dɪ'naɪəl/.

SPEAKING

1

Communication activities, Student's Book page 139

- Ask students to turn to page 139 at the back of the book. They read the five paragraphs and answer the question.

2

- Pairwork. Put students into A and B pairs. Ask them to choose a different situation about life changes on page 139 from their partner. They read their situation and make notes on the ways they might benefit from the move.

3

- Students now read about their partner's situation on page 139, and make a notes on the ways their partner, and any other people mentioned in the text, would not benefit from the move. They should then think of alternative solutions to their partner's situation.
- Go round monitoring and give help where needed.

Roleplay

4

- Students read the instructions and do the roleplay. Make sure that Student A understands that they have to explain the reason why they want to go ahead with the decision, while Student B has to dissuade them from doing so. Students then swap roles.

5

- Students discuss what they think the best course of action would be in each case.

6

- Pairwork. Students discuss the questions with a partner.
- Ask students if they found out anything interesting from their partner in their discussion.

DID YOU KNOW?

1

- Pairwork. Students read the information and discuss the questions with a partner.

Web research tasks

Methodology guidelines: Web research tasks, page xiv

- Ask students to research charities which help people at certain times of their life. British charities include *Age Concern, Children In Need, Childline,* and *Honeypot*.
- Ask students to research one of the charities above, or a charity from their own country, and present their findings to the class.

Web search key words

- charity; old age/middle age/teenager

IF YOU WANT SOMETHING EXTRA ...

Photocopiable activity, page 214
Teaching notes, page 193

Answer key

1 Review

Student's Book page 164

1

1	achievement	6	urgency
2	survival	7	dissatisfaction
3	pleasure / satisfaction	8	responsibilities
4	awareness	9	adaptation
5	offence	10	inaccuracies

2

1 A 2 C 3 B 4 C 5 A 6 C 7 B 8 B

3

1	is being	5	've made
2	comes	6	be having
3	's coming	7	had
4	've been doing		

4

Corrected version

My youngest boy, David, starts school next week. He's a bit nervous about it all, and to tell you the truth, so **am** I. My other two never seem to worry about anything, and **neither** / **nor** does their father. David obviously takes after **me** in that respect. We know, though, that he's got the same class teacher as **the one** Paul had two years ago, so **that**'s good. **Her** name's Miss Appleby. She's a caring person and a very good teacher – at least I think **so** and I know most of the other parents **think so** / **do** too. There's a two-week period of adaptation at the beginning, and it may be that David will come home at midday during **this** / **that** time. If **so**, I've arranged for my mum to pick him up and look after him.

2A | Memory

What the lesson is about

Theme	How good your memory is and ways to improve it
Reading	Three texts on improving memory
Vocabulary	Memory & memories
Grammar	Gerunds & infinitives

If you want a lead-in ...

Discussion starters

Methodology guidelines: Discussion starters, page xiv

- *What is your earliest memory? What is your favourite memory?*
- *Which of the following are you good at remembering? Names, faces, facts and figures*
- *Do you have any techniques for remembering things? What are they?*

Test before you teach

Methodology guidelines: Test before you teach, page xiv

- Write the following words on the board:
  easy had better deny can hope
  can't help forget it's no use
- Put students in pairs and ask them to decide whether the words are followed by the full infinitive, the bare infinitive or the gerund.
- During feedback, ask students if they can remember any rules as to why the words are followed by certain constructions.
- Answers: easy – full infinitive, e.g. *It's easy to understand;* had better – bare infinitive, e.g. *We had better go now*; deny – gerund, e.g. *He denied stealing the car; can* – bare infinitive, e.g. *I can see you*; hope – full infinitive, e.g. *I hope to see you soon*; can't help – gerund; e.g. *I can't help being clumsy*; forget – full infinitive, e.g. *I forgot to send the letter*; It's no use – gerund, e.g. *It's no use trying to help him.*

Vocabulary: memory & memories

1

- Students choose an appropriate alternative to complete the statements so that they are true for themselves.
- Students then discuss their sentences with a partner.

Language notes: memory & memories

- To ***learn (something) by heart*** is to remember it without having to read or check it.
- ***Vivid*** means very clear; ***vague*** means unclear.
- ***Fond memories*** are happy ones.
- ***Bittersweet memories*** are memories that are both happy and sad (for example, memories of a wonderful holiday, but with a boy/girlfriend who later left you.)

Extra task: sharing memories

- Ask students to write down a vivid memory, a vague memory, a fond memory and a bittersweet memory. Ask them to tell their partner about each.

Reading

The reading is three texts about different methods for improving memory. The first text is from a book written by memory expert Dominic O'Brien who has devised exercises to help people remember facts and figures. There is an interview with Dominic O'Brien in the next lesson, 2B. The second text is a scientific report which says that in the future it will be commonplace to use cognitive enhancing drugs to improve memory and mental performance. The third text, an extract from a newspaper article, argues that the correct diet plays a vital role in memory and mental ability.

1

- Students read the three texts and choose which method for improving memory they find the most and least appealing. They then discuss their choices with a partner and give reasons for their opinions.

Pre-teach key words: memory/memories

- Brainstorm words connected with memory to the board and draw a mind map. To do this, write *memory/memories* in the middle of the board and draw a circle round it. Draw four short lines from the circle and write *verbs, adjective collocations, idioms, expressions* at the end of each line. Then ask students to tell you words and phrases they know.
- Alternatively, make this a dictionary research task. Students must look up 'memory/memories' in their dictionaries and use the information they find to complete the mind map.
- Here is a possible finished mind map:

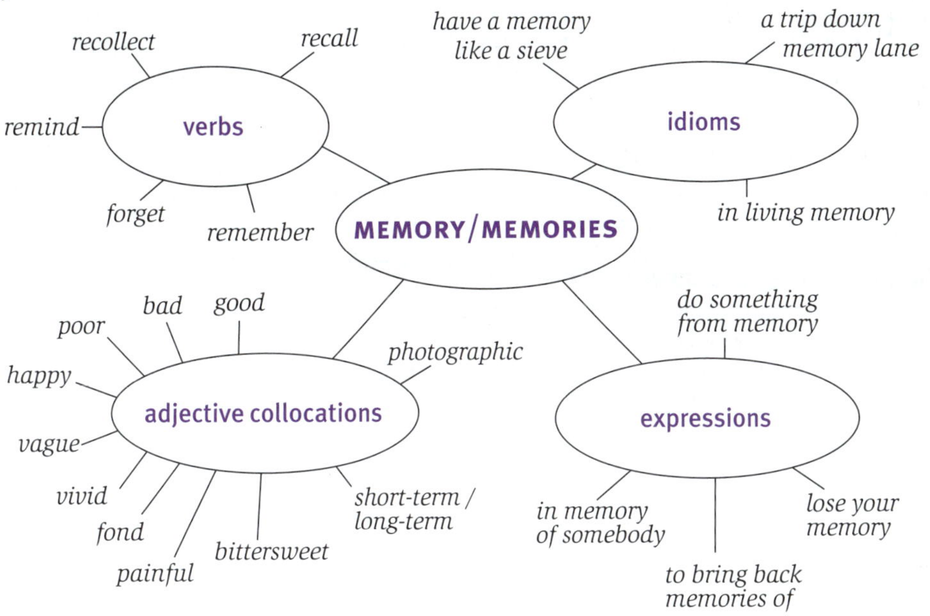

2

- Ask students to read the statements for each text first before reading the text they refer to again. They put a tick or cross next to the statements to show which are stated or not stated in the text.
- They can then check their answers with a partner before you check with the class.

1 ✗ 2 ✗ 3 ✓ 4 ✓ 5 ✗ 6 ✓ 7 ✓ 8 ✗ 9 ✗

Alternative procedure: jigsaw reading

- You could make this activity into a jigsaw task. Give students one minute to glance through the texts and say which three different memory improvement methods are being described. Then divide the class into pairs. One third of pairs reads A, one third B, and one third C. The pairs discuss the questions in exercise 2 which are relevant to their text. Divide the class again, this time into groups of three, with an A, B and C student in each group. Students then explain their texts to their new group members.

Language notes: reading

- During feedback, you may wish to check the following words and phrases:
- If something is ***stimulating*** it encourages interest.
- To ***show off*** is to behave in a way designed to attract other people's admiration.
- To ***sail through*** an exam is to pass it easily.
- ***Supple*** means flexible.
- To ***boost*** something is to improve it.
- … ***from the fringe to the norm*** means from the unusual and experimental to the usual and every day.
- ***Foggy*** means unclear and confused.

3

- Groupwork. Students discuss the question in small groups.

Possible answers:

- Common memory techniques include: remembering people and their names by linking their name and appearance, so 'Blue Belinda' because she has blue eyes; remembering facts or words by imagining them in a story or a picture; using acronyms as a shorthand – for example, remembering a list of verbs by making a word out of the first letter of each verb; organizing things you must remember into a mind map; linking people, facts or words with a colour or image; using a little poem to remember facts or dates (Columbus sailed the ocean blue, In leap year 1492).

Cultural notes: memory

- Alzheimer's disease is a serious illness affecting the brain, which makes it difficult to remember things. It gets worse over time and affects older people in particular.
- *Eternal Sunshine of a Spotless Mind* is a film starring Jim Carrey and Kate Winslett. It presupposes that you can go to a clinic and have bad memories erased from your brain. In the film, Jim Carrey, whilst undergoing the treatment, fights against losing his memories. The moral is that memories are what make us what we are – even the bad ones.

GRAMMAR: gerunds & infinitives

Language reference, Student's Book page 24
Methodology guidelines: Grammar boxes, page xiv

1

- Students look back at text A and match the highlighted verbs to the uses in the Grammar box.

A
full infinitive after certain verbs
to remember, to sail through
full infinitive after certain nouns
to show off
bare infinitive after modal verbs
become
bare infinitive after verb *help*
forget
gerund as subject
improving
gerund after preposition
making

- Ask students to find further examples of full infinitives, bare infinitives and gerunds in texts B and C. Then write them down under the headings used in exercise 1.

B
full infinitive to express purpose
to treat (people), to help (people)
full infinitive after certain verbs
(need) to improve
full infinitive after certain adjectives
(able) to forget
bare infinitive after modal verbs
(may) move, (could) usher
bare infinitive after *help*
(help people) forget
gerund after a preposition
(for) boosting

C
full infinitive to express purpose
to communicate
full infinitive after certain nouns
(ability) to store
full infinitive after certain verbs
(needed) to make
bare infinitive after modal verbs
(cannot) give, (would) train, (may) have, (will) slow
bare infinitive after *make*
(make you) feel
gerund as subject and object
eating (the right foods)

Language notes: gerunds & infinitives

- There are some rules for these uses of the full infinitive, bare infinitive and gerund: The full infinitive is used after certain adjectives e.g. *It's easy to do* and nouns e.g. *He made the decision to leave*. Gerunds are used after prepositions, e.g. *He insisted on talking* and certain verbs, e.g. *He considered applying for the job.* The bare infinitive comes after modals, e.g. *He could swim*.
- For the most part, students must learn and remember which form follows which verb. You may wish to point out that verbs are generally followed by gerunds when the gerund form describes an action which happens before the verb, e.g. *He denied taking the money* – the *taking* came before the *denying* and verbs are generally followed by the full infinitive when the infinitive form describes an action which happens after the verb, e.g. *He agreed to help* – the *helping* comes after *agreeing*. This is particularly clear when using verbs that can take two forms, e.g. *I remember phoning Kate.* (I phoned her and I remember doing it.) *He remembered to phone Kate.* (He remembered he had to phone her and then did it.)
- At this level, it is a good idea to get students to contrast the choice of form in English with the choice of form in the students' first language(s). Tell students to focus on and remember any forms that are different from how they would naturally use them in their L1.
- It is worth pointing out the form when verbs are followed by objects and negatives:
  John asked me not to come.
  Subject + verb + object + *not* + full infinitive

Extra task: gerunds & infinitives

- Ask students to form a table with three columns in their notebooks or vocabulary books, headed *gerunds*, *full infinitives*, and *bare infinitives*. Ask them to record verbs which are followed by these forms in the appropriate column whenever they come across them.

2

- Students complete the sentences with the correct form of the verbs in brackets.
- They can then check their answers with a partner before you check with the class.

1	wondering	5	agreeing
2	to get	6	to inform
3	phoning	7	laughing; crying / to cry
4	to become	8	forgetting; to buy

3

- Students complete the sentences using an appropriate verb form so that they are true for themselves.

4

- Pairwork. Students discuss their sentences with a partner.

Extra task: noughts & crosses

- Play noughts and crosses with gerunds and infinitives. Draw a noughts and crosses table on the board and write nine verbs from the lesson in the squares. Divide the class into two teams, (the X team and the O team). The X team must choose a verb and challenge the O team to make a correct sentence using the verb. If the O team produce a correct sentence, after conferring, they win the square. Rub out the verb and write O in the square. If the O team produce an incorrect sentence, the X team win the square. Then the O team choose a verb and the X team must make a sentence. Continue until one team has won three squares to form a line vertically, horizontally or diagonally.
- Alternatively, put students in pairs to play the game.
- Here is an example of the game:
  At the start of the game:

might	hope	let
avoid	refuse	deny
can't	agree	can't stand

Team X have won:

X	O	let
O	X	O
O	agree	X

Methodology advances
Teaching Advanced students – some pitfalls

- *It's worth noting a few of the common reasons why teachers may 'crash and burn' when teaching at Advanced level – not least so you can avoid them yourself.*

Not admitting you don't know

- *Of all the things that seem to get in the way of teaching high levels, this often seems to be the big problem. Faced with a language question that you can't answer, it's usually best to acknowledge this and then do something about it – such as offering your best guess (and admitting it's a guess), saying you'll find out before the next class, handing out some reference books for students to check, looking it up yourself, and so on. The alternative of covering up your ignorance and pretending that you do know something (and making up answers, fudging answers or giving unclear and incomplete explanations) seems to be something that students quickly see through. This tends to lead to low student trust and ever weaker student-teacher interaction. But before you start saying that you don't know lots of things ... make sure you read the next point!*

Not knowing enough

- *Having given all that encouragement to admitting ignorance (in the paragraph above) I now need to point out that there is a definite limit to how much you are allowed not to know. To be a successful Advanced teacher you do need to have an appropriate level of language awareness. While it's fine to have problems with rare, obscure, unexpected or odd items, your students will be puzzled or worried if they find that you have repeated or significant problems with more basic grammar.*
- *If you are in this situation, having been given a class that, in terms of language knowledge, you really don't feel up to teaching, it means that you need to put extra time into lesson preparation. Get to grips with the grammar points in the lesson before you go in. Read the language notes in the Student's Book and this Teacher's Book so that you feel familiar with the particular area. Go through the vocabulary and make sure you are comfortable with all the items. You can sidestep many potential problems by undertaking this sort of careful preparation.*

Letting students get into 'catch out the teacher' mode

- *This is a discipline problem that really only occurs in high level classes of teenagers or young adults. Because they haven't come across the issue at lower levels, it may take an unsuspecting teacher by surprise.*
- *Some Advanced students start playing the game of trying to spot and expose a teacher's weaknesses in language knowledge or skills. Stronger more confident class members (such as those who have lived in an English-speaking country for a year) sometimes feel that their own knowledge is superior to their teacher's and try to exploit this, perhaps for amusement or for 'scoring points' to bolster their own self-image in the class. This typically involves asking things that are not genuine issues the student wants to know about but questions that are intended to chip away at the limits of the teacher's knowledge. The student who keeps asking you for extremely obscure vocabulary items that he doesn't seem very interested in, and who then turns round to smile at other students, may be trying this.*
- *How to deal with it? Well, firstly you have to recognize it – and it can be tricky to spot that a question isn't something that a student is genuinely curious about. You don't want to pick on an innocent student – or discourage the student who really wants to find out about language items. However, when your intuition suggests that a student is trying to catch you out, the safest strategy is probably to (a) admit that you don't know (as described in the first section above), (b) simply turn the question back on them by saying something like, 'That's interesting. I have no idea. Please take three minutes and look it up in these two books and report back when you have an answer.' By not getting flustered, by not trying to pretend to have knowledge you don't have and by putting the onus of finding an answer back on the questioner, you are quite likely to defuse the problem and put a stop to further efforts to derail you.*

Getting the pace wrong

- *Pacing a lesson well is a problem for the teacher at every level, but is a particular issue at high levels. Advanced students can sometimes be very fast (so can easily get bored) but they can also be very slow, really trying to understand something challenging and going to great lengths to make sure they get it right. The same individual may operate at both extremes, depending on factors such as how interested they are, how valuable they feel the subject matter is, how they feel and so on. There is no easy answer for a teacher, but here are a few hints.*
- *As far as possible take your pace from the students in class. Follow their pace rather than lead. Be prepared for sudden, dramatic shifts in pace, and go with them. For example, sometimes students get very interested in a language point that had never occurred to you as worth spending time on. The pace might suddenly totally slow down while students look at the item, think about it, ask questions, and so on. Unless you really need to move on, try to allow this; this is the place where some real learning is going on.*
- *Talk with students about pace and find out what they think about how fast things should go. If there is a general preference for working quickly, play devil's advocate a little and argue the case that some Advanced level work requires slow careful focus and thinking.*
- *Plan shifts of pace yourself. It is sometimes effective to work very very fast, e.g. through material that seems easy for the class, perhaps polishing off two exercises in three or four minutes rather than taking a more normal, careful approach. Sudden fast work can help to energize a class and make them focus more carefully.*

IF YOU WANT SOMETHING EXTRA ...

➋ *Photocopiable activity, page 215*
➋ *Teacher's notes, page 193*

2B | Memory man

What the lesson is about

Theme	Playing cards & techniques to memorize cards in card games
Speaking	Groupwork: using Dominic O'Brien's technique to memorize cards
Listening	Interview with Dominic O'Brien – a memory expert
Vocabulary	Playing cards
Pronunciation	Chunking

If you want a lead-in ...

Discussion starters

Methodology guidelines: Discussion starters, page xiv

- *Do you like playing cards? Which game(s) do you play? How do you play that game?*
- *Have you ever played cards for money? When? Who with? How much did you win? What techniques do you use when you are playing cards?*

Pre-teach key words: cards

- Bring in to class as many packs of cards as you can. Divide students into small groups and give each group a pack. Tell each group to play with their cards for a couple of minutes. After two minutes, ask students to tell you what they did with the cards. Try to elicit as many words connected with cards as you can. If students aren't sure about the word, ask them to show you. Then tell them the word.
- Elicit to the board: *card, pack, deal, shuffle*, etc.

Introducing the theme: memorizing

- Prepare an OHT with 20 random words on it. (You could choose words from this and the previous lesson, e.g. *forget, vivid, bittersweet, shuffle, deal*, etc.) Cut up the OHT into separate pieces, each containing one word.
- Ask students to study the words for three minutes turn off the OHP. Tell students to write down all the words they can remember.
- As feedback, ask which words students remembered. Put the words onto the OHP as students recall them. Ask students if they used any memory techniques to help them.
- If you do not have access to an OHP, you can write the words on the board.

Vocabulary: playing cards

1

- Pairwork. Students work with a partner to match the words to the playing cards in the photo.

From left to right: joker; jack of hearts; king of diamonds; two of spades; ace of clubs; seven of hearts; queen of clubs; ten of diamonds

2

- Students complete the text using the nouns and the correct form of the verbs in the box.

1	pack	6	draw
2	suits	7	hand
3	face	8	shuffled
4	count	9	odds
5	dealt	10	bet

Extra task: describe the game

- Ask students to think of a simple card game which doesn't involve complicated rules. They explain the card game to their partner, and find out if their partner knows this game.

Cultural notes: blackjack

- Blackjack is a card game which is played in casinos all over the world. It is based on an earlier game called *vingt-et-un* ('twenty-one'), which was first played in French casinos in the early 1700s. In casinos, players play against the 'dealer', a casino employee who deals the cards then takes bets.
- The origin of the word 'blackjack' is interesting. In order to encourage players to play the new game, casinos in the United States offered bonus payouts if players won with particular hands. If a player's hand consisted of the ace of spades and a black Jack (either the Jack of clubs or the Jack of spades), they won a 10-1 bonus. Early players of the game started to call this hand a 'blackjack' and the name soon became used to describe the game as a whole.

Listening

The listening is a three-part interview with Dominic O'Brien, a World Memory champion. In Part 1 he describes what is involved in the championship and the type of people who take part in it. In Part 2 he describes the techniques he uses to memorize material. In Part 3 he describes his gambling experiences in Las Vegas and his learning experiences at school.

1

- Ask students to close their books and to name all the playing cards that they have seen on that page of the Student's Book.

2 1.7

- Explain that students are going to listen to an interview with a memory expert. Students listen to Part 1 of the recording and complete the gaps in the notes with a number.
- They could then compare their answers with a partner before you check with the class. Play the recording again if necessary.
- They then say which of the tasks and achievements they heard in the recording impressed them the most.

1	three / 3
2	two thousand / 2,000
3	twenty-five / 25
4	five / 5
5	two hundred / 200
6	twenty-eight and a half / 28.5 / 28½
7	fifteen / 15
8	two thousand eight hundred and eight / 2,808
9	three / 3
10	eight / 8

1.7

Part 1
I = Interviewer D = Dominic
I: Dominic, you've won the World Memory Championships no fewer than eight times. Could you perhaps start by telling us what is involved in these championships? What do you have to do?
D: Well, the World Memory Championships, er, started in 1991, and there were seven of us then. Um, these days there are three days and ten events. And to give you an idea, there are marathon events and sprint events. So, for example, the first one you have to memorize about a two thousand digit number. You have one hour to look at it, another hour and a half to recall it. This is like a marathon memory event. You then have an hour to memorize as many packs of playing cards as possible, usually about 25 decks in an hour. You have to memorize, er, a hundred historic dates, these are fictitious dates, and you have to put the year and the fact to them – you've got five minutes, so this is a sprint one. There are other ones where you have to memorize a spoken number. They put a CD in of 200 numbers read at one digit a second – very difficult if you consider that you can only hold about seven or nine digits in your short term memory. But we manage to do that. Erm, and then you have the fastest time to memorize a single deck of cards. And my personal best is 28 and a half seconds.
I: Goodness. What kind of people take part in these championships?
D: Erm, there's a broad range of people. Er, there are quite a few students having said that. Erm, I suppose the age range is somewhere between 15 and 35. I'm … I'm one of the older ones. I'm nearly 50 now, erm but you get er professional people, traders, a psychiatric nurse, memory trainers, but a lot of students as well.
I: Now, you also got yourself into the *Guinness Book of Records*. And to do that you memorized 54 packs of cards, that's 2,808 cards in a single sighting. How did you manage that?
D: Er, very slowly. I did this a few years ago, and yes, you're right. The 54 decks were shuffled into each other and you're only allowed a single sighting of each card. Now, I started off at nine o'clock in the morning doing this, and I finished at nine o'clock at night. That's just looking at each card, so there was lots of reviewing going on in my head. I then spent the next three hours trying to recall all 2,808, which I did. And I made eight errors, which is what Guinness allows. You're allowed to make a half per cent margin of error, so I made eight errors, and that is, at the making of this er audio, is still the current record.

3 1.8
- Students listen to Part 2 of the recording and answer the questions.
- They could then compare their answers with a partner before you check with the class. Play the recording again if necessary.

1 association, location (journeys) and imagination
2 Bill Gates, the ten of diamonds, is in the bedroom presenting him with a million-dollar cheque.
Kylie Minogue, the queen of clubs, is on the staircase practising for a night club event.
James Bond, the seven of hearts, is in the bathroom hiding in the shower and after an international spy.
3 Top memorizers do not have a brain which is physically different to the norm and they do not have an exceptional IQ, but they do use more parts of their brain than other people, in both the left and right hemispheres.

1.8

Part 2
I: What techniques do you use to memorize the material?
D: There are three things really involved. It's the use of association, so if I say 'key', you think of 'door', 'rabbit' you think of 'carrot'. That's association. The second one is the use of location. I use journeys, familiar journeys, a journey round my house, a journey round a golf course, to store information, to keep the sequence going. And the most important ingredient is the use of imagination, something that we all possess. Erm, and that combination works very well.
I'll … I'll just give you a brief example. Let's say er in playing cards … let's say you have three cards: the ten of diamonds, erm the queen of clubs and the seven of hearts. Now the ten of diamonds to me is Bill Gates, the richest man in the world, and the queen of clubs is Kylie Minogue, if you know her, erm the singer, and the seven of hearts would be er an international heart throb like erm James Bond – double oh seven. So that's the association. Now to get the three in sequence, I would have a journey round my house take … taking the bedroom, bathroom, staircase, etc.
So if we shuffle the cards up and the first one is the ten of diamonds. I would imagine Bill Gates being in my bedroom, maybe presenting me with a million-dollar cheque. How wonderful! Go to the second location, which would be the bathroom, and there we find the seven of hearts, which would be James Bond. He's hiding in the shower. He's after an international spy, for example. And the third stage, which is on the staircase, I find the queen of clubs, which is Kylie Minogue. Maybe she's practising for a … a night club event. So I'm using two things here, I'm using the erm imagination, but I'm also using left brain logic as well, giving them a reason why they're there. Now the journey preserves the order of the information.
I: And you're using quite a lot of humour as well.
D: I think so. I try to use the whole of my brain, not just the spatial, imaginative, but I'm trying to use sequence and logic and reason. You've got two brains, by the way. You've got a left and right hemisphere, you might as well use them both.
I: You've just mentioned the two sides of your brain, Dominic. I understand you were the subject of a brain study a few years ago.
D: Yeah, back in 2001, the Institute of Neurology approached me, er actually nine others as well, nine other top memorizers. And they wanted to know what was going on in our brains when we were memorizing all this massive amount of information. And they wanted three questions answered. The first one: are our brains physically different to the norm? Secondly, do we have exceptional IQ? And the third one: are we using different parts of our brains?
So the first question is, er no, our brains aren't physically different, mine isn't. I was put through this tunnel, it's called 'Functional Magnetic Resonance Imaging', so they look at your brain, slice by slice. They didn't find any silicon chips there or anything. Nothing extraordinary.
The second question, er no, I'm not intellectually superior over and above my memory abilities, so no high IQ there. You don't have to be a genius to do this.
But thirdly, yes, we are using parts of the brain, er left and right hemisphere, over and above the norm, er and particularly in a thing called the hippocampus. Erm, this is not surprising, it's something I'd always suspected, because I use erm journeys, so there's spatial facility there. I also use sequence, left brain function, reason, as I mentioned earlier, the use of imagination as well. So it's the two hemispheres working very well together, and I think the Institute of Neurology have proved this.

4 1.9

- Students listen to Part 3 of the recording and decide if the statements are true or false. They then correct the false statements.
- They could then compare their answers with a partner before you check with the class. Play the recording again if necessary.

1 True
2 False – 100,000
3 False – He says his profession as a card counter did not last very long, as he was banned for winning so much.
4 True
5 False – He says the opposite is true; he was diagnosed with dyslexia and he found it difficult to concentrate.
6 False – He began when he was 30.

Alternative procedure: students take control

- If you have a small class, and access to two or more recordings and audio players, this is a good opportunity to hand over control of the lesson to the students. In small groups, let students play the recording themselves. They can listen as much as they like, and pause or rewind as often as they like, in order to find all the information. During feedback, find out about your students' listening ability by asking how often they had to listen.

Extra task: vocabulary

- You could lead-in to this listening by pre-teaching some key words. For example, ask students to tell you the difference between *marathon/sprint; fictitious; factual* and *number digit* (67 is a number; 6 and 7 are its two digits).

Cultural notes: listening

- Bill Gates is the founder of Microsoft and the world's richest man.
- Kylie Minogue /mɪnəʊg/ is an Australian pop star.
- A ***heart throb*** is an attractive male film star or pop star.
- ***Dyslexia*** is a medical condition affecting the brain that makes it difficult to read and spell.

1.9

Part 3

I: Could you tell us about your gambling experiences in Las Vegas? Is it true you were barred from a number of casinos?

D: It is true. Erm, somebody suggested to me, as I can memorize all these packs of playing cards, then surely I could clean up at the casinos. So I took six months out and I studied the game of Blackjack or Twenty-one and erm when I commit myself to something, I'm a bit of a perfectionist. I have to spend a lot of time doing it. In fact, I dealt out a hundred thousand hands of Black Jack, trying to work out all the permutations. I also used the computer to work out odds against the casino – any two hands. And I committed all these tables to memory and then I went into the casino and found that I could … I could win. I had an edge over the … over the dealer. Erm, unfortunately my profession as a card counter, as they're called, didn't last very long, as I was winning more and more money. And then I got a blanket ban. So a few years ago I was commissioned by erm er British television, er production company to go to Las Vegas. In fact we travelled across America, and I got thrown out of thirteen casinos, er, but we turned 20,000 dollars into 30,000 dollars by the use of card counting, which is a skill. This is something I developed and something you could do too.

I: Finally, Dominic, could you tell us about your learning experiences at school? I imagine you must have been an A-grade student.

D: Well, everybody assumes that, but the opposite is true. In fact, I was diagnosed with dyslexia as a child. Erm, I found it very difficult to concentrate. We didn't know much about dyslexia in the sixties. I also think I had Attention Deficit Disorder as well, I was easily distracted, I was always looking out of the window. I much preferred to be out in the big wide world, playing football or tennis or … or painting or doing something like that. I found it very difficult to concentrate on what the teacher was saying and also on the written word. It took me four attempts to pass English language. So I would say the moral of the story here is, if I can achieve success rather late in life – I didn't start training my memory until I was thirty – then that gives hope for everybody else. It's never too late to start training your memory.

I: That's excellent advice. Thank you very much Dominic.

Methodology advances Working with long or complex Student's Book listening texts

- *As your students will be discovering, the listenings at this level can be quite challenging. For example, let's look at the recordings you will work on in this unit. This lesson contains a listening text (interview with Dominic O'Brien) that is more than seven minutes long and contains long individual turns (i.e. one person speaking at length) and some quite complex specialist concepts and terminology (e.g. functional magnetic resonance imaging). It also includes lots of features of natural, spontaneous native speaker speech such as hesitations, false starts and sentences that don't look much like standard written English sentences – all three features exemplified by this short extract: 'So the first question is, er no, our brains aren't physically different, mine isn't.' Lesson 2D contains lively exchanges with interruptions, disagreements and a lot of implied attitudes.*
- *While many students will have had practice in dealing with difficult listening work over the years, others may not have had the same level of exposure, perhaps because their learning was over-focussed on grammar, vocabulary and reading. If you find that your students struggle with some of these Student's Book listenings, you may want to have some extra ideas for working with them up your sleeve. Here are some suggestions:*

Before you do the Student's Book tasks

- ***'Best guess' predicted answers*** *Get students to predict answers to questions. Ask them to write down their 'best guess' for each question, and then compare their ideas with others, before they listen. For example, in this lesson students could fill in their estimates of answers for the gaps in exercise 2. This makes the actual listening also an enjoyable sort of informal competition: who predicted closest to the right answer?*
- ***Detailed introduction*** *Rather than just introducing the recording in general terms, tell the students in more detail exactly what they are going to hear on the recording (without actually revealing the key content).*

For example, after students have read the Student's Book introduction to part 1 of the recording in this lesson, you could go on to say: 'First of all he's going to talk about how the world memory championship has grown over the years and about the kind of tasks they have to do. Then he describes the kind of people that take part in these championships and how he won a world record.' By signposting the basic structure of what they are going to hear, an introduction like this will help students to find their bearings within a long recording, which in turn will help them to pick out details more easily.

While doing Student's Book tasks

- ***Replay in segments*** *Play the recording all the way through first time, but then – after allowing students to compare answers with a partner, before you check answers with them and without asking: 'Do you want to hear it again?' – start playing the recording again, pausing every 20 or 30 seconds at a natural pause point for at least ten second's pause. Keep quiet yourself. Let students talk to each other here, but don't ask or answer any questions or get into conversation. Don't ask when students want you to restart after a pause, just start playing it again when you feel it's the right time. The pauses reduce the intensity of a long listening, give extra thinking time and a chance for students to quickly check points with others.*
- ***Use student teachers*** *Invite an average or weaker level student to be the 'teacher'. This person is responsible for controlling the CD player and for reaching consensus on each answer, which he/she should write on the board. The student, not being sure of the right answers him/herself is forced to listen to a range of ideas and to go at the real pace of the class (something it's often more difficult for the real teacher to do). You may be surprised by the fact that this technique often takes much longer on areas you expected to be easy, and much less time on some you thought hard. (N.B. Although it may feel like the intuitive choice, don't appoint the strongest student to be teacher as they are likely to simply put up their own answers and ignore the views or problems of the class as a whole.)*

After listening work

- ***Raising awareness about achievement*** *While students can often see what they have learnt in grammar or vocabulary, their achievement in skills work may seem less tangible. Raise awareness at the end of concentrated work on listening by asking students to look back at the lesson and write one or more gap-fills for these sentences:*

1 After this lesson I think I am better at listening to ___(genre)___ and understanding ___(what sort of content)___ .
2 The most challenging things for me in this recording were ...

SPEAKING

1

Communication activities, Student's Book pages 140 & 147

- Groupwork. Put students into A and B groups. Ask them to turn to their respective pages at the back of the book and to read the instructions.
- They then pair up with someone in their group and take it in turns to tell their story to each other.

2

- Pairwork. Students now pair up with someone from the other group. They turn to their partner's page and test whether they can name the cards in the correct order and tell the story of the journey which helped them remember the cards in the correct sequence.

3

- Pairwork. Students discuss the questions with a partner.

Extra task: memory techniques

- Ask students to choose a set of vocabulary or grammar forms that they find difficult to remember. (It could be verb + gerund / infinitive forms from Lesson 2A.) Tell them to devise a way of remembering the set of words or grammar for the next lesson. In the next lesson, find out how successful some of your students have been.

PRONUNCIATION: chunking

1 **1.10**

- Play the recording and point out the slight pauses Dominic makes between each group of words, which are marked with a line (/), to help the listener make sense of what he is saying.

2

- Students now practise chunking by reading the tapescript in exercise 1.

3 **1.11**

- Ask students to look at tapescript 1.11 on page 156. They mark each chunk with a line (/).
- Students then listen to the recording to compare their text. They could then practise saying the text out loud with a partner.

Suggested answer:
I'll ... I'll just give you a brief example / let's say / er in playing cards / let's say you have three cards / the ten of diamonds / erm / the queen of clubs / and the seven of hearts / now the ten of diamonds to me / is Bill Gates / the richest man in the world / and the queen of clubs is Kylie Minogue / if you know her / erm the singer / and the seven of hearts would be er / an international heart throb like erm / James Bond – / double oh seven / so that's the association / now to get the three in sequence / I would have a journey round my house / take taking the bedroom / bathroom / staircase, etc.

IF YOU WANT SOMETHING EXTRA ...

Photocopiable activity, page 216
Teacher's notes, page 194

2c | Bicycle history

What the lesson is about

Theme	Transport & the history of the bicycle
Speaking	Groupwork: comparing three methods of transport and their impact on our lives today
Reading	*The rise of the bicycle*: a magazine article about the greatest technological innovation since 1800
Vocabulary	*Way*

If you want a lead-in ...

Discussion starters

Methodology guidelines: Discussion starters, page xiv

- *When and where do you think the bicycle was invented?*
- *How do you think the bicycle changed society?*

Test before you teach

Methodology guidelines: Test before you teach, page xiv

- Ask students to tell you as many different phrases as they can think of using the word *way*. Brainstorm and write them on the board.

Pre-teach key words: bicycles

- Using the pictures in the Student's Book, or, better still, a large picture of a bicycle or a drawing which you could put on the board, try to elicit and label as many parts of a bike as you can.
- Try to elicit the following: *wheels, tyres, (wire) spokes, gears, chains, seat, handlebars, pedals, brakes, bell.*

Speaking

1

- Groupwork. Put students into groups of three. They each choose one of the methods of transport pictured and argue with their partners why their method of transport has the most positive impact on our lives today.

2

- Students discuss whether their views about the method of transport they choose in exercise 1 correspond with their real views.

Cultural notes: transport images

- Picture A shows an early steam locomotive. The 'Rocket', invented by George Stephenson, was the first truly successful train, winning a competition in 1829.
- Picture B shows the first aeroplane, invented by Wilbur and Orville Wright, which made its maiden flight at Kitty Hawk, North Carolina, in 1903.
- Picture C shows the first gasoline-powered car. Karl Benz and Gottlieb Daimler patented the first cars in Germany in 1886.
- Picture D shows a woman sitting on a 'scorcher', a Victorian bicycle, in St James' Park, London.
- Picture E shows a man riding a 'penny farthing', the first bicycle built for riding at speed.

Reading

The reading text looks at the history of the bicycle, the changes in its design and why it was the greatest technological innovation since 1800.

1

- Pairwork. Students discuss the two comments about the effect of the bicycle in the 19th century.

2

- Students read the article and compare the ideas expressed in the article with the ideas they discussed in exercise 1.

3

- Students read the article again and match the headings to the paragraphs.
- If you think your class will have problems, tell them to read each paragraph in turn and then look back at the sentences for clues to do with reference words, grammar, etc. Do the first one as an example with the class.
- Students could compare their answers with a partner before you check with the class.

1 f 2 b 3 h 4 a 5 g 6 c 7 e 8 d

Extra task: vocabulary

- Ask students to find the following phrasal verbs, connected with cycling, in the text, and explain their meaning:
  hop on (get on quickly)
  pedal off (go away by using your pedals)
  push… along (move by pushing the ground with your feet)
  speed (sped) off (go away quickly)

Cultural & language notes

- ***Mate*** is a colloquial word for a friend. It is used here anachronistically.
- A ***dandy*** is a fashionable young man.
- A ***rupture*** is a tear in the bodily tissue.
- ***Bicycling*** is an old-fashioned term for cycling.
- A ***suffragist*** was a woman who took part in public protests about giving women suffrage (the right to vote) in the early 1900s; also called a *suffragette*.
- To ***emancipate*** someone is to free them.
- A ***corset*** is a stiff piece of underwear worn by women to make their waists look thin.
- A ***tenement*** is a block of flats; the word is often used to describe huge, overcrowded blocks, notably in nineteenth century London or New York.

4

- Groupwork. Students work on their own. They choose a technological innovation from 1800 to today which they think has had the greatest impact on the world. They make of list of reasons for their opinion.
- Students then take it in turns to tell the rest of the group their reasons for choosing their innovation. The group then decides which of the three innovations they think is the greatest and the reason why.

Alternative procedure: debate

- With more advanced classes, you could organize this as a more formal debate. Divide the class into two debating teams, team A and team B. Write on the board, *This house believes that the plane has done more to change the world than the car*. Team A must defend the motion. Team B must argue against it. Team A have five minutes to think of reasons why the plane is more important. Team B must think of why it isn't. Once students have a few arguments, tell each group to nominate a spokesperson. The spokesperson for A must stand up and make a speech in favour of the motion. Team B's spokesperson must then stand up and argue against. At the end, have a free vote and decide which team's argument was most convincing.

VOCABULARY: *way*

1

- Students look back at the highlighted expression *paving the way* in paragraph 7 of the text and say what they think it means.

To create a situation that makes it possible or easier for something to happen. (Definition taken from the *Macmillan English Dictionary*) Here literally, because the literal meaning of to pave is 'to put a hard flat surface on an area of ground'. The writer is alluding to the laying of road surfaces.

2

- Students complete the sentences with the adjectives in the box.
- Students could then compare their answers with a partner before you check with the class.

1 wrong	4 roundabout
2 long	5 big
3 bad	

3

- Students complete the sentences with the correct form of the verbs in the box.
- Students could then compare their answers with a partner before you check with the class.

Alternative procedure: dictionary research

- You could do exercises 2 and 3 above as dictionary research tasks. After they have filled the gaps with the expressions that they know, get students to look up *way* in the dictionary, and try to find any expressions they are not sure about.
- Using the dictionary, get students to categorize the expressions with *way* according to the categories in the Language notes below. Ask them to add any other useful expressions they find in the dictionary.

Language notes: way

- According to the *Macmillan English Dictionary*, the expressions with *way* can be placed in the following defining categories (useful phrases not in the exercises are in italics):
  1. method/manner
     in a roundabout way, get her own way, change her ways
  2. aspect/attitude
     in more ways than one, have it both ways
  3. direction/distance
     the wrong way round, *on your way, lose your way*
  4. means of going in/out
     force your way in, stand in someone's way
  5. area/position
     get in the way, keep out of the way
  6. situation/condition
     in a bad way, *the way things are*
  7. phrases
     go back a long way (meaning a long time), know your way round, work your way up, go out of your way, give way, *have a way with words, go your separate ways*

1 get	4 work
2 changed	5 goes
3 knows	6 give

4

- Ask students to look back at the sentences in exercise 3 and decide which ones describe themselves either now or in the past.

5

➲ *Communication activities, Student's Book pages 147 & 154*

- Pairwork. Put students into A and B pairs. Ask students to turn to their respective pages at the back of the book. They read the instructions and the list of topics.
- Students then take it in turns to talk about their list of topics without using the adjectives, nouns or verbs given. Their partner must guess which of the topics they are talking about.

Web research tasks

➲ *Methodology guidelines: Web research tasks, page xiv*

- Ask students to decide what they think was the greatest technological innovation of the 20th century. Then ask them to research the innovation on the internet and find answers to the following questions:
  Who invented or discovered it?
  What is the story behind its invention and development?
  How did it affect or change society?
  In what ways does it still affect society today?
  Why do you think it is so important?
- Ask some students to present their findings to the class in the next lesson.

Methodology advances Dictionaries

- *Successful high-level students need to be effective users of dictionaries, whether it's a good printed dictionary such as the new edition of the* Macmillan English Dictionary (MED), *an online dictionary such as (would you believe) the* Macmillan English Dictionary Online *or a beeping calculator look-alike in their pocket such as the ... well, I'll let you choose your own!*
- *A student who only goes to the dictionary for definitions is missing out on quite a lot of opportunities to improve their use of language. By offering a little training and practice in effective dictionary use in class, you offer ways for students to become more effective language users and more autonomous students. The table below summarizes some areas you might want to focus on with your class.*

Some things that Advanced students can get from dictionaries	***What they need to know or be able to do***	***Implication for the teacher***
They can learn typical collocations. Knowing the word on its own isn't enough. How does it go together with other words?	*Students will need to understand that the dictionary offers more than example sentences, but actually demonstrates regular going-together patterns.*	*Do exercises specifically focussed on collocation. The MED has 500 special collocation boxes which list thousands of strong collocates, showing the way words behave and combine with one another.*
They can learn how a new word is pronounced and recognize problems or incorrect sounds in their own pronunciation of a word.	*Students need to be familiar with phonemic symbols and be able to quickly read pronunciation from them.*	*It's worth spending time teaching these if students don't know them (and then offering lots of familiarization practice, e.g. transcribing words or saying them aloud from phonemes) so that students become able to do this fluently and successfully.*
They can learn where the main and secondary stresses are in a word. They can find out why some words they feel they know are often misunderstood by others.	*Students will need to know how stress is marked in the dictionary and be able to make use of this information in their own pronunciation.*	*Make sure students know what the stress symbols show. Practice making use of these when saying new words. Don't model words yourself – see if students can get perfect pronunciation just from reading the dictionary entry.*
They can expand their vocabulary and improve their language awareness.	*Students need to choose the right words at the right time and to use them correctly and idiomatically.*	*Show students the 'Expand your vocabulary' and 'Improve your writing skills' sections in the* MED. *Also show them the useful 'Metaphor' and 'Get it right' boxes'.*
They can learn new uses for familiar words.	*Students tend to think that the main problem is learning new things, whereas the real high level issue is discovering the extraordinary range of things you can do with supposedly familiar items.*	*Lead activities that focus on this, e.g. taking one familiar word such as ground, table, book, etc. and basing exercises on getting students to explore the vast range of possible uses (see Methodology advances: exploring the grammar of a word, page 105).*

Go to www.macmillandictionaries.com for more information about the *English Dictionary for Advanced Learners*.

If you want something extra ...

➋ *Photocopiable activity, page 217*
➋ *Teacher's notes, page 194*

2D | Memory stores

What the lesson is about

Theme	Comparing traditional museums with modern interactive museums
Speaking	Roleplay: committee discussing proposals for a new museum
Listening	A conversation about different types of museums
Grammar	Comparisons
Did you know?	Statues

If you want a lead-in …

Discussion starters

Methodology guidelines: Discussion starters, page xiv

- *What are the most famous museums in your country? What can you see in them?*
- *What is the best museum you have ever been to? Why is it good?*
- *If you were to design a museum, what would you try to achieve?*

Test before you teach

Methodology guidelines: Test before you teach, page xiv

- Write the following sentence starters on the board:
  It's bigger …
  It looks just …
  She's not as …
  It's by far …
  It's slightly…
  It's not such…
- Ask students to work in pairs to finish the sentences in any way they like.
- As feedback, correct wrong answers, and discuss what makes the right answers correct.

Listening

The listening is a conversation between three people about interactive museums, their popularity especially amongst children, how they attract visitors to museums and a comparison between interactive museums and traditional museums.

1

- Pairwork. Students read the texts about four different museums and choose which one they would most and least like to visit. They then compare their choices with a partner and give reasons for their opinions.

2 1.12

- Explain that students are going to listen to three people talking about these museums in the photos. Before they listen, ask students to read the sentences they have to complete.
- Play the recording. Students listen and complete the sentences, using between one and three words in each gap.
- They could then compare their answers with a partner before you check with the class. Play the recording again if necessary.

1 time machine
2 tenth
3 (a) leather (worker); (a) rubbish (tip)
4 a book
5 interactive
6 scientific discoveries
7 look at things
8 target audience
9 advertisement
10 close (down)

1.12

E = Emily T = Tom H = Hannah

E: So, um, so yep you go through the doors and what happens?
T: Oh yeah, you go down the steps and you go, it's like you're going back in time 'cos you're climbing down into an archaeological trench almost …
E: What do you mean – is there sort of like different rocks and stuff on the walls?
T: Yeah, they have, it's like, it's pretend but they have, like um, er artefacts built into the walls and things and then you go in a kind of little capsule that's like a … they pretend it's a time machine and it shakes and you see a little film of going back in time and so on … a woman gives you a little talk about the Viking times and York and then you go out of the capsule and you have to sit in a little um a little car like a roller coaster and you get locked in it, and, like a safety bar and you go round very slowly, it's not like like a ride, but as you go round the museum you're actually being showed round a Viking street – they've got like dummies and re-built houses and little er models of of the street as it was, er you know, in the tenth century when the Vikings were there.
E: I guess actually getting in a buggy is slightly better than having to walk around a museum, isn't it?
H: Yeah!
E: It's like … tiring …
T: Yeah, I mean … it's not a huge place but it just keeps it, it just keeps it and and it keeps it interesting and the buggy kind of twists and turns to make sure you're looking at the right bit ….
E: Oh right!
H: But what I've heard about, um, Jorvik that's different is that you can actually smell the, er different smells that you would have at that time … as well, which sounds really good …
E: Really? Weird!
T: Yes, it is weird …
E: How does that … what, you go into a different room and it smells different?
T: Yeah, it's … it's all one big room but with a track along the ground but as you go round this mock-up, like a a a re-built version of the street as you go past each house it smells different. You'll see one house has got a leather worker in it and it's just a puppet, just a mannequin, you know, but as you go past his house it smells a bit of leather and then a bit further down the street you go past a rubbish tip and it's got – it smells a bit of rubbish – it doesn't smell very nice …
E: Oh how horrible!
T: … there's a puppet of a man sitting on a toilet and … yeah! He shakes the toilet door at you as you go by and he shouts at you in old Norse and he smells. It's great – it really keeps it alive I think.
H: It sounds good definitely but I think on one … on the other hand going to one of these museums is a little bit like seeing the film of a book – I mean it's sort of a bit you're disappointed when you actually go and it's particularly if you … if you like using your own imagination, as I do.

T: Yeah, it's true, but I think, I think the point of something like Jorvik is to get, children especially, is to get everybody to engage their imagination and then you come out the other end and there's an actual traditional museum, with displays and, um, things written on the walls, and someone gives you a talk about, there's a bit more in-depth, you know, so it is, it's a kind of introduction to the whole idea.
E: Well, it's kind of, it sounds like, yeah, quite a balance between education and interactive because some museums are just, you know, nowadays are just all flashing, all singing, all dancing …
H: Yeah, it seems to be the way most museums are going these days, is to have interactive content, I think it's becoming more and more popular definitely …
E: Have you, have you been to one like that?
H: All of the London museums are like that now, I think, even even the more traditional ones are, they're sort of trying to get rid of their 'dusty, dusty, vases on … on shelves' image and kind of give more people to do and more interaction I think.
T: Like where?
H: Um, the Science Museum in, in London is by far the best museum I've ever been to – it's really, really good and they've just got all of these different, um, exhibits about every aspect of science and you can press buttons and you can sort of, you can use pictures of yourself to find out how you'd look at 65 and …
T/E: Really?
H: … and all of these things. And it feels like you're sort of making little scientific discoveries by yourself – of course you're not because you're being led through it – but it's nice to have a little bit of …
T: Sounds great!
E: Well, I don't know though, I dunno. I mean, do we really need all of this button-pushing? I mean why can't people … I mean the traditional thing was you go to a museum and you look at things … Why can't people just do that?
T: I think that's fine to some extent – I think there's room for both of these things, I think, especially for children, the button-pushing, interactive side of things really keeps things alive …
E: It's all so gimmicky though, isn't it, like computer games and reality TV … and now you go to a museum and you press loads of buttons …
T: … it just makes them feel that things are alive. I think it's much more … and I just think that the traditional ways are nowhere near as as good for getting things to come alive in a child's imagination as the as the modern displays. There are really good ones, I mean, some of them you know aren't as effective, but the Natural History Museum, the erm, the British Museum. Things like the Victoria and Albert Museum, with its Kylie exhibition that's coming up.
H: Oh yes. Yeah, I saw that on the internet actually. I really want to go to that. It looks erm really interesting.
E: Is there is there quite a lot of it on the internet? You can see what's what's going to be …
H: I think it's becoming more popular definitely. I mean you can have anything on the internet now and it was just a matter of time before you get sort of picture collections of museum items and things. And I think this Kylie thing, because of its sort of target audience, works very well on the internet as well, I think.
T: I don't think it would be …
E: It's popular culture …
T: Exactly. I don't think it would be a good thing if if it turned out to be all there was, was virtual museums, but I think there's room for these things to co-exist. I mean, because the thing about the virtual museum, like looking at the Kylie exhibition on the on the website, it's an, it's an interesting advertisement for the museum, but it's not like the real thing, it's not quite, not quite the same experience, and I think if that starts to put children off going to, going to the actual museum themselves it's got to be a bad thing, but as a, as a part of the experience it's a good thing.
E: Yeah, I guess it's just a popular … you know, just to just to cater for popular taste really, isn't it?
H: Yeah, yeah.
T: But if it brings people in to look at, you know, if they see the Kylie museum, the Kylie exhibition and they learn about Tudor costumes and, you know, historical things like that then it makes a lot more …
E: What was that, there was a, I'm sure there was a, it's sort of reminding me of another pop … Was there a pop museum?
T: Hmm.
H: Oh, in in Sheffield, was it?
E: Yeah, yeah.
H: I remember that.
T: There was one …
E: What happened to that? Did that …? I don't think that's around any more, is it? Did it close down?
T: I think it … It flopped, didn't it?
H: Yeah, it closed.
T: It closed down. Because I think they envisaged getting, I don't know, twelve million people through, and they only got a couple of million people through. And that kind of proves the point, that if something is set up just to cater to popular tastes, like you said, then it's not necessarily a success. People perhaps want the more in-depth experience.
E: It's quite quite ironic, though, that a that a museum that's set up to cater for popular culture should … you know, maybe that proves you know a point a little bit about the traditional museums. You know.
H: What do you put in a National Pop Museum, anyway? I mean ..
T: Robbie Williams.

3

- Pairwork. Students discuss the questions with a partner.

Extra task: discussion

- Ask students if they have changed the mind about which museum they would like to visit, having listened to the speakers discuss them.

Extra task: discussion

- If you are in an English-speaking country, bring in some leaflets about museums and exhibitions. Ask students to work in small groups and read the leaflets then discuss which place they'd like to visit. Alternatively, you could download some web pages that advertise British or American museums, and hand these out for discussion.

Language notes: listening

- ***Artefacts*** are old, historically important objects.
- If something is ***gimmicky***, it is intended to impress (usually by using modern ideas or technology) but isn't useful.
- If something ***flops***, it is a failure.
- To ***cater for/to popular culture*** is provide the kind of entertainment that the general public enjoys.
- You may wish to point out the words the speakers use to try to describe the ride at the Jorvik Centre: ***capsule*** (small enclosed space on a space vehicle); ***time machine***; ***buggy*** (a small vehicle with four wheels that travels over rough ground, e.g. a golf buggy, a beach buggy); ***roller coaster*** (a fast fairground ride). Point out that so many different words are used because there is no accurate word for the vehicle they went round in, and the speaker is trying to help his friends picture it.

Cultural notes: museums

- The Jorvik Viking Centre is located the historical city of York, in northern England. It is an interactive museum which houses exhibits on what life was like in Viking times.
  It is situated on the site of the remains of a Viking city. In 866, Vikings from what is now Denmark invaded the north-east coast of England, defeated the Saxons, and renamed the Saxon city 'Jorvik'. The language they spoke was 'Norse'. Vikings and Saxons continued to fight over the city until England was conquered by the Normans (from northern France) in 1066.
  Look up: www.jorvik-viking-centre.co.uk.
- The Science Museum is in Kensington, London. It was founded in 1857. The first jet engine was invented by Frank Whittle in 1930. Stephenson's Rocket is one of the earliest steam trains. It dates from 1829. Crick and Watson were the two scientists who mapped out the DNA molecule in 1953, creating the model you can see in the museum, and opening up the field of genetic research. Look up: www.sciencemuseum.org.uk.
- The Victoria and Albert Museum (the V&A) in Kensington, London, is one of the world's largest and most important collections of art and design. The museum is named after Queen Victoria (1837-1901) and her husband, Prince Albert. Kylie – the exhibition ran from February to June 2007. It displayed the dresses worn by the world famous Australian pop star in some of her elaborate stage shows. Look up: www.vam.ac.uk.
- The National Centre for Popular Music in Sheffield, northern England was an interactive museum of contemporary music and culture. It opened in 1999 and closed a year later, after failing to attract the predicted number of visitors. It became a live music venue and is now a students' union and community radio station.
- Robbie Williams, a pop star who was formerly in the boy band Take That, is one of Britain's most successful recording artists.

Methodology advances
Listening – features of native speaker speech (1)

- *Don't assume that spoken English is just written English said aloud. It is more like another language, with its own grammatical rules and conventions. Here are some brief notes on features of fast, fluent dialogues that may cause comprehension difficulties for students. You can find examples of all of these in the conversation between Emily, Hannah and Tom in this lesson. Or alternatively you could challenge your students to find examples of each of them, in so doing raising awareness of features of native speaker speech.*
- ***People don't usually talk in perfectly constructed sentences.*** *There are typically lots of false starts, repeated sections, unsaid words and so on. Sentences are often incomplete.*
- ***Sentences are often started by one person and then finished by another.*** *In real life, except in formal situations such as radio interviews, people tend not to speak in long individual monologues. Rather, they cooperate to build up meaning over a period of time. Frequently one person will begin saying something and then, perhaps when they hesitate a bit or are searching for a word, someone else will join in and take up the same theme.*
- ***A lot of language of approximation is used.*** *When we don't know exact information, we use vocabulary and expressions that allow us to be vague or imprecise, e.g.* about, nearly, sort of.
- ***There tends to be a lot of repetition.*** *Whereas, in written English, people try hard to avoid repetition by using synonyms, in spoken English we tend to repeat words and whole phrases, and often more than once. This probably arises from a wish to be clear and help our listener understand us more easily.*
- ***There are many fillers and hesitation devices.*** *Speakers usually try to avoid silence mid-speech, so instead use a variety of hesitation devices (e.g.* er, um, ah*) and fillers (e.g.* well, you know, that is to say, actually*). When a speaker needs a long pause, it is normal to vary the items used rather than simply repeating the same one.*
- ***There is a lot of deixis.*** *Deixis refers to language that can only be understood from the context that it is in. At its simplest, words such as you, him, that, there are deictic, as they only make sense when we are aware (from the immediate situation) which specific you, him, that, there are referred to. Recorded conversations are sometimes hard to follow or interpret because we can't see the context in which language is used and we often have to guess what is being talked about.*

GRAMMAR: comparisons

➲ *Language reference, Student's Book page 24*
➲ *Methodology guidelines: Grammar boxes, page xiv*

1

- Students read the sentences and add the missing word in the correct place.
- They can then check their answers with a partner before you check with the class.

1 With his red cheeks and even redder nose he looked just **like** a clown.
2 The older he got, **the** less tolerant he became.
3 It's not quite such **a** well-written book as her last, but the storyline is every bit as intriguing.
4 My new broadband connection enables me to download films much **more** quickly than before.
5 In science this year we have to do quite **a** lot more homework than last year.
6 With these roadworks it takes me twice as long **as** usual to get to the office.
7 The land is farmed in very much **the** same way as it was in the Middle Ages.
8 The beaches were nowhere near as good as last year and the hotel was far and **away** the worst we've ever stayed in.

2
- Students complete the sentences with the words in the box.

1 than	4 about
2 in	5 with
3 as	6 to

3
- Students discuss whether they agree or disagree with each of the statements in exercise 2.

4
- Students use the expressions in bold in exercise 2 to write sentences giving their own opinions.
- They then discuss their opinions with another student.

Language notes: comparisons

- ***Like*** is a preposition and means *similar to*. It is followed by nouns, pronouns and gerunds. In comparative sentences, it is gradable and can function in the same way as an adjective, e.g. *He is more like his mother than his father.*
- ***As*** is a conjunction and is followed by a verb phrase (or clause). In comparison, it can also be used before a prepositional phrase, e.g. *as in 2007*. ***As … as*** expresses equality, e.g. *She's as old as I am.*
- Notice that, in spoken English, ***like*** is commonly used to give examples, e.g. *I want to go somewhere hot, like Greece*. It is also commonly used with verb phrases like ***as***, e.g. *Peter always listened to his patients, like a good doctor ought to do*. Some grammarians would argue this is an inaccurate use. However, be aware that it is commonly accepted in spoken English.
- ***Such*** is always followed by a noun, e.g. *We have such bad luck*. Students often confuse its use with that of ***so***, which is followed by an adjective, e.g. *We're so unlucky.*
- There are many modifiers, used before comparatives, superlatives, ***as … as*** and ***the same (as)***. Students simply need to learn which ones collocate with which.

Speaking

1

➋ *Communication activities, Student's Book pages 140, 147 & 152*

- Groupwork. Tell students that there is going to be a new national museum in their area, and three committees are going to prepare a proposal for the museum. Put students into three small groups, A, B and C, and ask them to turn to their respective pages at the back of the book. For large classes, divide the class up into two or three groups. Then divide these groups into the three committees.
- Students read the situation. They choose one of the options, or a suggestion of their own. They then prepare notes for the meeting on their proposal, using the questions to help them.
- Go round monitoring and give help where needed.

2
- Students form new groups with one member from each committee. They then take it in turns to present their proposal to the rest of the group.
- When all committee members have presented their proposal, each committee member explains why their proposal would be the most successful. They should try to use the language on comparisons from the Grammar box in their discussion.

3
- Students vote for one of the proposals as a whole class. Remind them that they cannot vote for their own proposal.

Did you know?

1
- Pairwork. Students read the information and discuss the questions with a partner.

Cultural note: Nelson's Column

- Trafalgar Square was designed by Sir Charles Barry, who was also responsible for the Houses of Parliament. Building started in 1840 and finished five years later. Barry didn't like the concept of Nelson's Column. He was overruled and the column was built to celebrate the life and victories of Admiral Lord Horatio Nelson, one of Britain's greatest naval leaders. Nelson won a number of naval battles in the late eighteenth and early nineteenth centuries, culminating in the Battle of Trafalgar, off the Spanish coast in 1805. Nelson died of his wounds during the battle. The victory effectively prevented Napoleon, emperor of France, from carrying out plans to invade England.

If you want something extra …

➋ *Photocopiable activity, page 218*
➋ *Teaching notes, page 195*

Answer key

2 Review

Student's Book page 165

1

A

1 a lot
2 the same
3 as
4 far / a lot
5 such
6 quite

Not needed: so & like

B

7 by far
8 like
9 near
10 every
11 so
12 more

Not needed: most & each

2

1 goes
2 around
3 get; give
4 worked
5 wrong
6 long

3

b six of spades
c nine of clubs
d ace of diamonds
e joker
f king of hearts
g queen of spades
h jack of clubs

4

a of; up; down
b for; by; back
c about; to; to

5

1 no use worrying about it
2 seemed not to believe me
3 looking forward to seeing Sally next week
4 on to become a successful coach
5 your ability to keep (so) calm
6 has difficulty pronouncing my name
7 had / 'd better get ready

3A | Consumer society

What the lesson is about

Theme	Money & getting into debt
Speaking	Groupwork: discussing attitudes to money and spending
Reading	*'I didn't just say: give me the dough'*: a newspaper article about Karyn Bosnak, who set up an internet site to ask for donations to clear her debt
Vocabulary	Money
Grammar	Adding emphasis with auxiliary verbs

If you want a lead-in ...

Pre-teach key words: money

- Write *money* on the board. Then put students in pairs and ask them to think of as many verbs as they can that collocate with money, e.g. *get, give, win, earn, spend, lose.* After three minutes ask each pair to compare their words with another pair. During feedback, find out which group of four came up with the most correct collocations.
- Ask students to divide the verbs they think of into words with a positive meaning e.g. *earn, win* and verbs with a negative meaning, e.g. *lose, waste.*
- You could do this activity as a dictionary research task.

Introducing the theme: being in debt

- Introduce 'Karyn' – a young woman who is $20,000 in debt. Ask students to tell you ways that they would advise Karyn to get out of debt. Write ideas up on the board, e.g. *get a job, borrow money from a bank/relative, go into bankruptcy, go abroad,* etc. This gets students thinking about the theme, and creates a prediction task for first reading, *Did you guess Karyn's solution?*.

Vocabulary & speaking: money

1

- Students underline the word in each group which doesn't collocate with the word or words in capitals.

1 set aside	3 donate
2 run up	4 wisely

2

- Groupwork. Students discuss the questions in small groups.

Extra task: collocations

- Write the following on the board: *a bill, a claim, a fine, a loan, a mortgage.*
- Students work in pairs to use their dictionaries to check the meanings of the words, and say how they are relate to the theme of debt.
- Ask students to research which verbs collocate with the different verbs. During feedback, discuss differences, e.g. you pay off a debt or a loan, but you pay a bill or a fine.
- Some collocations:
  pay/settle a bill
  make a claim (an official request for money)
  pay a fine
  take out/obtain/arrange/pay off/repay a loan or a mortgage (money borrowed to buy a house)

Language notes

- ***Waste, squander*** and ***fritter away*** have similar meanings. ***Squander*** suggests that you use money in a very irresponsible way and lose it all. ***Fritter away*** suggests that you waste money over a period of time, spending small amounts on useless things, until there is none left.
- ***Settle*** is more formal than ***pay off***. ***Run up*** suggests building up debts over a period of time.
- ***Raise*** suggests gathering money from a number of sources, whereas ***obtain*** suggests getting it from one source
- ***Freely*** implies 'without worrying about it', ***lavishly*** implies 'on luxurious things', ***heavily*** means 'in large amounts'.

Reading

The reading text is the story of Karyn Bosnak and the success of her internet site. On the site she told her story of how she got into $20,000 worth of debt by overspending on designer goods, and invited people to send her donations of money to clear her debt. The site became national news. Many people sympathized with her and sent donations. With the donations and selling her own possessions on eBay™, she was soon able to pay off her debt.

1

- Explain that students are going to read an article about Karyn Bosnak. Ask them to read the quote from the article and to say what they think her mistake connected with money might have been.

2

- Students read the text quickly and answer the two questions. Tell them not to worry about the gaps in the text while they are reading as they will complete them in the next exercise.

1 To set up a website and ask people to help her pay her debts. She got the idea from a notice that her flatmate had spotted outside a supermarket, which begged for $7,000.
2 Students' own answers

3

- Students read the text again and complete it with the correct sentence beginnings.
- If you think that your class will have problems with this exercise, tell them to read each paragraph in turn and then look back at the sentences for clues to do with reference words, grammar, etc. Go through the example with them first.
- Students can then check their answers with a partner before you check with the class.

1 g 2 d 3 a 4 f 5 c 6 h 7 b 8 e

4

- Ask students to look back at the article and find the highlighted words and expressions. Remind them to use the context to work out the meanings of these words. They could then discuss with a partner what they think the words mean.

See language notes below.

Language notes: reading

- To ***bail someone out*** is to help a person out of a difficult financial problem.
- To ***plough through*** is to finish something that takes a long time and is difficult or boring.
- To ***have someone on*** is to try to make someone believe something that is not true, as a joke.
- A ***hick*** (American slang) is an insulting word for a person who has always lived in the country and does not know about life in the cities.
- ***Clothes buying binges*** are big shopping trips. A ***binge*** is an occasion when someone does too much of something they enjoy (e.g. drinking alcohol, eating, shopping).
- ***This sucks*** means 'This is terrible'. To ***suck*** (American slang) is to be very bad or annoying.
- If you are ***in the black***, you have money in your bank account, or have more money than you owe. To ***return to the black*** is to get out of debt.
- To ***panhandle*** is to beg for money from people who pass in the street.
- To ***have a chuckle*** is to have a laugh. To ***chuckle*** is to laugh quietly, especially in a private or secret way.

5

- Pairwork. Students discuss the questions with a partner.
- Ask students if they found out anything interesting from their partner in their discussion.

Extra task: discussion

- Divide the class into small groups. Tell them they need to raise $10,000 to pay off debts, start a business, or buy a car. Ask each group to come up with a 'get rich' scheme on the internet in order to raise the money. Ask one group member to present their idea to the class. Vote on who had the best idea.

Language & cultural notes

- ***Dough*** /dəʊ/ is slang for money.
- A ***shopaholic*** is someone who can't stop shopping.
- A ***guileless ingenue*** is a young woman who has little experience in the world and has no real plans.
- ***Empty-headed*** means stupid; a ***bimbo*** (slang) is an offensive term for a woman who is unintelligent but attractive.
- ***Cute*** (American English) means attractive.
- A ***buck*** (slang) is a US dollar.
- ***eBay***™ is a website where you can auction off personal belongings or buy things from other people.
- A ***busker*** is someone who performs in the street for money, juggling or playing the guitar, for example.
- ***Gucci***™ and ***Prada***™ are Italian fashion houses. ***Burberry***™ is a British fashion house.

GRAMMAR: adding emphasis with auxiliary verbs

Language reference, Student's Book page 34
Methodology guidelines: Grammar boxes, page xiv

1

- Students add *do*, *does* or *did* to the verbs in bold to add emphasis. You could then ask them to read the sentences out loud, emphasizing the auxiliary verb.

1 I **do think** he's right on this occasion.
2 She **did tell** me but I can't remember.
3 If anything **does go** wrong, phone me.
4 I **do like** your hat.
5 I **did do** my homework last night.
6 **Do stop** worrying!

2

- Students use the sentences in exercise 1 to write a short dialogue.
- They then practise reading their dialogue to a partner, stressing the auxiliary verbs.

3

Communication activities, Student's Book pages 138 & 146

- Pairwork. Put students into A and B pairs and ask them to turn to their respective pages at the back of the book.
- Explain that students are going to contradict what their partner says. They take it in turns to read out their sentences, which their partner contradicts.
- Go through the example with the students, reminding the students who are contradicting the sentence to stress the auxiliary verb and to add another comment.

Possible answers:

Student A

1 I **can** tell you what to do – I'm your mother and I don't care how old you are.
2 I **do** care about it – in fact, I'm an active member of Greenpeace.
3 He **hasn't** got a contagious disease – it's just a bad cold.
4 I **did** know, but I obviously couldn't talk about it to anyone.
5 She **is** working – she's got a part-time job in a bar.
6 It **does** snow sometimes – don't you remember that week in January last year?

Student B

1 I **am** going to the party and you can't stop me.
2 I **did** tell you – you just weren't listening, that's all.
3 He **doesn't** look like Matt Damon – he's far too tall.
4 She **will** get it – she's easily the most qualified candidate.
5 I **have** combed it – I just have naturally curly hair.
6 I **do** love you – but I'm not very good at expressing my feelings.

Language notes: adding emphasis with auxiliary verbs

- Point out that ***do***, ***does*** or ***did*** go before the verb and, as with forming negatives and questions, change its form, e.g. *He likes chips./He does like chips.*
- Make sure students attempt a wide, expressive intonation pattern and stress the auxiliary when attempting to say the sentences.

IF YOU WANT SOMETHING EXTRA ...

➋ *Photocopiable activity, page 219*
➋ *Teaching notes, page 195*

3B | Rubbish!

WHAT THE LESSON IS ABOUT

Theme	Rubbish & recycling
Speaking	Pairwork: discussing rubbish and recycling in your area
Listening	A radio programme about rubbish and recycling
Vocabulary	Rubbish
Speech feature	Fronting
Did you know?	PlasTax – a tax on plastic bags in Ireland

IF YOU WANT A LEAD-IN ...

Discussion starters

Methodology guidelines: Discussion starters, page xiv

- *Where do you put your rubbish?*
- *Do you sort or recycle rubbish? In what ways?*
- *What is national or local government policy on recycling? How enthusiastic about recycling are people in your country?*

Pre-teach key words: rubbish

- Write two sets of words on the board. Set A (on the left hand side of the board): *rubbish, waste, litter, refuse, scraps, crumbs, scrap metal, dust, junk;* Set B (on the right hand side of the board): *dump, bin, basket, tip, skip, recycling centre*
- Put students in pairs to discuss the different meanings of the words. Use comprehension check questions to help them. For example, *What do you call paper rubbish?* (litter) *What do you call rubbish from the garden?* (refuse) *What do you call the remains of food/bread?* (*scrap/ crumbs*) *What do you call an old, broken chair?* (junk)
- Ask students to match the types of rubbish to the containers you can put them in.

SPEAKING & VOCABULARY: rubbish

1

- Pairwork. Students describe each pair of photos, talking about the similarities and differences in them. They then speculate on what might be happening in each one.

Extra task: speculating

- You may wish to briefly revise the language of speculation on the board before asking students to do this task.
- Write the following on the board:
  It might/could/may be...
  ... might be + -ing ...

2

- Students discuss as a whole class which of the photos has the greatest effect on them and why.

3

- Tell students to read the whole paragraph first each time before they choose the correct alternative.
- They can then check their answers with a partner before you check with the class.

1	scraps	6	dustcart
2	bank	7	collection
3	tip	8	piles
4	skips	9	litter
5	put out	10	drop

Extra task: discussion

- Discuss the following questions with your class: *Are there any significant problems with rubbish and rubbish collection in your area? What are they? What can people and government do to improve the situation in your area?*

LISTENING

The listening is a radio programme about getting rid of household waste. The presenter talks to a representative from a waste management service about initiatives to control the amount of waste that goes to landfill sites and ways to encourage recycling. She then talks to workers at the recycling centre about the sort of things that are recycled, what these can be made into and the sort of things which can be sold. Finally, she talks to members of the public who have come to the centre looking for things to buy.

1

- Students discuss the questions as a whole class.

2 1.13

- Students listen to the recording about the recycling initiative and answer the questions.
- They could then compare their answers with a partner before you check with the class. Play the recording again if necessary.

1 The initiative consists of selling waste to the public at their Household Recycling Centres.
2 The principle objective is to prevent landfill.
3 a) organic matter: It is turned into compost and sold to the public.
  b) a fishing boat: A huge one was brought to the centre, where it was sold for £150.
  c) flashy jewellery: This is what Gerry, the site manager, looks out for. He has taken a lot home.

1.13

P = Presenter **FB** = Francis Beard **GT** = Gerry Taylor
S1 = Student 1 **S2** = Student 2 **M** = Man

P: Hello, I'm Carole Baker, and welcome on this bright, but rather cold December morning to *Hotpoint*. Now, today I've abandoned the warmth of our London studio and come down here to the south of Dorset so that I can talk ... rubbish. Domestic rubbish, that is, household waste, and I'm inside the gates of one of the county's eleven Household Recycling Centres. Now, it's not quite nine o'clock yet, the gates are still closed but there's already a substantial queue of people waiting outside to come in. With me to explain why, I have Francis Beard from the Dorset waste management services. Good morning, Francis.

FB: Morning, Carole. Well, yes, this is just one of our initiatives to reduce the amount of household waste which ends up on rubbish dumps, or landfill sites as we call them now. Our Recycling Centres are all managed on behalf of the Council by private contractors, and we encourage them to recover as much waste as possible for reuse and recycling. And as part of this, we allow the contractors to sell whatever they can first.
P: So that's why these people are here, then, to see if they can pick up any bargains?
FB: That's right. The thing is, you see, every household in Dorset throws away, on average, more than one tonne of waste a year – which is about the same weight as a family car. Now, with space at a premium, the whole question of landfill is clearly problematic, so anything we can do to reduce that has to be a good thing. That's our main aim – to keep rubbish out of landfill sites. And if we can sell it, it doesn't have to be buried.
P: But if you can't sell it, presumably you try and recycle as much as possible.
FB: Oh yes, indeed. In Dorset we recycle 34% of all household waste – that's one of the best rates in the country. Anything which can be recycled is sorted by hand and then sent to different factories around the country. Plastic bottles can be made into clothes, cans can be used to make goods such as fridges and cutlery or more cans, and textiles are sent to developing countries or else turned into fillings for toys or stuffing for furniture. And then of course there's compost.
P: Compost?
FB: Yes, we don't have the resources here to produce it ourselves, so we send organic matter, like garden waste and kitchen vegetable scraps, to a special composting facility where it decomposes and decays to make compost. Compost is extremely rich in nutrients and ideal for helping plants grow in the garden – we sell bags of it to the public here at our recycling centres. So it comes back to where it started.
P: Now, Gerry Taylor, if I can bring you in here. You're the site manager, aren't you, Gerry?
GT: That's right, Carole.
P: Now, you were telling me earlier about the kinds of things that people bring to the tip here. Some of them are pretty amazing, aren't they?
GT: Yeah, well, we, we, er take just about everything – except trade waste, that is – you know, rubbish from small businesses. Has to be household – and, er, tyres from cars and suchlike, can't take them. We get everything from clothes, crockery and furniture to all sorts of electronic waste – 'e-waste' they call it – things like fridges and cookers, computers, tellies, DVD players … at the moment we've got a couple of mountain bikes over there, there's a full set of golf clubs and er, oh yeah, er the other day, we had a fishing boat here.
P: Really!? A fishing boat!
GT: Yeah – huge it was. We only just managed to get it through the gates. Now why anyone would want to bring a fishing boat here I have no idea. He could have tried selling it himself. We had no trouble getting rid of it – somebody came in the next day and snapped it up. £150 he paid for it, and very happy he was too!
P: And you too, I imagine – that's all profit for you.
GT: That's right, but as a rule we normally keep prices fairly low, a few quid, that's all. And that money goes straight back into site management. As Mr Beard says, it's all about keeping the rubbish out of landfill sites, it's not about making profits.
P: And do you ever buy any of the items yourself?
GT: Ah, well, that's one of the perks of the job – it's free for those of us that work here. We can help ourselves. We get first choice on the stuff, and every day we sort through the skips before the gates open.
P: So, what have you taken home?
GT: Furniture mainly, tables, chairs, stuff for the garden. And I got my music centre from here, too. But the general public can't buy that kind of thing – we're not allowed to sell electrical goods.
P: Why's that?
GT: Something to do with health and safety regulations – I just can't do it. Anyway, what I mostly look out for is flashy jewellery. Sometimes someone chucks out an old chest-of-drawers and forgets to empty it out first. It doesn't happen every day but I've taken home rings, bracelets, necklaces, that kind of thing. It's all been fake up to now unfortunately, not worth much, but 'beggars can't be choosers', can they?
P: No, indeed. Now, one thing I'm curious to know is what kind of people come to the recycling centre to buy things. I can see that the gates have just been opened, so I'm going to talk to some of the people coming through. … Er, hello, can I ask you what you've come looking for this morning?
S1: Oh hi, er, yeah, we've just rented a flat, an unfurnished one. We're both students. At the moment all we've got is a wooden crate – that's our table – a couple of chairs we got from a rubbish skip in our street and er, er, what else have we got Jenny?
S2: Two beds made out of pallets …
S1: Oh yeah, that's right, really comfortable they are, but nothing to put our clothes in. So that's why we're here.
P: Well, good luck, let's hope you find something.
S1 & 2: Thanks.
P: Here's a gentleman on his own. Excuse me sir, could you tell us what you've come looking for?
M: Oh, anything really – I've got my own junk shop down in the High Street …

3 1.13

- Students listen to the recording again and decide if the sentences are true or false.
- They could then compare their answers with a partner before you check with the class. Play the recording again if necessary.

1 False – Private contractors run the centres on behalf of the Council.
2 True – It recycles 34% of all household waste.
3 False – It is produced in a special composting facility. It is only sold at the centres.
4 True – 'Trade waste' is not accepted.
5 True – 'That's one of the perks of the job – it's free for those of us that work here,' says Gerry.
6 False – They are not allowed to sell electrical goods.
7 False – 'It's all been fake up to now, unfortunately, not worth much.'
8 False – They have come to buy something to put their clothes in.

4

- Pairwork. Students discuss the questions with a partner.

Language & cultural notes

- ***Dorset*** is a county on the southern coast of England.
- The ***Council*** (short for County Council) is the local government for the area which is responsible for waste management among other things.
- A ***landfill site*** is a place where rubbish is buried in the ground.
- If you ***snap (something) up***, you buy it at a bargain price.
- A ***quid*** is a colloquial term for a pound (sterling).
- A ***perk of the job*** is a benefit or advantage you get from your job.
- ***Flashy jewellery*** is bright, expensive-looking jewellery.
- To ***chuck out*** (slang) is to throw away.
- The expression ***beggars can't be choosers*** means that if you get something or are given something without paying for it you should be happy with it even if it isn't exactly what you want.

SPEECH FEATURE: fronting

Language reference, Student's Book page 34

1

- Students rewrite the sentences to create emphasis, beginning with the words in italics.
- They could then compare their sentences with a partner before you check with the class.

1 Really expensive it was.
2 Six hundred euros it cost me.
3 How lovely it is to see you again.
4 What an awful man he is.
5 How she puts up with him I just don't know.
6 Why they decided to buy me a walking stick I couldn't tell you.

Language notes: fronting

- Fronting involves placing an object, complement or clause at the start of the sentence to give it emphasis. The problem for students is in getting the form right. One way to support students here, when doing exercise 1, is to tell them to mark where they need to divide the given sentences before fronting them:
  For example:
  1 It was / really expensive.
  Really expensive it was.
  4 He's / an awful man.
  What an awful man he is.
  5 I just don't know / how she puts up with him.
  How she puts up with him I just don't know.
- Point out that we often front to make things sound more interesting, e.g. *Huge it was* or to show annoyance, indignation or surprise. In this respect, you might want to point out expressions like *Why on earth*... or *How on earth*...e.g. *Why on earth he does it, I've got no idea.*

Extra task: stress & emphasis

- You may wish to briefly drill some examples so that students are clear about how to stress and emphasize these phrases.
  For example:
  Really expensive it was.
  What an awful man he is.

2 1.14–1.15

- Students listen to the recording and say what objects are being described by the two people.

Woman – car
Man – suitcase

1.14–1.15

Woman
Four years old it is, and it's only got 7,000 miles on the clock. Apparently, he had an operation on his leg not long after he bought it, so it's been sitting in the garage these last few years. Why he didn't ask more for it, though, I really don't know. Maybe he didn't realize its true value. £4,000 we paid for it, and its book price is well over twice that – a real bargain, don't you think? And the boot's enormous – with three young children, we need lots of space to put their things in when we go away anywhere. So of course, we're absolutely delighted.

Man
What a ridiculous present this is! Why on earth he thought I'd want one of these I cannot imagine. I mean, I don't *like* travelling. I've never been one for hotels – like my own bed too much. And look at it – it's not even very good quality. Made of cheap plastic it is. Five quid that must have cost him. And he chose the smallest one he could find, of course – there's just about enough room in that for a pair of pyjamas and a toothbrush. How you're supposed to get anything else in there, I just don't know. What a cheapskate he is. Always has been, always will be.

Language notes: listening

- The ***boot*** is the compartment for carrying luggage etc at the rear of a car.
- A ***cheapskate*** is a mean person who doesn't like spending money.

3

- Students look at tapescript 1.14–1.15 on page 156 and underline all the examples of fronting.

See tapescript in exercise 2 above for answers.

4

- Students work on their own and write a description of something they bought or were given. Tell them that they must not mention what it is. They should include some examples of fronting, using the words in italics from exercise 1, in their description.
- Go round monitoring and give help where needed.

5

- Students could now work in small groups and take it in turns to read out their description for the other students to guess what it is.

Extra task: reactions

- Write five situations on the board:
  I've just won £1000.
  My boy/girlfriend has left me.
  I've lost my wallet.
  I'm going on holiday tomorrow.
  I've been fired from my job.
- Divide the class into groups of four. One student in each group announces one of the situations from the board. The other group members must improvise sentences with fronting to express their support, surprise or indignation. Then a different student announces another situation.
- You could extend this task by eliciting and writing up other situations. You could support by writing a few 'expression starters' on the board: *How... What an idiot/ a fool/a hero... Why on earth ... How on earth ... Why anyone...*

Methodology advances
Listening at C1 level

- *Some of the listening texts in Straightforward Advanced are quite long and challenging, involving complex monologues or natural native-speaker interaction. This reflects the fact that a truly Advanced level student is expected to be good at processing lengthy and perhaps dense material in a variety of genres and accents. The following are some of the 'can do' statements for listening from the Common European Framework at C1 level.*
  - Can understand enough to follow extended speech on abstract and complex topics beyond his/her own field, even when it is not clearly structured and when relationships are only implied and not signalled explicitly, though he/she may need to confirm occasional details, especially if the accent is unfamiliar.
  - Can easily follow complex interactions between third parties in group discussion and debate, even on abstract, complex unfamiliar topics.
  - Can follow most lectures, discussions and debates with relative ease.
  - Can understand a wide range of recorded and broadcast audio material, including some non-standard usage, and identify finer points of detail including implicit attitudes and relationships between speakers.

  material from Council of Europe
- *This is quite a challenging list of abilities. Apart from an occasional need to check a detail, the C1 listener is capable of following almost everything that they hear, even if it is quite specialist. If you feel that your class are struggling with this, you may find it important to spend more time working on listening in class. Here are a few general thoughts:*
- *The best way to improve listening is to listen. If students are weak at listening, the simple answer is to do more. Make listening a regular feature of almost every lesson. Build confidence.*
- *Supplement the many listening texts in the coursebook with extracts you find elsewhere. internet talk radio programmes and podcasts often provide excellent 'real world' material. BBC radio 4 and 7 (www.bbc.co.uk/ radio) are particularly good for documentaries, plays and other speech radio.*
- *Students need to feel that they have achieved something from every listening text they hear. If you supplement the course with additional listening material, help students by offering tasks and questions that focus them and help them to find meanings. Try to avoid saying 'just listen' before playing a long recording. Students will listen better if you can get them to think about a topic, perhaps by setting questions that direct them to concentrate on certain areas.*
- *If students struggle with the speed and complexity of listening, don't respond by offering 'easier' recordings. Adjust the length rather than the complexity. It's better to break difficult listening texts into shorter sections rather than to seek out less challenging material. Students need to get practice in listening to real English.*
- *Also consider 'live' listening tasks such as the teacher lecture described in the Methodology advance on content teaching, see page 147.*

Did you know?

1

- You could begin this discussion by asking students how much rubbish, and what kind of rubbish, they generate each week.
- Pairwork. Students read the information and discuss the questions with a partner, giving reasons for their answers.

Cultural note: PlasTax

- The success of the PlasTax in the Republic of Ireland has encouraged much debate and interest in Europe. Tesco, Britain's largest supermarket, has expressed support for a similar tax in Britain. In contrast, the British Plastics Federation believes there would be little logic in taxing plastic carrier bags, as they do not consider them to be a significant litter problem or to have a significant impact on the environment.

Extra task: debate

- You could have a class debate about this issue. Divide the class into Group A (who must prepare arguments in favour of a PlasTax) and Group B (who must prepare arguments against a PlasTax). Each group takes turns to present their argument. At the end have a vote on the issue.

If you want something extra ...

➲ *Photocopiable activity, page 220*
➲ *Teaching notes, page 196*

3c | Competitive eating

What the lesson is about

Theme	An eating competition & doing things to excess
Speaking	Pairwork: roleplaying an interview with Sonya Thomas, a world eating champion
Reading	*Me and my big mouth*: a magazine article about Sonya Thomas
Vocabulary	Excess

If you want a lead-in ...

Discussion starters

Methodology guidelines: Discussion starters, page xiv

- *What's the most food you've ever eaten in one go? What was the occasion?*
- *What's your favourite food? Do you have a 'comfort' food? What is it and why is it comforting?*
- *Is there any type of food that you just can't stop eating once you stop?*

Test before you teach

Methodology guidelines: Test before you teach, page xiv

- Write *over* and *under* on the board. Ask students to work in pairs to think of as many words as they can which begin with these prefixes. Give the students four minutes. During feedback, find out which pair thought of the most correct examples.

Introducing the theme: competitive eating

- Write the following questions on the board:
  What do you think competitive eating is?
  Where do you think it might be popular?
  What sort of people might be good at it
  How would you prepare for a competitive eating contest?
- Ask students to discuss the questions in small groups or as a class, depending on the size of your class.
- You could use these questions to create a prediction task for the reading.

Speaking

1

- Students look at the photos and read the information. Ask them what they think about the contest.

2

Communication activities, Student's Book pages 141 & 152

- Pairwork. Divide the class into two groups, A and B, and then into pairs of A/B students. Ask the pairs in each group to turn to their respective pages at the back of the book and to read the instructions.
- Pairs A prepare the interview questions about the competitive eating contest, and pairs B prepare answers to questions they think they might be interviewed about. Set a time limit of five minutes for them to complete their questions or answers.
- Go round monitoring and give help where needed.

3

- Students now work with a different partner, so that an interviewer from a pair A is talking to an interviewee from a pair B, and roleplay the interview.

Alternative procedure: different roles

- Write the following words on the board before doing the roleplay:
  sympathetic humorous appalled disapproving critical
- Tell the 'magazine journalists' to choose one of the adjectives to describe the tone of the interview they are about to conduct. That way, when doing the interview, the interviewers are not merely asking questions, but responding to what Sonya says depending on the emotion they are role playing.
- Ask a few of the magazine journalists to report what they found out about Sonya to the class.

Reading

The reading text is about Sonya Thomas who is America's record-breaking eating champion, and her incredible ability to consume large quantities of food in record times, despite being thin. The text gives a commentary on an event in which Sonya eats 46 crabcakes in ten minutes.

1

- Students read the article and find out which questions from their roleplay were answered in the text.

2

- Students read the text and decide if the statements are true or false.
- They could then compare their answers with a partner before you check with the class.

1 True – 'Yet as unlikely as it seems, What is even more remarkable and Sonya ate an astonishing 40 crabcakes in twelve minutes.'
2 False – 'It is that record she is here this morning to defend.'
3 True – 'The first time I did it, it was just for fun. It just came out good so I thought, 'OK, let's do it'.'
4 False – No such claim is made: we only learn of one theory which attempts to explain why the very thin Sonya can eat so much in such a short time.
5 False – 'The so-called sport of eating contests – while dating back decades to events held at county fairs …'
6 False – 'She eats with one hand, using the other to take sips from a bottle and Food and water and a combination of the two drip down faces …'
7 True – 'At every eating contest, there are medics on hand.'
8 False – 'She is thrilled.' She says she slowed down and that she could eat more but there is no suggestion of discontentment with her performance.

3

- Students look back at the highlighted verbs in the text and match them to the definitions.
- They could then compare their sentences with a partner before you check with the class.

1 confides	5 dunk
2 grabs	6 licks
3 wolfing down	7 pondered
4 masticating	8 choked

4

- Pairwork. Students discuss the questions with a partner and give reasons for their answers.
- Ask students if they found out anything interesting from their partner in their discussion.

Possible criticisms are that competitive eating is bad for your health. It may cause long-term problems; It glamorizes and condones eating too much which may lead to other people over-eating, particularly children; People have died during competitive eating contests in Japan; It is being exploited by a New York marketing company.

Extra task: discussion

- Ask students if they can think of any other 'so-called sports' which are in bad taste or may be bad for your health?
- Discuss them as a class.

VOCABULARY: excess

1

- Pairwork. Students discuss the questions with a partner. Tell them that they can use a dictionary if they need to.

2

- Students complete the sentences with the prepositions in the box.

1 to	4 with
2 in; of	5 over
3 to	6 in

3

- Pairwork. Students discuss each of the statements in exercise 2 with a partner.
- They can then choose two of the statements which they agree with the most.

Language notes: excess

- The *Macmillan English Dictionary* lists about fifty uses of *over* (as an affix meaning too much/in excess) plus a verb or adjective. Note that *over* is used as an affix with other meanings too, such as *above* (overhang), *from one side to another* (overarching), *on top of* (overlap), and *to recover* (overcome).
- Here are some other common examples of *over* (as an affix meaning too much/in excess) plus a verb or adjective:
  over + verb: *overact, overcharge, overcook, overdo, overheat, overload, overflow, overstate*
  over + adjective: *overactive, overblown, overcrowded, overdone, overpowering, overqualified, overweight, overwrought*
- Note that the main stress here is on the main syllable of the verb or adjective, and there is secondary stress on the first syllable of *over*: overpriced /ˌəʊvə(r)ˈpraɪst/
- ***Overexposed*** means seen in the media so often that you lose interest in it.
- ***Binge drinking*** is drinking a lot of alcohol in a short period of time (a common social problem in British towns where young people go to pubs, get very drunk and cause problems in the street).
- ***Junk mail*** is mail (such as promotional or advertising material) that is sent to you when you don't want it.

Extra task: guess the meaning

- Write the examples of *over* + verb and *over* + adjective, listed in the Language notes, on the board, in two lists. Ask half the class, in pairs, to guess the meaning of the *over* + verb words, and the other half to guess the *over* + adjective words. Then ask the pairs to check their answers in dictionaries.
- Divide the class, so that students are in new pairs with partners who have researched different sets of words. Students must explain their sets of words to each other.

Extra task: recalling words

- At the end of the lesson, ask students to close their books and see how many of the *over* words they can remember from exercise 1.

IF YOU WANT SOMETHING EXTRA ...

Photocopiable activity, page 221
Teaching notes, page 196

3D | A cautionary tale

What the lesson is about

Theme	Becoming wealthy, being wealthy & losing all your wealth
Speaking	Groupwork: imaging living on Nauru
Listening	A radio programme about the story of the island of Nauru; how it became rich and then lost all its wealth
Vocabulary	Adjective affixes
Grammar	Cleft sentences

If you want a lead-in ...

Discussion starters

Methodology guidelines: Discussion starters, page xiv

- *What are the positive and negative aspects of living on a small tropical island?*
- *How can tropical islands create jobs and generate revenue?*
- *How can tropical island communities maintain their heritage and move with the times?*

Pre-teach key words

- Write the following words and phrases on the board:
  tropical idyll *riches to rags*
  high quality phosphate
  squandering money
  mined-out ruin
  low life expectancy
- Put students in pairs to predict what the 'cautionary tale' might be about from the phrases.
- As feedback, encourage a few pairs to predict the story, but don't confirm or deny at this stage.

Speaking

1

- Ask students to read about the situation on the island of Nauru, and give them a few minutes to imagine what life might be like on the island and how they might live their life on that island.
- Groupwork. Students discuss how they would spend their time on the island and what they would do with all their money. Tell them to consider what would be the positive and negative aspects of such a life.
- During feedback, ask the students whether they would continue to work or not, and if not, what would they do.

Listening

The listening text is a radio programme in six parts about the story of the tiny Pacific island of Nauru, made wealthy because it was found that the island was rich in phosphate. As a consequence, the inhabitants of Naura led a luxury lifestyle and they became lazy and obese. However, the phosphate eventually ran out and the government lost a lot of money. The mining destroyed the island and Nauru has now become one of the poorest countries in the world.

1 1.16

- Explain that students are going to listen to a radio programme in six parts about the island of Nauru. Ask them to read the six topic headings first and then listen to the recording and put them in the order that they hear them.

Correct order: 2, 5, 1, 6, 3, 4

1.16

Part 1

P = Presenter RC = Rob Crossan

P: Now on *Foreign Correspondent*, Rob Crossan travels to the tiny Pacific island of Nauru, and tells a cautionary tale of a country which went from riches to rags in just three decades.

RC: The best way to find Nauru on a map is to go north-east from Australia until you reach the Solomon Islands, then north-east again until you come to a tiny pinprick of an island in the middle of the Pacific Ocean – that is Nauru. What strikes one first about the island is its size: it measures just twenty-one square kilometres and has a population of some 12,000. Yet for such a small nation, Nauru has an incredible set of world-beating statistics. It is the smallest republic in the world, and the only one not to have a capital. According to recent reports, its people are the most obese on earth. It is also expected to be one of the first places that will disappear under the rising tides caused by global warming. Now, though, the island is beginning to come to the world's attention as a lesson in what happens when suddenly you get everything you have ever wanted. For Nauru, once the richest nation in the world, is now one of the poorest.

Part 2

The first outsider who laid eyes on Nauru was British sailor John Fearn in 1798, who named it 'Pleasant Island', because of its attractive environment and the friendliness of the Nauruans. German traders seized control of the island in 1888, but it was an Australian, Albert Ellis, who, at the close of the 19th century, made the discovery from which Nauru is still reeling. An odd-looking piece of rock that he took back to Sydney turned out to be a high-quality phosphate, made from guano, millions of years of accumulated bird droppings – a must for successful agriculture and a substance of which there was very little in Australia's soil. The first 11,000 tons of phosphate were shipped to Australia in 1907: the profits were split between the Australian and German governments and locals were powerless to stop the island's transformation from tropical idyll to industrial quarry. It was only in 1968, when the island was granted independence by Australia, that the Nauruans could begin to benefit from their riches.

Part 3

The Seventies and Eighties were golden years for Nauru. While Chinese labourers extracted the phosphate, which the government sold with huge profits, the locals led a life of luxury, eating imported Australian meat pies, drinking beer and driving 4 x 4s drunkenly around the island's one road, or chartering one of Air Nauru's five jets for trips to Fiji and Australia. All the islanders did in the way of exercise was walk to the government offices once a week to collect their share of the profits, a totally tax-free sum of money. I spoke to local man Warwick Pitcher, who grew up during this period. 'Nobody was that bothered about school,' he said, 'as we knew we would always have whatever we wanted as long as we lived on Nauru.' He told me his father collected his money every Friday and the family would enjoy a big meat feast as soon as the supply boat came in from Australia.

Part 4
But as the Nauruans relaxed, the island was being destroyed by the phosphate mining, and eventually the phosphate began to run out. Conmen descended on Nauru, either tricking or forcing the government into squandering money on a variety of ill-advised rescue schemes. These included the purchase of numerous properties abroad that were then left to rot, and buying a fleet of planes that flew empty around the Pacific in a failed attempt to make the island a centre for air travel. The island also became a tax haven, attracting millions of dollars' worth of illegal money and causing it to be blacklisted by the United States as a base for money-laundering.

Part 5
The poverty on the island is painfully obvious. Jeeps and motorbikes from the Eighties lie rusting on the roadside, the money to repair them having long since vanished. The grass on the island's golf course is knee high. The smart wooden pavilion of the government building is crowded every morning with Nauruans, chatting and smoking, waiting for a cash handout to buy rice. Ministers sit indoors, drowning in paperwork as they themselves struggle to survive on the government salary of £60 a fortnight that everybody earns, including the current president, Ludwig Scotty, who has the unenviable task of recovering the mined-out ruin of Nauru.

Part 6
President Scotty lives in a converted outhouse, a small hut which looks no bigger than a garden shed. I visit him in his office at Government House and find a worried-looking but amiable man with the obligatory bulging Nauru waistline and dark glasses. 'I am probably the poorest president in the world,' he tells me. 'This country is no longer in a coma, but we are still in intensive care.' He tells me his imaginative plans to bring tourists to Nauru. 'Topside' is an incredible sight,' he enthuses, referring to the mined-out area that covers 85% of the island, 'and I think people would be interested in seeing it – and there is good fishing off the coastline.' I ask him about the obesity problem on Nauru. 'We lived in a land where we didn't have to cook anything for ourselves,' he explains. 'We just ate junk because we could all afford to. Now our life expectancy is very low and nobody can afford chips and chocolate any more.'

Language notes: listening

- A ***pinprick*** is a very small spot.
- ***What strikes one*** is what your immediate impression of something is.
- If you are ***reeling***, you are in shock.
- ***Guano*** is solid waste from birds, used as fertilizer.
- A ***4x4*** (four by four) is a four wheel drive vehicle.
- ***Left to rot*** means left to decay and fall apart.
- To ***blacklist*** someone or something is to put them on a list, to show that are under suspicion or excluded from something.
- ***Money laundering*** is the practice of hiding the origin of money obtained from illegal activities by putting it into legal businesses.
- ***Mined-out*** means mined until there is nothing left.

2 **1.16**

- Before students listen to the recording again, ask them to read through the questions and discuss them with a partner. Point out that there is one question for each part of the recording. Do not confirm their answers until they have listened a second time.
- Students listen to the recording and make brief notes on the questions.

1 It's the smallest republic in the world and the only one not to have a capital. According to recent reports, its people are the most obese on earth. It is also expected to be one of the first places that will disappear under the rising tides caused by global warming. Once the richest nation in the world, it is now one of the poorest.
2 It was formed from high-quality phosphate, made from guano, millions of years of accumulated bird droppings. It's an important substance for agriculture which Australia's soil lacks.
3 The profits were shared out to the locals, which they collected from the government offices once a week. It was a totally tax-free sum of money. The Nauruans led a life of luxury – they ate imported Australian meat pies, drank beer, drove 4 x 4s, had trips to Fiji and Australia and didn't bother about school.
4 The purchase of properties abroad that were then left to rot, buying a fleet of planes that flew empty around the Pacific in a failed attempt to make the island a centre for air travel, creating a tax haven, which attracted millions of dollars' worth of illegal money causing the island to be blacklisted by the United States as a base for money-laundering.
5 Chatting and smoking outside the government building waiting for cash handouts to buy rice.
6 Visits to 'Topside', the mined-out area of the island, and fishing off the coastline.

3 **1.16**

- Students listen to the recording and check their answers.
- Pairwork. Students discuss the questions with a partner.
- Ask students if they found out anything interesting from their partner in their discussion.

Extra discussion task

- Ask students *Who you think is most responsible for the disaster that has happened on Nauru? The Nauruans? The Nauruan government? The Australians and/or the Germans? Conmen and speculators who tricked the Nauruan government? Why? What can / should the world community do to help Nauru?*

Cultural notes: Nauru

- Nauru (pronounced /nəˈruː/) or the Republic of Nauru is officially the world's smallest island nation and smallest independent republic. It covers about 21 km^2, and is found in the Micronesian South Pacific. Micronesian and Polynesian people were the first to inhabit the island. It became a German colony in the late nineteenth century. After the First World War, it was administered by Britain, Australia and New Zealand until it gained independence in 1968. Nauru used to have rich phosphate reserves, which was the main source of revenue for the island. Since these ran out, the government has tried all sorts of ways to obtain income, including becoming a tax haven. Since 2001, the Australian government has provided aid in exchange for an offshore detention centre in Nauru that holds and processes asylum seekers trying to enter Australia.

GRAMMAR: cleft sentences

Language reference, Student's Book page 34
Methodology guidelines: Grammar boxes, page 00

1 1.17

- Students rewrite the sentences, emphasizing the underlined part of the sentences.
- Play the recording. Students listen and check their answers.

> 1.17
> 1 It was when she remembered a notice her flatmate had spotted that Karyn came up with her idea.
> 2 All I need is $1 from 20,000 people.
> 3 One thing I'm curious to know is what kind of people come to the recycling centre to buy things.
> 4 What I mostly look out for is flashy jewellery.
> 5 All we've got is a wooden crate.
> 6 What is remarkable is that Sonya is the overall eating champion.
> 7 Sonya ate 20 crab cakes in 12 minutes. It is that record she is here this morning to defend.
> 8 The first outsider who laid eyes on Nauru was British sailor John Fearn.

2

- Students complete the sentences using their own ideas.

Language notes: cleft sentences

- Cleft or divided sentences add emphasis to a noun, person, time phrase or clause. They use the following structures:
  It is/was … (John) who …
  It is/was … (in 1999) that …
  What … is/was …
  The thing/Something (that) … is/was …
  The person/Someone (who) … is/was …
- The forms are fairly complex, so getting right them is difficult. Students will need plenty of practice in changing base sentences to cleft sentences. However, the forms are grammatically regular so, once they have the hang of them, students should be able to manipulate them confidently.
- Students often work through this sort of exercise, manipulating form, without thinking about why words or phrases are emphasized. Write the following sentences on the board and ask how they are different in terms of emphasis:
  It was only in 1968 that the Nauruans could begin to benefit from their riches.
  The Nauruans only began to benefit from their riches in 1968.
  (Answer: The second sentence is neutral in tone, whereas the first sentence gives the impression that it's introducing an interesting or startling fact; it emphasizes ***only*** and the year, giving a sense of shock that the Nauruans should have to wait so long to benefit)
- Stress and intonation are important here. The main stress is on the piece of information being emphasized, so, in the sentence below, the main stress is on ***did***. Students need to start their voice tone high and stress key information as they produce the sentence.
  *What they **did** was to ship the **phos**phate to Austra**lia**.*

Extra task: emphasizing key information

- You may wish to drill some of the sentences the students produced in exercise 2. Ask different students to read out a sentence they have written and then restate it, emphasizing key information, and asking students to repeat.

3

- Pairwork. Students read out their sentences to a partner, giving more details about their opinions.

Methodology advances
Are Advanced students a threat?

- *Although some teachers (e.g. at a university) may spend almost all their time working with Advanced students, many others (e.g. at a secondary school) very rarely come across genuinely advanced students. If you are in the latter category and are suddenly given an Advanced class to teach, this can feel worrying, or perhaps even threatening, particularly if you are newly qualified or teaching an advanced grammar point such as cleft sentences for the first time. A teacher might have thoughts like these:*
  - *They'll know as much or more language than I do.*
  - *They'll ask difficult questions.*
  - *They'll show up my weaknesses.*
  - *I won't be sure of my ground with Student's Book material.*
  - *I'll stumble and get confused.*
  - *I've no idea what they need.*
  - *My old teaching tricks and techniques won't work with an advanced class.*
  - *It's all going to go horribly wrong.*
- *Well, my first response to all of this is Don't Panic! If you recognize any of the worries above, then also be reassured by knowing that they are fairly common doubts as a teacher approaches an Advanced class for the first time.*
- *The second response is to state that this Teacher's Book gives you a lot of additional support in the shape of comprehensive language and cultural notes and extra ideas for language activities. It is designed to give you a lot of additional information and to help make teaching advanced students a less daunting prospect.*
- *The third response is that all good teaching is also a learning experience for the teacher, and high level teaching particularly so. It seems to me that those teachers who are most successful at Advanced classes are the ones who are seen to be also participating in and enjoying the shared learning experience. Language questions will arise that are exciting and challenging for everyone – students and teacher. Finding a way to revel in these and 'swim around' in the issues, rather than feeling that you need to have all the answers instantly at your fingertips, can lead to a new way of working that is collaborative and encourages students to take part in an exploration rather than being merely passive listeners and followers (see Methodology advances: Teaching Advanced students – some pitfalls, page 17).*

VOCABULARY: adjective affixes

1

- Students complete the extracts with the correct adjective form of the words in capitals. Point out that one of the adjectives needs a negative prefix.
- They could then compare their answers with a partner before you check with the class.

1 cautionary	4 unenviable
2 successful	5 imaginative
3 numerous	

Extra task: strong & weak collocations

- Ask students to use their dictionaries to check how 'strong' the collocations are between the adjectives in exercise 1 and the nouns they collocate with in the exercise and the listening text.
- Students should find that *global* and *warming*, and *cautionary* and *tale* have 'strong' collocations as they are given as examples in the *Macmillan English Dictionary*. In contrast, successful and agriculture are weak collocations.
- Ask students to find other strong collocations for these words in the dictionary, e.g. *cautionary remarks, successful business, numerous occasions*.

2

- Students form adjectives using the same suffixes as in exercise 1 for all three of the nouns in each group. Go through the example with the class first to make sure that they understand what they have to do.
- Give students plenty of time to complete the exercise as it is more complicated than they might think.
- They could then compare their answers with a partner before you check with the class.

1 representative; informative; comparative
2 advisable; forgettable; applicable
3 literary; voluntary; imaginary
4 advantageous; courteous; humorous
5 harmful; powerful; faithful

Language notes: adjective affixes

- *-al, -ary, -ful, -ous, -able* and *-(at)ive* are common adjective affixes, as are *-y, -ive* and *-ible*. There are no rules as to when each should be used. Students simply need to learn them.
- You may wish to contrast the following adjectives which have the same root but different affixes and meanings:
  forgetful (describes a person who can't remember things)
  forgettable (describes something that is quickly forgotten)
  imaginary (describes something that is not real)
  imaginative (describes someone who is creative and thinks of new ideas)
  comparable (similar to/can be compared to)
  comparative (relative to/used to describe forms such as *bigger*)
- Note the stress, marked on the words in the answer key.

3

- Students complete the text with the correct form of the words in brackets and the suffixes in the box. Point out that they will have to use a negative prefix for a couple of words.
- They could then compare their answers with a partner before you check with the class.
- Students discuss the question as a whole class.

1	substantial	6	sensible
2	unexpected	7	irresponsible
3	financial	8	homeless
4	persuasive	9	rainy
5	knowledgeable	10	unpredictable

Language note: sensitive v sensible

- Note that ***sensitive*** (emotional and easily upset or caring about others) and ***sensible*** (practical and reasonable) are false friends, particularly to speakers of romance languages, and, consequently, may cause confusion here.

Extra task: 'affix' tennis

- Write the following affixes on the board: *-al, -ary, -ful, -ous, -able, ive, ative, -y, -ible.*
- Put students in pairs, A and B. A serves an affix *(-al)*. B must return with a word e.g. *original*. A returns with another word e.g. *personal*, and so on until one student can't think of another adjective. The person who said the last word wins the point: 15-0. 'A' serves another affix, and another point is played. As in tennis, the winner is the first player to win four points, with a two point margin, so, at 40-40 (deuce) players continue to play until someone has a two point lead.
- Theoretically, you could continue to play until someone wins a set. However, two or three games are probably enough. Students may serve the same affix more than once, but they can't play with the same words, so, if *-al* is served a second time, B can't say *original*.

Web research tasks

➲ *Methodology guidelines: Web research tasks, page xiv*

- Nauru is an island in Micronesia in the Pacific. Ask students to choose another island in the region and research it on the web. Students can choose from the following islands: Saipan, Guam, Yap, Koror, Palau, Chuuk, Pohnpei, Kosrae, Majuro, Tarawa, Kiribati, Kiritimati, Kanton.
- Ask students to make notes under these headings: political structure, history, people, economy. Does their island have a similar history of exploitation and mismanagement to Nauru?
- Ask students to present their findings to the class.

Web search key words

- [name of island]; politics; history; economy

IF YOU WANT SOMETHING EXTRA ...

➲ *Photocopiable activity, page 222*
➲ *Teaching notes, page 196*

Answer key

3 Review

Student's Book page 166

1

1	imaginary	6	unexpected
2	unforgettable	7	infectious
3	harmful	8	introductory
4	powerless	9	Facial
5	receptive	10	rising

2

1 e 2 c 3 a 4 g 5 b 6 d 7 f

4

1	dust	4	binge
2	rubbish	5	money
3	litter	6	debts

5

1	overdrawn	4	overpaid
2	overslept	5	overpriced
3	overrated		

6

1	what	6	broke
2	a bore	7	How
3	All	8	do
4	do	9	would
5	that	10	spend

4A | Voicing complaints

What the lesson is about

Theme	Complaining
Speaking	Discussing photos of people complaining; recalling when you made a complaint
Reading	Three blog entries in which the bloggers complain about different things
Vocabulary	Ways of speaking

If you want a lead-in ...

Pre-teach key words: annoyance

- Write *annoyed* and *annoying* on the board. Then brainstorm other words students know with a similar meaning. Elicit (or give) the following words: (for *annoyed*) *angry, irritated, cross, mad, furious, incensed, fed up, frustrated, upset;* (for *annoying*) *irritating, frustrating, infuriating, upsetting.*
- Ask students to work in pairs to put the words in order to show strength of meaning, e.g. *irritating* - > *annoying* - > *infuriating.*

Introducing the theme: complaining

- Write the following on the board: *standing in queues, waiting for a bus, getting a parking ticket, getting junk mail, train delays, people who are late, unwanted phone calls from salespeople.*
- Ask students to work in pairs and small groups to discuss the following questions: *How do you feel in these situations? Do you have a story about one of these situations?*
- During feedback, ask a few individuals to share feelings and stories with the class.
- You could combine this exercise with the 'key words' exercise above. Get students to use the 'key words' to describe their feelings.

Speaking

1
- Pairwork. Students look at the photos and take it in turns to describe them to their partner. Remind them to talk about why they think the people might be complaining, the way in which they are complaining and how the people might be feeling to make them complain.

2
- You could start off the discussion by telling students about a time when you complained about something. Tell them where you made the complaint, who you complained to, what the complaint was about and finally what the outcome was.
- Tell students to think about a complaint they made, where they made the complaint (e.g. in a restaurant, a shop, a train station, an airport, at school), what the nature of their complaint was and who they complained to.
- You could also ask them if they have ever filled out an official complaint form and what happened as a result of their complaint.

Reading

The reading texts are three blog entries in which people are complaining about something. In the first entry, the blogger complains about their local bus service and how unreliable it is. In the second entry, the blogger complains about salesmen trying to sell you things on the phone or on the street. In the third entry, the blogger talks about how much they hate circuses.

1
- Students read the three blogs. They discuss the questions as a whole class and give reasons why they sympathize or not with each blogger.

2
- Students read the texts again and match the sentences to the relevant blogger.
- They could then compare their answers with a partner before you check with the class.

1 B 2 A 3 C 4 A 5 C 6 B 7 C 8 A 9 B 10 A

3
- Students look back at the text and underline the words and expressions which the bloggers use to express irritation.
- They could then compare their answers with a partner before you check with the class.

A I've had it up to here with ...; I'm sick to death of ...; it's so infuriating ...; it annoys me to think that ...; fed up
B If there's one thing that gets on my nerves it's ...; It drives me mad when ...; ridiculous
C Don't you just hate ...?; what I object to are ...; irritating; they really get up my nose; pathetic

Language notes: reading

- If you've ***had it up to here with*** someone, you are really annoyed with them.
- If someone ***(really) gets up your nose***, they irritate you.
- ***Shambolic*** means disorganized/chaotic.
- ***Masquerades*** means *pretends to be.*
- A ***misnomer*** is an inappropriate name.
- ***Full-to-bursting*** means so full people can't move.
- To ***lay on*** something is to provide it.
- To ***kick up a fuss*** is to complain loudly.
- ***Fliers*** are advertisements on small sheets of paper that are handed out in the street or left on car windscreens.
- To ***vent your anger*** is to show/release your anger.
- If something ***freaks you out***, it scares or shocks you.

Extra task

- To check exercise 3, and prepare for exercise 4, write some of the expressions from the text on the board as sentence starters and then ask students to complete them with their own ideas. For example:
I've had it up to here...
I'm sick to death...
It's so infuriating...
It annoys me...
I'm fed up...
It drives me mad...
Don't you just hate...

- Make sure students are following these phrases with the correct prepositions or clauses (e.g. *I'm sick to death of + -ing*).
- Ask different students to read their sentences aloud. Encourage them to speak with feeling.

4
- Groupwork. Tell students that it is now their chance to complain about something that irritates them, or to have a 'good moan', like the bloggers. Give them a couple of minutes to think about something that really irritates them.
- Before they start, point out the words and expressions they found in exercise 3, which they can use while they are having a good moan to their partner.
- You could then get feedback from the students on anything they discussed which they feel they would particularly like to moan about and share with the class. This activity may last some time.

Alternative procedure: guided discussion
- Give students something to moan about. Write four or five things on the board. For example:
  buses *homework* *programmes on TV*
  parents *bills* *neighbours*
- Ask students to discuss (and moan about) each in turn.

Extra task
- Play 'Just a minute'. Divide the class into groups of four or five, and make each group sit in a circle if possible. Write a list of things to moan about on the board (see above). One student must start moaning about the first subject (buses) and continue talking for one minute. Give a clear start signal and time the students. Other members of each group must listen and can interrupt by saying 'Stop!' if the speaker hesitates badly, repeats him or herself, or starts talking about a different topic. If somebody interrupts (and can briefly explain why) they must take over and continue talking about the topic until the minute has finished. The winner is the student speaking at the end of one minute.
- Repeat the game two or three times.

VOCABULARY: ways of speaking

1
- Students look back at the text and match the definitions a and b to the verbs in bold.

1 a 2 b

2
- Students complete the sentence beginnings with their appropriate endings.
- Don't check the answers at this stage. This will be done in the next exercise.

1 c 2 e 3 a 4 b 5 h 6 g 7 d 8 f

Extra task: ways of speaking
- Ask students to cover up the sentence endings a–h, and see if they can remember the ways of speaking from just the beginnings.

3 1.18
- Students listen to the recording and check their answers to exercise 2.
- They then practise saying the utterances as they heard them in the recording.

Language notes: ways of speaking
- To ***shriek*** is to shout in a loud, high voice (when scared or excited).
- To ***bellow*** is to shout in a very loud, deep voice.
- To ***whisper*** is to speak very quietly (so others can't hear).
- To ***snap*** is to speak in a short, sharp, angry way.
- To ***stutter*** is to repeat sounds of words without control (e.g. d-d-day) because you are nervous or have a speech problem.
- To ***sigh*** is to make a long, soft sound when sad and disappointed, or tired and relaxed.
- To ***grunt*** is to speak in low, short sounds (when miserable and reluctant to talk).
- To ***whine*** is to complain in a high, annoying voice.

Extra task: act out the word
- Ask students to act out each word to show that they understand. For example, say *sigh*. Students say *aaah* (in a sad way).
- Alternatively, ask students to match the verbs to the sort of people who might express themselves in these ways. For example, disappointed lover (sigh), excited schoolchildren (shriek), angry headmaster (bellow), bad-tempered granddad (grunt), nervous student (stutter), spoilt child (whine), angry parent (snap).

4
Communication activities, Student's Book pages 141 & 150
- Pairwork. Put students into A and B pairs. Ask them to turn to their respective pages at the back of the book and to read the instructions.
- They then take it in turns to read out the sentences in the manner of the verb in brackets. Their partner guesses what the verb is.

5
- Students complete the sentences with the words in the box.
- They could then compare their sentences with a partner before you check with the class.

1 lips	4 word; teeth
2 tongue	5 mouth
3 voice	

6
- Students work on their own and use the words in bold from the sentences in exercise 4 to write sentences that are true for themselves. They then discuss their sentences with a partner.

Extra task: expressions
- Ask students to compare the expressions with their own first language. Do they have similar expressions in their L1?
- Ask students to work in pairs to choose one word out of *lip(s), tongue* and *mouth*. They look their chosen word up in the dictionary and find two or three other useful expressions using the word. Ask pairs to explain words they have found to other students in the class.
- Some expressions are: *button your lip, my lips are sealed, pay lip service to; bite your tongue, hold your tongue, lost your tongue, a slip of the tongue, tongue in cheek; all mouth, big mouth, down in the mouth, mouth-watering.*

IF YOU WANT SOMETHING EXTRA ...
Photocopiable activity, page 223
Teaching notes, page 197

4B | Voice complaints

What the lesson is about

Theme	People who have medical problems with their voice
Listening	A radio interview discussing types of voice complaints
Vocabulary	Voice
Grammar	Reported speech
Pronunciation	Voiced & unvoiced sounds

If you want a lead-in ...

Pre-teach key words: voice

- Draw the diagram below on the board. Then elicit and label the different parts of the mouth and neck shown in the diagram.

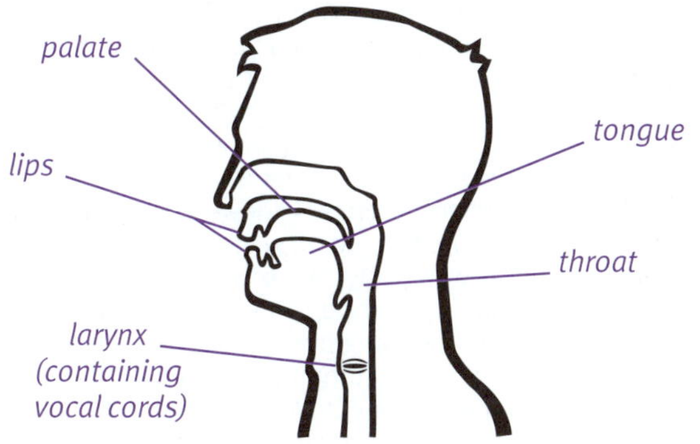

- Tell students that it is a good idea to copy this diagram on to a large sheet of paper or card. They can use it to check key vocabulary before doing the listening, and use it again as a reference to show how voiced and unvoiced sounds are formed when doing the pronunciation section.

Introducing the theme: voice complaints

- Ask students, *In which jobs is the use of the voice very important?* Elicit *teacher, actor, singer, call centre worker, radio broadcaster, fitness instructor, politician.*
- Ask, *How do these people use their voice? What sort of voice is best suited to these jobs? What sort of problems do these people have with their voices?*
- Put students in small groups to discuss the questions then have feedback as a class.

Vocabulary: voice

1

- Pairwork. Students read the list of ways you can use your voice. They then discuss examples of situations in which they can use these ways with a partner.

Possible answers:
lower – in a library or church, or when you don't want someone to hear you
raise – when you're angry with someone or want to be heard when you're in a noisy place
strain – teaching in a classroom, or giving a talk or presentation, when you've been using your voice for a long time
disguise – if you don't want to talk to someone who has phoned you and you pretend to be someone else

2

- Students put the adjectives describing types of voice into pairs that have similar meanings.

1 shaky / trembling; deep / booming; soft / gentle; flat / expressionless; hoarse / croaky; squeaky / high-pitched

3

- Students then think of a famous person or someone they know who fits each pair of adjectives, and compare their ideas with a partner.

4

- Students discuss how they would describe their own voice and in what circumstances their voices change.

Extra task: changing voices

- Choose one of the texts in 4A. Ask a student to stand up and start reading a text in a clear voice. After a few moments, give an instruction, e.g. *Lower your voice* or *Speak in a squeaky voice*. The student must obey the instruction and change his or her voice while continuing to read the text. Give another instruction. Then, after a minute, ask the student to sit down and another to stand up and take over.
- Divide the class into groups of four. In each group, one student reads a text while the others give instructions about how to change his or her voice.

Listening

The listening is a radio interview with a voice expert about the problems people can suffer from with their voice by overusing it and injuring it. She talks about the type of damage we can do to our voice and what we can do to prevent injury to it.

1

- Students discuss the question. Ask them to think of all the difficulties that might happen if they lost their voice for a prolonged period and what they would have to do to overcome the problems they would have.

2 1.19

- Ask students to read the list of topics before they listen to the radio interview. They then listen to the interview and put the topics in the order in which they are discussed.
- They could then compare their answers with a partner before you check with the class. Play the recording again if necessary.

1 Number of people affected
2 Types of people affected
3 Examples of voice complaints
4 Possible treatment
5 Surgery for cosmetic purposes
6 Threats to the voice at work
7 Taking care of our own voice
8 Exercising the voice

1.19

P = Presenter EW = Ellen Wainwright

P: … that report there on complaining from Julie Somersdale. Now, we move on from the subject of voicing complaints to … well, the whole area of voice complaints, that is, medical problems with our voice. According to a recent report, one in three workers in the world's modern economies rely on their voice to carry out their job and around one in four experiences voice problems on a regular basis. Now, I'd certainly include myself in those figures – in the last year or so I've been decidedly hoarse on more than a couple of occasions. But why do so many of us suffer in this way? With me to help answer that question is voice expert, Ellen Wainwright. Ellen, why is the voice taking such a beating?

EW: Well, as you mentioned, the most important tool for many of us now is our voice, particularly as we shift to more service-based economies. Broadcasters like yourself are at risk of course, but so too are people like shopworkers, receptionists, politicians, performers, fitness instructors and teachers. In fact, the report singles out teachers and call centre workers as the most regularly affected types of worker. Too much talking in the wrong environment can lead to voice loss, and in some cases, more serious damage.

P: What kind of damage can people suffer to their voice?

EW: Well, there is a whole range of complaints, including 'odynophonia', which is soreness in the throat that makes speaking painful, and 'vocal cord paresis', which is partial paralysis of the vocal cords. There's also, of course, 'laryngitis' – inflammation of the larynx, that organ in our throat which actually contains the vocal cords. People like catchy names they can remember, though, and we've now got a new term that's come into the language to describe this phenomenon – 'repetitive voice injury', based of course on the more familiar RSI, or 'repetitive strain injury'. It covers all manner of ills, but basically means overuse of the voice.

P: And are these problems treatable?

EW: Well, unfortunately, in some cases permanent damage can be caused – chronic laryngitis, for example, can mean having to give up work. Generally, though, people with prolonged voice loss can recover some or all of their ability to speak with the help of a good speech therapist. Occasionally, an operation such as vocal cord surgery may be needed.

P: Not very pleasant. Though I saw recently that people are actually opting to have vocal cord surgery in order to make them sound younger. Apparently, they can turn old shaky voices into strong clear ones by injecting collagen into the vocal cords to bring them closer together.

EW: Yes, that's the so-called 'voice lift' – another kind of cosmetic surgery. Once you've had your face lift, you can have a voice lift to match. The vocal cords become stiffer with age and move further apart – and this helps put that right. This can occur in younger people too, when their vocal cords become damaged, and that is the original, more serious purpose of this kind of surgery. But of course, as with everything, prevention is ten times better than cure, and if we look after our voice, we can avoid the need for any intervention of this type.

P: And how do we go about that? I mean, a teacher has to speak if she wants to do her job, and she probably has to raise her voice to make herself heard. And the poor call centre worker inevitably has to talk all day on the phone.

EW: Well, there are two considerations here: what our employers can do for us, and what we can do for ourselves. The working environment is crucial in all of this, and the employer has a responsibility to make sure conditions are right. Centrally-heated offices in winter with low humidity are bad for the vocal cords and can lead to throat infections. Erm, high levels of background noise in factories, for example, can cause voice strain if we're forced to shout above it – that's particularly true of people who have to give instructions. And teaching in overlarge classrooms with poor acoustics can have the same effect. In the case of the call centre workers – well, they often don't have enough breaks to enable them to drink an adequate amount of water. The employer should ensure that this is possible.

P: Yes, and I'll be talking to mine right after the programme. Now, Ellen, what can we do ourselves. How can we look after our voice?

EW: Well, I've mentioned water already. That's essential if we want to keep our vocal cords well lubricated. And try and avoid anything with caffeine – things like coffee, tea or soft drinks with caffeine in them, as these dry out the vocal cords. That's the first point. Also, if you feel you've been speaking too much, try asking a question or two – that puts the onus on the other speakers and gives you a bit of a rest. And when you speak, don't push your voice from your throat – instead, your navel, your tummy button should move towards your backbone. If not, you won't get the best from your voice and it may suffer damage.

P: And how about vocal exercises, the kind of thing actors or singers do before they go on stage? Do they help?

EW: Certainly. Vocal warm-ups are excellent for helping voice projection and ensuring you use your voice correctly. Proper breathing from the diaphragm and a good posture are important though. Make sure you keep your head up, your chin level and your shoulders sloping, not dropped or hunched. Oh, and relax – that's very important.

P: And not very easy! Can you give us a couple of examples of vocal warm-ups?

EW: Yes, alright. Well, the obvious one is: *Do re me fa so la te do*. Then there are those that combine the same vowel sounds with different consonants: *Ma me mi mo mu, Ba be bi bo bu, Ta te ti to tu*. And then you have sentences such as *Bring back my bonny baby's beautiful blue bonnet*.

P: Marvellous, Ellen. Unfortunately, on that note, we have to finish I'm afraid. But if you want to find out more about looking …

Language notes: listening

- To ***opt*** is to choose.
- If something is ***lubricated***, it is kept wet so that it works properly (usually, lubricated means well-oiled).
- ***Onus*** means responsibility/duty.
- ***Hunched*** means bent over.

3 1.19

- Students listen to the interview again and complete each gap with one word. Tell students to read the sentences first very carefully as they won't hear the exact words in the script as they are in the sentences.
- Students then look at the tapescript 1.19 on page 156 and check their answers.

1	four	6	lift
2	teachers	7	humidity
3	speaking	8	acoustics
4	injury	9	dry
5	speech	10	posture

Alternative procedure: prediction

- If students need more guidance, put them in pairs and ask them to guess what the missing words are before listening. If they can't guess, tell them to at least predict what part of speech the missing word might be (noun, verb, number, etc).

4
- Pairwork. Students discuss the questions with a partner.

Extra task: discussion

- Ask students, *What sort of voice do you enjoy listening to? Which famous person has a voice which you find particularly interesting or attractive?*

GRAMMAR: reported speech

➲ *Language reference, Student's Book page 44*
➲ *Methodology guidelines: Grammar boxes, page xiv*

1
- Students use the verb at the end of each line to report the direct speech.
- They could then compare their answers with a partner before you check with the class.

1 He regretted having left / leaving the cake next to the radiator.
2 She advised me not to wear a pink shirt with my green trousers. *or* She advised (me) against wearing a pink shirt with my green trousers.
3 She predicted it would rain the next / following day.
4 He refused to sing karaoke with his mother.
5 He suggested that the authorities should provide more litter bins in our parks.
6 She wondered why some people had to get so angry when they drove.
7 He claimed (that) he could name the capital city of every country in the world. *or* He claimed to be able to name the capital city of every country in the world.
8 She reminded me to hand in my essay (on) the following Friday. *or* She reminded me that I had to hand in my essay (on) the following Friday.
9 She accused the government of failing to keep its promise to reduce inflation.
10 He estimated there were about 700 students in the school. *or* He estimated there to be about 700 students in the school.

Extra task: reported speech

- Before asking students to do these exercises, you may wish to revise reported speech with your class. First, write the following on the board:
  I stayed here yesterday.
  She said that…

  Do you like chocolate, Tom?
  She asked…
- Put students in pairs to complete the reported statement and question. Tell them that there is more than one possible answer. Write the correct answers on the board then ask students to explain the rules they have put into practice. (See language notes that follow for answers and rules).

Language notes: reported speech

- *I stayed here yesterday* becomes:
  1 *She said that she had stayed there the previous day.*
  or 2 *She said that she stayed here yesterday.*
  Rules: 1 Pronoun changes (here, **I** to **She**); Tense changes (here, past to past perfect); Words referring to place (**here** -> **there**) and time (**yesterday** -> **the previous day**) change. 2 Here, the speaker chooses not to go one tense back or change the place and time references because, presumably, the speaker is still 'here' and it's still the day after 'yesterday'.
- *Do you like chocolate, Tom?* becomes:
- 3 *She asked him (Tom) if he liked chocolate.*
  or 4 *She asked him if he likes chocolate.*
  Rules: 3 Pronoun changes (**you** -> **him**); Use *if* with a yes/no question; go one tense back (present -> past); change question form to statement form. 4 There is no need to change tense if the 'liking' is still true.
- There are many reporting verbs in English, each of which have particular verb patterns which need to be learnt by students.

2
- Students use the phrases in bold in exercise 1 to write three sentences of their own, which are true for themselves or reflect their own opinions.

3
- Students then read out their sentences to a partner and compare and discuss the sentences. Ask them to make brief notes about what their partner says.

4
- Students now work with a different partner and report the conversation they had in exercise 3 using reported speech.

Methodology advances
Grammar at C1 level

- *Although the* Common European Framework *mainly describes real world actions that users can do with language, there are also a few descriptors that are concerned directly with grammatical knowledge and the ability to use grammar accurately and successfully:*
  - Can select an appropriate formulation from a broad range of language to express him/herself clearly, without having to restrict what he/she wants to say.
  - Consistently maintains a high degree of grammatical accuracy; errors are rare and difficult to spot.

  material from Council of Europe
- *This is certainly far less detailed than the descriptions offered for listening, writing and other skills – and for many teachers this might seem odd.*
- *The* Straightforward *Student's Book takes the view that you cannot improve your ability at language skills purely by working at the four skills. A sound grammatical and lexical knowledge underlies a student's ability to be a good listener, reader, writer and speaker. The more fine-tuned his/her knowledge of the language is, the more he/she will understand or be able to produce. For this reason, the coursebook, while offering a lot of work on skills, also devotes a substantial space to focussing on language structures and offering practice on them. Most students and teachers recognize the value of such work.*
- *A lot of Advanced level study is working on adding to or fine-tuning items that have already been partly learnt. There is some useful grammar that will be*

brand-new, but there is still a lot of exploration to be done with supposedly familiar items. One challenge is to get students actually using a wider range of language themselves, i.e. language items that they know, but avoid using. Many students will have found 'safe' structures that they can produce with few errors and it's only natural that they should often choose to stay in that safe zone. Encourage them to move beyond that and expand the range of items they regularly use.

- *Here are just a few thoughts to bear in mind when you teach grammar.*
- *Knowing about the language is useful but it's pointless without being able to use it. Keep in mind that the study and explanations are valuable, but don't spend all your time on these at the expense of giving students lots of chances to use the items.*
- *The single most useful hint about teaching grammar I've been given in the last twenty years is to think of it as a skill rather than as knowledge. In other words, teach grammar as something that you need to do and have to practise doing in order to get better at it, not just as something to file away in your brain.*
- *For some practical ideas, see Methodology advances: Practical grammar ideas, see page 72.*

PRONUNCIATION: voiced & unvoiced sounds

1

- Ask students to read the information about voiced and unvoiced sounds. They then look at the pairs of sounds and decide which is voiced and which is unvoiced. Tell them to touch their throat with a finger while saying each of the words out loud, so that they can feel their vocal cords vibrate when saying voiced sounds.

1	/f/ unvoiced	/v/ voiced
2	/d/ voiced	/t/ unvoiced
3	/k/ unvoiced	/g/ voiced
4	/ð/ voiced	/θ/ unvoiced
5	/ʃ/ unvoiced	/ʒ/ voiced

2

- Students circle the word in each group which is pronounced differently and say if it is voiced or unvoiced. Go through the example with the class first to make sure that they understand what they have to do.
- Again tell students to touch their throat when they are saying the words out loud so that they can feel which words are voiced and which words are unvoiced.
- They could then check their answers with a partner before you check with the class.

1	those (voiced – /ð/)	6	league (voiced – /g/)
2	health (unvoiced – /θ/)	7	missing (unvoiced – /s/)
3	of (voiced – /v/)	8	Stephen (voiced – /v/)
4	choose (voiced – /z/)	9	tension (unvoiced – /ʃ/)
5	picked (unvoiced – /t/)	10	measure (voiced – /ʒ/)

Language notes: voiced & unvoiced sounds

1 **Voiced /z/ & unvoiced /s/**
At the start of a word, the sounds /s/ and /z/ are equivalent to their spelling, so *zoo* starts with a voiced sound and *soap* starts with an unvoiced sound. However, in the middle or at the end of a word, the letter 's' is sometimes pronounced /z/ (*easy*) or even /ʒ/ (*measure*). In plurals and the third person, the 's' at the end is pronounced /s/ after unvoiced sounds, (*pets, leaps, thinks*), but /z/ after voiced sounds, (*eyes, opens, closes*). Elsewhere, the pronunciation of 's' varies, with no rules, so, for example *choose* and *nose* have a voiced /z/ sound, but *loose* and *dose* have an unvoiced /s/ sound. Similarly, when 's' is doubled, as in *kissing*, the 'ss' is generally an unvoiced /s/, but there are exceptions, such as *scissors* and *dessert*. Note also that when the spelling is 's' between a vowel and 'ure' the pronunciation is a voiced /ʒ/ (*treasure, leisure*).

2 **Voiced /ð/ or unvoiced /θ/**
At the start of a word, 'th' tends to be voiced when it is an article (*the*), a determiner (*this, that, these, those*), a conjunction (*though*) or a pronominal adverb (*thus*). In other cases it is unvoiced (*three, think, thoughtful*).

3 **Voiced /ð/ or unvoiced /θ/ at the end of a word**
'Th' tends to be unvoiced at the end of a word, (*seventh, both*). However, if 'th' is followed by 'e' at the end of a word, it is voiced, (*bathe, loathe*).

4 **Voiced /v/ & unvoiced /f/.**
Students sometimes get confused between /f/ which is unvoiced and /v/ which is voiced. In English, spelling and pronunciation are equivalent here, so words spelt with an 'f' are pronounced with an unvoiced /f/, (*knife, wife*), whereas words with a 'v' are pronounced with a voiced /v/, (*knives, wives*). An exception is the word 'of' which, when weakly stressed, is generally pronounced /əv/. Note also that 'ph' is usually pronounced /f/, (*phonology*), and 'gh' is sometimes pronounced /f/, (*rough, tough*, but not *through*).

5 ***-ed* endings**
After voiced consonants, '-ed' is pronounced with an unvoiced /t/ sound, (*liked, stopped*), but after an unvoiced consonant, '-ed' is pronounced with a voiced /d/ sound, (*rowed, bombed*). Note that *-ed* is only pronounced /ɪd/ after 't' or 'd', (*rated, folded*).

6 **The spelling of /g/ & /k/**
The voiced sound /g/ has many spellings: 'g' (*goat*), 'gh' (*ghost*) or 'gu' (*guest*). The unvoiced sound /k/ can be spelt 'c' (*cost*), 'ck' (*black*), 'ch' (*chemist*), or even 'cc' (*accrue*) or 'qu' (*critique*).

3

- Students practise saying the tongue twister three times in succession. You could ask for volunteer students to say the sentence out aloud to the class.

4

- Students now write their own tongue twister using one of the pairs of sounds from exercise 1.
- Students invite other students to say their tongue twister.

Possible answers:
Fearless Vic fell for feisty Val.
Sid sat on the sad settee.
Big Jack's black jag.
I have another brother south of Louth.
She should measure Sheila's treasure.

IF YOU WANT SOMETHING EXTRA ...

➲ *Photocopiable activity, page 223*
➲ *Teaching notes, page 197*

4c | In the limelight

What the lesson is about

Theme	Acceptance speeches at awards ceremonies
Speaking	Ranking different ways of being in the limelight
Reading	*And the winner is ...*: speeches at awards ceremonies
Vocabulary	Emotional reactions

If you want a lead-in ...

Discussion starters

Methodology guidelines: Discussion starters, page xiv

- *Do you watch the Oscar ceremony or read about it in the press? Why? What do you enjoy about it?*
- *Can you remember who has won an Oscar recently and why? Who do you think should have won an Oscar and why?*
- *Which of the following words would you use to describe Oscar night?*
  glamorous ridiculous phoney hilarious
  gripping dull magical
  How would you describe it?

Pre-teach key words: crying

- Write *crying* on the board and brainstorm other verbs that have a similar meaning. Then add a few other words that the students don't know. For example:
  weep, sob, wail, shed tears, howl, moan, snivel, blubber, whimper.
- Ask students in pairs to check the words in their dictionaries and discuss the different ways of crying that they refer to.
- This prefigures the Vocabulary activity (and could be done just before it).

Introducing the theme: in the limelight

- Ask students to think of a time in their life when they were 'in the limelight'. Write the following questions on the board and ask students to think of what they are going to say in response to them:
  What was the occasion?
  What did you have to do?
  How did you feel before, during and after?
  How did it go?
- Put students in small groups to talk about their 'limelight' moments.
- During feedback, ask one or two groups to describe the most interesting limelight story they heard.

Speaking

1

- Students work on their own and rank the activities in the list from 1 (the one they would be most willing to do) to 6 (the one they would least like to do).

2

- Pairwork. Students compare their list with a partner, giving reasons for their choices. They also discuss whether they enjoy being in the limelight, and why or why not.
- Have a class discussion to find out who enjoys being in the limelight, and why.

Reading

The reading text is a humorous criticism of awards ceremonies and how some people become over-emotional while giving acceptance speeches, whether the ceremony is for the Oscars awards or for something more mundane. It talks about the growth of awards ceremonies covering all sorts of achievements, where people are given the chance to make speeches and feel like major celebrities.

1

- Students discuss why they think that the Oscar ceremony is such a popular television event.

2

- Students read the article and choose the phrase that best summarizes its content.

1 b (Our fascination with awards ceremonies)

3

- Students read the article again quickly and underline the correct alternative in each sentence.
- They could then compare their answers with a partner before you check with the class.

1 superficial aspects
2 overemotional
3 have a tendency to cry
4 annoyance
5 the broad appeal of such events
6 took things very seriously
7 become the focus of attention

Language notes: reading

- If someone's ***jokes fall flat,*** no one laughs at them.
- ***Simpering*** means being nice about people, but in a silly, insincere way.
- ***Lachrymose*** means full of tears.
- ***Blubbering*** is crying in a noisy, uncontrolled way.
- ***Lounging*** means lazing around doing nothing.
- ***Sniffles*** are the noises you make when breathing through your nose when crying or when you have a cold.
- ***Swanky*** means luxurious and expensive.
- ***Unsung heroes*** are heroes that nobody knows about or praises.
- ***Back-slapping*** is congratulating (often insincerely).
- If we ***kid ourselves***, we let ourselves believe something that isn't true.

Cultural notes: awards

- 'In the limelight' means getting a lot of interest and attention from the press and media
  Invented in 1825, limelight was used in lighthouses and as stage lighting by burning a cylinder of lime which produced a brilliant light. In the theatre, performers 'in the limelight' on stage were seen by the audience to be the centre of attention.
- The Academy Awards ceremony (also known as the Oscars) is the most well-known film awards ceremony in the world. The awards are presented every year by the Academy of Motion Picture Arts and Sciences in Los Angeles. Winners are given a small statuette, nicknamed an 'Oscar'.
- Gwyneth Paltrow /'pæltrəʊ/ is an American actress and singer, who was born in 1972. She lives in the United Kingdom with her husband, Chris Martin, lead singer of the UK band, Coldplay, and their two children, Apple and Moses. Her most famous films include *Sliding Doors*, *Shakespeare in Love* and *The Talented Mr Ripley*.
- *Shakespeare in Love* is a romantic comedy film about Shakespeare young William Shakespeare who falls in love with one of his actors (Gwyneth Paltrow). Shakespeare in Love won a number of Academy Awards, including Best Picture and Best Actress (for Gwyneth Paltrow).
- *Eastenders* is a long-running British soap opera set in a working class area of the East End of London. Along with its rival soap, *Coronation Street*, which is set in Manchester, it is one of the most watched programmes on British TV.
- Big Brother is a popular reality TV programme in which a group of strangers are locked in a house together (hence 'inmates') for a number of weeks. Viewers watch their every move (or lack of movement) and vote to evict housemates they don't like.
- Stockport /'stɒkpɔː(r)t/ is a town near Manchester in the north-west of England, and Basingstoke /'beɪzɪŋstəʊk/ is a commuter town to the west of London.

4

- Pairwork. Students discuss the questions with a partner.

Extra task: speeches

- 'Do a Gwyneth'. Tell the class that they have just won the award of 'English Student of the Year' at the annual English Schools Award Ceremony. Divide the class into groups of four and tell each group to write an acceptance speech. Tell them that they can be emotional, witty or cynical in their speech – it's their choice.
- When students have prepared, ask them to nominate one person from their group to stand up and make the speech. After the speeches, decide who was wittiest, most emotional, etc.
- You could write some useful phrases on the board. For example:
  It's wonderful to be here …
  I'd like to thank …
  I can't believe that …
  I'm shocked/overwhelmed/so happy that …
  I wouldn't be here today if …

Methodology advances
Reading at C1 level

- *Here are some of the descriptors from the Common European Framework for Reading at C1 level:*
  - Can understand in detail lengthy, complex texts, whether or not they relate to his/her own area of speciality, provided he/she can reread difficult sections.
  - Can understand any correspondence given the occasional use of a dictionary.
  - Can understand in detail a wide range of lengthy, complex texts likely to be encountered in social, professional or academic life, identifying finer points of detail including attitudes and implied as well as stated opinions.
  - Can understand in detail lengthy, complex instructions on a new machine or procedure, whether or not the instructions relate to his/her own area of speciality, provided he/she can reread difficult sections.

material from Council of Europe

- *As a broad generalization, students who reach Advanced level classes in schools tend to be pretty good at most of the things that language teachers refer to as reading skills and they are usually able to deal successfully with a wide range of text types and reading strategies. Reading as a skill is not typically the main problem; the problem is more often to do with (a) unknown lexis – or students being misled by known lexis used in ways that students are not familiar with (e.g. combining with other words to make a new expression) and (b) subject matter containing use of references (e.g. cultural, historical or technical references) that are not familiar to the reader. The reading text in this lesson, for example, contains many cultural references.*
- *Having said that, there are still reading skills and strategies that are worth working on. These are often in the area of understanding messages that are not overt or explicit in the text. Interpreting the implied or unstated attitudes that lie beneath the surface of a text can still be quite problematic for even very good readers. It is good to raise awareness of these areas with advanced level students, asking questions such as: 'What do you think is the attitude of the writer to (award ceremonies)? Use the text to justify your answer.'*

VOCABULARY: emotional reactions

1

- Students look at the words from the text and say which emotional reaction they describe. They find more words and expressions from the text that refer to the same reaction.

The words from the text describe crying.
Other expressions that refer to crying: a performance so self-indulgently *lachrymose*; cast members come over all *tearful*; the moment the *sniffles* started; *tears flowed*

2

- Students choose the correct alternative to complete the sentences.
- They could then compare their answers with a partner before you check with the class.

1	to	6	by; over
2	out	7	out of
3	with	8	to
4	out	9	up; in
5	up; with	10	down

3

- Groupwork. Students first work on their own and choose five of the sentences from exercise 2. They must think of an example for each of the sentences which is true for themselves.
- Students then describe their examples to the group who guess which sentences they are illustrating.

Extra task: talks

- Write the following on the board:
  a *shock*   *a happy day*   *an upsetting time*
  a frightening experience
- Ask students to prepare to talk about a time in their lives which refer to one of the headings above. Ask them to incorporate two or three of the phrases in exercise 2 in their talk.
- Students tell their stories in groups, or, if your class is small, in open class.

Web research tasks

➋ *Methodology guidelines: Web research tasks, page xiv*

- Ask students to research last year's Academy Awards Ceremony. Ask them to find Best Film, Best Director, Best Actor and Best Actress. Ask them to try to find out what the director and actors wore and said, and how they felt and reacted.
- Students discuss their findings in class.

Web search key words

- Academy Awards/Oscars; Best Film; Best Actor; Best Actress

IF YOU WANT SOMETHING EXTRA ...

➋ *Photocopiable activity, page 225*
➋ *Teaching notes, page 197*

4D | Speech!

What the lesson is about

Theme	Giving speeches
Listening	Speechwriting tips & five speeches
Grammar	Modal verbs 1 (*must, might, may, could*)
Did you know?	The Queens' Speech & State of the Union Address

If you want a lead-in …

Discussion starters

Methodology guidelines: Discussion starters, page xiv

- What's the best speech you've ever heard?
- What makes a good speech?

Test before you teach

Methodology guidelines: Test before you teach, page xiv

- Find an interesting magazine picture of a person, ideally one in which some strong emotion is being shown – upset and crying, worried-looking, etc. Put it on the board and ask students to build a profile of the person. Ask, *How might this person be feeling? What do you think might have happened? Where do you think she might be and why?* Elicit lots of ideas, and encourage the use of modal verbs of speculation.
- Alternatively, write the questions on the board next to the picture, put students in pairs or small groups to discuss, then ask some students to present their 'speculations' to the class.

Introducing the theme: speeches

- Play 'thirty second speeches'. Write the list of topics below on the board:
  my favourite sport   my hobby   my home town
  my favourite holiday destination   my family
- Divide students into small groups. Then ask a person from each group to stand up and make a speech about the topic for thirty seconds. Say *stop*, then another student stands up and makes a speech about the next topic. This is a good way of getting students warmed up and speaking.

The listening is in two parts. In Part 1 an expert is giving a talk on how to prepare speeches, write and deliver them. In Part 2 he allows his audience to listen to extracts from five different speeches: a wedding speech, an 80th birthday speech, a book award acceptance speech, a 50th wedding anniversary speech and a retirement speech.

Listening

1

- Groupwork. Students discuss the questions in small groups.

2

- Explain that students are going to listen to a man giving a talk about how to write speeches. Before they listen, they discuss the type of advice he might give on writing a speech.

3 **1.20**

- Ask students to read the text first and try and predict the type of information that would be required to complete each gap. Then play the recording for the students to complete the notes.
- They could then compare their answers with a partner before you check with the class. Play the recording again if necessary.

1 preparation	6 thirty seconds
2 (the) occasion	7 (famous) quotation
3 humour / jokes	8 too many points
4 (their) names	9 read out / aloud
5 confidence	

Extra task: discussion

- Ask students to think about a good/bad speech they've heard. Did the speaker follow the advice? What was the result?

1.20

Part 1
OK, right, well, let's begin. Now, today, I'd like to start by passing on a few basic tips for writing and giving speeches. And then a little later we can listen to some actual speeches and see how well, or how badly they compare. Now the first, and to my mind the most important stage of writing a speech is <u>preparation</u>. I really cannot stress this enough. Don't just sit down with a pen and paper and charge straight into the first line of your speech – <u>prepare</u> the main points you want to make first. You'll save yourself an awful lot of time and frustration, and you'll be much clearer and much more confident about what you want to say.

Now what you say and how you say it, depends largely on three main factors: <u>the occasion</u>, the audience and the purpose of your speech. Now let's take <u>the occasion</u> first. Different rules apply depending on whether you're giving a birthday speech, retirement speech, best man speech, business presentation, and so on. This will determine for example how you dress, how much you smile, and indeed whether you include <u>humour</u> or not. Now this may not always be entirely appropriate – even the best <u>joke</u> or the funniest of comments is not always guaranteed to have your audience roaring with laughter. And the audience is a key factor here – make sure you know who they are and target your speech at them accordingly. By this, I don't mean of course that you have to know all <u>their names</u> – simply that you understand the type of people they are. Certainly, though, if you are familiar with the audience and you do know <u>their names</u>, then by all means use them in your speech. Mentioning specific people will help involve them in the whole process and build a bridge between yourself and those who are listening to you. And it'll do your <u>confidence</u> no end of good, too. As for the purpose of your speech, be clear about your goals and consider any social conventions you need to observe. You may for example give the most wonderful best man speech, but if you forget to toast the Bride and Groom you will have failed in your duty.

Now, when you come to actually writing the speech, a good beginning is crucial. In fact, I'd go so far as to say that the first <u>thirty seconds</u> are the most important. You have to win their attention, engage their interest from the very start if you want them to sit up and listen to you. And there are a number of ways to achieve this. You might for example consider making an interesting or controversial statement, asking a question, making a comparison, using a famous quotation or even telling a joke. Remember, though – whatever you do, make sure it's appropriate to the occasion and the audience. As for the middle or body of your speech, the best way to structure it is as a sequence of different points that you want to make. Try to make one point lead on to the next in a logical progression and make sure you don't include too many – that might confuse your audience, or worse, make them bored. It's much better to have a small number of points that are well made and which leave an impression on the listener. And that brings us onto the end of the speech, which, like the beginning, is crucial to its success. Always try to ensure your audience go away with good memories of your speech. End on a positive note and maybe leave them with something to think about, some kind of comment which they can turn over in their mind.

And one final point before we move on to delivery. It's always advisable to read out your speech while you're writing it. By reading it aloud, you'll be able to check straight away if it sounds natural or not, and whether you sound like a talking book or a real person.

Now, are there any questions before we get on to the subject of delivering the speech?

4

- Students now discuss what type of advice the man in the recording might give on delivering a speech. Point out that this is hypothetical – they will not hear the man giving his advice.

Suggested answers:

- use notes / cue cards to help you remember the main points
- consider dress and appearance (you are on show)
- speak clearly but don't shout; don't allow nerves to cause you to speak too rapidly
- use pauses to emphasize a point, or to allow the audience to react to a fact, joke or anecdote
- make eye contact with the audience; move your eyes across the whole room so that you appear to be speaking to everyone directly
- don't wave your hands around nervously; use hand gestures effectively

5 **1.21–1.25**

- Students listen to the extracts from five different speeches and answer the questions for each one.
- They could then compare their answers with a partner before you check with the class. Play the recording again if necessary.

Part 2

1 The father of the bride on her wedding day; quotation, using names (and social convention)
2 Granddaughter on her grandmother's 80th birthday; finishing on a positive note, leaving guests something to think about
3 Writer who has just received a book award; beginning with a question, use of humour
4 Daughter on her parents' 50th wedding anniversary; interesting statement, comparison
5 Employee at his retirement / leaving party at work; use of humour, use of names

1.21–1.25

Part 2

Speaker 1

… and many of you have travelled a long way to be here, particularly David and Elisa, who've come all the way from sunny Spain. So I'd like to thank them and all of you for helping to make this such a wonderful day for my daughter, Lara, and her brand new husband, Neil. Now, I've been doing a bit of homework, and I can tell you that it was Lysander in Shakespeare's *A Midsummer Night's Dream* who said that 'the course of true love never did run smooth'. And certainly, no one ever pretended that relationships were easy, but I have every confidence that Lara and Neil will give it their best shot and do everything they can to make theirs a long and happy marriage. Now, if we could all raise our glasses, I'd like to propose a toast to Lara and Neil and wish them all the very best for the future.

Speaker 2

… that despite all our differences there is one thing Peter and I do both agree on, and that's that you have truly been the best grandmother anyone could ever hope for. We both have very fond memories of time spent with you as children – the things you taught us, the games you played with us and the stories you told us from your own childhood. So we're very pleased to have been able to return the favour and do something a little bit special for you today. Just one final thing before we get you to blow out the candles on the cake: I think it's true to say that some of the good things in life get even better with age: and by that I mean cheese, wine, whisky, and of course, you Gran. Happy 80th!

Speaker 3

Thank you. Thank you – thanks very much … Now, where would we be without books? It's a good question, isn't it? Where would we be without books? I know where I'd be – at the local job centre looking for work, most probably. You see, when I told my father I was going to be a novelist, a writer of books, he said: 'That's great son. Just make sure you get a proper job as well.' And I'm ashamed to say I didn't take his advice. Still, it could have been worse, Dad. I might have become a poet or something. Anyway, I'd like to dedicate this award to him, my father, wherever he is, and reassure him that things are working out OK for me. I'd also like, of course, to thank everyone at Harris Holt, my publishers, especially my editor Tina Charles for her work on the manuscript …

Speaker 4

Now, you may not know this, but it was on this day, the 31st March in 1889 that the magnificent Parisian monument, the Eiffel Tower was inaugurated. What you will know, of course, is that exactly 50 years ago the 31st March was also a monumental day for my mother and father, George and Betty. For that was the day when they each pronounced those immortal words 'I do' at St Mary's Church here in Portslade. And just like that enormous metal structure on the banks of the River Seine, their marriage has remained solid and firm throughout both the good and the bad times. What's more, together they have been a tower of strength both to myself and to my family and I'm sure that you will all agree with me when I say …

Speaker 5

Goodness me, this is all rather overwhelming – I really had no idea the company employed so many people. And I've been working in the human resources department for over 25 years! Joking apart, though, I can only deduce that during my time here I must have done something right for so many of you to want to be here with me on my final day. Either that, or you've turned out en masse like this just to make sure I keep my promise and really do leave the building for good. Well, let me assure you I have just emptied my desk, but no Mike, I'm afraid I can't let you have my executive toys – those are going to my granddaughter. Now I'm not going to bore you with lots of details about …

6

Communication activities, Student's Book page 140

- Pairwork. Ask students to turn to page 140 at the back of the book. They choose one of the situations and write a brief speech. Point out that they should include at least one of the techniques from the Speech Writing Tips. Set a time limit for them to complete their speeches.
- Go round monitoring and give help where needed.

7

- Students listen to each others' speeches. Remind them of the chunking techniques they practised in Unit 2 which they should try and use when they are delivering their speeches. For each of the speeches, the students listening should answer the questions from exercise 5.

GRAMMAR: modal verbs 1

Language reference, Student's Book page 44
Methodology guidelines: Grammar boxes, page xiv

1

- Students complete the sentence beginnings to the sentence endings.
- They could check their answers with a partner before you check with the class.

1 f 2 d 3 a 4 h 5 b 6 c 7 g 8 e

2

- Students match the grammar points in the grammar box with the sentence endings a–h in exercise 1.
- They could then check their answers with a partner before you check with the class.

a 1 – *must* for making deductions
b 5 – *may have* to express contrast
c 2 – *might* to express possibility
d 3 – *could have* to talk about a past possibility
e 6 – *might as well* to suggest best course of action
f 4 – *could have* to express annoyance
g 2 – *may have* to express possibility
h 3 – *could have* to talk about a past possibility

Language notes: modal verbs 1

- We use ***must*** and ***can't/couldn't*** to make logical deductions. For example:
  They must be brothers. They look so similar.
  She can't be on a diet. She's eaten all the cake.
  There is some reason why the speaker is sure what he is saying is true (in the case of ***must***) or untrue (in the case of ***can't/couldn't***). We use ***might, may*** and ***could*** when we are unsure – it is only a possibility.
- Notice that the modal verbs tend to be stressed. This is particularly true in the case of ***might*** and ***could*** to express annoyance – the emotion is expressed by strongly stressing the modals. For example:
  You ***could*** *have warned me!*
- When we are talking about situations in the past, we use ***must have/might have/may have/could have***.
  I must have been a good mother. All the children turned out OK.
  John might have called, but the answer phone wasn't on.
- ***May*** and ***might*** can be used to express contrasting ideas as in the sentences below:
  She might be a good boss, but she doesn't know how to manage people.
  You may be 18, but I'm still your father.
  In these sentences, ***may*** and ***might*** don't relate to possibility; what is said here is true. Instead, we use them to show that the first fact has little bearing on the situation. The sentences could be rewritten as follows:
  Although she's a good boss, she doesn't know how to manage people.
  It doesn't matter that you're 18; I'm still your father.
- The phrase ***may/might as well*** suggests that that there is nothing to lose by following a particular course of action.
  I might as well go to the park. There's nothing else to do.

3

- Pairwork. Students choose four of the completed sentences from exercise 1 and have four separate conversations with their partner.
- Go through the example with the class first to make sure that they understand what they have to do.
- Tell students to use a different sentence to start each conversation.

Extra task: game

- Play 'It could have been worse'. Write the following situations on the board: *It was quite cloudy when we were on holiday./I missed school because I had a cold./I got a speeding fine yesterday./I went very red in the sun yesterday./I slipped and fell over.*
- Put students in pairs. They must think of as many nightmare scenario 'things that might have happened' as they can. For example, for the first situation, *It might have rained/snowed; There might have been a hurricane; The hotel could have been destroyed in a terrible storm*, etc.
- In feedback, find out who has the most imaginative responses.

Did you know?

1

- Pairwork. Students read the information and discuss the questions with a partner.

Cultural notes: official speeches

- The State Opening of Parliament is a colourful and historical event which takes place when Britain's politicians officially return to parliament after their summer break. This is usually in November. Dressed in crown and robes, the Queen or King (the current monarch is Queen Elizabeth II) makes a speech from the throne in the House of Lords. Although the speech is made by the Queen, it is actually written by the government of the day, and announces their forthcoming policies for the next political session. Everybody knows what's in the speech before she reads it. The speech is given in the presence of members of both Houses of Parliament (the upper house, called the House of Commons and the lower house, called House of Lords). At the beginning of the State Opening, an official with the title of Black Rod goes to the House of Commons to demand the presence of the 'commoners' in the House of Lords to hear the speech. As he approaches the Commons the door is closed. This is a symbol of the independence of the House. Black Rod bangs on the door (with his black rod) and the politicians then open the door and make their way to the House of Lords to hear the speech.
- The State of the Union address happens every year, usually in January. In it, the President of the United States makes a speech on the status of the country and on laws that will be introduced in the next year. The speech is made to Congress (composed of a lower house, which is called the House of Representatives, and an upper house, which is called the Senate).
- Many other monarchies have speeches from the throne, notably Norway and the Netherlands. The Emperor of Japan makes a short, non-political speech at the state opening of the Japanese parliament. In countries that are part of the commonwealth, such as Canada, Australia and New Zealand, a speech is made by the Queen's representative.

Extra task: presentations

- If you have a class of mixed nationalities, ask students to prepare and present a short presentation (or speech) on the political system and politics in their country.
- Tell the rest of the class to listen, take notes, and think of questions to ask at the end.

If you want something extra ...

➲ *Photocopiable activity, page 226*
➲ *Teaching notes, page 198*

Answer key

4 Review

Student's Book page 167

1

1 C 2 A 3 B 4 D 5 C 6 D 7 A 8 B
9 C 10 D 11 D 12 C 13 A 14 A

2

1 might / may not have understood you *or* might / may have misunderstood you
2 couldn't / can't have been speeding
3 could have saved a piece of cake for me
4 may / might as well throw it away
5 could have danced
6 might want to live in a flat but I don't

3

1 asked ~~for~~ to be moved
2 insisted ~~in~~ on buying
3 suggested (that) we (should) leave *or* advised/ recommended us to leave
4 refused ~~him~~ to buy him
5 admitted to stealing
6 denied ~~of~~ having

5A | Entrepreneurs

What the lesson is about

Theme	International entrepreneurs & global companies
Speaking	Discussing entrepreneurs
Reading	*Ingvar Kamprad: Leader of the flatpack:* an article about the founder of Ikea, the Swedish furniture company
Listening	Profiles of four entrepreneurs
Grammar	Relative clauses

If you want a lead-in ...

Discussion starters

➊ *Methodology guidelines: Discussion starters, page xiv*

- *What do you know about Ikea? Where is it based? What does it make and sell?*
- *Is there a branch of Ikea in your country? Have you ever been there? What did you buy? What do you think of their products?*

Test before you teach

➊ *Methodology guidelines: Test before you teach, page xiv*

- Write four sentences on the board:
  Roman Abramovich is Russian.
  He is a billionaire.
  He owns Chelsea football club.
  Chelsea Football Club is based in London.
- Ask students in pairs to make one sentence which contains the information in all four sentences. Elicit two or three good sentences to the board, and briefly discuss how they put the sentences together, noting the use of relative clauses.
- Possible answers: *Roman Abramovich is a Russian billionaire, who owns Chelsea football club, which is based in London./ Roman Abramovich is a Russian billionaire, who owns London-based football club Chelsea./ Chelsea is a London-based football club, which is owned by Roman Abramovich, a Russian billionaire.*

Pre-teach key words: money

- Write the following 'money' words from the text on the board:
  wealthy *frugality* *penny-pinching* *a fortune*
  a discount *low costs* *make a profit* *extravagance*
  low prices *luxury*
- Ask students in pairs to categorize the words. They could, for example, choose to categorize in terms of 'having money', 'spending money' and 'not spending money'.
- During feedback, ask pairs how they have categorized the words and discuss meanings.

Speaking & listening

1

- Pairwork. Students work with a partner and match the famous people to the area of business which made them successful.
- Groupwork. They then work in small groups to discuss what else they know about each of these famous people.

1 b 2 d 3 a 4 c

Cultural notes: famous entrepreneurs

- Oprah Winfrey /'əʊprə 'wɪnfri/ is a billionaire talk show host, actress and publisher. Her programme *Oprah*, is most viewed talk show in the history of television.
- Roman Abramovich /'rəʊmən æ'bræməʊvɪtʃ/ is a Siberian oil billionaire and politician, who owns London football club Chelsea.
- Richard Branson is owner of the *Virgin* brand – his portfolio includes a music label, a train company, and an airline.
- Michael Dell owns the *Dell* personal computer company.

2 2.1–2.4

- Students listen to the recording about the famous people to check their ideas. Ask them to make notes on their achievements while they are listening.
- They could then compare their notes with a partner before you check with the class. Play the recording again if necessary.

2.1–2.4

Oprah Winfrey
This billionaire and media entrepreneur founded Harpo Productions Inc. in 1988. The company has produced a number of films, many of which she has appeared in, as well as her own hugely popular talk show, broadcast in over 100 countries. Her *O* magazine is one of the USA's top women's lifestyle publications with a monthly circulation of over two million, and her lifestyle website is home to the largest book club in the world. She is also one of the partners in Oxygen Media Inc., a cable channel and interactive network with programmes designed primarily for women.

Richard Branson
His internationally recognized brand name can be found on anything from credit cards to mobile phones, trains, airlines and music megastores. In 1970, at the age of twenty, he set up a record mail order business and then opened his first record store soon afterwards in London. In 1972 he formed his recording label, the first release being the hugely successful *Tubular Bells* by instrumental artist Mike Oldfield. He took to the air in 1984, offering cheap cross-Atlantic flights, and in September 2004 he set up his space tourism company, Virgin Galactic. He is also an adventurer and has made several unsuccessful attempts to fly around the world in a hot air balloon. He became a 'Sir' in 1999, when he was knighted for services to entrepreneurship.

Roman Abramovich
This self-made man had a difficult start in life. Orphaned at the age of four, he was brought up by his maternal grandparents in the harsh environment of Komi, in the Arctic Circle. He built up his financial empire in the 1990s, becoming the majority shareholder in Sibneft, a large

oil company, and acquiring shares in a number of other companies, including the airline, Aeroflot. He also entered politics, becoming regional governor of the impoverished Far East region of Chukotka in December, 2000. Outside of his native country, however, he is perhaps best known as the owner of the English Premiership football club Chelsea, into which he has injected large sums of money.

Michael Dell
He studied at university to become a doctor, but went on to become the most profitable personal computer manufacturer in the world. With an initial capital of just $1,000, he began selling affordable computers to students from his university bedroom in 1984. He then developed an innovative approach to business. His company designs and manufactures computers based on a customer's own specifications; they are then sold directly to the consumer without going through retailers. The company's earnings are now over $40 million a day, and it is the largest online commercial computer seller in the world.

3
- Students discuss the questions as a whole class.

Extra task: presentations
- In a mixed nationality class, ask students to make brief presentations to the class about a famous entrepreneur from their country. Encourage other class members to ask questions.
- If you have a class with students from the same country, divide them into small groups of three or four to think of an entrepreneur, and prepare to describe why and how they became famous. Ask one student from each group to stand up and make a brief presentation about their entrepreneur without saying who it is. The rest of the class must guess the entrepreneur's identity.

Reading
The reading text is about the founder of the Swedish furniture store Ikea, Ingvar Kamprad. Kamprad also talks about his business philosophy. He explains how he became interested in business as a young boy and how he set up his company, and he talks about how flatpack furniture was started.

1
- Explain that students are going to read about the furniture store Ikea and its founder. Find out if students have been to an Ikea furniture store. Ask them what they know about it and what they think of it.
- Ask students to look at the words in the box and discuss what possible relevance they could have to Ikea and its founder, Ingvar Kamprad.

2
- Students read the text and check their ideas in exercise 1. Tell them not to worry about the gaps at this stage.

18.5 billion – the money Ingvar Kamprad is estimated to have
vineyard – his only extravagance is a small vineyard in Provence
frugality – providing customers with low prices and strict control of costs at every level in his company
cigarette lighters – he traded in cigarette lighters when he was growing up
revolution – the change to a more disposable attitude to furniture
300 million – the number of Ikea's customers worldwide
cult – what the employees of the company refer to Ikea as

3
- Ask students to read the sentences first. They then read the text again and complete the gaps with the correct sentence. If you think your class will have problems, tell them to read each paragraph in turn and then look back at the sentences for clues to do with reference words, grammar, etc.
- They could then compare their sentences with a partner before you check with the class.

1 b 2 d 3 a 4 e 5 g 6 c 7 f

4
- Students look back at the highlighted phrases in the text and use the context to work out what the phrases mean.
- They could then compare their answers with a partner before you check with the class.

build up – accumulate
set up – establish
turning out – producing
hit upon – suddenly think of
passed down – given to younger members of a family
hands out – gives to different people in a group

5
- Pairwork. Students discuss the questions with a partner.
- Ask students if they found out anything interesting from their partner in their discussion.

Extra task: discussion
- Put students in groups of four or five. Tell them that they are entrepreneurs and ask them to set up their own companies.
- Write the following on the board;
  What sector will you work in (oil, communications, furniture, etc)?
  What will make you stand out from the rest?
  What will you call your multinational?
- Give students a few minutes to think about their answers to the questions, then ask each group to tell the class about their company. During feedback, decide which group had the best idea.

Language notes: reading
- ***Penny-pinching*** means frugal or mean with money.
- If someone ***tinkers with*** something, they make slight changes to it.
- ***Transient*** means not lasting very long.
- ***Taboo*** means forbidden or disapproved of.

Cultural notes: Ikea

- Ingvar Feodor Kamprad /kæmp'rɑːd/ was born in 1926. He is the richest person in Europe and the fourth richest person in the world, with an estimated personal fortune of around $18.5 billion.
- Whilst Kamprad preaches frugality, he does own expensive properties, particularly that of his home in Switzerland, and before buying the Volvo, he did have a Porsche ...
- Sweden has one of the highest tax rates in Europe. Its top earners' income tax rate is 60%.
- Ikea is a great success story. Its products are modern and utilitarian, cheap but with attractive design features, and most of the products are self-assembly. IKEA is an acronym comprising **I**ngvar **K**amprad's initials, and the first letters of his home village, **E**lmtaryd, **A**gunnaryd. At the time of publishing, the chain has 254 stores in 35 countries, mostly in Europe, and in the United States, Canada, Asia and Australia.

GRAMMAR: relative clauses

Language reference, Student's Book page 54
Methodology guidelines: Grammar boxes, page xiv

- Students read the sentences from the text in the Grammar box and answer the questions.

a The relative pronouns in sentence 1 introduce a non-defining relative clause. These give information of secondary importance and commas are required before and, if necessary, after the relative clause. No commas are required in 2 or 3 as the relative clauses contain information which is essential to our understanding of the sentence.
b The relative pronouns in 2 and 3 could be replaced by *that*. *That* cannot be used in non-defining relative clauses such as that in 1.
c *that / which* (*He began importing and selling anything that / which he thought he could make a profit on.*) This omission is only possible in defining relative clauses where the relative pronoun (*which* or *that*) refers to the object (*anything*) of the verb in the relative clause (*make a profit on*).
d *He began importing and selling anything on which he thought he could make a profit.*
e a) *whose*
b) *which*

1

- Students add the missing word in the correct place in each sentence.
- They could then compare their answers with a partner before you check with the class.

1 The managing director, **who** worked his way up through the company from the factory floor, now earns over £1 million a year.
2 He was banned from driving for two years, **which** meant he lost his job as a sales representative.
3 I don't think I know anyone **whose** attitude to work is quite so positive as his.
4 It is very difficult to determine the extent to **which** charity concerts help resolve the problem of poverty in developing countries.
5 I can't remember when exactly my fascination for astronomy began – I think it's something (**which** / **that**) I've always been interested **in**.

Language notes: relative clauses

- There are two types of relative clauses: defining and non-defining. A defining relative clause is essential to the meaning of the sentence. For example:
  Kamprad is a man ***who worked hard to achieve his success.***
  If we removed the relative clause from this sentence, we would learn nothing about Kamprad except that he is a man.
  By, contrast, a non-defining relative clause adds extra, non-essential information:
  Kamprad, ***who earned his millions through the furniture chain****, IKEA, is still careful with money.*
  In this sentence, the fact that Kampard earned his millions through a furniture chain is incidental, and could be omitted.
- We use the relative pronoun *who* for people and *which* for things. In defining relative clauses, *that* can be used instead. The *who, that* and *which* can be omitted in defining relative clauses when it is an object
  The man (who/that) we saw on TV owns this company
  The books (which/that) I lent you explain everything.
- Common errors include:
  1 defining identified nouns. For example, in the sentence *My younger sister, who is tall, is a model,* students may think *tall* is defining, but the noun is already identified so this should be a non-defining clause.
  2 overusing the pronoun e.g. *The man who I met* is correct but awkward in spoken English.
  3 inserting subject pronouns unnecessarily, e.g. *The teacher who he set the exam.*

2

- Students work on their own to complete the sentences in an appropriate way. They then compare their sentences with a partner.

Language notes: relative clause phrases

- Notice that all these phrases are followed by a clause. Possible answers
- ...it got to the point where I had to leave/resign/say something.
  (***point*** means moment/situation)
- ...in which case I'll go travelling/I'll take the company to court)
  (***in which case*** means *If this (situation) happens*)
- ...the way in which it was organized/the police responded
  (***the way*** means 'the method')
- ...a number of cases where they have invaded people's privacy/they have caused a fight (***case*** means situation/circumstance)
- ...the day when I started school/I met my girlfriend.

Extra task: relative clauses

- Ask students in pairs to think of an entrepreneur and/or a major company. Tell them to write four or five sentences about the person or company, using relative clauses.
- Ask some pairs to read out their sentences to the class.

Web research tasks

Methodology guidelines: Web research tasks, page xiv

- Ask students to research a famous entrepreneur. They can use someone they know or choose one from the list below: Bill Gates, Donald Trump, Rupert Murdoch, John Paul Getty, Ray Kroc, Sam Walton, Henry Ford
- Ask students to present their findings to the class.

Methodology advances
Business English skills

- *Although* Straightforward Advanced *is a general English course, a small amount of business English will probably be useful to all students. Unit 5A and 5B look at a number of basic business topics, concepts and language. If you have some students who ask you for more business focus, you might like to consider integrating some business work into the main course programme. This can often be done by adding in short extension tasks connected to the main themes of a lesson.*
- *If you start by using the first suggestion below, groups of students will then have a 'company' of their own that they can continue using through other lessons. This avoids the need for lengthy set-ups for future business tasks; instead, you can just say 'use your company'.*

Create a class company

- *Ask students to work in groups of five or six and create an imaginary company. They should initially decide basics such as company name, individual roles (e.g. which student is Director), key products or services, future plans, etc. Once each group has their own company, you can make use of this in a range of future practice (see below).*

Take part in formal meetings

- *Work on the language and skills of formal meetings by adding short extra discussion tasks that could be done in the style of a business meeting, e.g. in lesson 6A, ask students to imagine their company is worried that its desk-bound workers aren't getting enough exercise. Have a meeting to discuss whether it's something the company should get involved in and possible ways to help them get in shape. In lesson 6D, ask students to have a meeting to discuss whether their company should provide crèche facilities for its workers.*
- *Another interesting way of getting practice in speaking at formal meetings is to organize a meeting to make real class decisions, e.g. if you need to decide what policy the class should have on setting and doing homework, rather than just discussing it informally, organize it as a formal meeting with an agenda, negotiation and final decision.*

Write formal letters and emails

- *Similarly to the ideas for meetings, many coursebook topics can be adapted to provide practice in formal writing, e.g. in lesson 7A, write a letter from Marie Stubbs to the students' company enquiring about a particular product or service that might be useful for the school, (or alternatively, write from your company to Marie Stubbs, offering some goods or services that you have). In lesson 7D, write a report about a series of small crimes (e.g. theft) that have happened on company premises and make suggestions for how to respond to the problem.*
- *Also take up any real-world opportunities that present themselves for your students to write real letters, e.g. persuading, arguing a point, complaining, inviting, and so on.*

If you want something extra ...

➋ *Photocopiable activity, page 227*
➋ *Teaching notes, page 198*

5B | A new business

What the lesson is about

Theme	Getting financial help to set up a business
Speaking	Making a pitch
Listening	Interview with a contestant from the TV show *Dragon's Den*
Vocabulary	Setting up in business
Speech feature	Question tags

If you want a lead-in ...

Discussion starters

➋ *Methodology guidelines: Discussion starters, page xiv*

- *What sort of innovations or inventions are we likely to need in the future? What sort of businesses are likely to be successful?*

Pre-teach key words

- Write the following sets of three words on the board: *design/manufacture/invest* and *product/brand/logo*
- Ask students to discuss the meanings of the words in pairs.
- Ask students to say how these words can be used to describe a common product, a can of cola for example.

Introducing the theme: new businesses

- Ask students to work in pairs or small groups. Tell them that they have one million dollars to invest in a new invention, innovation or business. Tell them to take two minutes to decide what they would like to invest in. Tell them to think about what sort of products or inventions will be required in the future, and what sort of businesses are likely to be successful.
- Ask one person from each group to tell the class what they decided.

Vocabulary: setting up in business

1

- Students complete the text with the words in the box. Remind them not to change the words in any way.
- They could then compare their answers with a partner before you check with the class.

1 set up	7 strike
2 plan	8 share
3 target	9 build
4 secure	10 source
5 pitch	11 identity
6 return	12 design

Alternative procedure: reading for gist

- Ask students to read the text for gist first, without looking at the words in the box, and guess what words are missing. Then ask them to look at the words in the box and put them in the text.

Extra task: collocations

- Ask students to find collocations connected with 'business plans' in the text.
- Possible answers: set up in business; put together a plan; achieve goals; provide information; pitch ideas; obtain a good return; strike a deal; develop the brand; design the logo/prototype.

Listening

The listening is an interview in three parts with Paddy Radcliffe. He talks about his invention, the Snowbone, and how he and his business partner gave a sales pitch on a British TV show and convinced an investor to invest money in the product and to help them develop it.

In Part 1 Paddy Radcliffe describes how he came up with the idea of the Snowbone and what it is. He also describes how he met his partner and how they developed a business plan for it. In Part 2 he talks about the experience of being on the TV show *Dragons' Den*, and how he and his partner managed to convince one of the investors to help them. In Part 3 he talks about what effect the investment had.

1

- Pairwork. Students look at the photo of the Snowbone and discuss the questions with a partner.

Extra task: discussion

- Discuss the following questions with the class: *If you had to sell the Snowbone to somebody, how would you describe its best features? Would you invest in this product? If so, why?*

2 💿 **2.5**

- Explain that students are going to listen to an interview with Paddy Radcliffe, the managing director of the company which developed the Snowbone. Students listen to Part 1 of the interview and decide if the sentences are true or false.
- They could then compare their answers with a partner before you check with the class. Play the recording again if necessary.

1 False – It comprises 'a handlebar, much like the front fork of a bike'
2 True – 'it was my partner Nick who really came up with the idea'
3 False – 'young guys aged between 16 to 25, maybe slightly older'
4 False – 'there are about one and a half million new snowboards sold worldwide every year'
5 False – Nick was a designer from the Royal College of Art.
6 True – 'So once the course had finished. I put myself full time into trying to get the business off the ground.'

Language notes: listening

- ***Bindings*** are part of the ski or snowboard that holds the foot in place.
- A ***BMX*** is a type of strongly-built bicycle suitable for doing stunts with.
- To ***give it a go*** means to try it.

2.5

I = Interviewer PR = Paddy Radcliffe
Part 1

I: Paddy, your product is called the Snowbone. Can you tell us exactly what it is and, and, how you how you came up with the idea?

PR: Sure. Erm, very basically, it's a handlebar attachment for a snowboard. Erm, you take the bindings off any normal snowboard and attach two footplates onto the snowboard and then to the front footplate attaches a handlebar, much like the, the front fork of a, of a bike. And that, that allows you to go down the slopes on a board-bike hybrid basically.

I: U-huh. Erm, and how did you come up with that idea.

PR: Well, it was my partner Nick who really came up with the idea. He's er, erm an industrial products designer, erm, he's an avid snowboarder, erm, and he wanted to try and develop something that added a little bit more to the snowboarding experience.

I: So, who is your target market? Who is the Snowbone aimed at?

PR: Erm, initially we're looking to aim it at the extreme sports market. Erm, so that's young guys aged between 16 to 25, maybe slightly older, guys or who are or perhaps involved in snowboarding or other snow sports, er, maybe involved in mountain biking or BMX.

I: BMX, that's a, that's a kind of bike, isn't it?

PR: Yeah. It's a sort of street bike, er, a bike for stunts. Erm, there's a worldwide market for, for snowsports that's worth about five billion pounds, erm, and it's, so it's a fairly sizeable market. Er, of that, erm, snowboarding, well, there are about one and a half million new snowboards sold worldwide every year, split broadly between Europe, North America – Canada and the USA – erm and the Far East – Japan, South Korea – and increasingly snowsports are becoming popular in China as well.

I: Right. Could we just go back, Paddy, and talk about your partner, Nick. Could you tell us how you, how you teamed up with him.

PR: Sure. Erm, I was doing a-an MBA a couple of years ago.

I: That's a, MBA, that's a Masters of Business Administration, isn't it?

PR: That's right. It's basically a, a business qualification. Erm, part of the course was to do a business plan, erm, and a team from the Royal College of Art er here in London, er basically a team of inventors and designers, came up to er to the to the course er with their various ideas and projects, the idea being that they would bring their ideas and the and the business students would write the business plans for those various ideas.

I: Hm hm.

PR: Erm, it was then that I met Nick, he brought the Snowbone up. Erm, I met him, we got on as people, erm, I liked the idea and took it on to write the business plan for it. Erm, the business plan developed, we got on better, erm, and the more that er we looked at the market and understood the market, felt that there was the potential for a business out there. So once the course had finished, we decided to give it a go, and I put myself full time into trying to get the business off the ground.

3 2.6

- Students listen to Part 2 of the recording and underline the correct alternatives in the sentences.
- They could then compare their answers with a partner before you check with the class. Play the recording again if necessary.
- Ask them if they have any similar TV shows in their country.

1	underwent	5	needed time
2	before	6	took to
3	an amount of money	7	third
4	reasonably well		

2.6

Part 2

I: Tell us about the experience on *Dragons' Den*, Paddy.

PR: Erm, it was an interesting experience for sure. Erm, we, we were invited by the BBC to go along and er and and audition for this show, erm, we passed the audition. Erm, the next thing we knew we were invited to a location in London to do the filming of it. Er, we arrived on the day, erm, not really knowing quite what to expect. We'd done a fair amount of preparation, erm, but we didn't really know what to expect and we were basically told that we might be hanging around all day, they couldn't say when we would go on and do our filming, we were there with other people who were going to pitch their ideas as well, so we settled down for for quite a long wait. Erm, the morning passed and we thought, 'well, it'll be lunch in a minute', but they said 'right, you're on in half an hour', so we, we, got got ourselves together and went into makeup, and then all of a sudden we were on. Erm, we walked up this this staircase, not knowing what was at the top of it. The cameras were rolling, erm, we reached the top and there were these five er business heavy hitters sitting there with large piles of cash sitting on the tables next to them, erm, and we went into our pitch. Er, we were allowed to do a five-minute pitch to the dragons, erm, it was a little bit of a double act between myself and Nick. Erm, it was fairly nerve-racking to be honest, but er we we knew our stuff and we'd done our preparation for our pitch, erm, and once we'd got er got through the pitch, which we did just about OK – I had to prompt Nick at one stage – erm then it was over to a sort of question and answer session with the with the dragons.

I: Hmm. And how long did that go on for?

PR: Erm, the the, in in total the question and answer session lasted about two hours. There was quite a lot of toing and froing initially just to, for them to understand what the product was all about, what the market was, er, and so on and so forth. Erm, and then slowly one by one, erm, some of the dragons decided that it wasn't quite for them and they didn't want to invest. Erm, there were one or two of them that showed a little bit of interest, er, an American chap showed some interest but then pulled out after about an hour and we were left with er the last dragon, er a lady called Rachel Elnaugh. Erm, and she seemed interested, she liked, she seemed to like the product, seemed to understand it, erm, just as importantly I think she she seemed to like us as individuals, which for investors is often a a fairly major criteria, that they they like the guys that they're going to invest in, erm, and we at that stage we got into a negotiation, as to how much we were after for investment, how much she was prepared to give, what sort of percentage equity she was wanting in the business, what sort of percentage equity we were prepared to give away, erm, and er that continued for for quite some time, erm, at one point they even had to er change the film in the camera because they had run out, and and given that as I as I said we'd gone on just before lunch, this was going in over lunch so everyone was getting hungry and it was all all quite tense and got more and more tense as time went by.

I: But she did eventually invest her money, didn't she?

PR: In the end she did, yes. We we we struck a deal. She was she was prepared to invest seventy five thousand pounds in return for a third share in the business.

Language notes: listening

- A ***heavy hitter***, in this context is a powerful business person – the phrase is derived from a baseball term that refers to a player who can hit the ball a long way.
- ***Percentage equity*** is a financial term meaning the percentage of shares in a company.
- The ***main drift*** is the main line of argument.
- A ***niche*** /niːʃ/ ***market*** is a market in which a specialized product is sold to a limited number of customers.

Cultural note: Dragons' Den

- *Dragons' Den* is an internationally successful television programme with series produced in Japan, the United Kingdom, Australia, New Zealand, Israel, Canada, and the Netherlands. The concept is simple; contestants, who think they have a good business idea or new invention, make a pitch to a panel of entrepreneurs – the 'Dragons'. The entrepreneurs are rich, successful, often famous business people, and if they like the pitch they offer investment and support to the successful contestant, in return for shares in their enterprise.

4 2.7

- Students listen to Part 3 of the recording and answer the questions.
- They could then compare their answers with a partner before you check with the class. Play the recording again if necessary.

1 It gave them credibility and the opportunity to talk to suppliers, as a result of which they were able to produce a prototype. They were also able to focus on marketing the Snowbone, developing the brand identity, the logo and a website.
2 The investment deal with Rachel didn't go through in the end and they didn't have the money they needed to take the business forward.
3 They've made contact with a firm of investors in London and a product development company in Taiwan.
4 Confident and optimistic, if the development costs in the plan put forward by the Taiwan company tie in with the proposed investment from the City of London firm.
5 You need to:
   - be fully prepared (analyze the market and be aware of the risks)
   - persevere, be tough mentally (be ready for knockbacks, ups and downs)
   - try and enjoy the lifestyle

Alternative procedure: roleplay

- Before playing the recording, divide the class into pairs, and ask them to roleplay the questions in exercise 4. One student is the interviewer, and the other student is Paddy. Tell the interviewers to change 'Paddy and Nick' to 'you' when they ask the questions. This breaks up the two long listening exercises, and creates a fun prediction task.

2.7

Part 3

I: So what impact did the programme have on the on the product, on the Snowbone?

PR: Well, we were obviously on cloud nine after after the programme er with this with this capital investment that we needed. Er, that gave us the opportunity to go out and try and source and talk to suppliers with the credibility of having investment behind us, so we were able to go out and er and find suppliers. It sounds easy, it's not easy at all. We rang around a number – they weren't interested, didn't understand. But eventually we did find some people who, who were prepared to help us, erm, and we developed our first manufacturing prototypes. Erm, that took probably about four months, er, of toing and froing and various product testing and so on, but we did end up with a product that was er useable and manufacturable. Erm, we were also able to go off and do some some marketing development, er we developed the the brand identity, the logo, er a website, erm so we got quite a lot of development er under way and things were going pretty well, erm. However, the deal wasn't actually finalized. Erm, we were having some costs covered by Rachel but erm, the full investment didn't actually go through in the end, which meant that erm about nine months after we'd actually done the filming for the show we were slightly back to square one in terms of the money that we required to take the business forward. Erm even though we'd erm taken it forward quite a long way. Erm, it's er it's been a bit of a struggle since then since the deal didn't ultimately go through, er but we've been plugging away and trying to keep our network up and take any opportunities we can for putting the idea in front of people who might be interested erm and those those efforts have paid some dividends. We've er more recently been in touch with erm a small firm of investors in the City of London, erm, they're reasonable guys, they seem intelligent people and they understand the product. Erm, we've also managed to source a er product development company out in Taiwan. The manufacturing costs will be much lower out there, ultimately, er and they at the moment are helping us to put together a a development plan so that we can take the prototype that we have now and er complete the development that we need to do so that we have a consumer ready product hopefully in the not too distant future.

I: And you're optimistic for the future?

PR: Er definitely yeah, if if er these guys out in Taiwan come back with the right sort of plan that er marries up with the the amount of money that these guys in the City are looking at putting in, then, very confident about the future, yeah.

I: So, Paddy, what advice would you give to other would-be entrepreneurs?

PR: Erm, I think the first thing is is, try and be as prepared as possible. It's it's not something that should be undertaken lightly, trying to set up a business, it's not an easy thing to do. If it was easy, everybody would do it and be millionaires but that's definitely not the case. So you need to be fully prepared. Make sure that you you know your stuff, that you've analyzed the market, that you know where the opportunity is, and that you're aware of the risks, because there are obviously a lot of risks involved. Erm because it's difficult, you need to have an awful lot of perseverance, you're going to get knockbacks, it's going to be difficult, erm, you're not going to have a lot of money to survive on, and it can be very very hard, so you need to you need to be tough mentally to be able to see it through, see through the hard times and hopefully er be able to reap the benefits at some stage down the line. Erm having said that, try and enjoy it. If you're going to be an entrepreneur, it's a bit of a lifestyle, so you have to enjoy the lifestyle and put up with the ups and the downs and really hang on to the ups and forget about the downs really. But ultimately if you feel that it's for you, give it a go because there's a whole entrepreneurial world out there that's just waiting to be discovered.

Language notes: listening

- If you ***plug away*** at something, you work hard without giving up.
- A ***knockback*** is a rejection.

Cultural notes: listening

- The City of London is London's financial district – one of the richest and most powerful in the world.
- More information about Paddy's product can be found at www.snowbone.com

5

- Pairwork. Students discuss the question with a partner and give reasons for their answers.

Extra task: discussion

- Find out if anybody in your class has entrepreneurs among family and friends. Ask them to tell the class about their experiences.
- If students have seen *Dragons' Den*, ask them to tell the class about any interesting 'pitches' they have seen.

Methodology advances
Student presentations (1)

- *In business terms a presentation refers to an occasion when one or more people formally give some information to others, usually involving a lecture-type monologue and often delivered with the help of projected computer displays (made with Powerpoint or similar programs). Some typical examples of presentations include: explaining a new product to potential buyers, talking through a proposed project with the people who will be involved with it or giving a report on the past year's work.*
- *In high level classes, getting students to prepare and give their own presentations is one of the most useful and most enjoyable ways of achieving a surprisingly large number of important aims. To name just a few: it allows students to work on things they are interested in; it encourages research skills; it makes them aware of the need to prepare carefully and to consider the best ways of integrating content and language; it encourages them to make choices and decisions themselves rather than looking for the teacher to sort everything out. In short, it both promotes autonomy and works on skills that will be useful for students keen on business English (but which are equally beneficial to students even if they aren't interested in business English).*
- *Here are two general sample ideas of topics for classroom presentations:*
- ***A grammar point I still find confusing or hard to use.*** *The teacher could make a list of possible grammar items – or students could choose the items themselves. The presentation could be structured as follows: (1) My experience with using this item. The sorts of problems I have. (2) A focus on the grammar and the key problems (3) Ideas to help memory and use. (4) Conclusions and suggestions for getting better at this.*
- ***An aspect of this unit's topic that is of interest to me.*** *Use the current coursebook topic as a starting point and encourage students to base a presentation around this theme, but taking it off in their own direction to reflect their own interests.*
- *See Methodology advances: Student presentations (2), page 95 for guidelines on working with presentations in class.*

SPEECH FEATURE: question tags

1 **2.8**

Language reference, Student's Book page 54

- Students listen to the sentences from the interview and mark the intonation pattern above the questions tags.
- Students then answer the questions and check their ideas with the Language reference section on page 54.

BMX, that's a kind of bike, isn't it?

But she did eventually invest her money, didn't she?

Language notes: question tags

- The key form rules here are that negative question tags follow positive statements, e.g. *It's cold, isn't it?* and positive question tags follow negative statements e.g. *You're not hungry again, are you?* The auxiliary verb used in the sentence is repeated in the question tag.
- Falling intonation is used to check information. Rising information is used to ask a real question, when we are unsure of the answer.
- After imperatives, use *can/will/could* and *would*, as below, e.g. *Shut the door, could you?*
- Note the exceptions to the form rules above:
  I'm takes the question tag *aren't I?* e.g. *I'm late, aren't I?*
  Let's takes the question tag *shall we?* e.g. *Let's think about it, shall we?*
- We use same way tags to express interest, surprise, anger or concern, e.g. *He's left, has he?* or *You've won the jackpot, have you?*

2

- Students complete the sentences with an appropriate question tag.
- They could then compare their answers with a partner before you check with the class.

1	aren't I	4	aren't there
2	have they	5	do you
3	will you / would you / can you / could you	6	hadn't we
		7	shall we

3

- Pairwork. Students look back at the sentences in exercise 2 and mark the question tags with either a rising intonation pattern or a falling one.
- Students then take it in turns to read out the questions in exercise 2, using the correct intonation. Their partner must respond to the question in an appropriate way.

4

- Ask students to read the information about same-way question tags.
- They then write four positive sentences for their partner to react to.

5

- Students take it in turns to read out their sentences to their partner, who responds using a same-way question tag. Tell them to exaggerate the tone of voice to show that they are expressing interest, surprise, anger of concern, and to try to keep each conversation going for as long as possible.

Extra task: question tags

- Write on the board: *My Night Out*. Then tell the following story:
  I went to my best friend's party last night. I was late so I drove there very fast. When I got there, nobody else had arrived. My friend was very upset. And I had forgotten to buy her a present. Then my friend told me that her boyfriend had texted to finish with her. To be honest, I thought it was funny, so I laughed.
- Tell the story a second time. This time tell the class to interrupt you with tag questions to express interest, surprise, concern, etc. For example, *Oh, she had a party, did she?/You were late, were you?*
- Ask students to prepare and tell similar *My Night Out* stories in pairs.

Speaking

1

➔ *Communication activities, Student's Book pages 142, 146, 151 & 153*

- Groupwork. Put students into the four groups, A, B, C and D. Explain that they are going to make a pitch for an idea or product, like Paddy Radcliffe on *Dragon's Den*, and to turn to their respective pages at the back of the book.
- Students choose one of the ideas or product from the box and prepare for their pitch using the points listed or any other points that they can think of.
- Go round monitoring and give help where needed.

2

- Students now form new groups, making sure that each group contains one student from the four original groups. They take it in turns to make a pitch to the group, i.e. the potential investors. Tell the students that at the end of each pitch, the 'investors' should question the student making the pitch about their idea or product.

3

- Students decide on one idea or product they think would make the best investment and why. Tell them that they cannot choose their own. You could also ask them why they would not invest their money in the other ones.

If you want something extra ...

➔ *Photocopiable activity, page 228*
➔ *Teaching notes, page 198*

5c | Women's work?

WHAT THE LESSON IS ABOUT

Theme	Housework – it's financial worth, & male and female attitudes to it
Speaking	Roleplay: housework rota
Reading	*A woman's work is never done*: a magazine article about the unfair division of housework
Vocabulary	Intensifying adverbs

IF YOU WANT A LEAD-IN ...

Discussion starters

Methodology guidelines: Discussion starters, page xiv

- *In your home, who does most of the housework? How is housework divided between people in your family or between people that you live with?*
- *How much do you do and what do you do?*
- *Who do you think should do housework, how should it be shared, and why?*
- *Have you ever had problems sharing housework? Why?*

Test before you teach

Methodology guidelines: Test before you teach, page xiv

- Write the following words on the board:
  marriage divorce wedding reception honeymoon husband-to-be fiancé blushing bride ex-wife seven-year-itch get hitched tie the knot
- Ask students in pairs to draw a web diagram to categorize the words. For example:

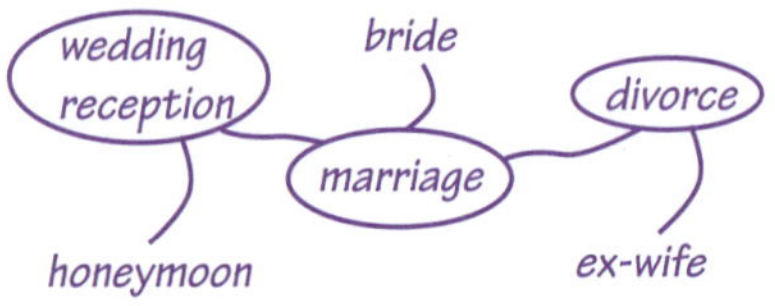

- Ask them to add other words to their diagram. Ask one or two pairs to present their diagram to the class. There will be several different versions of the diagram.
- Ask students to predict what the text is about from the vocabulary.

SPEAKING

Roleplay

1

Communication activities, Student's Book pages 141, 147 & 153

- Groupwork. Put students into groups of three, A, B and C. Ask them to read the information about the task and then to turn to their respective pages at the back of the book.
- Students read the instructions. Set a ten-minute time limit for them to agree on household duties for each member of their group and to make notes on their decisions.

2

- Students discuss the questions first in their groups, then as a whole class.

Extra task: discussion

- Ask students if they felt that their sex had any bearing on the outcome of the task.

READING

The reading text is about Susan Maushart and her book *Wifework*. In the text, she talks about her experience of changing from an independent career woman to a woman obsessed with housework after getting married. She claims that the high levels of divorce are caused by the unfair division of work within the home and believes that attitudes to woman and housework need to be changed for the institution of marriage to survive.

1

- Ask students to look at the photos and read the title and first paragraph of the text. They then make predictions about what the text will say on the topics of men, women and housework, and women and marriage.

2

- Students read the text and check their predictions in exercise 1.

3

- Ask students to read the statements first before they read the text again. They then read the text and tick the statements which are mentioned and put a cross next to the ones that aren't.

1✔ 2✘ 3✘ 4✔ 5✔ 6✘ 7✔ 8✘

Extra task: prepositional phrases

- Ask students to find prepositional phrases in the text. Then put students in pairs to discuss their meaning.
- Students should find the following:
  out of character = untypical
  at pains (to deny) = trying hard
  beyond a joke = not funny
  in a state of flux = in a changing state
  out of tune with = not sympathetic to or not agreeing to
  for the sake of (the children) = in the interests of
  from top to bottom = completely
  to go from bad to worse = to get even worse

Language notes: reading

- An ***archetypal Fifties housewife*** is a housewife typical of the 1950s, a period which, in retrospect, in the USA in particular, is seen as a decade when women were happy to stay at home, bringing up children, doing housework, and being decorous and charming for their husbands
- ***Jocks*** (American English) are ***underpants***.
- ***Nuggets***, in the context of the reading, are small, useful pieces

Cultural note: Susan Maushart

- Dr Susan Maushart is an American author and columnist. Although she was born in New York, she migrated to Australia in 1985, and has spent much of her career there. Perhaps her best known work is *Sort of a Place Like Home*, which was based on the testimony of aboriginal people she met in the Moore River settlement in Western Australia. It was made into a film called *Beyond the Rabbit Proof Fence*. Maushart's first feminist book was *The Mask of Motherhood*. This was followed by *Wifework: What Marriage Really Means for Women*. Her latest book is *What Women want next*.

4
- Pairwork. Students discuss the questions with a partner.
- Ask students if they found out anything interesting from their partner in their discussion.

Extra task: debates

- Ask students to work in pairs to write their own contentious statement about the issues raised in the text. For example, *Marriage is not in the interests of women* or *Women should be paid to do housework*.
- Debate one or two interesting statements as a class.

VOCABULARY: intensifying adverbs

1
- Students read the sentences and underline the adverb in each group which is different in meaning or intensity from the others.
- They could then compare their answers with a partner before you check with the class.

1	mildly	5	fairly
2	rather	6	reasonably
3	slightly	7	completely
4	particularly	8	vaguely

Language notes: intensifying adverbs

- In 1 to 5, the 'odd one out' is an adverb that is less intense than the other adverbs – all of which mean 'very very'.
- In 6, ***reasonably*** suggests 'sufficiently but not completely' capable, whereas the other adverbs suggest 'completely'. Note that ***quite*** has an intensifying function before non-gradable adjectives which are not normally used with adverbs such as 'very' or 'fairly'. For example: *She was quite brilliant!* means *She was absolutely brilliant.*
  With gradable adjectives, ***quite*** generally means 'fairly'. For example, *It is quite* **big** means It is reasonably big. However, ***quite*** has an intensifying function before some gradable adjectives which express the idea of completeness. These include *capable*, as well as *certain*, *determined*, *full*, *ready*, *right* and *sure*, as in the example below.
  You're quite right to complain to the manager.

2
- Pairwork. Students discuss the sentences in exercise 1 with a partner, saying how true each one is for themselves.

IF YOU WANT SOMETHING EXTRA ...

➲ *Photocopiable activity, page 229*
➲ *Teaching notes, page 199*

5D | Sexual discrimination

WHAT THE LESSON IS ABOUT

Theme	Sexual discrimination
Listening	Five people talk about sexual equality in the workplace
Vocabulary	Gender
Grammar	Hypothetical past situations
Did you know?	Women in the Anglican clergy

IF YOU WANT A LEAD-IN ...

Test before you teach

Methodology guidelines: Test before you teach, page xiv

- Write on the board *Regrets*. Then write: *If I ... Had I ... I wish ...*
- Ask students to tell you about any regrets they have about their lives. Depending on the age of your class, you could ask, *What do you wish you had done differently when you were 16/18/21?*

Introducing the theme: sexual discrimination

- Have a brief class debate about the topic. Ask, *Do you think there is discrimination in the workplace against women in your country? If so, in what ways? In what sort of jobs or professions do women face discrimination and why? Are there any jobs that are more suitable for men or women, and why?*

VOCABULARY: gender

1
- Pairwork. Students consider each of the words and tell their partner whether they think one sex is more suited to doing the job than the other. Tell them to give reasons for their opinions. You could pair the students up so that there is a male and female student in each pair, or put students in pairs of the same sex and then have a feedback session on their opinions.

2
- Students read the information and complete the table with the words in the box.
- They could then compare their answers with a partner before you check with the class.

male	female	neutral
policeman	policewoman	police officer
salesman	saleswoman	salesperson
fireman		fire fighter
air steward	air stewardess	flight attendant
headmaster	headmistress	headteacher

3
- Students could work in pairs. They read the sentences and change the underlined words into less offensive and more neutral words.
- Ask the students about their own language and if it has changed so as to be less offensive to women.

1 staff / personnel / workers
2 understaffed
3 working hours
4 manufactured / artificial / synthetic
5 humankind / humanity

4

Communication activities, Student's Book page 152

- Pairwork. Put students into A and B pairs. Ask them to turn to page 152 at the back of the book and to read the instructions.
- Student A chooses one of the jobs from exercise 1 or 2 and talks to their partner about the job for a maximum of five minutes without using the words *man, woman, he, she, his* or *her*. Student B asks questions to force Student A to use these words. If Student B is successful in doing this, then Student A must stop speaking.
- When Student A has finished speaking, they swap roles.

Language notes: use of they *to mean* he *or* she

- A good way of avoiding using *he, she, his* and *her* is to use *they* or *their*. For example, *They work in an office ... Their office is ...* Here, *they* and *their* do not refer to a group of people but are used to refer to one person without being gender specific.

LISTENING

The listening is five people talking about sexual discrimination. Speaker 1 talks about her experience of discrimination as a pregnant employee. Speaker 2 talks about his experience of discrimination as a male temp (temporary secretary) in the late 1970s. Speaker 3 talks about being paid less than a male employee doing exactly the same job. Speaker 4 gives his opinion as an employer about sexual discrimination and talks about how he treats his employees. Speaker 5 talks about the progress there has been since the 1970s.

1
- Students read the information and answer the question.
- You could then go on to discuss with the class if the situation for men and women in their country has changed in recent years, and if they think that there should be any further changes.

2 2.9–2.13
- Students listen to the five people talking about their experiences of the Sex Discrimination Act and say whether each speaker has a positive (P) or negative (N) attitude towards the current legislation.
- They could then compare their answers with a partner before you check with the class. Play the recording again if necessary.

1 P   2 P   3 N   4 N   5 P

2.9–2.13

Speaker 1
It quickly became clear when I was pregnant with Jamie that they were going to make life difficult for me. My boss said he felt 'let down' – can you believe it? – and he wouldn't give me time off work for antenatal appointments. And then when I got back from maternity leave, I found I'd been demoted to a junior position. Five years I'd been with them and that was the thanks I got. They were very obviously trying to force me out of the company. The Equal Opportunities Commission were very supportive and gave me funding to bring my case before the Employment Tribunal. If it hadn't been for the EOC and the Sex Discrimination Act, my fight wouldn't have been possible. But isn't it just incredible that something like this can still happen in the 21st century?

Speaker 2
When I was studying at university, I spent my summer holidays working as a temporary secretary. This was the late 70s and in those days male secretaries were even rarer than they are now. In one marketing firm I temped at, I was told by the personnel manager soon after I started that I wasn't needed anymore. He said it was better for the company's image to have women on the front desk. Blatantly sexist of course, and clearly against the law, but in those days I was very green and it never occurred to me that the Sex Discrimination Act might also apply to me. Had I made the connection, I would definitely have taken them to an employment tribunal. The SDA is such an important piece of legislation, and is obviously there for men as well as women. I just wish I'd realized that at the time.

Speaker 3
When I found out that the male sales reps in my company were getting a higher basic salary than me, I was furious. They were being paid 15% more for doing exactly the same job. I was even more upset when management refused to listen to my complaint. Part of me wishes I hadn't taken my case to the Employment Tribunal – the whole thing put a lot of pressure and strain on my family and myself, and it was both emotionally and financially very draining. OK, the result was positive and I received compensation, but I was fortunate – if I hadn't recently inherited some money, I might never have been able to take my claim to the Employment Tribunal. To my mind, the law doesn't go far enough to protect ordinary people – it depends too heavily on individuals to bring cases against offending employers. The Government could certainly do more to help.

Speaker 4
I can safely say that I have *never* discriminated against any of my workers because of their sex. That's not to say of course that all employers are like me, and yes, of course, we need laws to protect individuals against more unscrupulous types – I'm all in favour of that. But there needs to be a balance, and I don't think they've got that quite right yet. I mean, I have to be so careful – if I give promotion to a man, you can be sure there'll be two or three women knocking on my door the next day claiming they've been treated unfairly. And you know, last year, there was a woman here who told me the day after I gave her the job that she was three months pregnant. Now if I'd known that at the interview, I'd never have taken her on.

Speaker 5
We've come a long way since the 1970s. If the SDA hadn't been brought in, we almost certainly wouldn't have so many women in full-time employment now, and doing jobs they would never have dreamed of doing a generation or two before. I read the other day that nearly a quarter of all Britain's coastguards today are women – and before 1978 there wasn't a single one! Some things take a bit longer to change though. My sister works in the City and she tells me that although there's no active discrimination, there are certain differences in male and female culture which affect how you get on. She works extremely hard but she doesn't go to the pub after work, she doesn't like talking about football and she's not one for telling jokes. And she's convinced this has held her back. There are still a number of unspoken barriers in some male-dominated professions – the so-called 'glass ceiling'.

3 2.9–2.13
- Ask students to read the statements first so that they know what to listen out for. They then listen to the recording again and match the statements to one of the speakers. Point out that three of the statements are not required.
- They could then compare their answers with a partner before you check with the class.

1 f   2 b   3 d   4 a   5 h   Not needed: c, e, g

Cultural notes: sexual equality in the workplace
- Since the introduction of the Sexual Discrimination Act a number of social changes have taken place. The number of women in employment has increased by over a third from 9.1 million to 12.5 million. And in 1975, less than 2% of managers were women compared to over 30% today. Men's lives have changed too. Statutory paternity leave and pay was introduced in 2003 to enable fathers to be more involved in the care of newborn children. Fathers now spend two hours a day looking after children compared to just 15 minutes in 1975. However, despite the legislation, there are some areas where sexual inequality remains a major problem. The pay gap between the two sexes has hardly changed: women working part-time in Britain still earn 38.4% less per hour than men performing equivalent full-time work. In 1975 the figure was 42%. In addition, an estimated 30,000 working women each year were sacked, made redundant or forced to leave their jobs because they became pregnant. Despite the progress made in recent decades, in many workplaces sexual equality is still not a reality.

4
- Students read the three situations mentioned in the recording and for each one say how much sympathy they have for the speaker. Ask them to give reasons for their opinions.

GRAMMAR: hypothetical past situations

Language reference, Student's Book page 54
Methodology guidelines: Grammar boxes, page xiv

1
- Students complete the sentences from the recording with the correct form of the verbs in brackets.
- Students then look at tapescripts 2.9–2.13 on page 157 and check their answers.

1 hadn't been; wouldn't have been
2 hadn't taken
3 hadn't inherited; have been
4 hadn't been brought; wouldn't have

Language notes: hypothetical situations in the past

- We use the third or past conditional form and *I wish* + past perfect to hypothesize talk about imaginary situations in the past. For example:
  If I'd seen the play, I would have enjoyed it.
  I wish I'd seen the play.
  (The speaker didn't see the play in either case.)
- We can use the structure to express regret or explain why we did or didn't act in a certain way:
  I wish I'd gone to Turkey when I had the chance.
  If I'd know you were at home, I would have called you. (I didn't call you because I didn't know you were at home.)
- Students may be confused by the fact that the abbreviated forms of ***would*** and ***had*** look the same. Make sure you check this, pointing out that in the ***if***-clause the abbreviated ***I'd*** must be *had*.
- Before doing exercise 3, check the pronunciation of the abbreviated forms. It's a good idea to drill weak forms such as *I'd have* /aɪd əv/ and *I wouldn't have* /wʊdənt əv/.

2

- Students complete the sentences in two different ways about themselves, using *I wish* …, *If I'd* …, and *Had I known* …

3

- Pairwork. Students discuss their sentences in exercise 2 with a partner.

Extra task: discussion

- Write *Things I wish I'd known when I was 16* on the board. Ask students to think of four or five things that they wish they'd known. Then have a discussion in groups or as a class.

Methodology advances
Practical grammar ideas

Surgery

- *One of the most useful grammar activities at Advanced level requires no preparation from you (but does require a degree of courage as you throw yourself into the unknown!).*
- *Announce to students that on Friday once every fortnight (or at a time and frequency you wish) you will hold a grammar surgery. You will try and help with any language problems students bring along. You don't guarantee to know all (or any) of the answers, but you'll simply do your best to help. (And if no one brings along any problems, you'll just continue the course as normal).*
- *In the surgery itself, invite students to state their problem. If they have example sentences, write them up on the board, elicit ideas and answers from other students and where you can, offer help and explanations. Where you can't help, promise to try and find out and say you'll report back to them later.*
- *Finding answers to problems often seems to lead to something else interesting. I know some Advanced classes where the surgery (and activities arising from it) have grown and grown till they form a substantial part of the course.*

Translation contrasts

- *At lower levels teachers are typically encouraged to get students thinking and working in English without drawing parallels with their own language. However, students at higher levels often benefit from such analysis. Studying and comparing structures between two languages can help them to become clearer about the structure in the target language, noticing features that they perhaps hadn't picked out before. In particular, it can help them to notice how interference might be the cause of them making some frequent errors.*
- *A simple way to start working on this is: when students have just studied a particular structure, ask them to translate one (or more) of the example sentences into their language. Ask them to then pick out and list any distinctive differences between the way the item is made or used in one language compared with another. If the class contains students who speak the same language, they can compare and discuss their translations.*
- *An interesting extension idea is to collect in the translations. A week or two later, hand the translations back to students and ask them to translate them back into English. Will they reproduce the original English sentence correctly?*

Mediation roleplays

- *Mediation is the skill of helping two or more other people to communicate. For example, imagine that you speak German and English and you have two friends, one of whom only speaks English and one who only speaks German. Your role would be to help them communicate with each other, by translating and conveying messages between them.*
- *If you work with a monolingual class (or one where numbers of students speak the same languages) mediation can be a useful and much-needed real world language skill and can be exploited as a way of adding realistic practice to grammar lessons.*
- *When you have just studied a grammar item, ask students to think of a situation where someone might actually use it (e.g. past conditional sentences are often used in a work context when you analyse what could or should have been done in a past work situation).*
- *Explain the idea of mediation (as above) and elicit who three people might be in a dialogue that fits the situation they have already chosen (e.g. a manager, an employee on a work placement abroad and another employee).*
- *Immediately ask students to form groups of three and allocate roles. Remind them that one person only speaks one language and one person only speaks the other language. The third person can speak both. Let students roleplay the dialogue.*

Did you know?

1

- Pairwork. Students read the information and discuss the questions with a partner.

Cultural notes: the church

- A diocese is an area of a country that a bishop is in charge of. It is centred on the bishop's cathedral. It may contain a number of parishes, which are smaller areas centred on a church and its vicar (the Anglican term for a priest).
- The Anglican Communion is effectively an association of churches all over the world which have similar views to the 'mother church' in England, and to its primate, (or most important archbishop), the Archbishop of Canterbury. Each church recognizes each other's rites but is independent. It has over seventy seven million members, which makes it the third largest church grouping, after the Roman Catholic Church and the Eastern Orthodox Churches.
- The ordination of female bishops is an issue of controversy in the Anglican communion, accepted in some parts of the world, such as the USA, and opposed in other parts of the world, notably in Africa, which is the fastest-growing part of the communion

Extra task: discussion

- Ask students to describe an area of public life in their country in which there is debate about the role of women. In what ways are things changing?

Web research tasks

➲ *Methodology guidelines: Web research tasks, page xiv*

- Ask students to research an area of public life in Britain, the USA, or their own country, and find out how the role of women has changed. For example, they could choose the British parliament, and find out how many women MPs and ministers there are in comparison to 20 years ago.

If you want something extra ...

➲ *Photocopiable activity, page 230*
➲ *Teaching notes, page 199*

Answer key

5 Review

Student's Book page 168

1

1	prototype	5	business plan
2	logo	6	backing
3	return	7	supplier
4	idea	8	deal

2

Suggested answers (most common adverbs collocate first):
1 sorely / acutely disappointed
2 practically impossible
3 pitifully / acutely inadequate
4 fiercely competitive
5 vehemently / fiercely / fully opposed
6 perfectly / fully capable
7 acutely embarrassed
8 fully aware

3

1 If he'd ~~have~~ said
2 If only you ~~would~~ had / 'd come
3 If it hadn't been ~~with~~ for that hold-up
4 Had he ~~been~~ given
5 ~~Imagining~~ Imagine / Supposing
6 we'd have been able

4

1	why	7	which
2	what	8	when
3	which	9	which
4	who	10	where
5	whose	11	which/that
6	where	12	which

5

1 f 2 h 3 d 4 c 5 e 6 a 7 g 8 b

6A | Body care

What the lesson is about

Theme	Exercising without going to the gym; making it enjoyable rather than an ordeal
Speaking	Ranking leisure activities
Reading	*There's more than one way to stay in shape*: three texts on alternative ways to exercise
Vocabulary	Nouns from phrasal verbs

If you want a lead-in ...

Discussion starters

➋ *Methodology guidelines: Discussion starters, page xiv*

- *What sort of exercise do you do?*
- *How often do you go to the gym or sports centre? What do you do there? How much do you enjoy it?*
- *If you could design your own way of keeping fit, what would it be?*

Pre-teach key words: exercise

- Brainstorm words and phrases connected with exercise to the board. You could do this by miming the phrases (as far as you are able!).
- Elicit the following:
  do squats   do a handstand   do push-ups   do sit-ups
  do a forward roll   do a cartwheel   touch your toes
  work out   crouch   stretch   skip   jog   jump
  twist   lift weights
- Ask students which of these types of exercise they regularly do.

Speaking

1

- Students work on their own and rank the activities in the list from 1 (the one which would give them the most pleasure if they could do it tomorrow) to 8 (the one that would give them the least pleasure).

2

- Pairwork. Students compare their list with their partner and give reasons why they put them in that order.
- Students then discuss with the class any other activity which they would add to the list.

Extra task: discussion

- Build up a class list on the board of the most popular activities. Then decide how fit you all are as a class.

Reading

The reading is three texts about doing exercise without having to go to a gym. They describe how exercising can fit in with your everyday life and be enjoyable rather than an ordeal.

1

- Pairwork. Students read the three texts and discuss the questions with their partner.

2

- Students read the texts again and match the sentences to the correct text.
- They could then compare their answers with a partner before you check with the class.

1 B   2 A   3 C   4 B   5 C   6 A   7 B   8 A   9 C

Alternative procedure: jigsaw reading

- You could do this as a jigsaw task. Divide the class into groups of three. Each student in each group reads a different text. Then the groups do exercise 2 by sharing their information.

Language notes: reading

- To ***kill two birds with one stone*** is an expression that means to achieve two successful outcomes through one action.
- To ***wedge*** is to squeeze into a narrow space.

Cultural notes: punk rock

- The Ramones and Blondie were punk rock bands that emerged in New York in the 1970s. The Buzzcocks and the Undertones were British punk rock bands, both formed in 1975. Iggy Pop is an American punk rock pioneer who came to prominence in the 1970s, and is still performing.
- Skank is a form of dancing done by stepping forwards and backwards that first emerged in Jamaica in the 1960s, but was adapted by the punk movement. The pogo is a punk rock dance move which involves jumping aggressively in the air and shaking your head.

3

- Groupwork. Students discuss the questions in small groups.

Extra task: discussion

- Discuss the following questions as a class: *Have you heard of any other unusual ways of doing exercise? Can you describe them? Would you like to try them? Why? Why not? How can you make exercise fun and avoid it becoming boring?*

Vocabulary: nouns from phrasal verbs

1

- Read the information with the class.
- Students then choose the correct alternative to complete the sentences. Allow them to use their dictionaries if they wish.

1 checkouts	5 outlook
2 turnout	6 takeaway
3 downpour	7 outburst
4 upbringing	8 breakthrough

2

- Pairwork. Students discuss with their partner whether the sentences in exercise 1 are true or not for themselves or for their country. Tell them to go into as much detail on each sentence as they can.

3

- Students work on their own to write four sentences. Tell them that they should include one of the incorrect alternatives in exercise 2 in each sentence, but they should not write the word in the sentence. Instead they should leave a gap in the sentence where it goes, as in the example.

Language notes & possible answers

- A ***payout*** is money given as a prize or after a successful insurance claim. (*Following the accident, she was given a significant payout.*)
- A ***handout*** is a piece of paper with information on it given to students in class. (*The teacher gave the students an exercise on a handout for homework.*)
- A ***downturn*** is a reduction in economic activity. (*The economy suffered a downturn and many people lost their jobs.*)
- An ***uprising*** is a riot or revolution. (*There was an uprising on the streets of the city demanding change from the government.*)
- The ***outset*** is the beginning. (*At the outset, the expedition had plenty of supplies.*)
- An ***outfit*** is set of clothes that are worn together. (*Jo wore a lovely outfit, which included a skirt and jacket.*)
- A ***runaway*** is a person who has left home or escaped from somewhere. (*Jack was a runaway – he had left the children's home and lived on the streets.*)
- ***Getaway*** means escape. (*The criminals made their getaway in a fast car.*)
- ***Outcome*** means result. (*The outcome of the election was that the old government was still in power.*)
- An ***outbreak*** is the sudden start of a war or a disease. (*There was an outbreak of cholera in the region.*)
- A ***breakdown*** the failure of something (commonly a car, a marriage or communications) (*We had a breakdown and had to call a car mechanic to help us.*)
- A ***breakout*** is an escape from prison. (*There's been another breakout at Wandsworth prison.*)
- Note that the stress on all these compound nouns is on the first syllable.
  runaway **out**break

4

- Students show their sentences to their partner for them to guess what the missing word is.

Extra task: nouns from phrasal verbs

- Divide students into pairs or groups to research other nouns from phrasal verbs. Give each group a word, e.g. *break*, *pay*, *out*, or *hand*. Give the groups two or three minutes to find one or two compounds in their dictionaries. Then ask them to present their findings to the class.
- Possible answers: *break-in; breakup; payback; payoff; outfall; outlay; outlook; handover*

If you want something extra ...

➲ *Photocopiable activity, page 231*
➲ *Teaching notes, page 199*

6B | Medical care

What the lesson is about

Theme	Healthcare inventions
Speaking	Discussing health problems
Listening	Interview with an author on his book *Everything you always wanted to know about the history of healthcare, but were afraid to ask*
Vocabulary	Body collocations
Grammar	Passives 1
Pronunciation	Intrusive sounds

If you want a lead-in ...

Test before you teach

➋ *Methodology guidelines: Test before you teach, page xiv*

- Write these dates on the board: *1885, 1868, 1897, 1921, 1928.* Ask the students the questions below. They choose answers from the dates on the board.
  When was aspirin invented? (1897)
  When was penicillin (the first antibiotic) *discovered?* (1928)
  When was the first rabies vaccine developed? (1885)
  When was insulin developed to treat diabetes? (1921)
  When was antiseptic first used? (1868)
- Put students in pairs to discuss their guesses. Monitor and check their use of passive forms as they discuss.
- During feedback, give the correct answers, and ask if any students know any other important medical dates.

Pre-teach key words: body collocations

- Divide the class into small groups. Give each group one of the following words: *nose, teeth, feet, stomach, eye, ear.* Ask each group to brainstorm words that collocate with their word, then to use dictionaries to check and extend their collocations.
- During feedback, ask groups to share their favourite collocations.
- Some examples (for feet) are: *flat/bare/swollen/broken/wide/narrow/big/small/cold.*

Speaking & vocabulary: body collocations

1

- Pairwork. Students choose the word in each group which collocates with the part of the body in bold to describe a health problem.
- They could then compare their answers with a partner before you check with the class.

a	blocked	d	upset
b	rotten	e	strain
c	swollen	f	infection

2

- Pairwork. Students discuss the questions with a partner.

3

- Students complete the sentences about the parts of the body using the other words from the appropriate group of words in exercise 1.
- They could then compare their answers with a partner before you check with the class.

1	pierced	4	empty
2	wisdom	5	test
3	bare	6	plugs

4

- Pairwork. Students discuss the sentences in exercise 3 with their partner and say how true they are for themselves.

Methodology advances
Introducing online corpora

- *One of the most exciting developments for language education in recent years has been the increasing availability of information from online corpora. Here is a brief introduction to what they are and how they can be used.*

Definitions

- *A **corpus** (plural corpora) is a computer database that contains a vast collection of samples of spoken and written language all taken from real sources.*
- *A **concordancer** is a computer programme that accesses corpus information to produce lists that show specific requested data about an item (e.g. all the instances of sentences with another noun following the word* town*). By searching a corpus in this way you can find answers to many questions about how language is actually used (as opposed to how we think it might be used).*

Access an online corpus

- *As web addresses and access policies change frequently, I won't include any internet addresses here – but if you try one of these sets of search terms you should find some free-to-access corpora. (Note that some free corpora limit the number of output entries they produce.)*

Search terms

- *British National Corpus VIEW*
- *American National Corpus BANC*
- *Online English Concordancer*
- *Corpus Concordance Sampler*

- *Each programme works in slightly different ways so you will need to read the instructions and, if available, I suggest you follow any on-screen tutorials. However at the most basic level, you simply type in a word of your choice (e.g.* book*) and press enter. The programme then produces lists of that word with examples of text where it has been used. Some useful programs centre the key words in a single mid-screen column, which allows you to quickly compare collocating words in different contexts, e.g.*

for all your needs. A £10	***book***	*token will help to*
was going to be JK Rowling's last	***book***	*before she started working on a fresh*
would like to	***book***	*you for the party on the*

- *See Methodology advances: Using corpus information in class, page 82 for ways this data can be used in class.*

Listening

The listening is an interview with the author of the book *Everything you always wanted to know about the history of healthcare, but were too afraid to ask*, who describes his new book as a light-hearted look at the history of healthcare. He talks in particular about three inventions that we take for granted nowadays, and he discusses what people did and how they coped before these inventions.

1

- Groupwork. Allow students a couple of minutes to look at the words in the box and to imagine what the world would be like without these items. They then discuss the questions in small groups.

2 2.14

- Students listen to the interview and decide if the statements are true or false. They then correct the false statements.
- They could then compare their answers with a partner before you check with the class. Play the recording again for students to check their answers and to add any information that they may have missed.

1 True
2 False – the 1800s / 19th century
3 False – they used a chew stick
4 False – hair from the back of a pig's neck
5 True
6 False – shares some of the same ingredients as Roman toothpaste
7 False – unsafe as alcohol increases bleeding
8 True
9 False – not Wells but one of the participants on stage who had inhaled some of the gas
10 False – his attempt was 'a complete fiasco'; William Morton was the first

2.14

P = Presenter LE = Lee Evans

P: Hello and welcome to *Bodycare*. With me today is Lee Evans, who's just written a book with the rather attention-grabbing title of *Everything you always wanted to know about the history of healthcare, but were too afraid to ask.* Lee, why the long title?

LE: Well, as you say, it's attention grabbing, but also very importantly, it gives the reader an idea of the general tone of the book. If I'd called it *The History of Healthcare*, I'd have run the risk of frightening away precisely the kind of person who might be interested in reading it. This is not a serious, weighty volume for medical professionals with detailed descriptions of medical achievements through the ages. No, this is a much more light-hearted look at those aspects of healthcare which we're familiar with in our daily lives but whose origins we know embarrassingly little about.

P: Yes, I notice you write about the humble toothbrush, for example.

LE: That's right. Many of us, I'm sure, take the good old toothbrush and toothpaste for granted and assume they've been around for ever. But more modern types of toothpaste weren't developed until the 1800s and the first nylon toothbrush was introduced as late as 1938, almost immediately after nylon itself was invented.

P: So what did people use before that? Did they just let their teeth rot and fall out?

LE: Well, actually, no, in the case of the toothbrush, ancient Egyptians from around about 3,000 BC used a thing called a 'chew stick'. This was basically a twig or stick about the size of a pencil which they chewed at one end so that it became softened and frayed. And then of course they rubbed this against their teeth to get rid of food particles. And then, right at the end of the fifteenth century the Chinese came up with the first real toothbrush as we know it today. Only instead of nylon, they used the tough hairs from the back of a pig's neck – the Siberian wild boar to be precise – which they then stuck into a handle made of bamboo or bone.

P: Wasn't that rather painful for the gums?

LE: Yes, and in fact when they were introduced into Europe many of the refined and rather delicate upper classes preferred their brushes made from the softer horsehair. Can't say I really blame them, though.

P: No, indeed. And you mentioned toothpaste. What were the origins of that?

LE: Well, again this dates back to the ancient Egyptians, who used a mixture of wine vinegar and pumice stone.

P: That's the grey stone from volcanoes.

LE: That's right. And they ground this up into a powder along with eggshells and a few other ingredients and rubbed it into their teeth with their finger or a chew stick. But if you think that's unpleasant, spare a thought for the poor old Romans who cleaned their teeth with toothpaste made from human urine.

P: Really?! Urine?

LE: Yes, and they actually used it in its liquid form as a kind of mouthwash. But it wasn't such a silly idea. You see, modern dentists realized that urine contains ammonia, which helps whiten the teeth. And in fact, ammonia is still used as an active ingredient in toothpaste today.

P: Fascinating. Now your book contains a lot of interesting information like this on other everyday aspects of healthcare – you tell, for example, the history of glasses, the ambulance and even plaster casts, but I'd like, if I may, to ask you about the more serious issue of anaesthesia, to which you dedicate a whole chapter. Because anaesthetics are a relatively recent development, aren't they?

LE: That's right. Before their discovery in the middle of the nineteenth century, surgery was an extremely painful experience, an absolutely terrifying option for a patient. In fact, many preferred to put up with their illnesses rather than go through the ordeal of an operation.

P: Wasn't whisky used to help deaden the senses and relieve the pain?

LE: Yes, it was, but the problem with alcohol is that it increases bleeding and a patient was much more likely to bleed to death during an operation as a result. The medical world was desperate for a safe alternative.

P: And the patients too, no doubt. Now I see you mention in your book the discovery of three anaesthetics in particular: nitrous oxide, ether and chloroform. Tell us about those.

LE: Hmm, what's curious about all three of these is that they were already known to science, all three had been discovered long before their properties as anaesthetics were recognized. In fact, when nitrous oxide, or laughing gas as it's also known, was discovered in 1772, it was generally believed it would be deadly to humans. Nearly 30 years later, though, the British chemist Humphrey Davy actually plucked up courage and tried it out on himself – and rather than kill *him*, he found it killed the pain of his inflamed gum. But it was another 40 years or so before the full potential of nitrous oxide was realized by an American dentist called Horace Wells.

P: And how did that happen?

LE: Well, he was attending a demonstration of the gas and several people were invited up on the stage to inhale some. And Wells noticed that one of the participants who was under the influence of this gas had bashed his leg on a table but not seemed to feel any pain. So he went up to him at the end and he said 'You've hurt your leg, haven't you?' And the chap said, 'No, I don't think so.' But when he pulled up his trouser leg they saw an enormous gash there. He'd cut himself very badly and he was completely unaware – no sense of pain at all. So anyway, Wells put two and two together and very soon afterwards he took his discovery to the medical establishment – that was in 1844 – and performed what he promised would be the world's first painless tooth extraction.

P: And was it?

LE: Well, unfortunately, he hadn't administered enough nitrous oxide so the poor patient was writhing around in agony, kicking and screaming and shouting and the whole thing was a complete fiasco.

P: Oh dear. But laughing gas did, of course, eventually go on to be used as an aesthetic.

LE: Yes, it did, but the *first* aesthetic to be used *successfully* was ether, and sadly it wasn't Wells who performed the operation. In fact, his colleague William Morton is widely regarded today as the father of anaesthetics. Like Wells, he also chose a tooth extraction to prove his point to the medical establishment and once again it was in Massachusetts …

Language notes

- ***Attention-grabbing*** means highly interesting.
- The expression ***humble toothbrush*** means the 'simple' or 'ordinary' toothbrush. The phrase ***good old*** toothbrush is used to describe the toothbrush as something familiar and reliable. We can also use ***good old*** in front of a person's name, e.g. *Good old Jack. He never lets us down.*
- To ***pluck up courage*** is to raise enough courage to do something.
- To ***writhe around in agony*** is to move around, twisting and turning, in pain.

Cultural notes: Medical discoveries & inventions

- Nitrous oxide, ether and chloroform were all used as anaesthetics from the 1840s onwards. Whilst effective, they produce an excitable and slightly delirious state in the patient before they pass out, and a sick feeling afterwards. Today, other drugs are used as anaesthetics which work more effectively with fewer side effects.
- Sir Humphry Davy (1778-1829) was a renowned British chemist, who discovered the value of laughing gas as an anaesthetic.

3

Communication activities, Student's Book pages 142 & 148

- Pairwork. Put students into A and B pairs and ask them to turn to their respective pages at the back of the book.
- Allow them plenty of time to read the text and decide on the three major factual errors they want to include in their summaries. Make sure they include factual errors that are major ones. You could give an example of a major factual error and a minor factual error, which would be impossible to detect. For example, changing the dates by a century (a major factual error) and changing the date by a year (a minor factual error).
- Students then tell their partner about the history of glasses or ambulances and their partner tries to identify the mistakes.

Alternative procedure: paired reading

- With weaker classes, ask students to work with a partner on the same text and decide what changes to make. They then swap partners with one from a pair who has read the other text and summarize their text to them. Students try to find the mistakes in each other's summaries.

GRAMMAR: passives 1

Language reference, Student's Book page 64
Methodology guidelines: Grammar boxes, page xiv

1

- Students complete the passive sentences using one word in each gap.
- They could then compare their answers with a partner before you check with the class.

1	was	4	is
2	had; were	5	be
3	be		

2

- Students match the reason for the agent not being used with sentences 2–5 in exercise 1.
- They could then compare their answers with a partner before you check with the class.

a 4 b 2 c 3 d 5

Language notes: passives 1

- The passive is formed using the verb 'to be' and the past participle. The object of an active sentence becomes the subject of a passive one.
- The difficulty for students often lies in deciding when to use the passive. It is used to create a more impersonal style, or to focus attention on the action or the object of the action, rather than on the agent performing the action. Another reason that we use the passive, is that we like to give new information at the end, rather than the beginning of a sentence (see the extra task that follows).

Extra task: 'given/new' rule

- You may wish to check the difficult 'given/new' rule before doing exercise 3 by writing the following on the board, and asking students to say which sentence naturally follows the first and why:
  On the left, you can see a portrait of Elizabeth Cook.
  a Her husband painted it.
  b It was painted by her husband.
- Answer: The best follow-on sentence is b. The passive structure allows the new information to be revealed at the end of the sentence.

3

- Students rewrite the paragraph so that the information in bold appears towards the beginning of that sentence. Point out that they can make any necessary changes to verb forms and can decide whether to include the agent or not.
- They could then compare their answers with a partner before you check with the class.

1 the bone ends are put
2 the bones have to be held
3 this was achieved
4 The first splints were made by the Ancient Egyptians
5 the bandages used to be hardened
6 bandages have been soaked
7 These are gradually being replaced
8 Fibreglass enables the wearer

PRONUNCIATION: intrusive sounds

1

- Ask students to look at the sentences which include intrusive sounds /w/, /j/ and /r/ from the listening texts. Point out that in isolation the words *finger* and *for* don't normally end in /r/ in British English. Say the phrases aloud for students to listen and repeat.
- Pairwork. Students look at the extracts and discuss with their partner when the intrusive sounds /w/, /j/ and /r/ are added in connected speech.

When a word ends in vowel sounds like /uː/ or /əʊ/ and the next word begins with a vowel sound, /w/ is inserted.
When a word ends in a vowel sound like /iː/ and the next word begins with a vowel sound, /j/ is inserted.
When a word ends in the letter 'r', or vowel sound /ɔː/ and the next word begins with a vowel sound, /r/ is inserted.

2

- Students find the two intrusive sounds in each of the sentences from the recording. Tell them to say the sentences out loud quickly to help them hear the sounds.
- Go round monitoring and give help where needed.

1 With me today /j/ is Lee /j/ Evans.
2 Spare /r/ a thought for the poor /r/ old Romans.
3 Your book contains information on other /r/ everyday /j/ aspects of healthcare.
4 I'd like to /w/ ask you /w/ about anaesthesia.
5 All three /j/ of these were /r/ already known to science.
6 Several people were /r/ invited up on the stage to /w/ inhale some of the gas.
7 So /w/ anyway, Wells put two /w/ and two together.
8 William Morton is widely regarded today /j/ as the father /r/ of anaesthetics.

3 2.15

- Students listen to each sentence in turn and practise saying them.

Extra task: intrusive sounds

- Write the following on the board (they're all the names of actors/entertainers, some better known than others).
  Julie Andrews
  Jennifer Aniston
  Peter O'Toole
  Jenny Agutter
  Rosanna Arquette
  Louis Armstrong
  Francesca Annis
  Woody Allen
- Put students in pairs to decide what the intrusive sound is between first and second names, and to practise saying the names.

IF YOU WANT SOMETHING EXTRA ...

Photocopiable activity, page 232
Teaching notes, page 200

6c | Childcare

What the lesson is about

Theme	The ethics of adopting a foreign child
Speaking	Discussing adoption
Reading	*Natasha's story*: three extracts from the book *Welcome to Sarajevo*, a true-life story of a war correspondent in Bosnia
Vocabulary	*Care*

If you want a lead-in ...

Pre-teach key words

- Write the following pairs of words on the board, and ask students to work in pairs to discuss the difference in meaning between the paired words:
  correspondent/journalist *orphaned/abandoned*
  evacuee/immigrant *shelling/sniper fire*
- Ask students to predict the content of the text from the words.
- Answers: *journalist* is a general word, whereas a *correspondent* deals with a particular area of news (*political correspondent*, *foreign correspondent*); *orphaned* means your parents are dead, *abandoned* means you have been left alone; an *evacuee* is someone who has been moved out of a dangerous area, an *immigrant* is someone who has left their country and gone to live in another; *shelling* means firing shells which are explosives in a metal case whereas a *sniper* is someone who fires (shoots) at people from a hidden place.

Introducing the theme: war in Yugoslavia

- Ask students what they know about the former Yugoslavia and the conflict of the 1990s. Brainstorm what students know on to the board (write up names of places such as Sarajevo, for example) and encourage any knowledgeable students to share what they know with the class.

Speaking

1

- Groupwork. Students discuss the questions in small groups.
- Ask students if they found out anything interesting from their partners in their discussion.

Adopted foreign children and their parents

Parent	Country	Name
Ewan McGregor	Mongolia	Jamiyan
Madonna	Malawi	David
Gerhard Schröder	Russia	Viktoria
Angelina Jolie	Cambodia	Maddox
	Ethiopia	Zahara
	Vietnam	Pax

Reading

The reading text is three extracts from the book *Welcome to Sarajevo*. It is the true story of TV war correspondent Michael Nicholson during the Bosnian war in 1992. He was so shocked by the conditions at an orphanage he visited that he decided to rescue a child from it. In Extract 1 he talks about why he chose to adopt Natasha. In Extract 2 he describes fleeing Sarajevo with a coach load of children, and the trauma of parents saying goodbye to their children. In Extract 3 he describes the dangers of being arrested while trying to smuggle Natasha out of Bosnia.

1

- Pairwork. Students read the blurb from the book *Welcome to Sarajevo* and discuss the question.

2

- Students read the three extracts from the book and answer the questions.

1 Students' own answers.
2 Nicholson tells Vera Zoric that he chose Natasha because *she shines ... she doesn't seem to belong here ... she seems different to me.*

3

- Students read the extracts again and decide if the statements are true or false.
- They could then compare their answers with a partner before you check with the class.

1 F 2 T 3 F 4 F 5 T 6 F 7 T 8 F

Language notes: reading

- ***Insurmountable*** means impossible to deal with successfully.
- ***Irrevocable*** means impossible to change.
- If someone is ***tearful***, they are crying.
- ***Remorseless*** means continuing without stopping; showing no pity.
- To ***fuss*** is to worry about unimportant things.
- If you people are ***huddled*** together, they are standing very close to each other.
- To ***scribble*** is to write quickly and carelessly.
- To ***shrug*** is to raise and drop your shoulders in a gesture that means you are unsure.

Cultural notes: the Bosnian War

- The Siege of Sarajevo /ˌsærəˈjeɪvəʊ/ began on April 5th 1992 and ended on February 29th 1996. There has been no siege as long in the history of modern warfare. It was the central event of the Bosnian War which took place after the forces of the Bosnian government declared independence from Yugoslavia, creating the independent state of Bosnia and Herzegovina. About 12,000 people died in the siege, most of them civilians, and, as many others migrated, the population of the city fell by a third.
- The siege and the Bosnian War were part of a wider conflict between the different ethnic groups of the former Yugoslavia. In the 1990s, following the end of the Cold War, relations between the Orthodox Christian Serbs and the Moslem Bosnians broke down to such an extent that it ended in war and ethnic cleansing. Today, Serbia and Bosnia-Herzegovina, with Sarajevo as its capital, are separate countries.

4

➋ *Communication activities, Student's Book pages 143 & 149*

- Pairwork. Put students into A and B pairs and ask them to turn to their respective pages at the back of the book. Students read their extract about Zagreb or London Heathrow airport.
- Allow them time to look back at the main facts of the text. They then close their books and summarize their extract to their partner without looking back at the text.

5

- Pairwork. Students discuss the questions with a partner and give reasons for their answers. During feedback, you may wish to share the information about Michael and Natasha in the notes below.

Cultural note: Michael Nicholson

- Michael Nicholson is one of the world's most decorated foreign correspondents. He has been reporting for ITN (Independent Television News in the UK) for over 25 years and in that time has covered more wars and conflicts than any other British newsman, from Vietnam to Yugoslavia, fifteen in all. Natasha was adopted by the Nicholsons and grew up in Surrey. She went to the University of Bath and gained an HND in Sports Science. Now in her mid-twenties, she has returned to Bosnia more than once and visited the orphanage she was rescued from. In the British media, she has said she feels happy to have had a wonderful life in England, and feels ambivalent towards the mother who abandoned her.

Methodology advances
Using corpus information in class

- *Here are a few ideas for using corpus data in class.*

Basic use

- *Use a concordance on the computer to let students see additional real-life examples of language they are studying.*
- *If you don't have access to computers for all students to use, print off a concordance and photocopy it for use in class.*

Grammar

- *When studying a grammatical item, get students to go online and enter a typical example into a corpus to see what results come out. N.B. You can usually enter a string of words, e.g. 'Had I been' as well as a single item.*
- *Ask students to use a corpus to find five sentences using a specific piece of grammar. When they have these, ask them to write new sentences of their own, using the same grammar but changing the vocabulary so that the topic of the sentence changes.*
- *When students make a mistake in class using the wrong kinds of words with a grammatical construction, send them to a concordancer to check what kinds of construction are typically used. what kinds of construction are typically used.*

Lexis

- *Choose a common noun. Ask students to work in pairs and predict ten common adjectives that will appear directly in front of it. When the lists are ready, get students to check online.*
- *Try the idea above with many varieties of word combinations, e.g. noun and verb.*
- *Get one page of a concordance for a common key word (e.g.* bottle*) with all the appearances of this word in the central column. Photocopy the page, but with a strip of paper hiding the key word down the middle or the page. Hand the copies out to students and ask them to guess the missing word. (Repeat with a new word every day!)*
- *Similarly, you could photocopy a page and keep the key word in – but use correction fluid to white-out all prepositions in the words that come before the key word (or verbs, or adjectives, etc.).*

Writing

- *As an experiment for your class, when writing an essay, encourage them to try checking the corpus rather than a grammar book or dictionary. It's just possible they will find the information about typical collocations, patterns and uses will be more useful to them than the drier information in the traditional reference books.*

VOCABULARY: *care*

1

- Students choose the correct alternative to complete the sentences.
- They could then compare their answers with a partner before you check with the class.

1	of	4	to
2	about	5	with
3	for	6	in

2

- Students match the meanings listed to the expressions in bold in exercise 1.

1	look after well
2	not be at all interested in
3	look after well
4	a very long time
5	be more careful
6	not be worried about anything

3

- Pairwork. Students discuss with their partner how true the sentences in exercise 1 are for themselves.

Extra task: vocabulary

- Ask students to write their own personal sentences using the phrases with *care*. Ask them to share their sentences with a partner.

IF YOU WANT SOMETHING EXTRA ...

➋ *Photocopiable activity, page 233*
➋ *Teaching notes, page 200*

6D | Babysitting

What the lesson is about

Theme	Taking care of babies and children
Speaking	Questionnaire about babysitting
Listening	Radio interview with the owners of a babysitting agency
Vocabulary	Babies & babysitting
Grammar	Passives 2 (*need*, causatives, passive with infinitive)
Did you know?	Attitudes to children in the UK

If you want a lead-in ...

Discussion starters

Methodology guidelines: Discussion starters, page xiv

- *Have you ever been a babysitter? How often have you been a babysitter? Whose children did you look after? What was the experience like?*
- *What are the responsibilities of a babysitter? Do you think it is a job for both men and women?*

Pre-teach key words: babies

- Write *Babies* on the board and elicit words connected with babies. Ask, *What possessions do babies have? What noises do they make? What do they do?*
- As well as some of the words in exercise 1, try to elicit *toys, cry, crawl, toddler*, etc.
- You may also wish to pre-teach the near synonyms used in the listening: *babysitter, childminder; childcare, nanny.* (The role is more professional in the order given, so a *babysitter* is likely to be a teenager looking after children for an evening, a *childminder* is likely to be responsible for a group of children at a daycare centre or nursery, whereas a *nanny* is likely to be a full-time carer of a family's children). You could also introduce *au pair*, (a young person looking after a family's children abroad).

Vocabulary & speaking: babies & babysitting

1

- Students look at the picture and label it with the words in the box.

In clockwise order from top left: pushchair; feeding bottle; bib; high chair; teddy bear; dummy; nappy; cot; rattle; pram

2

Communication activities, Student's Book page 145

- Groupwork. Put students into small groups and ask them to turn to page 145 at the back of the book.
- Students read the situations and agree on the best alternative for each one, giving reasons for their decisions.
- Elicit a few examples of their decisions from the class.

3

- Groupwork. Students discuss the questions with their group and give reasons for their answers. Ask them if they have any funny stories about being a babysitter that they would like to tell the rest of the class.

Listening

The listening is an interview with a couple who have set up an internet company which specializes in providing a high quality babysitting service. They talk about how they recruit their staff and what training they give their babysitters who are not fully trained. Finally, they talk about how much they charge for their service, their customer care and how to get in contact with them.

1 **2.16**

- Explain that students are going to listen to an interview with the owners of a babysitting agency.
- Play the recording. Students listen and complete the sentences with one or two words in each gap.

1	a / one year	6	two hours
2	quality service	7	reality baby
3	childcare profession	8	roleplay(s)
4	interviews	9	six pounds
5	criminal record	10	surprise bag

2.16

P = **Presenter** **B** = **Barbara** **J** = **John**

P: ... just outside Canterbury and starting at 10.30. Sounds like a great day out for all the family. Now, if you're a parent and you like to go out now and then with your other half, but without the children, you'll know just how difficult it can be sometimes to find a babysitter. Fortunately, though, help is at hand. John and Barbara Walker have come along to the Radio South East studios to tell us about their babysitting agency *Childsitting Solutions*. Barbara, how long have you been operating in the South East?

B: Well, we're actually just coming up to our first anniversary – next week in fact.

P: Congratulations!

B: Thank you.

P: Any plans to celebrate?

B: Well, to be honest, we're so busy at the moment, we haven't really given it much thought. But no doubt we'll be opening a bottle of champagne to mark the occasion.

J: And we've just finished updating our website, so in a sense that'll be like a first birthday present to ourselves – and our clients, of course.

P: Right. So tell us a little bit about how the agency works – what would you identify as the secret of your success?

J: Well, we always said right from the beginning that we wanted to provide a quality service to our clients – and I think to a very great extent we've managed to achieve that. Parents keep coming back to us ... so ... well, they're obviously happy with the way we run things.

P: And when you say 'quality service', what do you mean exactly?

J: Well, clearly the most important asset we have are our sitters, and we take great care to ensure we have the right type of people working for us. Or at least Barbara does – recruitment is mainly her department.

P: So, Barbara, what kind of people do you take on? Are they all qualified childcarers?
B: Not all, no. Though something like 30% of all our sitters do have experience in the childcare profession – some are registered childminders or qualified nannies, there are a few primary school teachers and we even have a paediatric nurse on the books. A lot of these are people – women mostly – who are taking time out from their jobs to bring up their own children and need a bit of extra cash for the family budget.
P: And the other 70%?
B: Mainly young people who are thinking of going into some kind of job as a childcarer. Some are already training to do so, in fact. It's useful experience and it looks good on their CV.
P: Is there a minimum age?
B: Yes, sixteen. They have to be at least sixteen.
P: And how do you ensure these are the right people for the job? What vetting procedures do you have?
B: Well, I look through all the applications we receive and then decide which ones to call for interview. We do the interviews in four different towns in the region – Hastings, Ashford, Canterbury and Dover. John helps me out with some of them – I couldn't do them all by myself.
P: It's not easy to be in four places at once, is it!
B That's right. Though sometimes it would be a real advantage.
P: And apart from that? What else do you do?
B: Well, I take up the references – and I always do that by phone. I think you get a much better idea of someone's character by actually speaking to a previous employer or someone who knows the applicant.
P: Better than a letter.
B: Definitely. And then John gets in touch with the CRB.
P: What's the CRB, John?
J: The Criminal Records Bureau. Childcare is a very sensitive area, a big responsibility, so we have all our applicants checked out by the CRB to make sure they don't have a criminal record. And if they are discovered to have a record, we may not employ them. It depends on the offence, of course, but we want to be 100% certain that sitters are suitable people to have children in their care.
P: Yes, indeed. And I'm sure anyone using your agency will feel reassured by that. Now, I understand you also run babysitting classes. That's interesting. What are the main areas that you look at on the course?
J: Yes, these are for those of our sitters who don't yet have a recognized childcare qualification. It's a twenty-hour course run over ten weeks – so that's ten two-hour classes. We look at accident prevention, first aid, childminding skills ... Basically anything which is entailed in being a babysitter – and that really translates as entertaining the children, looking after their needs and keeping them safe.
P: Can you give us a couple of examples of what you do?
J: Well, one thing we use is a thing called a reality baby, not a real baby, but very lifelike, I can assure you, and ideal for teaching students what to do if a nappy needs changing or a baby needs to be fed or burped.
P: Sounds like a great idea – do they cry as well, these reality babies?
J: Oh, yes! We sometimes have her crying during a session – that way sitters get to realize just how distracting it can be.
P: Hmm. Nightmare. And what about older children – do you have 'reality toddlers' and 'reality teenagers'?
J: Not quite, no. But something fairly similar. When it comes to older children we use a lot of roleplay. That works really well when learning to deal with things like temper tantrums from toddlers or confrontation from teenagers.
B: We even do a role play where one sitter feeds strawberry yoghurt to another who's in the role of a one-year-old.
P: Strawberry yoghurt!
B: Yes. It gets very messy, I can tell you.
P: I can believe it! Great fun, though, I imagine. Now, we have to wind up soon, but before we do, I'm sure a lot of people listening will want to know how much they would have to pay for one of your sitters. Barbara, what sort of prices do you charge?
B: Well, the normal rate is six pounds an hour during the week, and then that goes up to six pound thirty an hour at weekends. We also charge an annual membership fee of fifty pounds, which works out at less than one pound a week.
J: Don't forget to mention the surprise bag.
B: Oh yes, that's right. Very important. For every visit, as part of the service, we provide our sitters with a small bag of toys and things – a surprise bag, we call it. It helps to break the ice at the beginning of the evening and distract children when mum and dad are walking out the door. The children can hang on to that – we don't ask for that back.
P: Good idea. And can parents choose which sitter they have? If there's one they particularly like.
B: Certainly, as long as they book well enough in advance. And of course, as long as that sitter is free on that particular night.
P: Of course, yes. Now, if you want to contact *Childsitting Solutions* or find out more about them, you can do so via their website, which is up on the screen in front of me. It's www dot childsitting solutions dot ...

Language notes: listening

- To ***vet*** is to check.
- To ***wind up*** means to finish.

Cultural note: listening

- Hastings, Ashford, Canterbury and Dover are cities in Kent, a county in the south-east corner of England.

Extra task: discussion

- Discuss some of the contentious points made in the recording. For example, *Do you think sixteen is an appropriate age to be a childminder? Do you think childminders should have qualifications? Do you think six pounds (about ten euros) is an appropriate hourly rate?*

2 2.17

- Students complete the sentences from the recording with the nouns in the box.
- Students then listen to the recording and check their answers.

1 hand	5 books
2 thought	6 references
3 doubt; occasion	7 touch
4 care	8 ice

3

- Students explain the meanings of the expressions in bold in exercise 2 in their own words.

Possible answers:
1 help is available
2 not thought about it much
3 it is very likely that / I expect that; celebrate
4 be very careful to
5 (in our files) working for us
6 contact those people who have offered to give information about prospective employees' abilities, personality, etc.
7 contacts
8 make others feel more relaxed and less shy or nervous

GRAMMAR: passives 2

➊ *Language reference, Student's Book page 64*
➊ *Methodology guidelines: Grammar boxes, page xiv*

1
- Students rewrite the sentences using an infinitive after the passive. They should begin each sentence with the underlined words.
- They could then compare their answers with a partner before you check with the class.

1 Michael Jackson is said to have a fascination for the fictional character Peter Pan.
2 Macauley Culkin, the *Home Alone* star, is known to have fallen out with his ambitious father.
3 Judy Garland's $500-a-week salary is believed to have been lower than that of the other *Wizard of Oz* stars.
4 Brooke Shields is understood to have dated Michael Jackson for a time.
5 Haley Joel Osmont was rumoured to have been picked by Spielberg to play Harry Potter.
6 The Olsen twins were once reported to be worth over $300 million.

Language notes: passives

- The pseudo-passive forms *have (something) done* and *get (something) done* are synonymous, although *get* is considered more informal and common in spoken English. Note that in spoken English *get* is often used in place of *be*, e.g. *He got thrown out.*
- Structures like *It is thought to be…* and *They were discovered to have…* are used to distance the speaker/writer from what is said.

2
- Students write three more sentences about the child stars and/or other stars from their own country, using the passive structure.
- Students then take it in turns to read their sentences to a partner who guesses who is being described.

Cultural notes: child stars

- Michael Jackson, born in 1958, is a pop star and global icon who has been involved in the music industry since the age of seven. He started as lead singer in the Jackson 5 and in the 1980s produced some of the world's best loved pop albums, notably the best-selling album of all time, *Thriller*. Between 1988 and 2005, Jackson lived on a huge Californian ranch, called Neverland after the fictional land in the Peter Pan stories. In 2003, a TV documentary called *Living with Michael Jackson* questioned his relationship with young children who came to stay on the ranch. He was tried and acquitted of the charges held against him in 2005.
- Macaulay Culkin /məˈkɔːli ˈkʌlkɪn/ is an American actor, born in 1980, best known for his roles as Richie Rich and as Kevin McCallister in *Home Alone*. Culkin has been estranged from his father since the age of 14, following a bitter custody battle after his parents split up.
- Judy Garland was an American actress and singer, who was born in 1922 and died in 1969. She was the archetypal child star, most famous for playing Dorothy in *The Wizard of Oz* (1939).
- Brooke Shields /brʊk ʃɪəldz/ is an American actress who was born in 1965. She was a big star in the late seventies and early eighties, appearing in films such as *Pretty Baby* (1978), *The Blue Lagoon* (1980) and *Endless Love* (1981). She has dated many famous people, and was married for a time to tennis star Andre Agassi. The rumours that she dated Michael Jackson arose from the fact that she was his date at the 1984 Grammy Awards.
- Haley Joel Osment /ˈheɪli: dʒəʊl ˈɒzmənt/ is an American actor, born in 1988, who had early success on TV before becoming famous as the little boy with mysterious powers in *The Sixth Sense*, a thriller made in 1999. Subsequently, he starred in *Pay It Forward* and *A.I.* Spielberg may have had him in mind to play Harry Potter, but the series of films was directed by Chris Columbus. (Rumour has it that Spielberg didn't get the job as author JK Rowling insisted on an all British cast.)
- Steven Spielberg is an American film director and producer. His most famous films include *Jaws*, *Schindler's List* and *Jurassic Park*. He has won an Academy Award winner three times and made more money than any other filmmaker in history. He is worth about $3 billion. However, rumour has it that he didn't get the job as director of the Harry Potter films because author JK Rowling insisted on an all British cast for the film versions.
- Mary-Kate and Ashley Fuller Olsen are fraternal twins who were born in the USA in 1986. They achieved huge success in the US sitcom *Full House*. Since then they have made a number of movies, usually appearing together.

3
- Students read the sentences and identify the two mistakes in each one. They then correct the mistakes.
- They could then compare their answers with a partner before you check with the class.

1 I ought to have my eyes tested at the optician's – I think my lenses need to be changed / need changing.
2 I used to get my shirts ironed by my mum, but she said I needed to learn to do it myself.
3 Our roof needs fixing /to be fixed – we had several tiles blown off in the storm last week.
4 The car needed a service / servicing / to be serviced so I took it to the garage this morning to get ~~got~~ it done.
5 I had my keys stolen yesterday so now all the locks need ~~of~~ changing.

Extra task: exchanging gossip

- Tell students to work in small groups and imagine that they are journalists on a gossip magazine. They must write some gossip about well-known people – it can be true or imaginary. Students exchange the gossip with another group and each group to decides which pieces of gossip they believe.

4

- Pairwork. Allow students a couple of minutes to think about four things of theirs that need something doing to them. Give them a couple of examples, e.g. *My house needs painting – I'll paint it myself. My hair needs cutting – I'll get my hair cut at the hairdresser's.* They then tell their partner which jobs they will do themselves and which ones they will have done by someone else.

Extra task: discussion

- Put students into pairs and tell them that they have just bought a house in the country, but it is in need of repair. Get them to brainstorm what might be wrong with the house and what they are going to get done.

Did you know?

1

- Pairwork. Students read the information and discuss the questions with a partner.

Cultural note: Charles Dickens

- Charles Dickens was a nineteenth-century English novelist. His books describe what life was like for poor people living in Victorian London. His most famous works include *David Copperfield, Great Expectations* and *A Christmas Carol.*

If you want something extra ...

Photocopiable activity, page 234
Teaching notes, page 201

Answer key

6 Review

Student's Book page 169

1

1 well	3 longer
2 less	4 good

2

1 teeth	5 eye
2 nose	6 ear
3 feet	7 nose
4 stomach	8 hand

3

1 breakthrough	4 outlook
2 turnout	5 outburst
3 downpour	

4

1 is thought (by police) to be living in Argentina
2 alleged to have been bribed by Dee
3 was claimed by the newspaper to have been dating the supermodel for over a year
4 was believed to be planning to kidnap the heiress
5 had our flat raided by the police at the weekend
6 needs cutting / to be cut
7 made to rewrite the essay (by the teacher)

5

1 pierced	9 breakdown
2 burst	10 pushchair
3 picks	11 throws
4 burp	12 smacking
5 checkout	13 yell
6 laughing	14 coming
7 bullying	15 mark
8 taken	

6

My wife, Heather, /r/ and I /j/ are coming up to /w/ our tenth wedding anniversary /j/ and we plan to go /w/ out for /r/ a meal in a posh restaurant to mark the /j/ occasion. Heather wants our two children, Sophie /j/ and Joe /w/ aged four /r/ and six, to go /w/ as well. How can I get her to /w/ understand that this is clearly /j/ a bad idea?

7A | Behaving badly

What the lesson is about

Theme	Bad behaviour at school and how to resolve it
Speaking	Describing your secondary school
Reading	*A new broom*: an extract from an autobiography of a headmistress who turns a failing school into a successful one
Listening	Five people describe bad behaviour at school and the subsequent punishment
Vocabulary	Schools
Grammar	Ellipsis

If you want a lead-in ...

Pre-teach key words: discipline

- Write the following forms of punishment on the board and ask students in pairs to put them in order from least to most severe:
  be/get caned *be expelled* *be suspended*
  get detention *be removed (from class)*
  be given lines *be told off*
- Discuss the punishments as a class. Which do students approve/disapprove of? Which are no longer used in schools?
- Ask students which form of punishment would be most appropriate in the following situations:
  not doing homework *talking in class*
  hitting the teacher *being rude to the teacher* *stealing*
  writing graffiti *setting off an alarm*

Introducing the theme: schools

- Find out how much your students know about the school system in Britain. It's likely that they know very little. Write the following on the board:
  a public school
  a comprehensive school
  a primary school
- Students work in pairs to think of questions they would like to ask you about the three types of school. Use the information in the Cultural notes on page 90 to answer their questions.

Speaking & listening

The listening is five people talking about different acts of misbehaviour at school and the subsequent punishment.

1

- Allow students a few moments to think about their secondary school. They then circle the most appropriate adjective for them which describe each of the topics to do with secondary schools in bold.

2

- Pairwork. Students explain their choices in exercise 1 to their partner, giving examples from their own experience of secondary schools.

Language note: speaking

- A ***single-sex*** school is one attended by only boys or only girls (not mixed).

Extra task: collocation

- Ask students to work in small groups to think of other adjectives that collocate with the nouns given. Ask them to research their ideas using a dictionary.
- Possible collocations: comprehensive/high/junior/primary school; experienced/knowledgeable/motivating teachers; bright/attentive/motivated pupils; tough/strict discipline; conventional/unconventional/teaching methods

3 **2.18–2.22**

- Students listen to the recording about student misbehaviour at school and the punishment that they received for it. They answer the questions for each of the five speakers.
- They could then compare their answers with a partner before you check with the class. Play the recording again if necessary.

1 abuse scratched on colleague's car door – pupil expelled
2 fight between two classmates – bully suspended for a week; victim of bullying let off with a warning
3 smoking on way to school – received three strokes of the cane
4 playing truant, messing around, being abusive and being disruptive – no punishment; moved to Learning Support Unit
5 setting off fire alarm – an hour's detention; had to pick up litter

2.18–2.22

Speaker 1
Here's an example of how bad things have become where I teach. One of my colleagues, Juliet – a chemistry teacher – had a really nasty shock a few weeks ago. She went out to her car at the end of the school day and found that someone had scratched something really offensive with a key or something on one of the doors. You can imagine how upset she was – especially since she'd recently had the whole car repainted. They caught the nasty little individual though – it was one of Juliet's Year 10 pupils who she'd recently given a detention to. He was expelled – of course – but I think the Head should have taken the matter further and called in the police.

Speaker 2
There was a fight in my class the other day – during Maths, it was. This lad, Darren Smith, he's a right bully, and he kept punching and kicking this other lad, Steven Beggs, who sits in front of him. Beggs is normally dead quiet, and he never gets into trouble or anything. But for some reason he just exploded – he stood up and started hitting Smithy really hard – punching and kicking him back. He went mad. And the teacher had a right job pulling him off – he just couldn't separate them. Anyway, once they'd sorted it out, Smithy – the one who'd started it, you know, the bully – he got suspended for a week. Dead right too, I think – I hate bullies, I do, and the school's really cracking down on them now. Beggsy just got let off with a warning.

Speaker 3
When I was about fifteen I got caned for smoking on the way to school. Somebody living near the school reported me and I had to go and see the headmaster. He gave me three strokes, three very painful strokes, on the backside, and I had the marks to prove it for over a week afterwards. Of course, at the time I thought this was grossly unfair, particularly since I wasn't even on the school premises when I was smoking. Looking back though, and especially given what goes on in schools nowadays, I think it's essential to have strict rules and rigid discipline – and that includes corporal punishment. The softly-softly approach just doesn't work.

Speaker 4
Up until last week my eldest daughter had a couple of really disruptive girls in her class – when they actually bothered to turn up at school, they were constantly messing around or being abusive to teachers and generally making it impossible for anyone to get on with any work. Fortunately, they've been excluded and placed in the school's Learning Support Unit – that's a special kind of class where children with serious behavioural problems get lots of individual attention, and things like help with anger management and sessions on how to relate to others. All sounds very progressive, but I'm a bit sceptical myself – I'm not sure to what extent a leopard can change its spots. And I'm dreading the day when the school thinks their problems are solved and they get put back into Janie's class.

Speaker 5
I had to stay behind after school for an hour last Tuesday. An hour's detention. There were three of us altogether and we all had to go round the school picking up litter. I mean, you know, that's like *really* logical, isn't it? You set off a fire alarm and you have to pick up litter for an hour – stupid if you ask me.

4
- Students listen to the recording again and say how the speakers felt about the punishments that were given to the students.

1 feels the police should have been called in
2 approves
3 disapproved then; approves now
4 sceptical; not happy that pupils will be reintegrated into her daughter's class
5 feels it was illogical and stupid

5
- Pairwork. Students discuss the question with a partner.
- Students can then feedback their ideas to the class.

Extra task: discussion

- Ask students to share any stories they have about how they were disciplined at school. Did they ever do anything bad? How were they punished?

Reading

The reading text is an extract from an autobiography by Marie Stubbs who became the headmistress of an inner-city comprehensive in London. The school was threatened with permanent closure because the staff couldn't control the students' behaviour. In the extracts, Marie Stubbs describes how she dealt with the situation and what changes she made to the school to save it from closure.

1
- Students read the text and answer the question. Tell them not to worry about the gaps in the text at this stage, as they will be completing them in the next exercise.

- puts up posters in different languages encouraging good behaviour
- organizes a May Ball for Year 11 pupils at a top London hotel
- buys benches and tables for the playground; paints basketball courts and football pitches there
- redecorates the school with bright colours
- plays music over the Tannoy™ system
- buys books and allow pupils to take them home (one teacher projects books onto screen in cafeteria)
- puts suggestion boxes around the school

2
- Ask students to read through sections a–f. They then look back at the text and choose the correct section for each of the gaps in the text.
- They could then compare their answers with a partner before you check with the class.

1 b 2 e 3 a 4 f 5 d 6 c

3
- Pairwork. Students discuss the meaning of each of the highlighted words and expressions in the text with their partner.

The following definitions are taken from the *Macmillan English Dictionary*. They appear in the order that they occur in the completed text:

on the brink of – about to, on the point of; *the brink* is the point in time when something very bad or very good is about to happen
putting my feet up – sitting down and relaxing, especially with your feet raised off the ground
turn it round (v) – make it stop being unsuccessful and start being successful
stagger (v) – arrange for events or activities to start at different times
pull together (v) – work together to achieve something
embroiled (adj) – involved in a difficult situation
gets a grip on – holds tightly
soothing (adj) – making you feel more calm and more relaxed
catching glimpses of – seeing someone or something for a moment only
flippant (adj) – treating a serious subject or situation in a way that is not serious, especially when this annoys other people
hush (n) – a sudden silence
sprung up (v) – from *spring up*: to appear or to be produced suddenly and quickly

Language notes: reading

- The title of the text, ***A new broom*** comes from the phrase ***A new broom sweeps clean.*** This means that a new person can bring about a complete change.
- If something is ***pitted***, it has small marks or holes in it.
- ***Magnolia*** is a creamy white colour. If it's washed-out it means it's pale and lifeless, probably because it hasn't been repainted for ages.
- ***Overwrought*** means very upset or emotional.
- A ***template*** is a pattern or example for something.
- ***Swarming*** means moving in large groups (like bees).
- ***Embroiled*** means involved in a difficult situation.

Extra task: vocabulary

- Ask students to find 'school' words in the text. For example:
  term playground pupils assembly Governor

Cultural notes: British school system

- The state school system in Britain consists of **primary** schools (for four to eleven-year-olds) and **secondary** schools (for eleven to sixteen-year-olds, or eighteen-year-olds if 'A' levels are taught there). Occasionally, students attend a middle school between the ages of eleven and fourteen, but this has been largely phased out. The majority of state secondary schools are **comprehensive** schools. This means that they take children of all abilities, usually from the surrounding area. A minority of state secondary schools are **grammar** schools, which means that the intake is selected by means of an entrance exam. Most British schools are secular. However, there is a minority which are religious, for example Roman Catholic, Church of England, Jewish or, increasingly, Moslem.
- Private schools in Britain are generally called **independent** schools, but can also be referred to as **fee-paying** or confusingly, **public** schools. They are more likely to be single sex, though this is dying out as co-educational schools (mixed sex) become more popular. Private primary schools are called **preparatory** schools.
- Education is compulsory in British state schools until the age of sixteen when students take exams called GCSEs (General Certificate of Secondary Education). The majority of students stay on to take exams at eighteen called 'A' levels.

Cultural notes: Marie Stubbs & St George's Catholic School

- Marie Stubbs is a former head teacher and author of the book Ahead of the Class. In the book, Stubbs recounts her experience of taking the helm at one of the most troubled schools in Britain, St George's Catholic School. The previous head teacher, Philip Lawrence had been fatally stabbed after intervening in a fight on the school grounds. Seventeen months after Stubbs was appointed the school was taken off the list of failing schools, drawn up by Ofsted (the governmental department in charge of school inspections).

Cultural notes: reading

- Maida Vale /ˌmeɪdə ˈveɪl/ is a leafy London village not far from Regent's Park and Notting Hill – it is an expensive, fashionable part of the city which has pockets of exclusive lifestyle shops, cafés and restaurants.
- Lord of the Flies is a novel by British Nobel prize winning author William Golding in which a group of boys, stranded on a deserted island following a plane crash, gradually descend into primitive behaviour.
- Farsi is the first language of Iran.
- Yoruba, with over 22 million speakers, is the first language of the Yoruba people (a large ethnic group of West and Southwest Africa). It is spoken, among other languages, in Nigeria, Benin, and Togo.
- May Balls are formal dances in which students dress up smartly and to celebrate the end of their school year. They are more common in universities than schools – the university with the oldest and most famous tradition of May Balls is Cambridge. Nowadays the balls can involve rock concerts and other shows.
- B&Q is a well-known do-it-yourself superstore chain in Britain which sells garden furniture, shelving, painting materials, etc.
- Bob Marley was upbeat reggae superstar singer-songwriter of the 70s and 80s.
- Enya is an Irish singer with a gentle, mournful voice who sings melodic, new age folk songs.

4
- Pairwork. Students discuss the questions with a partner. In multi-national classes, you could ask students of the same nationality to pair up first and discuss the questions. They can then discuss the problems of indiscipline in their countries with pairs from another country, or as an open class.

Extra task: discussion

- Ask students, *What punishments are typical in your country? How do you think teachers should deal with disruptive students?*

GRAMMAR: ellipsis

➋ *Language reference, Student's Book page 74*
➋ *Methodology guidelines: Grammar boxes, page xiv*

- Students read the sentences and write in the word(s) omitted from each one.
- They then read the sentences again and identify which of the following statements is incorrect.

1 I
2 keep the books
3 confident they will behave well
4 his; informed his mother and (his) father
5 go to the May Ball; go to the May Ball
6 open (now)

The incorrect statement is the last one: *be* cannot be omitted after a modal verb – see sentence 6.

1

- Students read the sentences and cross out the words that can be omitted. Encourage them to say the sentences out loud as they do the exercise.
- They could then compare their answers with a partner before you check with the class.

1 I can't play a musical instrument but ~~I~~ really wish I could ~~play a musical instrument~~.
2 A: Do you watch a lot of television?
B: I don't ~~watch a lot of television~~ now but I used to ~~watch a lot of television~~ (before).
3 I often spend the evening at home on weekdays but ~~I~~ never ~~spend the evening at home~~ on Saturday.
4 A: Will you still be in bed at 10 on Sunday morning?
B: I may well ~~still~~ be ~~in bed at 10 on Sunday morning~~. I don't get up till late.
5 I don't smoke. ~~I've never smoked and I'll probably never smoke.~~ I never have and ~~I~~ probably never will.

2

- Pairwork. Students look back at the sentences in exercise 1 and tell their partner how true they are for themselves.

Language notes: ellipsis

- We use ellipsis (which means omitting words from a sentences) to avoid repetition when the meaning is clear. It is often used:
  - at the end of a noun phrase
  If your computer isn't working, use Dave's (computer).
  - at the end of a verb phrase
  I thought I knew his name, but I didn't (know his name).
  - with question words
  She did the work, but I don't know how (she did it).
  - with relative pronouns
  Is that the school (that) you went to?
  - after *and* and *but*
  Thank you for the excellent food and (the excellent) wine.
  With infinitives, we use *to* to avoid repeating the whole verb phrase. For example:
  Are you going to learn German?
  I'd like to (learn German) but my school doesn't offer it.
- Other areas where ellipsis is used include short answers, e.g. *Are you tired? Yes, I am.* and with *as if/though* and adjectives, e.g. *He walked away quickly as if (he were) afraid of something.*

Extra task: ellipsis

- Write the following questions on the board:
  Do you eat out often?
  Are you going to do your homework this evening?
  Is it the end of the lesson yet?
  Do you think the teacher can swim?
  Have you ever lived abroad?
- Ask students in pairs to take turns asking the questions. They must answer using ellipsis.

IF YOU WANT SOMETHING EXTRA ...

➲ *Photocopiable activity, page 235*
➲ *Teaching notes, page 201*

7B | Rudeness

What the lesson is about

Theme	Behaviour, manners & rudeness
Speaking	Collaborative activity: poster campaign to improve manners
Listening	Conversation between three people on the subject of rudeness
Vocabulary	Good & bad behaviour
Speech feature	Ellipsis in conversation

If you want a lead-in ...

Discussion starters

Methodology guidelines: Discussion starters, page xiv

- How polite are you? In what situations are you polite?
- Can you think of a situation in which you have been very rude or one in which someone has been very rude to you?
- Do you think it is important to be polite and have good manners these days?

Test before you teach

Methodology guidelines: Test before you teach, page xiv

- Write five 'ellipted' phrases on the board:
  More tea? *Should be by now.* *Anybody else?*
  Doesn't take much. *You still here?*
- Ask students in pairs to decide what full sentences or questions they could be 'ellipted' versions of. Elicit a few good suggestions and discuss as a class.
- Put students in new pairs to write a short dialogue using the phrases. They can use any other phrases they like but their 'play' must contain all five phrases. For example:
  You still here?
  Umm ... afraid so.
  More tea?
  No thanks ... etc.
- Ask a few pairs to act out their dialogue for the class.

Vocabulary & speaking: good & bad behaviour

1

- Students complete the questions with the nouns in the box.
- They could then compare their answers with a partner before you check with the class.

1 queues	5 hooligans
2 manners	6 trouble
3 behaviour	7 offence
4 parties	8 language

2

- Groupwork. Students discuss the questions in exercise 1 in small groups.

Language notes: good & bad behaviour

- To ***form an orderly queue*** means to make a well-organized queue.
- ***Rowdy*** means noisy and aggressive.
- ***Loutish*** means stupid, ignorant, noisy and aggressive.
- ***Foul*** means bad/rude.

Cultural notes: rudeness

- In Britain, good table manners involve not talking with your mouth full, using a knife in the right hand and a fork in the left, and not shovelling food with your fork, and keeping your elbows close to your sides. On more formal occasions, it may also involve choosing the correct knife or fork to eat different courses, holding your wine glass by the stem not the bowl, and even passing things round the table in the correct order.
- In British English we use the phrase, *form/stand in a queue*. In US English it is *stand in line*.
- The British word 'hooligan' became an international word when gangs of British football 'fans' caused violence at football matches and in cities across Europe in the 1980s. As a result, huge changes were made such as all-seater stadiums (stadiums where everyone at the match has a seat; no one stands) and massive police presence at matches. Today, hooliganism in Britain still happens but is much controlled, and, in fact, other European countries now have greater problems with organised violence. The word, by the way, was first used in the 1890s to describe 'hooligan gangs' and many think it derives from an Irish family, the Hooligans, who lived in Southwark, South London, in the late nineteenth century and were notoriously tough and violent.

Extra task: collocations

- There are opportunities here for students to find other collocations for the words in the box. Ask students in pairs to look up the words in a dictionary and share interesting collocations with the class. For example, *form/stand in/jump a queue*, or *bad/good/lousy/offensive/rowdy/thoughtless behaviour*.
- Students could also look at synonyms of 'hooligan':
  lout *thug* *hoodlum* *ruffian*

Listening

The listening is three friends talking about rudeness in a variety of situations.

1

- Pairwork. Explain that students are going to listen to three people talking about rudeness. Ask them to look through the topics and then make predictions with a partner about the kind of things they think they might say about each topic.

2 2.23

- Students listen to the conversation and tick the topics in exercise 1 that the people discuss.
- They could then compare their answers with a partner before you check with the class. Play the recording again if necessary.

> - Rudeness to certain types of employee
> - The effects of city life
> - Saying 'please' and 'thank you'
> - Mobile phone abuse
> - Traditional etiquette
> - The essence of good manners
> - Negative influences

2.23

J = Jenny S = Simon L = Lucy

J: I mean, take my dad for example. He's a London bus driver. **Has to** put with all kinds of abuse – passengers having a go at him because they've had to wait twenty minutes in the rain, car drivers shouting and swearing at him because he's actually had the nerve to stop at a bus stop, would you believe, and, you know, hold them up a bit on their journey.

S: Maybe he doesn't indicate – you know, signal he's going to stop and all that.

J: Come on Simon! For goodness sake, he drives a bus, buses stop at bus stops, that's what they're there for.

S: Alright, Jenny. I know, I know. **Just trying** to offer an explanation.

J: Well, there isn't one really, is there? I mean, there's no excuse for all of that. He's just doing his job.

L: I think it's probably some kind of need we have to kick the cat when things aren't going right for us. You know, we've had a bad day at the office – a row with the boss maybe – we're feeling a bit grumpy so we take it out on the first person who's unlucky enough to get in our way – and that might be a bus driver like your dad, Jenny, or a shop assistant, a waiter, the person you buy your train ticket from ....

J: Hmm. Basically, anyone who's paid to help you.

S: Yeah, that's right. Ironic, isn't it? And another thing is that city life is so stressful nowadays, we kind of expect people to be impatient and rude, and so on. And because we think other people are going to be rude, we automatically go on the defensive and prepare to do battle.

L: Hmm, that's right.

J: But then it becomes a vicious circle – **creates** even more stress. I mean, it'd be much better if we could turn the whole thing on its head and all be nice to each other for a change. The world would be a much better place for it.

S: Well, **wonderful** if it could be like that, of course, but it's a bit idealistic, isn't it?

L: No, I don't think it is, really. I mean, good manners can be contagious too, and it doesn't take too much of an effort to be polite, does it?

J: Certainly not. Even if it's just a case of saying 'please' and 'thank you'.

S: Hmm. As long as it's not overdone.

J: What do you mean?

S: Well, I think sometimes parents put too much emphasis on all that stuff. **Always going on** at their kids – 'Don't forget to say please', 'What's the magic word?', 'I didn't hear you say thank you.' They get obsessed by the whole thing. I mean, good manners and being polite is much more than just mechanically repeating one or two words.

L: Yes, it is, but if you give enough attention to the smaller things, the bigger ones take care of themselves. I think if you always make a point of saying 'please' and 'thank you', then it'll have a positive effect on how you behave to others, whatever the situation.

J: Yes, and the same goes for 'hello' and 'goodbye' – some people don't even have the good grace to say a simple 'good morning' or even just 'hi' when they walk into a shop. I think it's so rude.

L: Hmm, they're almost denying the existence of the shop assistant – as if they weren't there. It's like when you see someone carrying on their mobile phone conversation while they're being served. Now that really is rude, I think.

S: Ooh, don't start me off on mobile phones. I've got a friend who texts other people while he's talking to me. No eye contact, of course – so I stand there making faces at him, you know, sticking my tongue out and all that – very childish, of course, but keeps me amused.

L: Doesn't take much, does it?

S: Ooh, catty.

J: And then there's all that shouting, of course. 'I'm on the train! I'll be home in ten minutes! I love you, darling!'

S: Hey, that was very good. Do that kind of thing very often on the train, Jenny?

J: Ha ha!

L: I think we're all in danger of forgetting our manners, here.

S: Yep, truce everyone! Let's change the subject. What about all that old-fashioned etiquette stuff like holding the door open for women, helping them on with their coat and all that? That's what my parents taught me, and now, apparently, it's not the done thing.

J: Oh, that's just insulting – treating women as if they're so pathetic they can't do anything for themselves.

L: Oh, I don't know. I like a bit of old-fashioned chivalry now and then. **Can't see** any harm in it really. What I object to is when people walk through the door and then let it slam in the face of the person behind. It's very dangerous, for one thing.

S: Yeah, especially those big heavy fire doors that swing shut. It's a wonder there aren't more people walking around with black eyes and broken noses.

L: Yeah, I think doors are probably quite a good test of manners, really. People pushing in front of you so they can get through the door first, or fighting to get on the train before everyone else has got off. Absolutely no consideration for others.

J: Hmm, yeah, you know, thinking about it, I reckon a lot of what we've been talking about is about that.

S: About what?

J: About a lack of consideration. I mean, it seems to me that good manners are about respecting other people – you know, imagining what it's like to be the other person and caring about how they feel.

L: Putting yourself in other people's shoes.

J: Yeah, that's right. It's about empathy, isn't it? Empathy and kindness. If people stopped to think what it must be like for my dad driving a boring old bus, listening to people moaning all day, they might be a bit nicer to him – smile at him and say 'hello', instead of shouting at him about how long they've had to wait.

S: Yeah, that's very true. It makes me think of the poor old referees who have footballers screaming abuse at them every week. A little bit of empathy would go a long way on the football pitch. Might see some better behaviour at matches.

L: Well, yes, exactly. Footballers are a perfect example of poor role models. If we're looking for people to blame for the bad manners we have to put up with nowadays, they'd be pretty near the top of the list.

J: Yeah, just behind politicians. Have you ever watched a whole debate on television, you know, from Parliament – I've seen better behaviour from a class of six-year-olds.

S: I think you're being unfair on the six-year-olds. No, I actually think reality TV shows would be at the top of my list. You know, programmes like *Big Brother*, and so on. I mean, the behaviour of these insignificant people is just ...

Language notes: listening

- ***Have the nerve to*** means dare to (used ironically here).
- ***For goodness' sake*** is an exclamation used to show annoyance or impatience.
- The phrase ***kick the cat*** means to take out your feelings of anger on the first person (or cat) you see.
- The word ***catty*** is used to describe someone who says cruel or unpleasant things about others.
- ***Barging*** means pushing.
- ***Bawling*** is screaming and shouting.
- ***Lousy*** means bad or poor.

Cultural note: parliamentary debates

- British parliament is very confrontational. In debates, the ruling party sit on benches facing the opposition party, and they take turns to score political points by criticizing each other.

3 2.23

- Students listen to the recording again and make brief notes on each of the topics they ticked in exercise 2.

Possible answers:
Rudeness to certain types of employee – Jenny speaks of abuse her bus-driver father receives. Lucy speaks of need to 'kick the cat' if things aren't going well, our rudeness to first person we come across, e.g. people in jobs like bus driver, shop assistant (i.e. people paid to help us).
The effects of city life – Stressful. We expect people to be rude so we go on the defensive and 'prepare to do battle'. Vicious circle – creates more stress.
Saying 'please' and 'thank you' – Like rudeness, good manners are contagious, including saying 'please' and 'thank you'. Can be overdone. Lucy says small things like this have a positive effect on how you behave to others.
Mobile phone abuse – Speaking on mobile when being served in a shop; texting other people in middle of conversation; shouting (e.g. when on the train).
Traditional etiquette – e.g. holding door open for women, helping them on with their coat. Jenny says it's insulting, Lucy likes a bit of old-fashioned chivalry. Doors a good test of manners: holding them open (dangers of not doing so), people pushing to get through, fighting to get on train before others get off.
The essence of good manners – Lack of consideration, respecting people, putting yourself in other people's shoes, empathy and kindness. Examples: bus drivers, referees.
Negative influences – Poor role models, e.g. footballers, politicians, people on reality TV shows.

4

- Pairwork. Students discuss the questions with a partner.
- You could then find out what forms of rude behaviour annoys the class most, and any differences between nationalities about what people consider as rude behaviour.

Extra task: discussion

- Divide the class into small groups. Ask each group to make a list of 'rude' behaviour in one of the following categories: in a car; on a bus or train; in class; while shopping; while eating in a restaurant. Ask students to present their lists to the class, and have a class discussion as to which behaviour they think is most rude.

SPEECH FEATURE: ellipsis in conversation

Language reference, Student's Book page 74

1 2.24

- Students match the questions with the replies. They then cross out any words that can be omitted.
- Play the recording. Students listen and check their answers.

1f ~~Is there~~ anything else you need for the journey?
~~I~~ don't think so. ~~Are~~ You coming to the airport to see me off?
2d ~~Did you have~~ any luck with the tickets?
No, ~~they were~~ sold out, unfortunately. ~~It's a~~ pity, really.
3h ~~Are you~~ sure you're alright?
~~I'm~~ absolutely positive. ~~I've~~ never felt better.
4a ~~Would you like a~~ cup of tea?
No, thanks. ~~I~~ never touch the stuff. ~~It~~ makes me feel sick.
5c ~~Is~~ your mum any better?
Yes, thanks. ~~She~~ should be home next week.
6g ~~Are you~~ coming out tonight?
~~I~~ can't, I'm afraid. ~~I've~~ got to work.
7b ~~Did you~~ enjoy your holiday?
Yes, ~~it was~~ fantastic! ~~We~~ just got back, actually.
8e ~~Have you~~ got any aspirins?
~~I'm~~ sorry. ~~I'm~~ afraid I can't help you.

2.24

1
A: Anything else you need for the journey?
B: Don't think so. You coming to the airport to see me off?

2
A: Any luck with the tickets?
B: No, sold out, unfortunately. Pity, really.

3
A: You sure you're alright?
B Absolutely positive. Never felt better.

4
A: Cup of tea?
B No, thanks. Never touch the stuff. Makes me feel sick.

5
A: Your mum any better?
B Yes, thanks. Should be home next week.

6
A: Coming out tonight?
B: Can't, I'm afraid. Got to work.

7
A: Enjoy your holiday?
B: Yes, fantastic! Just got back, actually.

8
A: Got any aspirins?
B: Sorry. Afraid I can't help you.

2

- Pairwork. Students practise reading out the exchanges in exercise 1 with a partner.

3

- Pairwork. Students work with the same partner. They choose the beginning or the ending of one of the exchanges from exercise 1 and write an eight-line dialogue which includes it. They should also include other examples of ellipses in their dialogue.
- Ask them to practise reading out their dialogue.

4

- Pairs then read out the dialogue to the class, without including the exchange from exercise 1. The other students guess which exchange from 1 the pair chose.

Language notes: ellipsis in conversation

- In speech, subject pronouns can be omitted, e.g. *Should be here in a minute.* – omits *he/she*, auxiliary verbs can be omitted, e.g. *You tired?* – omits *are*, and, sometimes, both pronoun and verb can be omitted, e.g. *Been there* – omits *I have*. The one difficult exception is that you cannot shorten questions that begin with *Am I* or *Is it*.
- Note that although this kind of ellipsis is frequently used in spoken English, we would not use any of the examples above in spoken English.

Methodology advances
Student presentations (2)

If you haven't done presentations in class before, here are a few guidelines and ideas for setting them up:

- *This is potentially one of the most engrossing and challenging things that students can do in class – but take care to set it up well. You don't want students feeling they are wasting hours of their time.*
- *Carefully explain the task, the timescale and the purpose to students, e.g.* You are going to research, write and give a ten-minute presentation next Wednesday. This won't be a quick instant talk, as you may have done before. I am expecting you to give an interesting high quality talk that has been well-prepared and is delivered effectively. We will use an hour of class time today and another hour on Thursday and one more on Tuesday next week. In addition you will need to spend some self-study time working on this.
- *Choosing the right topics is essential. Students need to feel interested and motivated, and this is most likely to happen if they are working on something that they feel a personal connection to.*
- *Unless you want to allow a completely free choice of topic you will probably want to set a general topic area (e.g. health, grammar problems, a famous person). You could then either prepare a 'menu' of possible presentation focuses or let students choose the specific focus they want entirely by themselves. In either case, it's probably important to allow a degree of choice. If you allocate specific titles to students they won't have the motivation that comes from having selected it themselves. Though, note that this is a guideline rather than rule. There may well be things that you believe students will find interesting once they get into them, which may, in the long run, prove more exciting than looking at something they already know well.*
- *Students will probably benefit from working in pairs so that they can support each other and share the load of writing, checking and delivering the presentation. However, the task is also suitable for keen students working on their own, and some may prefer this.*
- *Be explicit to students about the benefits that preparing and doing the presentation is likely to have for them. (Don't assume that students will automatically realize the value of it.)*

SPEAKING

Communication activities, Student's Book pages 143 & 149

1

- Groupwork. Put students into two groups, A and B. For larger classes, divide the class into two Group As and two Group Bs. Ask them to read the situation in their course book and then to turn to their respective pages at the back of the book.
- Students read the instruction about the tourist board poster campaign. They discuss the relative importance of each area and the effectiveness of each poster in their groups.
- Students then decide which three posters they would like to include in their campaign, any changes they want to make to the illustration or slogan, or if they want to design a completely different poster for any of the areas.

2

- Students now pair up with a student from the other group to tell them which poster campaigns they have chosen and why.

3

- Students now decide together on one poster for each of the campaigns, for home and abroad, to be used in a press release. Allow them a few minutes to prepare their talk. They then explain their choices to the class.

IF YOU WANT SOMETHING EXTRA ...

Photocopiable activity, page 236
Teaching notes, page 201

7c | Whodunnit?

What the lesson is about

Theme	A detective story
Speaking	Ranking types of books
Reading	*A missing person*: extracts from the book *A Dark Devotion* by Clare Francis about a missing woman
Grammar	Participle clauses

If you want a lead-in ...

Discussion starters

Methodology guidelines: Discussion starters, page xiv

- *What was the last book you read? Who was it by? What was it about? Where was it set? What genre was it? Would you recommend it? Why?*

Introducing the theme: whodunnit?

- Ask students to discuss the following questions in pairs or small groups.
  What's a whodunnit? (a detective story in which a detective has to find out 'who has done ...' a crime)
  What typically happens in the plot of a whodunnit?
  What is the detective at the heart of a whodunnit like?
  Who are the typical characters of a whodunnit like?
- Have a class discussion.

Speaking

1

- Students match the types of book with the book covers.
- They could then compare their answers with a partner before you check with the class.

1 F   2 B   3 A   4 H   5 C   6 E   7 D   8 G

2

- Students work on their own and rank the book types in exercise 1 according to how pleased they would be to receive them as a birthday present.
- They then compare their list with a partner, giving reasons for their choices.

3

- Pairwork. Students discuss their reading habits with a partner.

Extra task: mini survey

- You could turn this into a mini class survey. Ask students to walk round the class and interview at least five people, asking the questions in exercise 3. Students then sit students down with a partner, and ask them to share their data, and use it to put together a brief summary of class reading habits.
- Ask two or three pairs to briefly present their summary to the class.

Reading

The reading text is extracts from the book *A Dark Devotion* by Clare Francis. In the first extract on page 70, the protagonist Alex, who is a criminal solicitor, talks to her friend Will about the disappearance of Will's wife Grace, and about how he is being treated as a suspect by the police. In the three extracts at the back of the book, Alex talks to Grace's mother and Will's mother about Grace's relationship with her husband, and then with her own brother about his affair with Grace.

1

- Students read the extract from *A Dark Devotion* and answer the questions.

2

Communication activities, Student's Book page 154

- Students read the blurb on page 154 to check their answers to the questions in exercise 1.

Will – Grace's husband
Alex – a friend of the family, who is possibly a detective

3

Communication activities, Student's Book pages 144, 150 & 154

- Groupwork. Put students into groups of three and ask them to turn to their respective pages at the back of the book.
- Students read the extracts from the book. Tell them to make brief notes about the main facts in their extract.

4

- Students summarize their extracts to the other students in their group and then discuss what they think happened to Grace.
- The groups can then tell the class what conclusions they made about Grace's disappearance. You could then provide them with the information about what really happened. Photocopy the text below and hand out one copy to each group or student.

'I took hold of her arm. I said you will not do this thing. She tried to pull away, but I held on to her jacket. We pulled back and forth, her jacket tore. And still she tried to walk away. She tried to walk away! To go and do these terrible things she planned, but I kept hold of her jacket as though I was holding on to my life! My life, Alex! Then she pulled her arms from the jacket, she pulled free, suddenly, with a – jerk! She stumbled, she fell against the post. She was half over the gate. And then, Alex ...'
Part of me wanted to stop her there; the other part waited silently to hear the end.
'I pushed her. I did not mean to push her ... Well, I'm not sure what I meant to do. I was thinking of Will and Charlie, I was thinking that I loved them more than all the world. Perhaps I wanted her to have a shock – the water, the fall. I don't know, Alex! But I pushed her and she fell into the pool and she was still, no movement. She floated, face down. She must have hit her head – I don't know.'

Alternative procedure: comprehension

- With weaker classes, put a list of comprehension check questions on the board before you read the passage. For example:
  Who is speaking?
  What action lead to Grace's death?
  Why did the speaker take this action?
  How did Grace die?
- Allow students to discuss these questions briefly with a partner before going through them as a class.

Extra task: discussion

- Discuss students' reactions to the text from exercise 4. Do they think it is a good ending? Were they surprised by it?

Language notes

- ***Drummed into*** means taught repetitively.
- ***Tunnel vision*** is an inability to see anything more than a very narrow area of something.

Cultural note: Clare Francis

- Clare Francis, born in 1946, is a best selling writer of thriller and mystery novels. Before turning to writing, she was a famous yachtswoman, making a solo voyage across the Atlantic and taking part in the Whitbread Round the World Race before. At first, she wrote non-fiction works about her sailing experiences. Then she started writing fiction. Her first crime novel was called *Deceit*. It was published in 1993 and later adapted for television. *A Dark Devotion* was published in 1997.

GRAMMAR: participle clauses

➋ *Language reference, Student's Book page 74*
➋ *Methodology guidelines: Grammar boxes, page xiv*

1

- Students rewrite the underlined sections using the words in the box.
- They could then compare their answers with a partner before you check with the class.

1 <u>which</u> was drawn on an envelope
2 <u>Because</u> we didn't want to appear rude
3 <u>If</u> they are stored / <u>If</u> you store them in an airtight container
4 <u>with the result that</u> 30,000 residents were left without electricity.
5 <u>While</u> (I was) walking by the river yesterday
6 <u>After</u> discussing / he had discussed it further with his wife

2

- Students combine the pairs of sentences using participle clauses.
- Go round monitoring and give help where needed.

1 She tripped and fell, cutting her knee quite badly and spraining her ankle.
2 Having worked at the factory for over 40 years, he was devastated at the news of its impending closure.
3 This book is a first edition, signed by the author. / This book, signed by the author, is a first edition.
4 When told he had won the award, he broke down in tears.
5 Speaking to journalists after the trial, she said that justice had been done. / She spoke to journalists after the trial, saying that justice had been done.

3

- Students work on their own and complete each sentence.

4

- Pairwork. Students take it in turns to read out the clauses they added in random order for their partner to guess which sentence they have completed.

Language notes: participle clauses

- We can use participle clause instead of relative clauses, but students can get confused about when to use present participles (which generally replace active verbs) and when to use past participles (which replace passive verbs). You may wish to contrast the following sentences to highlight this:
  Students failed by the examination board can reapply. (who were failed – passive)
  Students failing the exams can reapply. (who failed – active)
- The other key area for students to grasp is that participle clauses are generally used when its subject is the same as the main clause. Compare:
  Having done a day's work, I went home. (I did the work. I went home)
  Having done a day's work, my friends came round. (They did the work then they came round – it can't be used to say *I* worked then *they* came round because this would involve a change of subject)

Web research tasks

➋ *Methodology guidelines: Web research tasks, page xiv*

- Ask students to research Clare Francis and other well-known whodunnit writers, such as classic detective fiction writers Arthur Conan Doyle, Agatha Christie and Georges Simenon or modern writers such as Ian Rankin, Ruth Rendell and Colin Dexter.
- Ask students to tell the class what the writer's detective is called, and what their most well-known novels are about.

IF YOU WANT SOMETHING EXTRA ...

➋ *Photocopiable activity, page 237*
➋ *Teaching notes, page 202*

7D | Crime report

What the lesson is about

Theme	Crime reports & court cases
Speaking	Discussing sympathy
Listening	Three reports on court cases and their verdicts
Vocabulary	Legal matters
Did you know?	Canadian Mounties

If you want a lead-in ...

Pre-teach key words: crime

- Write *crime* on the board, and brainstorm crimes that students know. You could use examples to try to elicit some crimes, e.g. *What do you call it when someone deliberately sets fire to something? – arson.*
- Elicit some of the following: *murder, manslaughter, arson, burglary, mugging, robbery, theft, shoplifting, fraud, forgery, vandalism, assault,* and *playing truant* (not a crime as such, but it is referred to in the text).
- Ask students to put the crimes in order from most to least serious.

Introducing the theme: crime

- Dictate the following crimes to the class: *A mugger with a knife stops an old lady in the street and steals her purse; a city investor deliberately transfers £1million from his clients' investment accounts to his own private account; a wife kills her husband after a violent argument; a drunk driver hits and seriously injures a child.*
- Ask students to work in small groups to discuss what punishment they would give each criminal.
- Discuss students' views as a class.

Listening

The listening is three radio news reports on court cases. The first report is about a pensioner who was cleared of assault for stabbing a burglar. The second report is about a mother who received a prison sentence because her daughter played truant. The third report is about a company fined for an environmental offence, and environmentalists calling for heavier penalties for these offences.

1

- Pairwork. Students read the headlines in the webpage and discuss the possible stories behind the headlines with their partner.

2 2.25–2.27

- Students listen to the recording and match the three reports with the headlines on the webpage in exercise 1, and write down who the people are in each of the reports. Pause the recording after each report and give students time to write down their answers.

Report 1 – *Pensioner used 'reasonable force' to defend himself*
Peter Simpson: pensioner who stabbed a burglar and was cleared of assault
James Boyle: the burglar
David Westwood: the judge in Peter Simpson's trial
Anna Coleby: member of the organization 'House Defence'

Report 2 – *Mother jailed for teenage daughter's truancy*
Sheila Danbury: mother who was sentenced to prison for failing to ensure her daughter attended school
Paula Banes: Educational Welfare Officer
Ian Stride: Sheila Danbury's lawyer

Report 3 – *'Polluters must pay more,' say environmentalists*
Sally Blofeld: environmental correspondent.
Jerry Wexford: member of environmental group, 'Action Now'
Daniel Roberts: spokesman for the Ambrian Water Authority

2.25–2.27

1
P = presenter JS = Jenny Sanders

P: A pensioner who stabbed a would-be burglar with a kitchen knife has been cleared of assault. Sixty-eight-year-old Peter Simpson had been charged with the offence following a failed burglary at his home in March. Having been knocked to the floor by James Boyle, an unemployed plumber, who had climbed in through an open window in the kitchen, Mr Simpson grabbed a knife from a drawer and stabbed the intruder three times in the leg.
In his trial last Monday, Boyle, who had stolen from a number of neighbouring houses in the same morning, pleaded guilty to six counts of burglary and one of attempted burglary. He was given a six-year jail term. Jenny Sanders was in court to hear Peter Simpson's acquittal.

JS: Former army officer Peter Simpson, explained how on the morning of March 15th he had heard a noise in his kitchen and gone to investigate. When he ordered 22-year-old Boyle to leave his home, the younger man had shouted insults at him and pushed him to the floor. Simpson said he had used the nearest available knife and applied his army training to overcome his attacker, without at any moment attempting to cause him permanent harm.
Judge David Westwood expressed regret that charges had been brought against Mr Simpson, who, he said, had clearly acted with reasonable force to defend himself and his property.
The incident has revived debate about exactly how far homeowners should be allowed to go when confronting intruders. Under current legislation, anyone can use what is described as 'reasonable force' to protect themselves against burglars who enter their homes. The government recently issued a set of guidelines explaining the law.

Speaking after the trial, Anna Coleby from the organization 'House Defence' insisted that householders should have the right to use any force they consider necessary to defend themselves and their homes, without having to worry whether it is reasonable or not. She said that burglars should lose all their rights when they trespass on other people's property and be prepared to face the consequences. Members of James Boyle's family refused to comment.

2

P = Presenter IS = Ian Stride

P: In the first case of its kind in the Radio Ambria area, a single mother has been jailed for allowing her daughter to play truant. Thirty-five-year-old Sheila Danbury was sentenced to 60 days' imprisonment by Brenton magistrates yesterday for failing to ensure that her eldest daughter attended school regularly.
Parents can be fined a maximum of £2,500 for each child playing truant, or imprisoned for up to three months. Speaking after the trial, Educational Welfare Officer Paula Banes said that the local education authorities had been working closely with Ms Danbury for over eighteen months and she had been warned repeatedly that she faced a prison sentence if she continued to allow her daughter to miss lessons.
Sheila Danbury was said to be shocked and upset by the decision. Her four children, including fourteen-year-old Sandra, who attended only 25% of classes in the last academic year, are currently being cared for by their aunt.
Earlier, I spoke to Ms Danbury's lawyer, Ian Stride, and asked him for his reaction to the sentence.

IS: Well, it's excessive. I think the, I think the legislation is there, or should be there at least to persuade, to convince parents of the need to send their children to school, but I but I really don't think a jail term will help to get my client's daughter back into the classroom. The very person the girl needs won't be there to encourage her.

P: Does your client regret not doing enough?

IS: Well, she did everything she could. She got the girl ready in the morning and drove her to the school gates, but even if she'd dragged her in screaming, she couldn't have forced her to stay. Clearly, the school has to accept some of the responsibility for that.

P: In a statement yesterday, the local education authority welcomed the decision, saying that it hoped it would send out a clear message to parents that truancy will not be tolerated. Ms Danbury's lawyer said his client would be appealing against the sentence.

3

P = Presenter SB = Sally Blofeld

P: Fines imposed on companies convicted of polluting the environment are insufficient, according to environmental groups. The criticism comes after yesterday's decision by Redford Magistrates to fine the Ambrian Water Authority £15,000 for allowing sewage to leak into Lake Carston last year. The leakage killed a large proportion of the lake's wildlife as well as making it unfit for water sports.
Our environmental correspondent, Sally Blofeld reports.

SB: In yesterday's court hearing, the Ambrian Water Authority pleaded guilty to allowing raw sewage to enter Lake Carston last November. The sewage had overflowed from a blocked sewer, causing the death of the lake's entire fish population as well as frogs and other wildlife.
The penalty brings the total of the company's fines for environmental offences to nearly half a million pounds this year alone, drawing criticism from the region's environmental groups. Jerry Wexford of 'Action Now' called for tougher penalties for organizations found guilty of causing pollution. He said that £15,000 was just a 'drop in the ocean' for large companies and urged courts to increase fines and impose prison sentences on company officials who are shown to be negligent. Larger fines, he said, would pay for the costs of clean-up operations, and jail sentences would serve as an encouragement to businesses to prevent such incidents occurring again.
Daniel Roberts, a spokesman for the water authority, accused the environmentalists of exaggerating the extent of the problem. He maintained that sewage leaks were inevitable, but had been kept to a minimum in the region. He also pointed out that the water authority had paid the entire bill for Lake Carston to be cleaned and was investing over a million pounds in new treatment technology.

3 2.25–2.27

- Students listen to the recording again and make notes on what was said by and/or about each of the speakers in the reports.

Suggested answers:

Report 1

Peter Simpson – He gave his version of events, saying his army training had enabled him to overcome the burglar. He aimed not to cause the intruder permanent harm.

James Boyle – He made no comments, but we do know that he pleaded guilty to all the charges made against him. He was sentenced to six years in prison.

David Westwood – He expressed regret that charges had been brought against Peter Simpson. He felt reasonable force had been used.

Anna Coleby – She said that householders should have the right to use any force they felt necessary to defend themselves and their homes. Burglars should lose their rights when they enter other people's homes, and face the consequences.

Report 2

Sheila Danbury – She made no comments, but she was said to be shocked and upset by the decision.

Paula Banes – She said that the education authority had been working with Ms Danbury for eighteen months and she had been warned repeatedly that she faced a prison sentence if she did not do more.

Ian Stride – He said he felt the sentence was excessive and would not improve the situation. Sheila Danbury had done everything she could and the school should accept some of the responsibility.

Report 3

Sally Blofeld – She explained how the incident occurred, its consequences for the lake's wildlife and the fact that the Ambrian Water Authority has been fined a total of half a million pounds this year.

Jerry Wexford – He said that such fines were too small ('a drop in the ocean') and that larger fines and prison sentences for company officials should be imposed.

Daniel Roberts – He accused the environmentalists of exaggerating the problem, and said that leaks had been kept to a minimum. He added that the water authority had paid for Lake Carston to be cleaned and was investing in new treatment technology.

4
- Groupwork. Students discuss the statements in small groups, giving reasons for their opinions.
- Groups then report their ideas to the class.

Extra task: discussion

- Ask students if they know what the law is in their country, relating to each discussion point. Do they think that the law is fair?

VOCABULARY: legal matters

1
- Students complete the sentences with the prepositions in the box. Point out that they will need to use two of the words more than once.
- Students then look at tapescripts 2.25–2.27 on page 157 and 158 and check their answers.

1 of	2 with	3 to	4 to; for	5 against	6 on; of
7 of	8 of				

2
- Students complete the sentences with the appropriate noun form of the verb in capital letters. Point out that they may need to use a plural form.
- They could then compare their answers with a partner before you check with the class.

1 trial	5 plea
2 accusations	6 convictions
3 arrests	7 charges
4 suspicion	8 sentences

3
- Pairwork. Students describe two recent high profile court cases in their country to their partner. Tell them that they should try and use as many of the verbs and nouns in exercises 1 and 2 as they can. Students might like to research court cases on the internet for homework first if they can't think of any. They then tell their partner about their court cases at the beginning of the next lesson.

Extra task: legal vocabulary

- Ask students to find other 'legal' words in the tapescript.
- Possible answers: given a six-year jail term, in court, acquittal, case, jailed, fined, warned, penalties.

SPEAKING

1
- Groupwork. Ask students to read the situations and to discuss the two questions in their groups.
- Go round monitoring and give help where needed.

Extra task: discussion

- Ask students if they can tell you about any miscarriages of justice they have read about recently. What was the crime or situation? What was the punishment?

DID YOU KNOW?

1
- Pairwork. Students read the information and discuss the questions with a partner.

Methodology advances
Word lists – reprocessing words and owning them

- *At the end of each unit in* Straightforward Advanced *you will find word lists that collect all the key items that have appeared in the lessons. These are obviously useful as a reference for students, but, although there aren't specific teaching ideas listed in the Student's Book, they have a lot potential for in-class exploitation (e.g. as a ten-minute activity at the end of a unit). This would have the advantage of both revising lexis and of bringing all the work in a unit to a neat conclusion.*
- *The truth is that few students are likely to remember all the new vocabulary items they meet. But re-meeting an item, especially a short time after the first meeting, is going to greatly increase the chances of it being remembered and successfully used.*
- *As a general principle, any tasks that ask students to look at words and 'reprocess' them in some way (i.e. think about them or do something with them that may increase memorability) are likely to be useful. Reprocessing tasks might involve selecting words, sorting words, making use of words, and so on.*
- *It will also be useful if you can find some way to help students to 'own' the words a little more, i.e. moving the words from 'something that I saw used in the Student's Book to 'something that I can comfortably use myself'.*
- *Here are some ideas for activities that encourage re-processing and owning lexis:*

Personal selections
- *Give students a few minutes working on their own to look through the word list and choose the three words they would find most useful to 'keep' and use themselves in future.*
- *When ready, pair up students who should now tell each other which three words they have picked and explain why they feel that these words are important to them.*
- *At the end gather some choices together from the whole class.*
- *It can be very interesting, enlightening and often surprising to hear which items students pick for themselves and their reasons. In my experience, it is rarely the items that I would have thought likely to be most useful for them.*

My sentences
- *When needing a quick way to practise vocabulary, teachers sometimes ask students to 'put this word into a sentence'. It's a simple and much-used classroom task though I often wonder how useful a random, context-free sentence like this might be. But with small variations it can become more effective.*
- *Ask students to look through the word list and find one item they believe that they could actually say this week in a conversation. They should think of the specific context where it will be said, e.g. where they are, who they are talking to, what they are talking about, why the item will come up in the conversation, etc. Emphasize that the word should feel absolutely natural and normal in the context.*

- *Make small groups with three or four students. One student in the group describes their context in detail. The others can discuss the item and say if they think the context is clear and will help them to recall the item.*
- *(Optional) The other students in the group act out a conversation according to the description just given. This can be followed by brief feedback, e.g. Was that what the original student meant? Did the vocabulary item fit naturally into this context?*

Personal sorting

- *Working in pairs, ask students to take a large piece of paper and draw three columns labelled: (1) Very important and useful – I must learn this; (2) Quite useful – probably worth remembering; (3) Not so important for me.*
- *Ask students to go through the word list and, after agreeing, write every item into one of the three columns. Explain that they should try not to put everything in column 1!*
- *Let pairs compare with other pairs and then discuss as a whole class. Remember that, in learning terms, it's not so important where they placed things. The simple fact that they have had to look again at a word and think about it is already a reprocessing activity and greatly increases the chances of all the items (even those in column three) being remembered.*
- *There are more ideas for working with word lists in Methodology advances: Word lists – definitions and dictations, page 154.*

IF YOU WANT SOMETHING EXTRA ...

➋ *Photocopiable activity, page 238*
➋ *Teaching notes, page 202*

Answer key

7 Review

Student's Book page 170

1

1 A popular television actor convicted of dangerous driving
2 John Hope, known to television viewers as 'Pricey'
3 leaving a trail of destruction
4 Hope, said to be depressed
5 causing extensive damage to the property
6 suffering from multiple fractures
7 When arrested by police
8 shouting
9 (When) Passing sentence
10 Having heard the evidence
11 Speaking to journalists after the trial, Hope's lawyer announced

2

1 orderly
2 rowdy
3 disruptive; lenient
4 best; foul; serious

3

1 C 2 D 3 C 4 B 5 A

4

Suggested answers:
A: ~~Would you~~ like an orange juice?
B: ~~I~~ can't drink it, unfortunately.
A: Why's that? ~~Is there~~ anything the matter?
B: ~~I've~~ got a bad stomach. ~~It~~ hurts when I eat or drink certain things.
A: ~~Have you~~ been to the doctor about it?
B: ~~I'm~~ going next week.
A: ~~It~~ might be an ulcer.
B: ~~I~~ hope not.
A: ~~Is there~~ anything else I can offer you?
B: ~~Have you~~ got any whisky?
A: ~~Are~~ you serious?
B: No, ~~I was~~ just joking!

5

Correct order: 1, 8, 10, 4, 7, 2, 9, 3, 5, 11, 6

8A | It takes all sorts

What the lesson is about

Theme	Describing people
Reading	Extracts from two novels where the main characters are described
Grammar	Noun phrases

If you want a lead-in ...

Discussion starters

➋ *Methodology guidelines: Discussion starters, page xiv*

- *Is there an unusual or eccentric person in your family who dresses or behaves unusually? If so, how would you describe him or her?*

Test before you teach

➋ *Methodology guidelines: Test before you teach, page xiv*

- Write the following pairs of phrases on the board and put students in pairs to say what the difference in meaning between each might be:

1 *a milk bottle*	*a bottle of milk*
2 *Tuesday's performance*	*the Tuesday performance*
3 *my aunt's house*	*my aunts' house*
4 *an intelligent woman*	*a woman of intelligence*

- Discuss answers as a class.
- Answers: 1 the container/the container and its contents; 2 a specific performance/a regular performance; 3 one aunt/two or more aunts; 4 Here, the second sentence is grander and more poetic.

Introducing the theme: descriptions

- Cut out pictures of various people from magazines. Hand out a picture to students in pairs in your class. Ask each pair to prepare to describe the person in the picture under the following headings: name, age, appearance, clothes, family, where they live, what they do, their life story, etc.
- Give students five minutes to prepare then ask a few pairs to present their person to the class.

Reading

The reading texts are descriptions of characters from two novels. The first is Mr Hilditch from *Felicia's Journey* by William Trevor and the second is Robert and Lizzie from *A Spanish Lover* by Joanna Trollope.

1

- Pairwork. Students describe the people in the pictures, what they look like and what they think their personality is like. They then match the items in the pictures to the person they think they would belong to; Mr Hilditch, or Robert and/or Lizzie.
- Don't check answers at this stage. This will be done in the next exercise.

2

- Students read the extracts from the two novels and compare them with their ideas in exercise 1. They then discuss how the descriptions in the extracts differ from how they described the people in exercise 1.

Mr Hilditch: A, C, E, F
Lizzie: B, G, H
Robert & Lizzie: F

3

- Students look back at the highlighted adjectives in the text and, using the context to help them, match them to the definitions.
- They could then compare their answers with a partner before you check with the class.

a deft	e ill-assorted
b rickety	f bursting at the seams
c skimpy	g rambling
d far-off days	h blurred

Language notes: reading

- To ***truss a chicken*** is tie it up and prepare it for cooking.
- ***Shrubberies*** are small bushes.
- A ***mantelpiece*** is the narrow shelf above a fireplace.

Cultural notes: reading

- *Bounty*™ and *Mars*™ are popular brands of chocolate bars.
- Spongeware is white pottery with a simple stamped design on it, often of flowers or shapes.

4

- Pairwork. Ask students to read the categories in the box, then to look back at the two extracts and discuss anything that was said about Mr Hilditch, Robert and/or Lizzie for each of the categories.
- From the information students now have about Mr Hilditch and Robert and Lucy, they discuss with their partner what type of personality they now imagine the people to have. Point out that they can use the adjectives in the box to help them.

Mr Hilditch
Age: 54
Physical appearance: fat; short pigeon-coloured hair; well-kept teeth; poor vision (wears spectacles); delicate fingers
Clothes: suit, waistcoat, striped tie tied in tight knot
Family: mother died, never knew father; he lives alone
Work: catering manager (previously an invoice clerk); has worked for same company for many years
House: detached house; his mother died in the house, suggesting he may have grown up in it
Furniture & decoration: huge mahogany cupboards and chests; ivory trinkets; second-hand Indian carpets; elaborately framed portraits of strangers
Habits: we learn that he polishes his shoes twice a day, smiles a lot, cooks for himself and enjoys eating

Robert & Lizzie
Age: in the illustration probably late teens / early twenties; now much older – college days referred to as 'far off days'
Physical appearance: in the photo, Robert wears a frown of seriousness; Lizzie is skinny with presumably long hair
Clothes: in the photo, fashionable clothes of the 1970s – Robert in bell-bottomed trousers and Lizzie in platform-soled shoes, skimpy jersey and huge floppy-peaked velvet cap.
Family: probably married now; they had a child, Harriet, in 1978; both sets of parents are mentioned, though we don't know if they are still alive now
Work: ran (still run?) their own shop, the Middleton Gallery; it seems they make at least some of the objects they sell
House: rented flat above the gallery
Furniture & decoration: furnished with ill-assorted items – the shop 'resembled the perfect seventies fantasy of an Anglo-Saxon rural idyll' with naïve watercolours, spongeware mugs and wooden spoons'
Habits: we learn rather about their work (e.g. patchwork making) than any everyday habits

Cultural note: William Trevor

- William Trevor was born in Ireland in 1928. He worked as a teacher and achieved some success as a sculptor before devoting himself to writing. Most of his novels are set in Ireland and England, and range in style from black comedies to stories about Irish history. Felicia's Journey (1994) is a dark story about a young Irish girl who falls victim to a sexual predator.

Cultural note: Joanna Trollope

- Joanna Trollope is a hugely popular English novelist who was born in 1943. She has written many novels, often about contemporary Britain in rural locations. *A Spanish Lover* (1994) is about the bond between twins and what happens as a result of their unique relationship.

5

➋ *Communication activities, Student's Book page 155*

- Pairwork. Put students into A and B pairs. Ask them to turn to page 155 at the back of the book and to read the instructions.
- Student A describes someone they know well to their partner, using the categories in exercise 4, as well as any other relevant information. Tell them not to include a description of the person's personality.
- Student B then tells their partner what they think the character of the person is like, and Student A says how accurate this impression is.
- Students then swap roles.

Extra task: describing a person

- Ask students to think of a famous person and prepare to describe their personality and appearance.
- Put students in small groups. They describe their famous person without saying who it is. The rest of the group must guess the identity of the famous person.

GRAMMAR: noun phrases

➋ *Language reference, Student's Book page 84*
➋ *Methodology guidelines: Grammar boxes, page xiv*

1

- Students match the noun phrases to the appropriate category in the grammar box. Point out that they will need to use one of the categories more than once.
- They could then compare their answers with a partner before you check with the class.

a 4 b 1 c 3 d 7 e 2 f 1 g 5 h 1 i 6

2

- Students read the descriptions, then identify the two mistakes in the use of noun phrases in each and correct the mistakes.
- They could compare their answers with a partner before you check with the class.

1 a children's *(things intended for people in general)* television programme *(commonly accepted compound nouns)* I used to enjoy
2 The last time I drank a glass of wine *(containers and their contents)* with my evening meal *(things that occur or appear regularly)*
3 the best Sunday *(things that occur or appear regularly)* newspaper *(commonly accepted compound nouns)* in my country
4 a piece of advice *(where no compound noun exists)* for car owners *(commonly accepted compound nouns)* in my area
5 tomorrow's *(things occurring at a specific time)* weather forecast *(commonly accepted compound nouns)*
6 a sportsman or (sports)woman *(commonly accepted compound nouns)* of exceptional talent *(to describe the characteristics of people or things)*
7 an area of great natural beauty *(to describe the characteristics of people or things)* within an hour's drive *(the duration of something)* of here
8 a rather ridiculous item of clothing *(where no compound noun exists)* that was once the height of fashion *(where no compound noun exists)*

3

- Pairwork. Students describe someone or something for each of the descriptions in exercise 2 to their partner.

Language notes: noun phrases

- There are a number of categorizing rules for noun phrases, covered fully in the language reference, but it is a good idea to focus on and compare some of these uses. For example:
  A *Saturday job* is something you do regularly, every Saturday but *Saturday's match* refers to a single event.
  A *milk bottle* refers to the container, but *a bottle of milk* refers to the contents.
  A *chicken sandwich* refers to chicken that is dead and cooked but a *chicken's egg* refers to a live chicken.

Methodology advances
Exploring the grammar of a word

- *What exactly is Advanced vocabulary? Does it mean learning increasingly obscure words and grammar? And if so, what on earth is the point of that?*
- *Most teachers will have met the student who delights in having notebooks full of increasingly odd, unlikely and largely useless words they have discovered. While this sort of curio collecting may have some value, I think it's worth persuading students that there is probably much more use in exploring the hidden depths of common, everyday items, i.e. items they think they know already.*
- *For example, this lesson looks at what happens when some familiar nouns come together in noun phrases (lesson 9D reviews some common adjectives used with particles).*
- *One way of exploring the hidden depths of familiar words is to look at what has been called 'the grammar of a word' – in other words, the patterns of other words that can come before or after a word.*
- *As an example, let's take just one common word – hand and try this useful task with your class. Start by writing the keyword (in this case hand) in the centre of the board (establish that, in this example at least, you are only dealing with the noun not the verb).*
- *Now ask students to think of any words or combinations of words that typically come before or after this word. Start writing them up, arranging the new words roughly into columns (depending on what part of speech they are) and discussing meanings as you go. Use dictionaries wherever they help. You might be surprised as the board quickly fills up with so many uses. (The diagram below just gives you a small sample of what you might find.) There is a lot to explore – as there is with many common words.*
- *Make a hard copy of the resulting diagram (perhaps on a piece of A3 paper) and pin it up on the classroom wall. Encourage students to keep alert outside class for more variations to add to it. Return to the diagram after a few weeks and see what can be added.*
- *A task like this helps your students become more familiar with, and more comfortable with using, the range of ways that a word is used. This is probably much more important learning than ten new items of obscure vocabulary that they are never likely to say.*

give			*a*	*helping*		*to*	*someone*
give	*someone*		*a*	*big*			
write		*in*	*an*	*elegant*			
hold			*the*	*winning*			
hold			*someone's*		*hand*		
set			*the*	*hour*			
get			*the*	*upper*		*over*	*someone*
ask		*for*	*someone's*			*in*	*marriage*
take	*someone*	*by*	*the*				
spend	*money*					*over*	*fist*

IF YOU WANT SOMETHING EXTRA ...

➋ *Photocopiable activity, page 239*
➋ *Teaching notes, page 202*

8B | Birth order

What the lesson is about

Theme	Family relationships; the importance of your position in the family
Speaking	Quotations about sisters
Listening	A conversation about birth order
Vocabulary	Character traits
Pronunciation	Changing word stress
Did you know?	Famous American siblings

If you want a lead-in ...

Discussion starters

Methodology guidelines: Discussion starters, page xiv

- *Do you have brothers and sisters? How many? Are they older or younger than you? What are they like?*
- *What was your relationship with your brothers and/or sisters when you were younger? In what ways were/are your personalities similar or different?*

Pre-teach key words

- Write the following pairs of near antonyms on the board and ask students to discuss the meanings as a class.
  kids/grown ups
  first-born/little sister
  goody-two-shoes/rebel
  siblings/only child
- Ask students to say which words describe them. (You could also add the following to check vocabulary that comes later in the unit: *spouse/partner; parent/relative; friendship/relationship*)

Speaking

1

- Groupwork. Students read the quotations and discuss the questions about the sisters in small groups.

2

- Students work on their own to complete the sentences so that they are true for them. They then compare their thoughts with the rest of the group.
- Groups could then choose the statement they liked best and read it out to the class.

Extra task: poster

- You could ask groups to make a poster with their thoughts on it. Groups put their poster on the wall then circulate to read and comment on other groups' posters.

Listening

The listening is a discussion about how the order in which you are born in your family (birth order) affects your personality, your attitude to life and to the risks you take.

1 2.28

- Students listen to the conversation about birth order and choose the correct alternatives to complete the sentences.
- Students could then check their answers with a partner before you check with the class. Play the recording a second time if necessary.

1 copy their parents' behaviour
2 her parents' high expectations
3 she fits the description in the article
4 strategies to attract attention
5 worries unnecessarily
6 helping to solve problems
7 consumers' buying habits

2.28

A = Ann R = Rob C = Christina

A: ... arguing all the time. They just couldn't get on – it was a real personality clash.
R: There was an article in the paper yesterday all about personality.
A: Yeah?
R: Yeah. It talked about how your position in the family ... you know, whether you're the oldest or youngest child ... how that determines the type of person you are and how you get on in life.
C: Yeah, I read that too. Birth order, it's called.
R: That's right, birth order. I thought it was really interesting.
A: What did it say?
R: Well, apparently, first-borns are more likely to be hard-working, conscientious types, you know, who do well in exams and get good jobs and so on, and their younger brothers and sisters are more ... have a more ... rebellious streak and they don't do as well as their older siblings.
C: And they tend to be more creative too. And more adventurous – they take more risks.
A: Who, the younger ones?
C: Yeah.
A: Why's that then? Why the difference?
R: Well, it seems fairly understandable really. I mean, first children get loads of attention from their parents and they can get kind of really close to each other. And a lot of them ... the children ... <u>they sort of mimic their parents and start behaving in the same way as they do</u> – you know, responsibly. Like grown-ups, adults.
A: Hm. Some adults.
R: Yeah, true, some adults. Anyway, by being good, and working hard at school they go on getting their parents' attention and approval. Which they like, of course, so they carry on being good and working hard and getting good marks ... and so it goes on.
C: And that was me to a tee. Conscientious Christina. Miss Goody-two-shoes.
A: That doesn't sound like you at all. I've always seen you as a bit of a rebel.
C: Well, yeah, I was – eventually – when I was about seventeen or eighteen. Just before I left school and went to university. <u>I just got fed up with all the parental pressure. They had all their hopes pinned on me</u>, and just let my younger brother get on with it, do his own thing. I really envied him that. Me, I was 'destined for great things,' as my dad always said.

R: But you were, I mean, you have – you've done very well for yourself.
C: Yeah, but, for example, they wanted me to study law, so I deliberately chose something very different – interior design – just to show them I still had a voice, that I could, you know, make my own decisions. And I started smoking, dyed my hair red, got a boyfriend they didn't approve of … all that kind of stuff.
R: You'll have to show us the photos some time – I can't imagine you with red hair.
C: It's not a pretty sight, I can tell you.
A: So why are younger siblings supposed to be more rebellious or … what was it? Creative?
R: Yeah. And adventurous.
C: Risk-takers.
A: Right. Because, I mean, I'm the younger of two sisters, and I'm not sure I'm that rebellious. I may get a bit stroppy now and then but I'm not really a rebel.
C: No, but you've done some pretty adventurous things – like hitchhiking round Europe … or … or that white-water rafting holiday you went on.
R: And you're creative – come on. I mean, I wish I could draw half as well as you.
A: Well, maybe. But I still think I'm fairly conventional. I've never really rocked the boat. Anyway, what reasons did it give, this article you read?
R: Well, it sort of confirmed a bit what Christina said about her brother. When the second one comes along, the excitement of having children has worn off – so the parents pay less attention than they did with the first, and the child has more freedom to develop as he wants … or she wants.
C: But they also want – and need – the attention of their parents, so they have to find other ways to make their mark. My brother didn't exactly rebel, but he was always clowning around, playing jokes on people, acting the fool – a right little entertainer – just so he'd get noticed. And I think that accounts for that very bubbly, outgoing nature of his.
R: And I think younger children have a more relaxed attitude to life as well – probably because there's not so much pressure on them from their parents. You're a lot more laid-back than your sister, aren't you, Ann?
A: Yeah, she has a real tendency to fuss – usually over very silly little things, too. Loses sleep over the smallest of problems. Basically, I think she suffers from a lack of confidence.
C: Hmm. Interesting. Because it mentioned that in the article too. Said that some first-borns develop a sense of anxiety when a brother or sister is born. They become anxious because they lose that exclusive attention they've been getting. They're frightened their parents aren't going to love them any more.
R: So they work even harder at school to please them, they get their approval … and so it goes on.
A: Oh dear. All sounds very complicated, doesn't it? What about you Rob? You're the second of three – it must be even more difficult for you?
R: No, I wouldn't say that at all. I mean, I never got all that suffocating attention my older brother John had to put up with. And by the same token I wasn't fussed over like my little brother Paul – even now we all treat him a bit like a baby – and he'll be 25 next month!
C: And married with his own two kids. And … er … are you a diplomat and peacemaker, like it said in the article?
R: Yeah, I guess I am. I've always liked the fact that my brothers come to me to sort out their differences – you know, if they've had an argument or something. And I do what I can, try and patch things up, get them to see each other's point of view, you know. I probably get on better with both of them than they do with each other.
A: And what about only children? Did it say anything about them?
R: Not really, no. But I guess they enjoy all the benefits of first children, without ever having to share any of the attention with a younger brother or sister.
A: Probably more confident as a result.
R: Yeah, probably. More successful too.
C: You know, what I found interesting about the article was that they're using all this information about birth order theory to improve marketing.
A: Yeah? How?
C: Well, they reckon that people born first are more likely to be attracted by a recognized brand name, or something that's been endorsed by a celebrity. I suppose that kind of fits in with their more conformist attitudes – you know, following the general trend, buying what they feel safe with. And their younger brothers and sisters, they'll be a bit more adventurous and be open to new ideas like … well, like internet banking when it first started, or anything that's a bit different.
R: Yeah, and apparently, it affects your health too.
A: You're joking.
R: No. I'm serious. Apparently, if you're a first-born, you're more likely to suffer from allergies. And if you're not, then your chances of having an accident …

2

- Groupwork. Students discuss the questions in small groups.

Language notes: listening

- If something is described ***to a tee***, it is described perfectly.
- To ***have hopes pinned on someone*** is to have very high expectations of them.
- ***Stroppy*** means bad-tempered.
- A ***bubbly*** person is lively and fun to be with.

Methodology advances
Listening – work on the details as well as the whole

- *Many teachers are nowadays trained to focus students away from worrying about catching every word in a listening text. This is sensible advice; it's usually much more important that students become proficient at finding the essential meanings in a text rather than worrying about small details that are probably unimportant.*
- *Having said that, there is certainly also a case, especially at high level, for working on catching ALL the details. Often by this level, students have become relatively good at getting the gist of what is being said, or at understanding all the key points. (For this reason,* Straightforward Advanced *does not always contain gist listening tasks, as in the conversation between the three friends in this lesson.) But they may also be missing some important nuances because that is also the limit of what they can do. It can be very revealing to do a really intensive listening task in class and let students discover how much they are not catching.*
- *Try this basic teaching strategy. First select a piece of material (choose a recording from an earlier lesson, one which proved challenging for your students). Pick out a short passage from it – just three or four sentences. Choose a section that has particular problems such as fast speech, weak sounds, swallowed sounds, contractions, hesitations, fillers, mid-sentence changes of direction, etc.*

- *In class, remind students about the original text and its subject. (You could initially replay the whole recording if you think it will help them to recall it.) Set intensive listening tasks that require students to listen very carefully to the extract you have selected. I typically use a sequence such as this:*
  - (a) *Ask students to listen and write down every word from the first sentence. Replay the recorded extract again and again until they are satisfied that they have an accurate answer (or give up). N.B. Depending on the actual extract, this may be very much harder for students than you (or they) expected.*
  - (b) *Pair up students to compare their answers. Replay the recording as necessary. Don't over-help. Don't confirm or deny answers. Let students struggle to get to their own answer.*
  - (c) *In the whole class, hear the students answers and confirm the correct version.*
  - (d) *Ask students to continue working in pairs. They listen again to the same sentence and compare it with the transcript they have written, marking every stressed syllable and the direction that the intonation moves in.*
  - (e) *(Optional) If students are good at using phonemes, ask them to listen again and make notes of any words that are pronounced with any changed, missing or unexpected sounds (see Methodology advances: Listening – Features of native speaker speech (2): pronunciation, page 127).*
  - (f) *Repeat the above stages with the second and third sentences. (N.B. Three sentences is probably enough; students are likely to find more than about 20–30 minutes of this very intensive listening tiring.)*

VOCABULARY: character traits

1 2.29

- Ask students to read the sentences from the recording first and then complete them with the nouns in the box.
- Students listen to the recording and check their answers.

1 types	5 tendency
2 streak	6 lack
3 nature	7 sense
4 attitude	

2.29

1 First-borns are more likely to be hard-working, conscientious types.
2 Their younger brothers and sisters have a more rebellious streak.
3 That accounts for that very bubbly, outgoing nature of his.
4 Younger children have a more relaxed attitude to life.
5 She has a real tendency to fuss.
6 She suffers from a lack of confidence.
7 Some first-borns develop a sense of anxiety when a brother or sister is born.

2

- Pairwork. Ask students to look back at the character traits in exercise 1. They then discuss with their partner to what extent they feel each statement is positive (P) or negative (N).

Possible answers:
1 P 2 N 3 P 4 P 5 N 6 N 7 N

3

- Students choose the adjective from the alternatives which does not describe an aspect of a person's character when used with the word in bold in each sentence.
- They could then compare their answers with a partner before you check with the class.

1 touch	4 temporary
2 put on weight	5 government
3 white	

Language notes: character traits

- We use ***streak*** to describe an aspect of someone's personality which is different from the rest of their character, whereas we ***nature*** describes their personality in general. For example, *She has a very easy-going **nature** but does show a tough **streak** when under pressure.*
- We use ***attitude*** to describe a person's opinions or feelings.
- If you have a ***tendency*** to do something, you are likely to do it often. For example, *She has a **tendency** to giggle when she is nervous.*

Extra task: writing a description

- Students tell their partner about three different people that they know of who possess one or more of the character traits from exercise 3.
- Ask students to write a short description of one of the people they discussed, using language from the lesson.
- Alternatively, ask students to write a description of a well-known person. Ask some students to read out their descriptions. Can the rest of the class guess who it is?

PRONUNCIATION: changing word stress

1 2.30

- Ask students to read the information, then underline the stressed syllable in the word *rebel* in both sentences. Tell them to say the sentence out loud and check that they have stressed the correct syllable.
- Students then listen to the recording and check their answers.
- Students then answer the question.

With the noun, the first syllable is stressed; with verbs the second syllable is stressed.

2 2.31

- Students could work in pairs. They decide together where the stress goes on the words in bold and mark it.
- Students then listen to the recording and check their answers.
- They then read out the sentences aloud. Make sure that they are stressing the words in bold correctly.

1 The chief **suspect** arrived at court under police **escort**, **protesting** her innocence.
2 I took the **present** back to the shop but they **refused** to give me a **refund** without a receipt.
3 The **produce** is **transported** across the **desert** in enormous refrigerated lorries.
4 The huge **increase** in personal debt was **recorded** in a recent **survey conducted** by the Institute of Finance.
5 The Republican caused a major **upset** by defeating Burns, but the Democrats **contested** the result and demanded a **recount**.

3

- Students now write five sentences of their own. Point out that each sentence must include at least one of the words in bold from exercise 2, but the words must have the stress on a different syllable.

4

- Students take it in turns to read out their sentences to a partner.

Language notes: changing word stress

- Words that are written the same but have different meanings depending on where the stress is placed are called 'homographs'.
- Emphasize the basic rule that the stress is on the first syllable when these words are nouns e.g. *a present*, but on the second syllable when these words are verbs e.g. *to present*. Point out the way that the weak stress /ə/ sound also plays a role here. For example, the 'o' in the noun ***produce*** has its full value, whereas in the verb ***produce*** it is pronounced with a weak stress /ə/ sound.
- Remind students that there are plenty of two-syllable words that have the same stress regardless of whether they are verbs or nouns. For example, in the text, ***order, mimic, study, water, reason, notice*** and ***pressure*** are stressed on the first syllable in both their verb and noun form, and ***design, account*** and ***result*** are all stressed on the second syllables.
- ***Survey***, as a verb, can be stressed on either syllable, depending on meaning. ***Survey*** is used to mean look at (*he* ***surveyed*** *the scene*) whereas ***survey*** is used to mean asking people questions (*20% of those* ***surveyed*** *said yes*).

Extra task: stress on word endings

- Another, and slightly more complex, area of word stress you could do as an extension task is to look at how the stress on words ending with *–ate* vary depending on whether they are used as verbs, adjectives or nouns. For example, the verb *articulate* has a secondary stress on the last syllable /a(r)ˈtɪkjʊlˌeɪt/ whereas the adjective has no secondary stress /a(r)ˈtɪkjʊlˌət/.
- Get students to use dictionaries to research the parts of speech and changing stress of the following: *graduate, designate, separate*.

Did you know?

1

- Pairwork. Students read the information and discuss the questions with a partner.

Cultural notes: famous political siblings

- George Walker Bush is the 43rd President of the United States, elected in 2001. His father, George H. W. Bush was US President from 1989-1993. Bush's siblings are also involved in politics. His younger brother, Jeb was Governor of Florida and his sister Dorothy is a fundraiser for the Republican Party. Bush has two other brothers, who are businessmen.
- Bill Clinton was the 42nd President of the United States between 1993 and 2001. His half-brother, Roger Cassidy Clinton, Junior, is ten years younger than Bill. Roger played in a rock band, served a year in jail for cocaine possession, and was arrested in 2001 for drunken driving.
- Jimmy Carter was president from 1977-1981. During and after his presidency, Carter championed human rights issues in the USA and overseas. His younger brother, Billy Carter worked in the family peanut-growing business, and had a colourful reputation in the media as a beer-drinking country boy. He famously backed an advertising campaign for Billy Beer, much to the embarrassment of his brother.

Web research tasks

Methodology guidelines: Web research tasks, page xiv

- Ask students to research other famous brothers and sisters on the web. How are they different? To what extent do they fulfil the stereotypes of older and younger siblings discussed in the unit.
- Suggested siblings: Michael and Ralf Schumacher; Owen and Luke Wilson; Kylie and Dannii Minogue; Ralph and Joseph Fiennes; Paris and Nicky Hilton; Jane and Peter Fonda; Julia and Eric Roberts; Prince William and Prince Harry

If you want something extra ...

Photocopiable activity, page 240
Teaching notes, page 203

8c | A close bond

What the lesson is about

Theme	The importance of modern day friendships
Speaking	Discussing different relationships
Reading	*End of a friendship*: a magazine article about friendships and relationships
Vocabulary	Relationships
Grammar	Attitude adverbials

If you want a lead-in ...

Discussion starters

➲ *Methodology guidelines: Discussion starters, page xiv*

- *Who are your closest friends? When and where did you meet them?*
- *What makes a friend? What do you expect from them? How important are they to you?*

Pre-teach key words

- Write the following on the board:
  friend lover acquaintance partner colleague spouse sibling best friend mate pen friend close friend flatmate
- Ask students to put the words in order from person closest to you to least close. During feedback, ask students what they expect from relationships with the different types of people.

Introducing the theme: friendship

- Prepare the following quotes on an OHT or handout:
  Happiness is having a large, loving, caring, close-knit family in another city.
  George Burns (American comedian)
  Contrary to general belief, I do not believe that friends are necessarily the people you like best, they are merely the people who got there first.
  Peter Ustinov (British actor and raconteur)
  It's no good trying to keep up old friendships. It's painful for both sides. The fact is, one grows out of people, and the only thing is to face it.
  W Somerset Maugham (British novelist)
- Ask students to discuss which ones they agree with and why. Have a general class feedback session.

Vocabulary & speaking: relationships

1

- Students choose the correct alternative to complete the questions.
- They could then compare their answers with a partner before you check with the class.

1 immediate; extended	4 stormy; breakups
2 rapport	5 links
3 terms	6 ties; relations

2

- Pairwork. Students discuss the questions in exercise 1. Tell them to give as much detail as they can on each one.

Language notes: relationships

- Your ***immediate family*** contains your mother, father, brothers and sisters.
- Your ***extended family*** includes aunts, uncles, cousins and grandparents.

Extra task: collocation

- There are a number of verbs that collocate with links and ties: *establish, build, forge (make), foster (encourage and support), develop, strengthen, break.*
- You could teach these extra verbs to students, or get them to research the words *links* and *ties* in a dictionary to see if they can find them for themselves.

Reading

The reading text is a magazine article in which the writer discusses modern day friendship. She talks about trying to maintain a friendship and the importance of friends for single people. She goes on to compare the relationships you have with friends with the relationships you have with your family and lovers.

1

- Pairwork. Students discuss the questions with a partner.

2

- Students read the article and answer the questions.

1. Tula ended the friendship with the writer. The writer had got married and Tula had made new friends after her partner left her. She reviewed her situation and decided that her friendship with the writer was not something she wanted to keep.
2. The writer was not keen to end the relationship and they maintain some contact – a couple of emails and a possible walk together.

Language notes: reading

- If you have been ***dumped***, someone has ended a relationship with you.
- ***Conundrums*** are puzzles.
- If a person or a group of people is ***your rock***, you can always depend on them for support.
- ***Heralded*** means announced or presented.

3

- Students read the article again and decide if the statements are true or false.
- They could then compare their answers with a partner before you check with the class.

1 False	2 False	3 True	4 True	5 False	6 True
7 False	8 False				

Extra task: definitions

- Prepare the following definitions on an OHP or write them on the board:
  a start liking
  b stop functioning
  c depend on for support
  d leave a partner suddenly
  e start a new stage in life
  f ask for help
  g be available
- Ask students to find the following phrasal verbs in the text then match them to the definitions above.
  fall apart walk out take to move on be around lean on turn to
- Answers:
  a start liking – take to
  b stop functioning – fall apart
  c depend on for support – lean on
  d leave a partner suddenly – walk out
  e end a relationship and start a new stage in life – move on
  f ask for help – turn to
  g be available – be around

4

- Pairwork. Students discuss the questions with a partner.

Extra task: discussion

- Ask students, *If you had to dump a friend, how would you do it?*

GRAMMAR: attitude adverbials

Language reference, Student's Book page 84
Methodology guidelines: Grammar boxes, page xiv

1

- Students work on their own to complete the sentences in a suitable way.

2

- Pairwork. Students compare their sentences with a partner.

Language notes: attitude adverbials

- Attitude adverbials can go at the start or at the end of sentences or before the main verb. For example:
  Surely he must know the truth.
  He must know the truth, surely.
  He must surely know the truth.
  The can also go between *be* and an adjective:
  His speech was certainly fantastic.
- Because these adverbs express our feelings about what we are saying, they are strongly stressed and have an intonation pattern that reflects the 'attitude' of the word. Therefore, *Amazingly, I...* should have an up and down intonation that shows surprise, whereas *Fortunately, I...* has a flatter intonation that shows relief. It is important for students to approximate the right stress and intonation when using these adverbials, so it is a good idea to get them to listen and repeat the example sentences given. This is particularly true of phrases beginning with *surely*, which needs to be said with strong stress and an indignant, rising intonation.
- Modal verbs are also used to express attitude. For example, in the sentence from the text, *I should have seen it coming: the phone calls not returned ...* The speaker is rebuking herself for failing to recognize something.

Extra task: contextualizing

- Write on the board some other phrases from the language reference (see below). Ask students to work in pairs to put them in meaningful contexts.
  much to my disgust oddly enough certainly regrettably foolishly obviously

IF YOU WANT SOMETHING EXTRA ...

Photocopiable activity, page 241
Teaching notes, page 203

8D | Singles

What the lesson is about

Theme	Being single & speed dating
Speaking	Matching men and women with compatible partners
Listening	Six people talking about being single
Vocabulary	Adverbs with two forms
Grammar	Discourse markers

If you want a lead-in ...

Pre-teach key words: singles

- Write the following on the board:
  a widow a spinster a divorcee a widower
  a bachelor a single person a single parent
- Ask students to say which are male, which female, and which can be either. Discuss the meanings. N.B. *spinster* (a single woman) and *bachelor* (a single man) are old fashioned terms. *Spinster*, in particular, is rarely used (except in an ironic sense, e.g. *30 today and still single – what an old spinster I am!*)

Introducing the theme: singles

- Divide the class into small groups. Write the following on the board in a list:
  living alone/living with your parents
  being single/being married
  going on holiday by yourself/going on holiday with friends
  working at home/working in an office
- Tell students to think which situations they'd prefer and why. Then ask one student in each group to tell their group their preference. After about 30 seconds, say 'change'. A different student must then talk about a different situation until you say 'change' again.
- During feedback, ask what the preferences of the majority were in each group.

Speaking

1

➲ *Communication activities, Student's Book pages 144 & 150*

- Groupwork. Put students in A and B groups. Explain that A groups are going to look at photos of four men and B groups are going to look at photos of four women. They are going to make guesses about the character and background of these people.
- Ask students to turn to the respective pages at the back of the book. Students look at the photos of the people and discuss what they think they might be like. They should consider each of the points listed.
- Students work with a partner from the other group. They describe each of the four men and women to each other and together they decide whether any of the men/women would be compatible with each other and why.

Listening

In the listening, six people talk about what it is like being single. They talk about people's perceptions of single people, the advantages and disadvantages of being single, whether they are happy about their situation or not, and the difficulty of finding the perfect partner.

1

- Students discuss the reasons they think people have for being single.

2 2.32–2.37

- Students listen to the recording and answer the question for each speaker.

1 H 2 N 3 N 4 H 5 H 6 N

2.32–2.37

Speaker 1
You see, the fact is, I don't need a man to feel complete as a woman. And some people just find that difficult to accept. You know, they still have this image of the single woman as some kind of lonely spinster, on the shelf, with only her dogs or cats to turn to. But that's just so old fashioned. For me, being single is a lifestyle choice and I don't need to be pitied. You know, I hate it when people say 'Oh, you poor thing, it must be terrible.' Well, no, actually, it isn't. Anything but. I like my own company and my life is very full, thank you very much. In fact, I think as a rule, women are much better able to cope on their own than men. We're far more self-sufficient.

Speaker 2
Well, yeah, OK, living with your parents does have its advantages, I suppose. I mean, I don't have to do any housework, my mum does all my ironing and she won't even let me near the kitchen. Even so, I'd rather be in my own place and sharing it with someone – you know ... a woman ... as in, er, 'serious relationship'. No disrespect to my mum, of course, but her hugs and kisses just aren't ... well, they're not the same, are they? Anyway, there's not much chance of a move in the near future, I'm sad to say. For one thing, I'll need to save up a lot more – property prices round here are sky-high at the moment and I just haven't got enough to pay a deposit. Plus, of course, I have to find someone to be in a serious relationship with. And I'm afraid I'm not having much luck in that department right now.

Speaker 3
When he walked out, I thought, 'Good riddance! I'm glad he's gone. I don't want him here and I don't need him here. I don't need anyone.' And if it was just me, if I only had myself to look after, I'd still feel the same way. But I've got my two boys to think of and they really need to have a man about the house. Darren, stop that this minute! Put it down. Now! You see – they're a bit of a handful. They need a dad and I need the extra pair of hands. Mind you, they're bone idle, most men, aren't they, so there's no guarantee the next one would be any better than the last. But of course, that's not the only reason for being in a relationship, is it?

Speaker 4
On balance, I'd say I'm better out of a relationship than in at the moment. Of course, I do enjoy the companionship of a steady girlfriend – I split up with someone recently, and I think one of the things I miss most is the regular conversation – you know, politics, the planet, a film we've seen – whatever. But my job's taking up a lot of my time at the moment – my boss keeps sending me away on business – Eastern Europe mostly – so I'm hardly ever around during the week. And anyway, there's a lot to be said for being single. I get to see my chums more often, for one thing, and we all go out partying and clubbing together at the weekend – a whole group of us. We have a great time. And there's not that same pressure to be somewhere or do something at any specific time – I don't feel tied down like I used to.

Speaker 5
To be perfectly honest I just couldn't imagine going out with another man, let alone being married to one. I mean, relationships are all about compromise, aren't they, and I'm just hopeless at that. Like, why should I have to spend the evening watching football on the telly or going out with his boring friends? I know, I know – I'm just selfish and inflexible, but at least I admit it. Let's be honest, though, men have some pretty unendearing qualities of their own. They leave their dirty handprints all over the walls, they spill coffee on the sofa and don't clean it off, and they go on and on about their problems as if everyone else was really interested. I should know, I've been married twice. No, it's not always easy being single, but that's how I want it. I'm much better off that way.

Speaker 6
Nine years to go to my retirement, and I still haven't found that elusive 'woman of my dreams'. I've tried – believe me, I've tried – but she just hasn't shown her face yet. Perhaps she's hiding from me. Haven't given up hope yet, though. In fact, I've just started going to a singles club – every Friday down at the Beach Hotel. The Tropical Bar. I've already got my eye on somebody. Dorothy, her name is – she works in Gamidges in Brent Street. I might pop in there one day this week and surprise her. Nothing to lose.

Language notes: listening

- ***On the shelf*** means unmarried and too old to get married.
- ***A bit of a handful*** means difficult to manage/control.
- ***Bone idle*** means very lazy.
- ***Chum*** is a colloquial word for friend.

3

- Ask students to read the statements first so that they know what to listen out for. They then listen to the recording again and match the statements to the speakers. Point out that three of the statements aren't needed.

1 c 2 g 3 a 4 i 5 d 6 f
Not needed: b, e, h

4

- Groupwork. Students discuss the statements from the recording in small groups.
- You could then open this up into a class discussion.

Extra task: discussion

- Ask students to discuss the situation in their own countries. Is the number of single people growing? Is it more acceptable for young people to leave home and live alone? Is there a growing number of older people who live alone instead of with their family?

GRAMMAR: discourse markers

➜ *Language reference, Student's Book page 84*
➜ *Methodology guidelines: Grammar boxes, page xiv*

1

- Ask students to read the information. Point out that the attitude adverbs they studied on page 81 are one type of discourse.
- Ask students to turn to tapescripts 2.32–2.37 on page 58 and match the highlighted discourse markers from speakers 1–3 to the explanations a–i.

a Adding extra information – *In fact*
b Making a general statement – *As a rule*
c Explaining what you have said – *I mean*
d Correcting what someone has said – *Actually*
e Returning to the original subject – *Anyway*
f Showing you do not intend to offend – *No disrespect to*
g Introducing information which should be obvious to the listener – *Of course*
h Enumerating a series of points – *For one thing* and *Plus*
i Contrasting with previous ideas – *Mind you* and *Even so*

Language notes: discourse markers

- Discourse markers are used to prepare readers or listeners for what is to come next, or connect what has been said or written to what was said or written before. They are generally used at the start of a sentence or to link two clauses.
- Here are some specific uses of discourse markers:
  to introduce a point, e.g. *To start with …*
  to add points, e.g. *for one/another thing, as well as that, on top of that**, in addition, moreover*
  to introduce extra reasons to support an argument, e.g. *besides, anyway*
  to make general statements, e.g. *as a rule, on balance, generally speaking, all in all, by and large*, on the whole**
  to make the most important point, e.g. *ultimately …*
  to indicate honesty, e.g. *let's be honest, let's face it*, quite honestly/frankly, in all honesty, to be honest/frank, admittedly*
  to introduce a contrast, e.g. *still, all/just the same*, even so*, mind you*, however, nonetheless*
  to clarify and explain, e.g. *I mean*, to put it another way*, that's to say, after all*
  to limit, modify or correct, e.g. *at least, anyway, actually, in fact*
  to change the subject, e.g. *by the way, anyway*
- The phrases with asterisks (*) are more idiomatic, and often, but not exclusively, used in spoken English.

2

- Students look at tapescripts 2.32–2.37 on page 58 again and explain the use of the highlighted discourse markers from the speakers 4–6. Students could work in pairs to do this exercise.

Suggested answers:
On balance – making a general statement to summarize
Of course – introducing information which should be obvious to the listener
Anyway – adding further weight to what is being said
For one thing – enumerating a series of points
To be perfectly honest – showing that you intend to speak sincerely
I mean – explaining what you have said
Let's be honest – showing that you intend to speak sincerely and inviting the listener to agree with you
In fact – adding extra information

3

- Students complete the texts with the discourse markers in the boxes. Point out that on a couple of occasions, more than one answer may be possible.
- They could compare their answers with a partner before you check with the class.

2	For one thing	9	Of course
3	To be honest	10	all the same
4	after all / to be honest	11	Mind you / Actually
5	anyway	12	Anyway
6	Generally	13	actually
7	At least	14	In fact
8	I mean	15	ultimately

4

- Pairwork. Students discuss with a partner how happy they would be in the three situations in exercise 3.

Vocabulary: adverbs with two forms

1

- Students read the information and the two sentences from speaker 4 in the recording. They then answer the questions.

1	mostly	2	most

2

- Students choose the correct adverbs to complete the pair of sentences.
- They could then compare their answers with a partner before you check with the class.

1	a easily	b	easy
2	a wide	b	widely
3	a light	b	lightly
4	a loudly	b	loud
5	a late	b	lately
6	a shortly	b	short
7	a high	b	highly
8	a hardly	b	hard

Language note: adverbs with two forms

- When adverbs have two forms, there is a difference in meaning; they cannot be used interchangeably. Here are the meanings of the adverbs from exercise 2:
  1a: If you are ***easily distracted***, you find it hard to concentrate on things.
  1b: To ***take things easy*** is to do things in a relaxed way.
  2a: ***Wide awake*** means completely awake. Note – in other contexts, *wide* does not mean *completely*.
  2b: If you ***travel widely***, you travel to many places.
  3a: If you ***travel light***, you don't carry much with you.
  3b: If you ***sleep lightly***, you are easily woken.
  4a: If you ***snore loudly***, you make a lot of noise in your sleep!
  4b: To ***laugh out loud*** is to laugh so that everyone can hear you.
  5a: If you are ***late***, you are not on time.
  5b: If you've been to the theatre ***lately***, you've been recently.
  6a: ***Soon*** means shortly.
  6b: If you ***cut short your holiday***, you come home early.
  7a: To ***aim high*** is to try to achieve something better than average.
  7b: ***Highly*** means very.
  8a: ***Hardly anything*** means almost nothing.
  8b: If you ***try hard***, you make a lot of effort.

3

- Pairwork. Students discuss how true the sentences in exercise 2 are for them.

Extra task: collocation

- Ask students to find other verbs and adjectives that these adverbs regularly collocate with by researching in their dictionaries. For example, *go easy*, *work hard*, *cry out loud*, *wide apart*.

If you want something extra ...

- *Photocopiable activity, page 242*
- *Teaching notes, page 204*

Answer key

8 Review

Student's Book page 171

1

1	nature; light	5	lack; short
2	streak; high	6	type; hard
3	attitude; easy	7	tendency; late
4	sense; loud	8	nature; wide

2

1	terms	4	breakups
2	family	5	rapport
3	relations/links	6	links/relations

3

1 five days' holiday / a five-day holiday; end of March
2 company's chief executive / chief executive of the company; man of great integrity; corruption scandal; source of shock
3 referee's decision / decision of the referee; last night's cup final; outbreak of violence
4 diamond wedding ring; coffee mug; kitchen cupboards / cupboards in the kitchen
5 look of surprise; people's faces / the faces of people; women's clothes, fancy dress party

4

1	for one thing	8	At least
2	on top of	9	To be honest
3	Mind you	10	Surely
4	Actually	11	mean
5	After all	12	Besides
6	Anyway	13	fact
7	ironically	14	Ultimately

9A | A place called home

What the lesson is about

Theme	Building a new town
Speaking	Groupwork: town planning and making a presentation about a proposed new town
Reading	*The city of tomorrow*: article about the architect Le Corbusier and his plan to rebuild the centre of Paris
Grammar	Modal verbs 2 (*will, would, shall*)

If you want a lead-in ...

Discussion starters

Methodology guidelines: Discussion starters, page xiv

- *What sort of architecture do you admire – modern or traditional? Which modern buildings do you like?*
- *How would you describe the architecture of the town or city where you live?*
- *In what sort of building and area would you prefer to live and why?*

Pre-teach key words: urban planning

- Write the following words from the text on the board:
  clean air skyscrapers overcrowding
  high-rise buildings urban sprawl tower blocks
  green space pollution ample accommodation
  slums sewage
- Ask students to work in pairs to categorize the words under three or four headings. Ask pairs to tell the class how and why they have chosen their categories.
- Ask the class to predict the text from these words.

Reading

The reading text is an article about the French architect Le Corbusier and his revolutionary plans to rebuild the centre of Paris. He intended to solve the problems of overcrowding and urban deprivation which existed in the city in the early twentieth century by building high-rise buildings and separating pedestrians from car drivers.

1

- Groupwork. You could ask the students to close their eyes for a minute or two and think of Paris and the images that come to mind. Ask them to think about the buildings, streets, parks, people, cafés, etc. Students then form small groups and tell each other about the images they thought of.
- Then ask them to imagine what Paris would be like if some of the famous places, such as the Eiffel Tower, the Arc de Triomphe, Montmatre, etc. were pulled down to make way for skyscrapers.

2

- Students look at the photo and read the introductory sentence to the text. They then discuss the questions in their groups. Don't confirm the answers at this stage. This will be done in the next exercise.
- When getting feedback from the class, ask students what they know about the architect Le Corbusier.

Cultural notes: Le Corbusier

- Le Corbusier was born in 1887 and died in 1965. His real name was Charles-Édouard Jeanneret. Though he was born in Switzerland, he became a French citizen later in life. He was an innovator of modern design and architecture. Le Corbusier wanted to improve ordinary people's lives, and believed that if his ideas for new ways of urban living were not adopted, there would be a revolution. Nowadays, his ideas are often thought of as leading to the construction of huge, soulless, inhuman estates, but, arguably complexes built to his design (such as Unite d'Habitation in Marseille) are popular and successful. It was projects by other developers, following his principles but using cheap materials, that resulted in poor housing and came to undermine his legacy.
- The article in the Student's Book was written by Alain de Botton. He was born in Zurich, Switzerland in 1969 and now lives in London. He writes about the ideas of important artists, philosophers and thinkers. (See www.alaindebotton.com).

3

- Students read the text and compare their ideas in exercise 2.

1 Because his ideas were so innovative, e.g. the skyscrapers, the city parks and the abolition of city streets.
2 To overcome the problems of poor housing and sanitation.

4

- Ask students to read through the sentences first before reading the text again. While they are reading the text, tell them to underline the parts which give them the answer. They then choose the correct alternative to complete each sentence.
- They could then compare their answers with a partner before you check with the class.

1 very near the National Library
2 lonely
3 extremely overcrowded
4 living conditions in cities
5 the uncontrolled development of the city
6 should not be hindered by pedestrians

5

- Pairwork. Students look back at the highlighted words and expressions in the text and discuss their meaning with their partner. They can then check their answers in a dictionary.

Definitions taken or adapted from the *Macmillan English Dictionary*:

dropped by – made a short visit to
whiled away – spent time in a relaxed way
ambling – walking in a slow relaxed way
drawn up – prepared and written
choked – filled so that it is difficult to move
in order – suitable or necessary for a particular situation
alleviate – make something less severe or serious
at a stroke – with a single action
dotted – in many parts of a place
winding – following a course that curves a lot
for the sake of – for the benefit of

6

- Students discuss the questions as a whole class.

Extra task: discussion

- Ask students, *Which buildings would you like to see demolished in your town or in your capital city?*
- You could also ask students for their views on Le Corbusier's plans. *Do you think that Le Corbusier's plans for Paris might have worked? Why? Why not? What would you say is right/wrong about Le Corbusier's views of architecture and how we should live?*

SPEAKING

Warning: this speaking activity can take between 40 to 50 minutes.

1

Communication activities, Student's Book page 139

- Groupwork. Explain that students are going to submit a plan for a new town. Ask them to turn to page 139 at the back of the book and to read the information about the cities.
- Students then discuss the points listed for their plan for the new town. Tell them to choose one student to take notes on all the points listed. They will also need to choose another member of the group to present their plan to the rest of the class in exercise 2.

2

- The student chosen to present their plan tells the rest of the class about it, explaining the various decisions they have made.

3

- Students vote on the best plan. Point out that they cannot vote for their own plan.

Alternative procedure: roleplay

- Write the following roles on the board:
  An architect who loves Le Corbusier
  A politician with traditional ideas
  A local homeowner
  A young person who can't find a house to buy
  A local builder   *An ecologist*
- Put students in the groups and ask them to choose a different role each. Tell students to play their role when discussing their plan.

Language notes: reading

- A ***site*** is place where building is planned or being undertaken.
- A ***cycle path*** is a path specifically built for cyclists to use.
- If you ***relocate***, you move to a different location.

Methodology advances
Speaking at C1 level

- *Here are some of the descriptors from the Common European Framework for Speaking at C1 level:*
  - Can give clear, detailed descriptions and presentations on complex subjects, integrating sub-themes, developing particular points and rounding off with an appropriate conclusion.
  - Can deliver announcements fluently, almost effortlessly, using stress and intonation to convey finer shades of meaning precisely.
  - Can handle interjections well, responding spontaneously and almost effortlessly.
  - Can express him/herself fluently and spontaneously, almost effortlessly. Has a good command of a broad lexical repertoire allowing gaps to be readily overcome with circumlocutions. There is little obvious searching for expressions or avoidance strategies; only a conceptually difficult subject can hinder a natural, smooth flow of language.
  - Can use language flexibly and effectively for social purposes, including emotional, allusive and joking usage.
  - Can argue a formal position convincingly, responding to questions and comments and answering complex lines of counter argument fluently, spontaneously and appropriately.

material from Council of Europe

- *These descriptors represent a stage that is significantly beyond just being able to take part in a discussion or a shop transaction. This list reminds us that if we are to help our students genuinely achieve C1, we will need to offer them practice in a range of speaking genres and encourage them to risk using techniques and strategies that they might well have been avoiding.*
- *While many students should be able to meet some of these targets successfully, there are probably aspects of others that might cause difficulties. Thinking of my own students, the phrases that strike me as problematic for them include:* using stress and intonation to convey finer shades of meaning precisely; there is little obvious searching for expressions or avoidance strategies; emotional, allusive and joking usage; and answering complex lines of counter argument.

material from Council of Europe

- *The CEF lists of 'can do' statements are a useful reminder of what a student should aim to achieve at a certain level. It is our job as a teacher to ensure that we do not just glide along offering safe tasks set at a much easier level. This is a particular problem with speaking as it is all too easy to set discussions or under-challenging communicative activities without really demanding that students extend their range. We need to show our students these descriptors and challenge them to take the risk of trying to reach that level.*

GRAMMAR: modal verbs 2

➋ *Language reference, Student's Book page 94*
➋ *Methodology guidelines: Grammar boxes, page xiv*

1

- Students complete the sentence beginnings with the appropriate endings.
- They could then compare their answers with a partner before you check with the class.

1 d 2 f 3 a 4 c 5 e 6 h 7 b 8 g

2

- Students identify the places in exercise 1.
- They could then compare their ideas with a partner before you check with the class.

Possible answers:
1 library / internet café
2 doctor's surgery / health centre / dentist's surgery
3 supermarket
4 sports centre / gym / swimming pool
5 museum / art gallery
6 theatre
7 school
8 bank

3

- Students look back at the sentences in exercise 1 and identify the function of each of the modal verbs in bold, using the terms from the grammar box at the top of the page.

1 habitual behaviour
2 refusal
3 annoying behaviour
4 suggestion / arrangement; intention
5 future from a past perspective
6 request
7 assumption
8 imaginary situation

Language notes: modal verbs will, would & shall

- Conditioned by years of conventional grammar study, students often think of *will* as a future tense and *would* as a conditional. However, at this level in particular, students should start thinking about these words as modal verbs with a range of meanings and uses depending on the context.
- You could categorize the uses of *will* as follows:
  Habitual behaviour: *I'll often have eggs at lunchtime* (typical); *She will keep biting her nails* (annoying).
  Future reference: *I think she'll do well* (prediction); *I'll go out later* (intention); *We'll all be old one day* (future fact)
  Degrees of willingness: *Will you help?* (request); *I'll help* (willingness); *I won't come* (refusal); *You **will** do as I say.* (command); *This window won't open.* (failure to respond)
- You could categorize the uses of *would* as follows:
  Habitual behaviour: *I'd go for long walks when I was a child* (typical); *He'd blow smoke all over the room* (annoying)
  Willingness: *Would you take a seat?* (request – here, *would* feels more formal than *will*); *She wouldn't take any notice of me.* (past refusal)
  Hypothetical or imaginary situations: *You'd be happier at home* (a hypothetical situation in the present); *I wouldn't wear that* (advice); *When I was eighteen I thought I'd live forever* (taking about the future from a past perspective)
- *Shall* is used with *I* or *we* to make offers, arrangements, suggestions and requests for advice e.g. *Shall we go?* One further use is to emphasize a future intention or prediction, e.g. *You shall work harder!* However, this use is not common.

4

➋ *Communication activities, Student's Book pages 154 & 142*

- Pairwork. Put students into A and B pairs and ask them to turn to their respective pages at the back of the book.
- Tell the students to look at the places in the box and to choose five of them. Allow them a couple of minutes to write similar sentences to the ones in exercise 1, which make reference to or are said in the places in the box. Point out that each of their sentences should contain a different use of *will*, *would* and *shall*.
- Students then take it in turns to read their sentences for their partner to identify the places.

Extra task: dialogues

- As an extension, get students in pairs to write a three-line dialogue, using *will*, *should* or *shall*, and set in one of the places mentioned. For example:
  A: What shall we have?
  B: I think I'll order the fish.
  C: Mmm. Good idea.
- Get students to act out their dialogues for the class. Can the rest of the class guess the location?

IF YOU WANT SOMETHING EXTRA ...

➋ *Photocopiable activity, page 243*
➋ *Teaching notes, page 204*

9B | Squatters

What the lesson is about

Theme	Homes, buildings & problems of finding somewhere to live
Speaking	Roleplay: a buyer finding faults when viewing a new home and the seller highlighting its positive aspects
Listening	A radio interview about squatting
Vocabulary	Describing homes
Did you know?	Listed buildings in the UK

Discussion starters

➋ *Methodology guidelines: Discussion starters, page xiv*

- *What sort of houses do people typically live in in your country? How would you describe them?*
- *What are traditional houses in your country like? What sort of houses did people live in a hundred years ago?*

Pre-teach key words: estate agent speak

- Prepare the following phrases on an OHT. They are all typically found in the speech or brochures of estate agents. Display the phrases to the class. (If you don't have access to an OHP, you could prepare the phrases as a handout.)
  What the estate agent said:
  1 Great location to enjoy the ambient nightlife
  2 The fourth bedroom would make a great study.
  3 The gardens are easy to maintain.
  4 It's an attractive old building with original features.
  5 It's convenient for local transport links.
  6 The property is built in a secluded location.
  7 It's a charming town house.
  8 It's a cosy cottage.
  9 It's close to local schools.
  10 A renovation opportunity
- Ask students in pairs to guess how the house hunter might describe the properties when they visit. Do one as an example.
- Feedback on students' answers, and read out the suggestions below:
  What the house hunter said:
  1 "The house was next door to the noisy local pub."
  2 "More suitable as a broom cupboard."
  3 "The garden was so small that investing in a lawnmower would be a waste of money."
  4 "This house hadn't had any renovations since it was built in 1926."
  5 "The house overlooked the M25 motorway."
  6 "It was in the middle-of-nowhere – barren and desolate."
  7 "*Charming* clearly means *tiny*."
  8 "Another word for *tiny*. The cottage's main entrance was built for a child!"
  9 "The noise from the playground was deafening."
  10 "Tear down and start again"

Vocabulary & speaking: describing homes

1

- Pairwork. Students read the choices of homes and tell their partner which one of the pairs of homes they prefer. Point out that their choice should not be determined by money.

2

- Students choose the correct alternatives to complete each sentence. Allow them to use their dictionaries to help them.
- They could then compare their answers with a partner before you check with the class.

1 newly; conveniently
2 condition; repair
3 thatched; antique
4 run-down; overgrown
5 cosy; tastefully
6 period; DIY
7 cramped; gloomy
8 poorly; rickety; threadbare

3

- Pairwork. Students answer the questions. First, they read the sentences in exercise 2 again and discuss which ones they think give a positive description and which ones negative. They then describe their own homes to their partner.

1 P 2 N 3 P 4 N 5 P

6 The house is made to sound positive, but the description implies that it is in poor condition and needs a lot of money spending on it. It is the type of description that one finds in an estate agent's details.

7 N 8 P

Language notes: describing homes

- ***Thatched*** roofs are made of straw.
- ***Antique*** is used to describe an object that is old and valuable; ***elderly*** is used to describe an old person.
- Houses that have been neglected are ***run-down***; machines ***break down*** when they go wrong.
- In an ***overgrown*** garden, all the plants have grown out-of-control.
- A ***cosy*** room is warm and comfortable. ***Cosy*** is usually used to describe a small area rather than a large one. In a ***draughty*** room, cold winds blow under the door and through the windows.
- ***DIY*** means 'do-it-yourself' – a DIY enthusiast enjoys renovating his or her own house.
- If a house or room is ***cramped***, there isn't much space to move around.
- ***Gloomy*** means 'dark'.
- ***Rickety*** means poorly-made and likely to break. People who are ill frequently or continuously are ***sickly***.
- A ***threadbare*** carpet is worn-out. (You can see the threads.)

Roleplay

4

- Pairwork. Put students into A and B pairs and ask them to read the instructions for their role. Allow them a few minutes to think about the negative or positive aspects of the house and what they are going to say about it. They then do the roleplay. Go round, helping them with any vocabulary they might need.

5

Communication activities, Student's Book page 155

- Students change roles. Ask them to turn to page 155 at the back of the book and to read the instructions for their role. Allow them a few minutes to think about the negative or positive aspects of the room and what they are going to say about it.
- They then do the roleplay. Go round, helping them with any vocabulary they might need.

LISTENING

The listening is a radio interview about squatting. The presenter first talks to a woman who works for the Squatters' Rights Association about why people squat, the type of people squatters are and what legal rights they have. The presenter then talks to a squatter about what it is actually like to squat.

1

- Pairwork. Students read the dictionary definition for *squatter* and discuss the questions on squatting.

Cultural note: squatters

- A squatter is anyone who lives in an unoccupied building without the owner's consent. Squatting is not illegal in Britain and squatters have certain rights. They cannot be evicted from a property without a court order. Under British law, any squatter who has been in a property for ten years is allowed to apply for freehold on that property. (This means that the house becomes theirs). If the person who owns the property objects, they must evict the squatters within two years, otherwise the squatter can apply for the freehold unopposed.

2 3.1

- Students listen to the interview about squatting and answer the questions. You could pause the recording half way through for students to take down the information on Annie Taylor first, before playing the part for Gerry Burnham.
- They could then compare their sentences with a partner before you check with the class. Play the recording again if necessary.

1 Annie works for the SRA – Squatters' Rights Association. She offers advice to squatters, and informs them of the legal aspects of squatting. The SRA recently published a study on squatting.
2 Yes. She says it's a question of necessity because of high property prices. She talks about it being absurd, criminal even that there are so many vacant properties and she agrees that it is hardly surprising that so many people decide to squat.
3 He got in through the kitchen window, having first established that the house was empty.
4 Gerry has mixed feelings about living as a squatter. He says it can be depressing when you first move into a house, and eviction is 'a bit of a hassle'. But being on the move makes it interesting and he says he has learnt to do DIY.

3.1

P = Presenter AT = Annie Taylor
GB = Gerry Burnham

P: Messy, long-haired layabouts in dirty, scruffy clothes; rowdy parties that keep the neighbours awake, and crumbling run-down houses and flats that bring down property values in the local area. That, at least, is the traditional image of squatters and the buildings they inhabit. But according to a recent study that's all changing. The number of squatters in the UK has risen dramatically in the last ten years, from around 9,500 to almost 15,000 – that's an increase of 60% – and around 10,000 of those are to be found in the London area alone. With me is Annie Taylor from the SRA, the Squatters' Rights Association, the group that carried out the study. Annie, why are so many people squatting?
AT: Well, several reasons, really. Principally, though, it's a question of necessity. Most people squat simply because they have to. Property prices and rents are currently just too high for many people and there is a serious lack of social housing up and down the country.
P: That's homes provided at low cost by non-profit organizations, right?
AT: That's right. Rented accommodation, mainly. There are over 100,000 families queuing up for this type of housing, so it's absurd – criminal, even – that there are so many empty homes in Britain – 750,000 at the last count. That's three quarters of a million unused flats and houses that are going to waste – in many cases because of property speculation.
P: Hardly surprising, then, that so many people decide to squat.
AT: Indeed.
P: And what type of people are they? How how would you describe this new generation of squatters?
AT: Well, for one thing there are more students squatting than before. Erm … but we're also seeing large numbers of graduates, young people in career jobs who just cannot afford to get on the property ladder. Erm, and then increasingly we're offering advice to people who come here from the Continent … from other European countries.
P: Interesting. And do you find yourself having to speak their languages as a result?
AT: We try. We do our best. But to be honest many of these people have a very good level of English, and all our technical, legal advice is printed out in a number of different languages, anyway. So … yeah … that means they're, they're clear on all aspects of squatting in Britain.
P: You mention there the legal aspects – because of course, what surprises many visitors to this country is that squatting here is a civil offence, not a criminal offence.
AT: That's right. You can legally occupy a vacant building as long as there's no sign of a forced entry. In other words, you mustn't break any windows or locks to get inside. And once you're in, then you have to prove you have exclusive access to the property, which basically means changing all the locks.
P: Uh huh? The law is very clear on that, is it?
AT: Yes, it is, but we also tell squatters to put up a copy of Section 6 on the outside of the building – on the doors and windows. Just in case.
P: And what is a Section 6?
AT: It's a document, a legal warning, spelling out clearly to the owner – or even the police – exactly what your rights are. It begins 'Take notice that we live in this property, it is our home and we intend to stay here'.
P: But the landlord can still evict you.

AT: Yes, he can, or she can. But they have to go through the courts and that can take time – usually up to four weeks, sometimes months. Even years, in some cases.
P: My goodness me. Thank you, Annie. Very enlightening. It's time now, I think, to bring in our other guest today – Gerry Burnham, who is a squatter. Good morning, Gerry.
GB: Morning.
P: Gerry lives in a squat – a semi-detached house – with three other people in Chiswick, West London. Gerry, how did you get into the property? Or rather, before that, how did you know it was empty in the first place?
GB: Well, firstly, er, it's er, it's a detached house, actually, not a semi. Only the best.
P: Sorry, yes, of course. I do beg your pardon.
GB: Anyway, er, my mates and I, we, er, we were about to be evicted from our last place so we went looking for somewhere else to live – house-hunting, like – and, er, we saw this place looking a bit run-down. The, er, the garden was overgrown and the whole place needed a coat of paint. It was, er, well it looked pretty abandoned really.
P: So you moved in.
GB: Not straightaway, no. You have to make sure it is really empty first. We gave it a couple of weeks. We, er, we looked in the dustbin every day to make sure no one was throwing any rubbish out, like, and, er, we watched the postman to see if he brought any letters or not.
P: Which he didn't, presumably?
GB: No, nothing.
P: So what did you do next?
GB: We got in through the kitchen window – it was in such a bad state, like, that it more less just fell open. Then we did what Annie was just talking about – changed the locks and all that.
P: And how do you feel about squatting? Because you're a computer programmer, aren't you? Can't you afford to rent?
GB: Well, I could, yeah, but in London all I'd get for my money'd be a tiny flat, with nothing left over to save. At least this way I'm putting money in the bank. Should be able to get a mortgage soon, with a bit of luck. Hope so, anyway.
P: So you can't wait to get out.
GB: Well, no, I wouldn't say that. I suppose I've got mixed feelings about it all, really. I mean, it's pretty depressing when you first move into a place – no running water, no gas, no electricity. Sometimes you never do get connected – especially electricity – they can be really difficult, they can, when it comes to squatters. Some refuse point blank. But then, you know, you're with your mates and little by little you get settled in, and before you know it you've made a little home for yourself.
P: And then you get evicted.
GB: Yeah, that's a bit of a hassle, but, er, it makes it all interesting as well, though. I mean, you're always on the move. Always busy, too – I've got quite good at DIY and all that, since I've been squatting, like. Fact, I think landlords benefit quite a bit from people like us. We do their houses up for them, keep them maintained and so on.
P: Yes, I'd like to come back to you, Annie, on that, if I may. I understand there are now squatting co-operatives, who move into places and actually restore them. Is that right?
AT: Yes, it is, particularly in the Manchester area. There are several groups of people, students mainly, who …

Language notes: listening

- A ***civil offence*** relates to private legal disagreements between people, rather than criminal law.
- To ***evict*** someone is to force them to leave the house or flat that they are occupying.
- A ***mortgage*** is a loan given specifically to buy a house.

3 3.2

- Ask students to read the sentences first so that they know what information they are listening for. Point out that they should add no more than three words to each sentence.
- Play the recording for the students to complete the sentences.

1	15,000 / fifteen thousand
2	social housing / low cost homes
3	three quarters of
4	(other) European
5	criminal offence
6	Section 6 / six
7	detached
8	dustbin / rubbish bin
9	mortgage
10	electricity

3.2

P = Presenter   A = Annie Taylor
G = Gerry Burnham

1
P: The number of squatters in the UK has risen dramatically in the last ten years, from around 9,500 to almost 15,000 – that's an increase of 60% – and around 10,000 of those are to be found in the London area alone.

2
AT: Property prices and rents are currently just too high for many people and there is a serious lack of social housing up and down the country.

3
AT: There are over 100,000 families queuing up for this type of housing, so it's absurd – criminal, even – that there are so many empty homes in Britain – 750,000 at the last count. That's three quarters of a million unused flats and houses that are going to waste.

4
AT: Erm, and then increasingly we're offering advice to people who come here from the Continent … from other European countries.

5
P: … what surprises many visitors to this country is that squatting here is a civil offence, not a criminal offence.

6
AT: Yes, it is, but we also tell squatters to put up a copy of Section 6 on the outside of the building – on the doors and windows. Just in case.

P: And what is a Section 6?
AT: It's a document, a legal warning, spelling out clearly to the owner – or even the police – exactly what your rights are.

7
P: Gerry lives in a squat – a semi-detached house – with three other people in Chiswick, West London. Gerry, how did you get into the property? Or rather, before that, how did you know it was empty in the first place?
GB: Well, firstly, er, it's er, it's a detached house, actually, not a semi.

8
GB: Not straightaway, no. You have to make sure it really is empty first. We gave it a couple of weeks. We, er, we looked in the dustbin every day to make sure no one was throwing any rubbish out, like, and, er, we watched the postman to see if he brought any letters or not.

9
GB: At least this way I'm putting money in the bank. Should be able to get a mortgage soon, with a bit of luck. Hope so, anyway.

10
GB: I mean, it's pretty depressing when you first move into a place – no running water, no gas, no electricity. Sometimes you never do get connected – especially electricity – they can be really difficult, they can, when it comes to squatters.

4
- Students complete the sentences from the recording with the words in the box.
- Students then look at tapescript 3.1 on page 159 to check their answers.

1 down	5 out
2 out	6 through
3 up	7 in
4 on	8 up

Language notes: listening
- To ***bring down*** something is to lower it.
- To ***carry out*** something is to perform a task.
- To ***spell out*** is to explain in detail.
- To ***go through*** the courts is to enter court proceedings.
- To ***settle in*** somewhere is to get used to living there.
- To ***do up*** a place is to decorate it.

5
- Pairwork. Students discuss the questions with a partner.
- You could extend this by asking students what they suggest their government could do to help first-time buyers get on the property ladder in their country.

DID YOU KNOW?

1
- Groupwork. Students read the information. They work in small groups and discuss the questions and give reasons for why they put the buildings and structures they have chosen on their list.

Extra task: discussion
- Divide the class into small groups. Ask each group to make a list of the top five buildings in the world, built in the last 100 years. This would work particularly well with an international class which would bring a variety of experience and opinion to the discussion.
- During feedback, ask groups to present their lists and explain why they have chosen those particular buildings. You could develop this into a class discussion with groups arguing as to which buildings are most important. Build a list of five agreed by the whole class.

Web research tasks
➲ *Methodology guidelines: Web research tasks, page xiv*
- Ask students to choose one of the buildings they selected in their top five and write a description of it and its importance based on their web research.

IF YOU WANT SOMETHING EXTRA …
➲ *Photocopiable activity, page 244*
➲ *Teaching notes, page 204*

9c | A place in the sun

What the lesson is about

Theme	The Caribbean & ecotourism
Speaking	Pyramid discussion: deciding on three activities to do on a day trip to Tobago
Reading	*A happy marriage*: a text on ecotourism in the Caribbean
Grammar	Inversion

If you want a lead-in ...

Discussion starters

➋ Methodology guidelines: Discussion starters, page xiv

- *Where do you usually go for your holidays? Do you go to the same place or do you go to different places each year? What type of holiday suits you?*
- *What activities do you enjoy doing on holiday?*

Pre-teach key words

- Write the phrases below on the board. Ask students to work in pairs to determine what each one means.
  all-inclusive holidays *beach erosion*
  homogenized resorts *complete renovation* *haggling*
  well-trodden tourist route *marine pollution*
- Answers: *All-inclusive holidays* are holidays where everything is covered in the price you pay. (You do not have to pay separately for any drinks, meals or snacks.)
  Beach erosion is the wearing away of beach rock, due to human or environmental activity
  Homogenized resorts are holiday resorts where people don't leave the hotel grounds.
  A *complete renovation* is a total redecoration and updating.
  Haggling is bargaining for a better deal.
  The *well-trodden tourist route* refers to the typical places that people visit when on holiday.
  Marine pollution is pollution of the seas and oceans.
- Ask students to say how the phrases might be connected and what the text might be about.

Speaking

1

- Ask students to imagine that they are on a Caribbean cruise and that they have one full day to spend on the island of Tobago. Ask them to look at the list of activities on page 152 at the back of the book and choose the ones that they are interested in.

2

- Pairwork. Students discuss their choices with each other and explain why they have made them. They then decide on three activities that they would like to do together.

3

- Students then join another pair of students. They agree on two of the activities that the group will do together.
- Students then compare their choices with the rest of the class.
- You could then find out if anyone has been to the island of Tobago and what they did there.

Reading

The reading text is about ecotourism in the Caribbean and measures taken by some of the hotels on the islands to be more environmentally friendly and to help the local economy.

1

- Pairwork. Students discuss the questions in order to predict the information in the reading text.

2

- Students read the text and compare the information in it with their ideas in exercise 1.

3

- Ask students to read the phrases first. They then read the text again and match the phrases to the correct sections A–C of the text in which they are mentioned.

1 C 2 A 3 C 4 B 5 A, C 6 B 7 A 8 B 9 A

4

- Pairwork. Students discuss the questions with a partner, giving as much detail as they can.

Language notes: reading

- To ***safeguard*** something is to protect it.
- ***Impeccable*** and ***immaculate*** mean perfect.
- A ***scavenger hunt*** is a game or activity in which people walk around beaches or woods finding and collecting rubbish.
- To ***compost*** is make fertiliser from waste products.
- ***Pillow shams*** are decorative fabric coverings for pillows, often designed with trims, flanges, ruffles, or cording. Not to be confused with simple pillow cases for sleeping on, shams are placed behind the sleeping pillows when the bed is made up.
- ***Skin deep*** means superficial.

Cultural notes: the Caribbean

- The Caribbean /kærɪ'biːən/ is the name for the many islands which are located in the Caribbean Sea to the east of Central America. Some of the islands are Spanish-speaking, e.g. Cuba, others are French-speaking, e.g. Martinique, and many have English as a first language, e.g. Jamaica and Bermuda.
- Tobago /tə'beɪgəʊ/, together with Trinidad /'trɪnɪdæd/ and several nearby islets, forms the Republic of Trinidad and Tobago. Tobago is the smaller of the two main islands. 42 kilometres long and 10 kilometres wide, it is to be found in the southern Caribbean Sea, northeast of the island of Trinidad and southeast of Grenada. It has a population of about 54,000. The capital is Scarborough.
- Barbados /bɑː(r)'beɪdɒs/, is an independent island state in the western Atlantic Ocean. It is the most easterly island in the Caribbean. It has a population of about 279,000 and its capital is Bridgetown.
- Robert Mitchum was a rugged, powerfully-built Hollywood actor, famous for his roles as gangsters and criminals in films such as Cape Fear and Out of the Past.
- Rita Hayworth was a dancer and actress who appeared in Hollywood musicals.

GRAMMAR: inversion

Language reference, Student's Book page 94
Methodology guidelines: Grammar boxes, page xiv

1

- Students rewrite the sentences beginning with the words in brackets.
- They could then compare their sentences with a partner before you check with the class.

Suggested answers:
2 Very rarely do you come across anyone nowadays who hasn't been abroad.
3 Only by living in a country where it is spoken can you really learn a language.
4 Under no circumstances should tourists be allowed to visit the Antarctic.
5 Not until you've tried French cuisine will you truly know what good food is.
6 Not only did I hate visiting monuments as a child, but I also couldn't stand going into museums.
7 Only recently have I started going on holiday without my parents.
8 Never again will I go (back) to that place I went to last year on holiday!

2

- Pairwork. Students discuss the sentences in exercise 1 with a partner and say how true they are for themselves.

3

- Explain that students have just had a disappointing fortnight's holiday in an ecotourism hotel in the Caribbean. Ask them to write five sentences complaining about different aspects of their stay.
- Students compare their sentences with their partner's. They could then write a joint letter of complaint to the hotel.

Language notes: inversion

- In the examples in the Student's Book, inversion is used for emphasis.
- The subject and auxiliary verb are inverted after the negative or restrictive adverbial placed at the start of the sentence. The adverbial is usually followed by an auxiliary verb and the subject. For example:
  Not since my school days *have I been spoken to like that.*
  Only if I begged him *would he have visited me.*
- The emphasized adverbial needs to be stressed strongly at the start of the sentence.

Extra task: a letter of complaint

- Ask students to write a letter of complaint to a travel company, using the five sentences they prepared in exercise 3.
- Alternatively, ask students to write a brochure extract for a Caribbean island. Ask them to research an island on the internet, e.g. Bermuda, Jamaica, Grenada, Martinique, and then write about it, using inversion to emphasize.

IF YOU WANT SOMETHING EXTRA ...

Photocopiable activity, page 245
Teaching notes, page 205

9D | Experimental travel

What the lesson is about

Theme	Experimental tourism
Speaking	Ranking alternative travel options
Listening	A conversation about experimental travel experiences
Vocabulary	Adjectives formed with particles
Speech feature	Vague language

If you want a lead-in ...

Discussion starters

Methodology guidelines: Discussion starters, page xiv

- *What's the most unusual holiday you have ever had? Where did you go? What was different about it? How/Why did you decide to go there?*
- *Have you ever had a holiday which went disastrously wrong? What happened?*

Test before you teach

Methodology guidelines: Test before you teach, page xiv

- Write the following on the board:
  out off on up
  Ask students to think of as many adjectives as they can which start with these words. For example, *online, upbeat, out-take*. Give them four minutes.
- Find out which pair has most words. Elicit them on to the board. Then ask the rest of the class to check them in a dictionary to see if the pair are the winners.

Speaking

1

- Students read the travel descriptions from *The Lonely Planet Guide to Experimental Travel*. They then match the descriptions to the travel options.

1 b 2 c 3 e 4 d 5 a

2

- Students work on their own and rank the travel options from 1 (for the one they would most like to do) to 5 (the one they would least like to do).

3

- Pairwork. Students compare their list with their partner's and give reasons for their choices.

Language & cultural notes

- ***Quirky*** means strange and unusual.
- ***Bora Bora*** is a tropical island in French Polynesia.
- If you ***stick your thumb out*** at the roadside, you are likely to be hitchhiking.
- ***Blind Man's Bluff*** is a children's game. One person is blindfolded and must try to touch the other players, who run away and try to hide.

Extra task: discussion

- Ask students if they know of or can devise other creative and experimental ways of travelling.

Listening

The listening is four excerpts from a conversation between friends, in which some of the ideas in the *Lonely Planet Guide to Experimental Travel* have been tried out.

1 3.3–3.6

- Students listen to the four conversations and for each excerpt, answer the questions. You could pause the recording after the first two excerpts and ask students for their answers. Then play the rest of the recording.

Excerpt 1: Blind Man's Bluff; yes
Excerpt 2: Slight-hitch Travel; no
Excerpt 3: Alternating Travel; yes
Excerpt 4: Eco Tourism; Emma did, Steve didn't.

3.3–3.6

Excerpt 1
I = Interviewer S = Sally A = Alison J = John

S: That's what they say and you know, I think wearing it really did kind of sharpen my other senses. I put it on when I was on the train to get used to it and I sort of became aware of every sound – every little knock or scrape – and I could smell every coffee or sandwich or whatever.
I: And what about when you got to York, Sally? What was it like?
S: Well, we did all the sights and everything – the cathedral, the city walls, the historic buildings and so on – except of course they weren't really 'sights' because I couldn't actually see them. Paul, though, did a marvellous job of describing everything to me and by the end of our day there I felt as if I knew the city really well.
A: What about things like eating and washing and all that – how did you get on with that?
S: Yeah, all those little things that form part of our daily routine – they were a real challenge. I had to sort of learn to sit down again or eat with a knife and fork. In this restaurant we went to, they had these tall kind of tube-shaped glasses and every time I reached out to pick mine up, I knocked it over and spilt everything all over the place. Disastrous!
J: Did you do anything else when you were there? Did you like go into any museums or anything?
S: Yeah, we did actually. Paul took me into an exhibition by some local sculptor – Anna Kirby, or something, I think her name was. It was all modern stuff, from local stone – lots of curves and holes and that sort of thing.
I: And he described everything to you?
S: Well, yeah, some things. But luckily for me, many of the works there were hands-on exhibits – which is great if you're visually handicapped.
J: Or a child.
A: Or an adult! It must be brilliant feeling your way around an exhibition.
S: Yeah, it really was something else. Paul had to describe the rest to me but it was the tactile experience I most enjoyed.
J: Obviously.

Excerpt 2
I = Interviewer D = Dave A = Alison T = Tom

I: Dave, you went a bit further than Sally, didn't you?
D: Yeah, not as far as the place I had on my sign, though.
A: What was that?

D: Tokyo
All: Tokyo!
D: Yeah, that was my 'faraway place'. It was a good conversation starter, helped break the ice and all that. But apart from that it's just like the normal version. Well, I imagine it is, anyway – I was a complete novice, you see – a real rookie.
A: Really? So what did you think of it?
D: Well, pretty dull really – not my cup of tea. I mean, I met some nice people and practised my languages and everything, but the bits in between, all that waiting next to busy roads, it's not my idea of fun. And it was really hard to get lifts, especially in France.
T: Maybe they just thought you were a bit crazy or something – standing on a French roadside trying to get to 'Tokyo'.
D: Yeah, maybe. Mind you, the ones who did pick me up were often madder than me. There was this one guy who kept swerving onto the wrong side of the road – I couldn't work out if he was doing it for fun or he was just a lousy driver, but we very nearly had a head-on collision at one point with this oncoming lorry.
A: Ooh, sounds hairy.
D: Yeah, it was. And then after that bit of excitement – if you can call it that – I had to wait for about four hours outside this town called Bar-le-Duc, or something. Great laugh – I got really cheesed off, I can tell you.
I: So how far did you get eventually?
D: Munich.
I: And then what? You gave up?
D: Well, some guy who gave me a lift there put me up for a couple of nights – he gave me a key and I could sort of come and go as I pleased – just like a hotel.
A: That was good of him.
D: Yeah, and it meant I could do a bit of good old, non-experimental, conventional sightseeing ...
All: Aha
D ... before I got the overnight train back to London.
All: What? Cheat!

Excerpt 3
H = Helen T = Tom
T: Helen, you actually flew to Lithuania, didn't you?
H: Yeah, I managed to get a cheap flight. And I also took in the main sights as well – like Dave.
All: Aah? Oh yeah?
H: Yeah, I wanted to compare the two types – as in 'experimental', you know.
T: Hm-mm. So what did you discover?
H: Well, the first day I did all the left-right business, and I have to say I was very pleasantly surprised. I had a lovely time, it was fascinating.
T: In what way?
H: Well, I saw all those parts of Vilnius that I wouldn't otherwise have seen if I'd just done the typical tourist thing – you know, all the bits of the city that are kind of off the main tourist routes. I saw some lovely old buildings with these really pretty courtyards and everywhere there was loads of greenery, you know, trees and grass and stuff like that.
T: Sounds lovely.
H: Yeah, it was. But I think what I enjoyed most about the whole thing was not knowing what I was going to discover every time I turned a corner. When I went sightseeing the next day, I knew what I was going to find because I'd already seen it in the brochures and things. This was different.
T: But presumably it wasn't all quite so pretty – I mean, you must have seen some unattractive places as well.
H: Oh yeah, of course. I mean I walked through some really ugly run-down housing estates – some of the buildings were in a terrible condition. But I mean you expect that in a city, don't you, wherever you are. And anyway, it all helped to give me a true flavour of the place, to see both sides of the coin. And as the day went on, I got to realize that there was always a park or a river or something close to every built-up area, so I never got down or fed up or anything.
T: And when did you decide to stop?
H: When I came to a brick wall. ... No, seriously, the book says something about carrying on until something blocks your path, and for me it was a brick wall in a dead-end street – I couldn't go left or right. I can't say I was sorry, mind – I was worn out. I'd been walking for something like six hours.

Narrator: Excerpt 4
I = Interviewer S = Steve E = Emma A = Alison T = Tom
S: I mean, the thing is, it's like, do you go where you want to go, or do you go where you think your partner will go, or do you go where you think your partner will think you will go?
A: Ooh, tricky.
T: Very.
E: Yes, and if I'd gone where I thought Steve would go, I'd have headed straight for the district with all the bars.
S: She knows me too well.
A: Got some good bars in Madrid.
E: Hmm. Quite. But that's not my idea of a good time.
S: No, and I figured that was what she'd think. So I went to all the main tourist sights instead.
A: You as well!
T: Looks like everyone did.
S: Yeah, I did the lot – the Puerta del Sol, Plaza Mayor, the Royal Palace ...
E: And I was following in his footsteps, would you believe? Though I didn't know it at the time, of course.
I: What, everywhere?
S: Yep. About ten minutes behind me, she was.
I: Wow! What a coincidence.
E: Not really – I mean, it's the tourist thing, isn't it? Everyone does what the guidebook tells you to. Understandable, really, I suppose. And anyway, I had a marvellous time. It's a lovely city, Madrid.
S: Better if you can see it with someone, though.
A: Oh, did you miss her?
S: Well, yeah, you know, I mean, it's a bit boring walking all day round a city on your own.
T: So you didn't bump into each other? You didn't meet up at all?
S: Well, yeah, but only because we cheated.
A: How come?
E: We had a plan B in case we didn't find each other. We didn't want to go to Madrid and not have a romantic meal together, did we? Lovely, it was.
S: Yeah, lovely and expensive.
E: Ooh, you old misery guts.

2 3.3–3.6

- Ask students to read the statements for each excerpt first. Then play the recording again, pausing after each excerpt for the students to decide of the statements are true or false.

1 False	2 True	3 True	4 False	5 True	6 False
7 True	8 True	9 False	10 False	11 True	12 False

Language notes: listening

- A ***rookie*** or ***novice*** is someone who is inexperienced in what they are doing.
- If you are ***cheesed off***, you are bored and annoyed.
- ***Misery guts*** is an expression used to refer to someone who is being miserable or negative.

Cultural notes: cities

- York is a historical city in north-eastern England, with Roman and Viking remains, and many medieval buildings.
- Vilnius is the capital city of Lithuania, one of the Baltic states in north-eastern Europe.

SPEECH FEATURE: vague language

1

- Remind students of the work they did on approximation in lesson 1B on page 8, which is another aspect of vague language.
- Ask students to complete the vague expressions in bold from excerpt 1 of the recording with the words in the box.
- Don't check the answers at this stage. This will be done in the next exercise.

1	kind	4	like; anything
2	everything; so	5	something
3	all	6	thing

2

- Students look at tapescript 3.3 on page 159 and check their answers to exercise 1.
- Then ask students to look at excerpts 2 and 3 and underline further examples of vague language. Point out that they need to focus on words and expressions which show vagueness only, and tell them that most of the expressions are the same as the ones they have already seen in the first extract.

Excerpt 2:
It was a good conversation starter, helped break the ice and all that.
I mean, I met some nice people and practised my languages and everything.
Maybe they just thought you were a bit crazy or something.
And then after that bit of excitement – if you can call it that – I had to wait for about four hours.outside this town called Bar-le-Duc, or something.
I could sort of come and go as I pleased.

Excerpt 3:
You know, all the bits of the city that are kind of off the main tourist routes. Everywhere there was loads of greenery, you know, trees and grass and stuff like that.
I'd already seen it in the brochures and things.
There was always a park or a river or something.
I never got down or fed up or anything.
I'd been walking for something like six hours.

Language notes: vague language

- People often use this kind of language in spoken English. It may be because they are uncertain of what they are saying or because they don't think it is necessary to expand on what they are going to say with specific examples or detail. People also use vague expressions to give themselves a chance to think, especially if they are feeling nervous.
- ***Like***, ***sort of*** and ***kind of*** are used to say 'not exactly'. ***Something like*** means 'approximately'.
- ***Kind of*** and ***sort of*** are often abbreviated to /kaɪndə/ and /sɔː(r)tə/ in speech.
- ***I mean*** is used to introduce an explanation or a correction of what you've just said.
- Vague language, in particular phrases such as ***like*** and ***and stuff*** is also a feature of 'teen speak'.

3

- Groupwork. Allow students a few minutes to imagine a place where they had their experimental travel experience and what happened on the trip. They could make a few brief notes if they want. They then take it in turns to describe their experience in small groups, using some of the vague expressions from exercise 1. Encourage the students listening to ask questions and to show interest in the travel experience being described.

Extra task: travel stories

- You could extend this task. Divide the class into groups of four. Each group has to plan an experimental travel trip and write it down briefly. They then hand their 'plan' to another group. The groups must then imagine going on this trip. Tell them to close their eyes and think about the trip as if it happened. Tell them to think of something funny that happened, and something disastrous. Then mix the students so that they are in groups with people who have a different story to tell. The students tell each other their stories.

Methodology advances
Listening – features of native speaker speech (2): pronunciation

- *As mentioned before, some listening material in this book contains fast, fluent, colloquial native speaker speech. This may cause some problems for your class, particularly if 'vague language' is involved, so it's worth making sure that you are aware what some of the language problems might be.*
- ***Stress*** *Perhaps the key skill in following fast speech is to successfully catch the stressed syllables. Stressed syllables tend to keep their expected vowel pronunciation, whilst unstressed ones may sound weak, swallowed or get lost completely. When a speaker is talking fast, it may seem to the listener that it is only the stresses that are being pronounced; the listener then has to mentally reconstruct the missing parts of what was said.*
- ***Elision*** *The faster the speech delivery, the more likely a speaker is to drop sounds. These lost (or elided) sounds are often at the end of words.*

- ***Assimilation*** *This term refers to the way that sounds completely change in fast native speaker speech. Here are two well-known examples:*
  Handbag is typically pronounced as if it was spelt hambag.
  Sandwich is typically pronounced as if it was spelt samwich
- *Here is one very short example of an extract of spoken English that illustrates all three of the features above:* What are you going to do with that tray? *might be pronounced in fast speech as:* /wɒdʒə gənə dʊ wɪðæ treɪ/. *(There are, of course, many other ways of saying it.) Compare this with an ultra-careful, slow, word-by-word pronunciation of the same sentence:* /wɒt ɑː(r) juː gəʊwɪŋ tə duː wɪð ðæt treɪ/.
- *We can quickly notice weak form vowels (e.g. the* /uː/ *of* you *becomes* /ə/ *in fluent speech), elision (e.g. the* /t/ *in* going to *has been completely lost) and assimilation (e.g.* /wɒt ɑː(r) juː/ *becomes* /wɒdʒə/*).*
- *You may be wondering why these are listed as potential problems for listening rather than for speaking. In fact, it doesn't matter very much if your students choose to use (or not to use) these features in their own speech – for while they could make a speaker sound more natural, they are by no means essential to meaningful communication. But when listening, if your students are expecting to hear* /wɒt ɑː(r) juː gəʊwɪŋ tə duː/ *but actually hear* /wɒdʒə gənə dʊ/, *they may well have comprehension problems. Raising students' awareness about what to expect when listening is actually the most important reason for studying such features of connected speech.*

VOCABULARY: adjectives formed with particles

1

- Students complete the sentences with the adjectives in the box.

1	uphill	6	sit-down
2	out-of-town	7	off-the-peg
3	out-of-the-way	8	online
4	indoor; outdoor	9	up to date
5	outspoken	10	comfortably off

2

- Pairwork. Students work on their own. They look back at the sentences in exercise 1 and underline the alternative they think their partner is most likely to choose.

3

- Students tell their partner what choices they made for them in the sentences in exercise 2, and explain the reasons for their choices. Their partner then tells them if they were correct.

Language notes: adjectives formed with particles

- Some adjectives formed in this way are hyphenated; others are not. There are no rules about when to use a hyphen, although many adjectives formed from phrasal verbs tend to be hyphenated.
- The stress tends to be on the particle when it is a suffix, e.g. fed up, head on, etc.

IF YOU WANT SOMETHING EXTRA ...

➋ *Photocopiable activity, page 246*
➋ *Teaching notes, page 205*

Answer key

9 Review

Student's Book page 172

1

1 D 2 C 3 D 4 B 5 A 6 C 7 B 8 B
9 A 10 D

2

1 struggle
2 exhibits
3 meal
4 traffic
5 collision
6 critic
7 place
8 superstore
9 suit
10 activities

3

1 d – down
2 h – up
3 a – into
4 f – on
5 e – up
6 c – out
7 g – out
8 b – through

4

Suggested answers:
1 had they had / enjoyed
2 will I lend her
3 when he got / arrived / left
4 have I cleaned / do I clean
5 should you leave
6 does he look like
7 did she thank me / has she thanked me
8 do I get / have / have I had

5

Students' own answers.

10A | Turning out well

What the lesson is about

Theme	Endurance races & achievements
Speaking	Groupwork: deciding on an endurance race to take part in and what equipment to take
Reading	*Made it!*: an article about two men with very different personalities who took part in a rowing competition to cross the Atlantic
Vocabulary	Success

If you want a lead-in ...

Pre-teach key words

- Write the words below on the board. Then ask students work in pairs to discuss each set of words. Do they have positive or negative connotations? What could these words describe?
  1 *an ordeal* *a challenge* *an adventure*
  2 *competitive* *laid-back* *non-confrontational*
- Ask students to predict what the words might have to do with the text.

Introducing the theme: endurance races

- Write the following on the board:
  mountain climbing *marathon running*
  long distance swimming *cross country skiing*
  hiking *rowing* *sailing*
- Ask students to say which of these they have done or would like to do.
- Ask, *Have you ever set yourself a challenge involving one of these activities? Where did you go? How did you prepare? What happened? How did you feel at the end?*

Speaking

1

➋ *Communication activities, Student's Book page 138*

- Groupwork. Students look at the photos of the endurance races and then turn to page 138 and read about the races. Ask if anyone would like to take part in any of these races.
- Put students into small groups. They then turn back to page 96 and do the task.
- Go round monitoring and give help where needed.

2

- Students choose a representative to tell the class what endurance race their group is taking part in and to explain their list of essential items they are going to take with them. Alternatively, the groups could join up with another group to talk about their race and to compare their lists.

3

- Students discuss the questions as a whole class.

Extra task: discussion

- Ask students to tell the class about any other long distance endurance races they know of, particularly in their own country.

Cultural notes: endurance racing

- The photos show the Iditarod trail sled dog race across Alaska, the Marathon des Sables in Morocco, the Race Across America, and Ben Fogle (on the left) and James Cracknell, having completed the Atlantic Rowing Race (see Communication Activities for details).
- GPS stands for Global Positioning System. GPS is a widely used navigation aid, which picks up microwave signals transmitted by satellite. A GPS receiver uses the information to determine its location, speed and direction.
- Other famous endurance races include the Tour de France (the world's premier long-distance professional cycle race); Paris-Dakar Rally (a motor vehicle race across the Sahara desert); the Whitbread Round the World Race (a race round the world for yachts); ultra marathons such as the Comrades Marathon in South Africa (an 89km race), the Antarctica Marathon and the Great Wall Marathon.

Reading

The reading text is an article about the unlikely partnership of Olympic gold medallist rower James Cracknell and TV presenter Ben Fogle who teamed up to take part in a 3,000 mile Atlantic rowing race. It describes their different personalities and the difficulties they faced as they took part in the race.

1

- Students read the text and answer the question. Tell them to underline the difficulties in the text as they read it.

> They have very different personalities, which led to disagreements: James is competitive, Ben is not.
> James succumbed to the psychological stress of ocean rowing.
> They encountered two tropical storms and a hurricane.
> They had to spend a lot of time in their cramped cabin.
> They both suffered injuries.
> They cut back on their rations as they thought they were going to take longer than expected.
> They didn't sleep very much.
> Their boat capsized and they lost a lot of equipment.

2

- Ask the students to read the sentences first. They then read the text again and choose the correct alternative to complete the sentences.
- You could then ask students how competitive they are, and if they are more of a Cracknell or a Fogle (or neither).

> 1 invited Ben to row
> 2 was used to a different kind of race
> 3 was pushing himself too hard
> 4 cry
> 5 they were unable to row
> 6 considered asking for help
> 7 had each benefited from the other's personality

Extra task: scanning

- Ask students to scan the text for descriptions of James (*gentlemanly, hyper-competitive spirit, insatiable will to win, a bully*) and Ben (*slower, useless at rowing, passion for tough challenges, non-confrontational, laidback [with a] subtle perspective on life*).

3

- Pairwork. Students take it in turns to tell each other about an occasion they spent with someone who had a very different personality to their own. Ask them to talk about what problems they had and how (or if) they overcame them.

Extra task: vocabulary

- This text has a good deal of vocabulary connected with challenge and success. Ask students to find words and phrases in the text connected with these areas.
- Answers: *finished third, come first, make it to (Antigua), seven-week ordeal, dangerous/tough challenge, accept the challenge, insatiable will to win, competitive spirit*

Language notes: reading

- If you ***bounce up to*** someone, you approach them in a lively, friendly way.
- To ***kill or cure*** in this context means that the endurance race would either kill James or cure his competitive spirit.
- If you are ***marooned***, you are left alone somewhere, with no way to escape.
- To ***fret*** is to worry.
- A ***spurt*** is a sudden burst of speed or energy.

Language notes: rise, raise & arise

- Note the use of ***rise, arise*** and ***raise*** in the text. They have a variety of use, but, basically, ***rise*** means move upwards, e.g. *The sun rose*, ***raise*** means make go up or put in a higher position, e.g. *She raised her hand* and ***arise*** means come up or develop, e.g. *A problem has arisen.*
- The examples in the text are: ***a cheer rose up*** *(became louder)*, ***raise money for charity*** *(collect)*, ***raise the alarm*** *(tell people there is danger)*, ***disagreements that had arisen*** *(developed/come up)*.

Cultural notes: Atlantic rowing race

- The Canary Islands are off the coast of west Africa, and Antigua is an island in the Caribbean Sea to the east of Central America.
- Ben Fogle is a TV presenter, who has appeared on BBC's Animal Park and Countryfile. He was also in Castaway 2000, a reality TV programme in which a group of people had to survive as a community on an isolated Scottish island.
- Jame Cracknell won gold medals in rowing events at the Sydney Olympics 2000 and the Athens Olympics 2004. Rowing is a significant sport in Britain, a country which has produced a large number of world champions and Olympic medallists in the sport.

VOCABULARY: success

1

- Students complete the sentences with the correct form of the verbs in the box.
- They could then compare their answers with a partner before you check with the class.

1 went; turned	4 did
2 paid; achieved	5 stand
3 gave	6 further

Extra task: vocabulary

- You could lead in to the vocabulary activities by drawing attention to following theme-related vocabulary in the reading text.
  made it! finished third overall the first (two man crew) to ... make it to Antigua reach the finishing line insatiable will to win take the lead come first competitive spirit
- Ask students to underline these phrases in the reading text which are to do with success, and discuss their meaning from the context.

2

- Students complete the sentences with the nouns in the box.
- They could then compare their answers with a partner before you check with the class.

1 future	4 flier
2 success	5 life
3 charts	6 region

3

- Pairwork. Students think of examples for six of the descriptions in exercises 1 and 2 and tell their partner about them.

Web research tasks

➋ *Methodology guidelines: Web research tasks, page xiv*

- Tell students to research a long distance endurance event that takes place in any country. It could be marathon running, hiking, rowing, cycling, sailing, rallying, horse riding, etc.
- Students make notes about the event: When and where is it? What does it involve? How do you enter the race? They must then think about how to prepare for the event and what they should take.
- Ask students to make presentations to the class about their event and how they are going to plan for it.

Web search key words

- [type of sport]; long distance; endurance

IF YOU WANT SOMETHING EXTRA ...

➋ *Photocopiable activity, page 247*
➋ *Teaching notes, page 205*

10B | What is success?

What the lesson is about

Theme	Defining success and how to achieve it
Listening	Six people's views about what success is and how to achieve it
Vocabulary	Three-part phrasal verbs
Grammar	Futures
Pronunciation	Contrastive stress

If you want a lead-in ...

Discussion starters

Methodology guidelines: Discussion starters, page xiv

- *Are you an ambitious person? What are your ambitions? Which ambitions have you already achieved?*
- *What would you say were the major achievements of your life so far? What else would you like to achieve?*
- *Have you ever won anything or come first at anything? How did you feel? Are you a competitive person who likes to win, or do you prefer to just take part and set personal challenges?*

Pre-teach key words: future plans, ambitions & expectations

- Write on the board:
  The future
  I'm thinking ...
  I'm hoping ...
  I expect ...
  I'm about ...
  I'm probably ...
  I should ...
  I aim to...
  I may well ...
- Ask students to choose five sentence starters and write something that is true about their future plans, ambitions and expectations. Tell students to share their ideas in small groups. Monitor and listen to see how well students use these forms.

Listening

In the listening, six people talk about success, what it means to them and how they think it can be achieved.

1

- Groupwork. Put the students into small groups. They read the questions and discuss how they would answer them.
- You could ask students to compare their ideas with the dictionary definition of *success* (the achievement of something that you planned to do or attempted to do).

2 3.7–3.12

- Ask students to look at the pictures. They then listen to the people talking about success and match the speakers to the pictures.
- They could then compare their answers with a partner before you check with the class. Play the recording again if necessary.

1 D 2 F 3 A 4 C 5 E 6 B

3.7–3.12

1
What is success? That's easy – you just have to look at my sales figures to know the answer to that. Best in the whole southern region, they are. I've sold more policies this quarter than anyone else on the sales team did for the whole of last year. Mick the Machine, they call me. They all say to me 'What's the secret, Mick – how'd you do it?' Of course, personality's important – you've got to have a bit of spark, you've got to know how to win people over. But most of all, I put my success down to self-discipline and perseverance. You've got to get up in the morning, get out there and do the business – it doesn't matter what the weather's like, how you're feeling, how unsure you are of pulling off a deal – you've just got to keep going.

2
A successful person for me is not someone who makes pots of money. Success is not about accumulating wealth, it's about achieving happiness. It means enjoying whatever you do. Life is so short, we have to make sure our stay on this planet is a pleasant one. Have a good time, let your hair down, that's what I say – as long as you treat others with respect. And if you want to enjoy life, you've got to adopt a positive outlook on everything. If things don't turn out well, don't let it get you down. We all come up against problems – we just have to face up to them, try and solve them. And we all make mistakes at some time – in all areas of our lives. The important thing is to try and learn from them, not let them destroy you.

3
I'll be 83 next month – and I've just signed up for a computer course. How about that, then? It starts next Monday. I told my son about it – I said 'I'm going to learn to use the computer,' and he said 'What? At your age? Never.' He seems sure I won't be able to do it but I know I will. You see, all through my life I've been successful – I've always got what I wanted. And the key to that success has always been the same – confidence. Being sure of yourself and knowing you can achieve anything if you really want to ... and you know, success for me here won't only be learning to use the computer – in a sense, that's the least of it all. No, I'll get most satisfaction out of proving that son of mine wrong.

4
Success is all about achieving goals – accomplishing what you set out to do. But it's not so much what you achieve as how you achieve it that counts. You have to earn your success. For instance, people tell me I'm an excellent cook – now, whether that's true or not is not for me to say, but it's always a great source of satisfaction to me when my dinner guests express their appreciation of one of my meals. I feel valued – and that, for me, is success, but particularly because I know that I've invested an enormous amount of time and effort in preparing the meal and organizing the whole evening. If I just threw something together in half an hour, they'd probably still enjoy it, but it wouldn't be quite the same, would it?

5
When, or rather, if I get to old age, I hope I'll have had a useful life. That for me is a true measure of success – doing something positive with your life and at the same time making the world a better place. My dad always said you should aim to leave a legacy when you've gone, something useful for people to remember you by. He wrote several books – very good ones too – but he wasn't suggesting that everyone has to do that. It could be something more simple,

like planting trees, doing up a house or even having children. ... I expect I'll have my own kids one day, but for now I'm happy just to keep it to planting trees. In fact, I'm driving up into the mountains with some friends of mine next week to do just that.

6
You often hear people say it's not the winning, it's the taking part that's important. That's fair enough, particularly if, like me, you're an amateur, rather than a professional. Though I reckon it's more the doing your best that's important – after all, there's no point taking part if you don't at least try to win. Round about this time next week I'll be setting off for Stockholm to take part in a European club competition. Success for me in Sweden will be knowing I've gone out there and given it my best shot, both for me and for my club – even if I don't win any medals – which is more than likely given the strength of the other runners! Anyway, to give ourselves the best chance of doing well, we've been training hard all season. Preparation is obviously an essential factor in achieving success.

3
- Students listen to the recording again and write notes for each of the speakers under the headings in the table.

	What is success?	How do you achieve it?
1	having good sales figures	self-discipline and perseverance
2	achieving happiness; enjoying what you do	adopting a positive outlook on everything; facing up to problems; learning from mistakes
3	getting what you want, (learning to use the computer); proving his son wrong	confidence; being sure of yourself; knowing you can achieve anything if you really want to
4	achieving goals; feeling valued	investing time and effort
5	doing something positive and useful with your life, making the world a better place	leaving a legacy, e.g. writing a book, planting trees, doing up a house, having children
6	doing your best	training, preparation

4
- Students work in the same groups. They discuss each of the speaker's views from the listening and say how much they agree or disagree with their views on success.

Extra task: vocabulary

- The listening text is rich in expressions, which you may wish to exploit. Prepare an OHT of the following or write it on the board. Ask students to match verbs in A with the rest of the expression in B. Ask them to do the same with C and D.

A	B
have	something together
throw	off a deal
pull	a bit of spark
give	yourself a chance

C	D
let	it your best shot
win	people wrong
prove	your hair down
give	people over

- Ask students to look at the tapescripts 3.7–3.12 on pages 161 and 162 to check their answers. Alternatively, check the answers with them, using the language notes below.

Language notes: listening

- To ***have a bit of spark*** means to have a quick, sharp, lively personality.
- To ***win someone over*** is to charm them into liking you or agreeing with you.
- To ***pull off a deal*** is to make a successful business transaction.
- To ***let your hair down*** is to have a good time.
- To ***prove someone wrong*** is to show them through your actions that they were wrong about you.
- To ***throw something together*** is to make something quickly, e.g. to make a quick meal.
- To ***give something your best shot*** is to try your hardest.
- To ***give yourself the best chance*** means to take every step you can to give yourself an advantage.

GRAMMAR: futures

➋ *Language reference, Student's Book page 104*
➋ *Methodology guidelines: Grammar boxes, page xiv*

1
- Ask students to look at tapescript 3.7–3.12 on pages 161 and 162. Point out that the highlighted words all refer to the future. Ask students to explain the choice of the verb tense used in each case.

It starts – The present simple is used to talk about timetabled or scheduled events.
I'm going to learn – *Going to* is used to talk about intentions or plans.
I won't be able / I will – *Will* and negative *won't* are used for making predictions.
I get – The present simple is used after time conjunctions to refer to the future.
I'll have had – The future perfect is used to talk about actions or events which have been completed by a certain time in the future.
I expect I'll have – *Will* is used after verbs of thinking like *expect, believe, doubt, think*, etc. This is a prediction.
I'm driving – The present continuous is used to talk about arrangements.
I'll be setting off – The future continuous is used to talk about actions which will be in progress at a certain time in the future.

2

- Students read the grammar box and then do exercise 3.

3

- Students choose the correct alternative to complete the sentences.
- They could then compare their sentences with a partner before you check with the class.

1	hoping	6	about
2	should	7	well
3	bound	8	hopeful
4	chance	9	is
5	hope	10	likely

Language notes: futures

- At this level, students should be familiar with the main verb tenses. One area that may be new is the uses of the future continuous, which you may wish to explain in more detail:
- It can be used to describe an action in progress at a time in the future. For example:
  I'll be sitting in the airport at this time tomorrow.
- It expresses regular or decided actions – speakers often choose to use the future continuous as a 'reassuring' future to say that something will happen because it always does in the normal course of events, as in the sentences below:
  We'll be shopping on Saturday. (It's something we always do.)
  On this course, we'll be looking at nineteenth-century fashions.
- It can also be used to ask about other people's plans.
  Will you be seeing Nathan on Saturday Night?
- Notice the variety of time expressions in exercise 3, which you could check with students:
  in the not too distant future
  by the end of the month (*by* means *before*)
  before the decade is out (a *decade* is ten years; *out* means 'over')
  this season (the football season happening currently)
  in the next few days
  at some time in the future
  in her forthcoming exams (*forthcoming* means 'approaching')
  in three months' time
  within a week (in less than a week)

4

- Ask students to choose five sentences from exercise 3. Explain that they are going to rewrite these sentences so that they are either true or express their own opinion. They rewrite the sentences by changing the underlined words. Tell them that they can also change the time expressions if they wish.

5

- Pairwork. Students discuss their sentences with a partner.

Extra task: writing about travel plans

- Prepare the following on an OHT or handout, or dictate it to the students. Ask the gist question, *Which country is the writer going to visit?* (Answer: Iceland)
  The flight from London should take about three hours. It's unlikely to be very hot, even though we're going in summer, but there will be many hours of daylight. We're looking forward to catching and eating our own salmon and trout and we're hoping to do some bird-watching, too: the island is home to many seabirds. We'll also be swimming in pools filled with water from natural hot springs. We're bound to enjoy it – we both love out-of-the-way places.
- Ask students to work with a partner to write a short paragraph like the one above. It could be about a town or country they intend to visit, a well-known event they're going to attend, or a celebrity's future plans. Ask them to include at least five future structures from the Language Reference section on page 104.
- Students read out their paragraph to another pair of students who must guess what or who they have written about.

PRONUNCIATION: contrastive stress

1 3.13

- Ask students to read the information about stress and then read out the sentence, stressing the words in bold. They then listen to the example sentence on the recording.

2

- Students work on their own and underline the contrastive stress in the sentences. Tell them to read the sentences out loud as they do the exercise.
- Don't check answers at this stage. This will be done in the next exercise.

3 3.14

- Students listen to the sentences and check their answers to exercise 2.
- They then practise reading the sentences aloud.

1. He seems sure I won't be able to do it, but I know I will.
2. It's not so much what you achieve as how you achieve it that counts.
3. When, or rather, if I get to old age …
4. He wrote several books, but he wasn't suggesting that everyone has to do that.
5. It's not the winning, it's the taking part that's important.
6. That's fair enough, particularly if, like me, you're an amateur, rather than a professional.

4

- Pairwork. Allow students a couple of minutes to prepare for this activity. Ask them to think of six things they know or believe to be untrue about their partner. Tell them to make a note of them if they need to be reminded, but not to read the notes out.
- They then take it in turns to tell their partner the things they think are untrue. Their partner should correct the untrue sentences using contrastive stress. However, if the sentences happen to be true, they can say *Yes, that's correct*.

Extra task: contrastive stress

- As an extension to exercise 4, (or as preparation), try this exercise. Write the eight words below on the board.
  competitive
  lazy
  French
  teacher
  coffee
  ten o'clock
  unfashionable
  magazines
  Put students in pairs. Student A must improvize a statement about their parters, stressing the key word. Student B must improvize a response, emphasizing a contrasting word. For example:
  *You're a **competitive** person.*
  *No, I'm not. I'm very **easy going.***

VOCABULARY: three-part phrasal verbs

1

- Pairwork. Students read the sentences from the recording. They then discuss the meaning of the three-part phrasal verbs with a partner.

See language notes

2

- Students complete the sentences with the correct form of the verbs in the box.
- They could then compare their answers with a partner before you check with the class.

1	makes; put	4	go
2	look	5	get
3	come	6	cracking

3

- Ask student to look back at the phrasal verbs in the sentences in exercise 2. They then match them to their meanings 1–6.

1 f; b 2 e 3 a 4 c 5 g 6 d

4

- Pairwork. Students discuss the statements and opinions in exercise 2 with a partner. Tell them that they should give examples where relevant to support their views.

Language notes: three-part phrasal verbs

- Three-part or phrasal-prepositional verbs are made up of verb + adverb + preposition.
- To ***put (it) down to*** is to attribute a cause to something. Literally, to ***sign up for*** something (e.g. a course, a voluntary project, etc) means to enlist in it, but more often than not we use the phrase just to mean that we have agreed to take part in something.
  If you ***come up against*** something, you meet a problem that you have to deal with.
  To ***face up to*** something unpleasant is to accept the situation and deal with it.
  To ***make up for*** something is to compensate for it or to say sorry.
  To ***put up with*** something is to tolerate it.
  To ***look up to*** someone is to respect and admire them.
  To ***come in for*** criticism is to receive criticism.
  To ***go in for*** something is to take part in it.
  To ***get away with*** something is to escape punishment for it.
  To ***crack down on*** means to deal with something strictly. In is often used in the context of crime.

Extra task: three-part phrasal verbs

- As an extension, write a set of verbs on the left of the board, and a set of particles on the right. Use the words below.
  Verbs: *go, come, get, make, put, look*
  Particles: *up, in, on, to, off, for, against, about, away, down, with*
- Divide the class into teams of four. Ask them to write as many sentences using different three-part phrasal verbs as they can in five minutes. Find out who has written most sentences. Let students check the phrasal verbs in their dictionaries.

IF YOU WANT SOMETHING EXTRA ...

➋ *Photocopiable activity, page 248*
➋ *Teaching notes, page 206*

10c | Going wrong?

What the lesson is about

Theme	Embarrassing incidents & the TV
Speaking	Groupwork: discussion about what to do in a difficult situation
Reading	*The Wrong Guy:* a newspaper article about an embarrassing case of mistaken identity at the BBC
Vocabulary	Television
Did you know?	The BBC

If you want a lead-in ...

Discussion starters

Methodology guidelines: Discussion starters, page xiv

- *What's the most embarrassing thing that has ever happened to you? Where were you? What did you do? Why was it so embarrassing?*
- *Have you ever felt embarrassed for somebody appearing on TV? Why? What did they do?*

Pre-teach key words: TV

- Write *TV* on the board. Put students in pairs or small groups to brainstorm as many words as they can think of connected to TV. Tell them to think about types of programme, people on TV, people who watch TV and words used to describe TV.
- After three or four minutes, ask some groups to tell you their best words. Write the most interesting words on the board and check their meaning.

Speaking

1

- Groupwork. Students read the situations and discuss in small groups what they would do in each of them and why they would take that action.
- Go round monitoring and give help where needed. Then elicit a few examples from the class.

Possible advice for situations 1, 3 and 5.

Situation 1: If safe to do so, turn off the heat and cover the pan with a lid or dampened tea towel. Never use water on chip pan fires as this will cause a fireball. If the fire gets out of control, call the Fire and Rescue Service on 999.

Situation 3: Sound the horn and flash the lights. Don't apply the brakes as you would burn them. Don't turn off the ignition, as this would affect the steering. If you have a mobile to hand and it is safe to do so, call the police. (This nightmare scenario came true for 26-year-old Kevin Nicolle as he was driving his BMW on the A1 in Yorkshire. He tried breaking, which reduced his speed, but the breaks began to burn. He phoned the police on a hands-free mobile. They advised him to put his hazard flash lights on and sent out a helicopter. After travelling at high speed for 84 kilometres, he crashed at a roundabout. He escaped unhurt.)

Situation 5: Wait until the fog clears, although this could be hours, or days. Alternatively, find a river or stream and follow its course down.

Alternative procedure: sharing information

- One way of organizing this is to divide the class into groups of six, and tell each group member to read one of the situations. Students then close books. Each student has to introduce their situation, from memory, elicit comments about it from other group members, and remember the best ideas. During feedback, ask group members to summarize what was said about their situation.

2

- Students take it in turns to tell each other about a time when something went wrong for them. Tell them to say how they felt at the time.
- Note that students will get a further opportunity in the next section to talk about situations when something went wrong.

Reading

The reading text is the true story of what happened in the last situation in Speaking exercise 1. A cab driver, waiting for a job interview as an IT assistant at the BBC, was mistaken for an IT consultant and was interviewed live on TV about a legal dispute concerning the computer company Apple, which he knew nothing about.

1

- Students read the text. They compare their ideas for the last situation in Speaking exercise 1 with what actually happened.

2

- Ask the students to read the statements first. They then read the text again quickly and mark the statement with a tick if it is stated in the text or a cross if it isn't.

1 ✔ 2 ✘ 3 ✔ 4 ✘ 5 ✔ 6 ✘

3

- Pairwork. Students discuss the questions with a partner.

Extra task: vocabulary

- Ask students to find and underline the words used to describe how Guy Goma felt in the text:
  shock fear guilt remorse embarrassment guile
- Check the meaning of the nouns, and ask students to tell you what they think the adjectives of the nouns are (*shocked, afraid, guilty, remorseful, embarrassed, guileful*).
- Ask students to say how they would have felt in this situation and what they would have done.

Language notes: reading

- ***Hapless*** means unlucky.
- Franz Kafka was an early twentieth century Austrian/Czech writer. His novels often depict a nightmare world of bureaucracy in which the central character is powerless to control his own fate. The phrase ***Kafkaesque nightmare*** is used to describe Guy Goma's experience as his situation spirals out of control.
- If you ***smell a rat*** you realize that something is wrong.
- A ***chap*** is a colloquial term for a man.
- To ***flit*** is to move swiftly.

Cultural notes: Guy Goma

- The interview with Guy Goma took place live on the BBC News 24 channel on May 8th 2006. He was asked three questions before the programme moved on to something else. You can find more information about Mr Goma, and watch the famous clip of his interview by going to his official website, www.guygoma.com. Interviewed after the programme, Mr Goma said that he would be happy to talk about any situation if invited back on the airwaves, but would appreciate time to prepare himself better.
- Max Clifford is a well-known British publicist or PR agent who represents many celebrities in their dealings with the media.

Methodology advances
Two odd reading ideas

Are your students getting a bit bored with doing reading texts in similar ways? Are you looking for a way to revitalize classroom reading work a bit? Try one of these slightly odd ideas!

'Impossible' reading

- *Choose an appropriate text (less than a page long) that has comprehension questions.*
- *In class, warn students that they will answer five (or however many) comprehension questions but will be allowed to read the text only once and with a strictly limited time. State the time limit of one minute and pause for the disbelief, complaints and moans about it being impossible! Stand your ground.*
- *Ask students to think about how they might best be able to get as many correct answers as possible even with such a tight time restriction. Their responses should include the ideas of (a) being as familiar as possible with the questions before they read, (b) having thought about what the possible answers might be, etc.*
- *Hand out the questions. When students have read them and talked together about their ideas of possible answers, hand out the text face down on the table. Tell students to turn it over when you say 'go' and turn it back when you say 'stop' (after exactly a minute).*
- *Let students write their answers individually for a few minutes. Ignore any complaints!*
- *After a while combine students into groups or four or five. Explain that the winning group will be the one that has written the most correct answers. Let them discuss and agree their answers, and only then, tell them that you will give them a further two minutes to check and confirm or change their answers.*
- *Repeat the quick reading technique, this time for two minutes, and allow a further group discussion.*
- *Collect in the students' written answers, then allow them to read the text normally.*
- *After students feel they have had a realistic time, go through the answers together and declare the winning group.*
- *Discuss whether students enjoyed the reading exercise or not. Ask them what skills they think it was designed to help them with. (Answers could include ideas from the following bullet point.)*
- *Although this seems at first glance an odd task, it has a number of serious purposes. It encourages students to read questions more carefully than they have ever done before. It gets them predicting in a more thoughtful way. It encourages efficient fast reading. It encourages focused speculation about meaning that has been missed in the reading. Incidentally, it also helps to build cooperation between students as the highest score will only be gained by the team that discusses and works best together.*

From the seed to the tree

- *Photocopy two different texts. If possible the layout and typeface should be the same. Roughly tear (not neatly cut) each text into small extracts. The extracts should contain about twenty to thirty words but will not end neatly at beginnings or ends of sentences.*
- *In class, make pairs and hand out one extract from each text to each pair. Explain that pairs have extracts from two different texts. Their task is to predict what each text is about and what the main point or argument is.*
- *When students have read the extracts, discussed them a little and reached their conclusions, join pairs together to make groups of four. They should now try to work out which extracts are from the same sources and discuss and agree what the two texts are about. Because each group can now see two parts from each text they may want to change from their original ideas. (If you have a large class, you could continue the activity with a further stage, by bringing together the groups of four into a larger group of eight.)*
- *Get feedback in the whole class. Make notes on the board as to all ideas about the two texts.*
- *Hand out the complete original texts for students to read as normal. When they have been read, check back with the guesses on the board. Did any group manage to successfully predict what the tree would look like from just seeing the original seeds?*

VOCABULARY & SPEAKING: television

1

- Students complete the sentence beginnings with their endings.
- They could then compare their answers with a partner before you check with the class.

1 e 2 b 3 a 4 h 5 c 6 f 7 g 8 d

2

- Pairwork. Students discuss each of the questions in exercise 1 with a partner, giving details and examples where relevant.

Extra task: vocabulary

- You could extend this area of vocabulary further by eliciting words students know, or by introducing the words below:
  reality TV historical drama docudrama chat show serial episode series presenter announcer quiz show host
- Ask students what they understand by the words. If necessary, they can check them in their dictionaries.

Language notes: television

- A ***couch potato*** is a lazy person who watches TV all day.
- To ***channel-hop*** is to use the remote control to switch from one station to station.
- ***Prime time*** TV is usually between six and ten in the evening– the time when audience figures are highest.
- If you are ***glued to the TV***, you are unable to move your eyes away from the screen, presumably because the programme is so interesting.

Cultural notes: British TV channels.

- In Britain, there are five free-to-air terrestrial TV stations: BBC1, BBC2, ITV (Independent Television), Channel 4 and Channel 5. With a set-top box, you can access more free terrestrial channels through the *Freeview* service.

DID YOU KNOW?

1

- Groupwork. Students read the information about the BBC and discuss the questions in small groups.

Cultural notes: the BBC

- The BBC shows no commercials as it is largely funded by the licence fee. In 2007, a colour TV Licence cost £135.50 and a black and white licence cost £45.50. Everybody with a TV set has to buy one, even a student in shared accommodation watching a TV in his/her room. It is, however, free for people over 75.
- As a result of its unique funding, there is a real feeling of ownership of the corporation among ordinary British people. The BBC has a certain obligation to provide quality and diversity in its scheduling, rather than simply airing programmes aimed to attract the highest number of viewers.
- For more information, go to: www.bbc.co.uk.

Methodology advances
You do it!

- *One of the best ways to learn anything is to try to teach it to someone else (as I'm sure most teachers have discovered at some point in their careers). So, why not apply this idea to the students in your class?*
- *Look ahead in your Student's Book, say at the next two lessons, and make a list of a number of distinct grammatical and lexical items coming up. Make sure the notes pinpoint the specific focus rather than just the general area. For example, in lesson 10D you could pick something like 'using must have to make deductions about the past' rather than the big and general title of 'modal verbs'.*
- *In class, make pairs and allocate one of these items to each pair. Explain that their job is to prepare a ten to fifteen-minute lesson. To do this they will need to:*
  - *(1) research the language using reference books, internet and any sources, but not the information in the Student's Book.*
  - *(2) think about what would be useful to teach the others in class (e.g. focus mainly on meaning and/ or form; focus on typical expressions that it is used in; or focus on typical mistakes).*
  - *(3) decide how it would be best to teach. Now this of course is the interesting one. It may be useful to get students thinking about how you have taught things over their course. Point out that teaching isn't just explaining. Teaching often involves interaction, question and answer, student tasks, guided discovery, and so on. Encourage students to make use of some of these techniques in their lesson.*
  - *(4) Teach it!*
- *Give help where appropriate during the three preparation stages. Guide students towards more accurate information, clearer focus and better teaching strategies. You could get students to privately do a mini rehearsal with you (perhaps in the corridor or in another room).*
- *Make it clear that you will not interfere or help during the mini-lesson itself (except perhaps to save students who are really digging a hole for themselves). For this period, sit back, enjoy the teaching and make notes.*
- *I suggest you follow each 'lesson' with a short feedback session. Invite feedback from teachers and students. How was the lesson? Was it clear? Did they learn anything useful? It's fine to point out any mistakes or problems but keep the general tone very positive and encouraging. Add your own comments, again mainly saying what they did well.*

IF YOU WANT SOMETHING EXTRA ...

➋ *Photocopiable activity, page 249*
➋ *Teaching notes, page 206*

10D | A stabbing incident

What the lesson is about

Theme	Unfortunate incidents & the opera
Speaking	Pairwork: telling a story about a stabbing incident from pictures
Listening	An interview with an opera singer about a stabbing during a rehearsal
Vocabulary	Not turning out well
Grammar	Modal verbs 3 (*must, should, need*)

If you want a lead-in ...

Pre-teach key words

- Use the pictures on page 102 to pre-teach key vocabulary from the text before starting the exercises.
- Pre-teach the following: *knife, stab, blade, handle, retract, wound, bloodstained, collapsed.*

Introducing the theme: not turning out well

- Ask students to think of any situations in their lives that have gone badly wrong. If necessary, give an example from your own life.
- Ask students to discuss the situations with their partners. *What happened? Whose fault was it? What were the results?*
- During feedback, ask students what lessons they have learnt from the situations described.

Listening & speaking

The listening is an interview with an opera singer who describes an incident that happened during the rehearsals of a production of *I Pagliacci*, in which he injured another singer with a knife when the push-button mechanism on it failed to work.

1

- Ask the students to look at the pictures and discuss a possible order for them to tell a story. Tell the students that the man in the blue t-shirt is holding a knife (not visible in the artwork) in pictures A and F. They could compare their order with a partner.

2

Communication activities, Student's Book page 152

- Ask students to turn to page 152 at the back of the book where they will find the final picture for the story. Ask them if this has affected their order and to change it as necessary.

3 3.15

- Students listen to the recording and put the pictures in the correct order.
- They could then compare their answers with a partner before you check with the class. Play the recording again if necessary.

1 C, 2 A, 3 F, 4 D, 5 H, 6 E, 7 G, 8 B

3.15

P = Presenter DR = David Randall

P: Now on *Personal Account*, the British tenor David Randall tells how during rehearsals for a production of *I Pagliacci* things didn't turn out quite as planned.

DR: The world of opera is much larger than life, and sometimes things can go very wrong. Take my Covent Garden debut in 1976. I was singing Don Ottavio in *Don Giovanni* when I fell through a trap door. I had to pull myself out, trailing yards of costume and singing: 'Tremble, tremble you vile beast'. And the time during the first-act love duet of *La Bohème* at the Coliseum when my trousers split. Trying not to laugh, I had to walk off stage backwards, holding Mimi in front of me. But nothing compares with November 1998, when I was in Milwaukee singing with the Florentine Opera Company. The production was *I Pagliacci* and I was singing Canio. In the final scene, I stab to death my unfaithful wife, Nedda, and her lover, Silvio. I'd been given my props when we started rehearsing, and these included a knife for the stabbing scene. It looked like a real commando knife and I wasn't happy: 'I can't use this,' I told them. 'It's far too dangerous.' But everyone assured me it was perfectly safe. The props man demonstrated a simple push-button mechanism that made the blade retract into the handle.

I used the knife to practise a stabbing motion with the American baritone Kimm Julian, who was playing Silvio. As we rehearsed the scene, he had a way of arching his body and pulling in his stomach which just didn't look right. After about twelve attempts, the director suggested we try it in slow motion. At the crucial moment, just as I'd done twelve times before, I pushed the button to make the blade retract. But when I looked down, I saw to my amazement that the blade was still out. I hadn't felt any resistance when I stabbed Kimm, so I thought everything must be OK. I asked him, 'I didn't get you, did I?' and he answered: 'No.' I just had time to think, 'Thank God,' when I saw Kimm's face turn white. He was sweating. Clearly, all was not well. He put his hand to his stomach, then took it out and looked at it, saw that it was bloodstained, and collapsed. I looked at the knife again – it was clean. But then I saw blood oozing from his stomach and soaking into his shirt and jeans. It was horrible.

The emergency services arrived along with the police. By then I was in tears – almost hysterical – thinking I'd killed Kimm. What happened next was like a farce as the director described to the police how I'd just found out that my wife was having an affair with this guy, so I'd stabbed him. He was giving them the plot of the opera, but the police took it seriously. They grabbed me and marched me off to another room. They were wearing holsters with guns. I felt very threatened. The next thing I knew I was being questioned about how long I'd known that this guy had been having an affair with my wife. Farce was turning into nightmare. I tried to explain that Nedda wasn't my real wife – Diana was at home in England with our children. But the police started accusing me of having a lover. After pleading with them to let me call Diana, they took me to a phone. Convinced by now that I had killed Kimm I cried down the phone to her, and the police stood nearby listening to every word.

Eventually, they realized their mistake and I was released. But the story leaked out, and while Kimm was undergoing surgery for a wound that had missed

his stomach by millimetres, I was being hassled by TV and radio stations. Back home in England, reporters turned up at our house, desperate to interview Diana and the children. Our nanny was hounded by a journalist asking her: 'Is he aggressive at home?' Then they got hold of our gardener, and he said: 'David? Oh yes, he's good with a knife.'
It seems funny in retrospect, but I could easily have killed Kimm. The blade had gone in three inches. Thinking about it still gives me the shivers. But horrific as it was, the incident led to fantastic publicity – the show suddenly sold out.
Kimm was only in hospital for a night, but he pulled out of the production. He took it all in the best of spirits. He even said to a journalist: 'David probably feels worse than I did.' Another baritone was engaged to play Silvio. And I got what I'd first wanted – a retractable toy knife. On the opening night, I was still shocked. As the moment drew nearer for me to stab Silvio, I felt really distressed, and I could sense the audience waiting too. But the critics gave me a fantastic review, which appeared alongside a photograph of me brandishing the knife at Silvio. When I got back to England I took lessons on a special way of tucking the knife up my sleeve. Now, if I'm singing a role where I have to use a knife, I feel in total control of my own destiny – and that of anyone I might need to stab.

Language notes: listening

- A ***tenor*** is the male singer who has the highest range of notes.
- A ***baritone*** is the male singer with a deeper range than a tenor, but a higher range than a bass (the lowest range).
- A ***trap door*** is a small door that covers an opening in the floor, through which actors appear and disappear.
- A ***commando*** is a soldier who attacks behind enemy lines.
- ***Props*** are objects used by actors on stage.
- The ***navel*** is small hollow in the middle of your stomach, where the umbilical cord used to be.
- A ***rehearsal*** is a practise session for a play, opera or musical performance.

Cultural notes: the opera

- *I Pagliacci* (The Clowns) is an opera composed by Ruggero Leoncavallo, which tells the tragedy of a jealous husband who kills his wife and her lover. It was first performed in 1892.
- Covent Garden Theatre or, as it is more commonly known, the Royal Opera House, was built in 1858. It is situated just off the north piazza of Covent Garden and is the third theatre on that site. (The previous two were destroyed by fire.) It underwent renovation in the 1990s and reopened in 2002.
- *Don Giovanni* is an opera composed by Mozart, which was first peformed in Prague in 1787. The story is based on the legend of Don Giovanni or Don Juan.
- *La Bohème* is an opera composed by Giacomo Puccini. It is based on *Scènes de la vie de Bohème* by Henri Murger, and it was first performed in Turin in 1896.
- The London Coliseum is a theatre venue which has been the home of the English National Opera since 1968.
- Milwaukee is the largest city in the state of Wisconsin, USA. It is located on the southwestern shore of Lake Michigan.

4 3.15

- Students listen to the recording again and choose the correct alternative to complete each sentence.
- They could then compare their answers with a partner before you check with the class.

1 amusing	4 committed adultery
2 seemed so authentic	5 the opera's success
3 Kimm change colour	6 David was still affected by

5

- Students complete the sentences from the recording with the correct form of *take* or *turn*.

1 turn	5 turning
2 Take	6 turned
3 turn	7 took
4 took	8 took

6

- Pairwork. Students discuss the meanings of the expressions with *take* and *turn* in bold in exercise 5.

1 happen as they were expected to
2 used to introduce an example
3 became white
4 accepted this as fact
5 changing into
6 arrived
7 accepted it very well
8 had / received

7

- Students work with the same partner and retell David's story, using the pictures to help them.

GRAMMAR: modal verbs 3

Language reference, Student's Book page 104
Methodology guidelines: Grammar boxes, page xiv

1

- Students read the sentences and complete them with the items in the box. Point out that they will need to use one of the items twice.
- They could then compare their answers with a partner before you check with the class.

1 mustn't	5 shouldn't have
2 had to	6 should have
3 must have	7 didn't need
4 must have	8 needn't have

Language notes: modal verbs, must, need and should

- It can be confusing for students that modal verbs often have very different past forms, or even more than one past form depending on their meaning. You could preview this by writing the following sentences on the board and asking students to rewrite them in the past.
  1 You must feel tired after all that work. (must have felt …)
  2 John must wear a tie at work. (had to …)
  3 The children mustn't speak in class. (couldn't/weren't allowed to)
  4 I don't need to do my homework this weekend. (didn't need to)
  5 We should go and see that play. (should have gone …)
- During feedback, give the correct answers then refer students to the grammar box for reasons why. For number 4, explain that need has two past forms: *didn't need to* and *needn't have.* For example:
  I didn't need to wash the car.
  I needn't have washed the car.
  In the first sentence, no action was taken, as it was unnecessary (maybe the car was already clean); in the second, an action was taken, but it later turned out to be an unnecessary one (perhaps it rained heavily after the car was washed).

2

- Pairwork. Students discuss the possible context for each of the sentences in exercise 1, and say what the word in bold refers to.
- Then ask students for their ideas.

Possible answers:
1 Parent talking about what he/she said to daughter: *it* might refer to an item of clothing.
2 Someone talking about childhood with brother: *it* might refer to a bicycle.
3 Teacher or ex-teacher talking about former school: *they* might refer to his/her pupils.
4 Someone talking about an umbrella (*it*).
5 Someone talking about an item of clothing that they want to take back to the shop: *it* might refer to the receipt.
6 Someone arrives late at a party to find the cake (*it*) has been eaten.
7 Someone talking about a visit to a youth hostel: *one* might refer to a sleeping bag.
8 Someone who has returned from a holiday abroad: *it* might refer to a language phrase book or dictionary.

Language notes: pronouns

- This is an exercise in pronoun reference. ***There*** must refer to a place, it to a singular thing, ***they*** to plural things or people, ***one*** to a singular thing.

3

Communication activities, Student's Book page 141

- Pairwork. Put students into A and B pairs. Ask students to turn to page 141 at the back of the book and read their roles.
- Students A then tells their partner about what went wrong and the consequences it had for them. Student B tells their partner what they should or shouldn't have done in order to prevent each of the problems occurring. Suggest that Student A responds to Student B's advice.
- You could give them the following example if necessary:
  Student A: *My car broke down on the motorway the other day. It was terrible – I had to wait an hour for the breakdown lorry to arrive. I missed an important meeting at work and my boss was really angry.*
  Student B: *You should have taken out your car insurance with a better company – then the breakdown lorry might have arrived sooner. And if your meeting was so important, then you should have tried to hitch a lift from another motorist.*
- They then change roles with Student B telling Student A what went wrong and Student A providing the advice.
- Go round monitoring and give help where needed.

Extra task: extended conversation

- Extend the conversation; Student A responds to Student B's criticism/retrospective advice. Student B then replies.

Methodology advances
Digging for fossils

- *One common problem at this level is that many errors seem to be fossilized, i.e. the student has repeated the error so much that it has become a fixed, unmovable part of their personal language. Even though they may have studied the language item many times and even if they understand exactly what is wrong, somehow they don't seem to be able to stop themselves making the mistake when under the pressure of speaking fluently.*
- *Many fossilized errors reflect a translation of a similar structure in the student's first language. For example, many Hungarians who otherwise speak English at Advanced level say sentences like 'We went with my mother to the shops.' when they are actually only talking about two people and the sentence should start 'I went …'. The error goes directly back to the structure used in Hungarian. Such translated-structure errors seem to be amongst the hardest to clear out.*
- *So what can be done? Well, perhaps not very much. Drawn-out correction and repeated study doesn't seem to make very much difference. Some language items simply seem to get stuck in this way. Arguably, there is a case for just relaxing and accepting that there will be some grammar that this happens with.*
- *If the student is very determined to correct the problem, one way forward might be to agree a non-intrusive way of alerting them to every occasion when the error happens.*
- *I had a student who regularly used phrases like 'If I will come …' despite knowing perfectly well that this wasn't grammatically possible. I agreed with her to simply hold my hand up for a second or two (as if about to wave) whenever I heard this error (but to do or say nothing else that focussed on the error). I did this on quite a few occasions, which frequently prompted self-correction by the student. After a while, we both noticed that the problem was recurring less often. I have to admit that it hadn't completely gone by the time the course finished, but this 'gently nudging' approach did seem to have had some effect.*

VOCABULARY: not turning out well

1

- Students complete the sentences with the correct form of the verbs in the box.
- They could then compare their answers with a partner before you check with the class.

1 came	4 work
2 fallen	5 went
3 make	

2

- Students complete the sentences with the nouns in the box.
- They could then compare their answers with a partner before you check with the class.

1 good	4 cause
2 flop	5 grief
3 mess	

3

- Students think about five situations they have experienced, witnessed or read about and write sentences about them using the expressions from exercise 1 and 2.

4

- Pairwork. Students discuss their sentences with a partner, giving as many details as they can.

Language notes: not turning out well

- If your hard work ***comes to nothing*** you achieve nothing through your efforts.
- If something ***falls through***, it fails to happen.
- To ***make it to*** means to reach.
- If things ***work out***, they succeed.
- A ***flop*** is a failure.
- If you ***make a mess of*** something, you do it badly.
- If someone is a ***lost cause***, he/she is beyond help.
- If you ***come to grief***, things go badly wrong for you.

IF YOU WANT SOMETHING EXTRA ...

Photocopiable activity, page 250
Teaching notes, page 207

Answer key

10 Review

Student's Book page 173

1

1 off; to
2 chance / possibility; came; made
3 out; through; went
4 lost; any
5 high; it
6 success; box
7 sense; achieved / fulfilled; out
8 up; on

2

Possible answers:
1 a exam
2 an golf tournament
3 a company
4 an article of clothing
5 a record
6 a film
7 a book
8 an opportunity to appear in a (TV) talent show

3

1 d 2 g 3 a 4 h 5 c 6 f 7 b 8 e

5

1 couldn't
2 mustn't / shouldn't
3 shouldn't / needn't
4 must / should
5 should have
6 didn't need to
7 needed to go / had to go
8 must be / must have been
9 need / have
10 must / should

6

Hi Paul

Only a few days to go until you ~~will~~ come over to stay with us – we're all really looking forward to seeing you again after so long. Hopefully the rain will have stopped by then – the weather's been terrible these last few weeks!

We're thinking ~~in~~ of taking you up into the mountains one day to go walking. It's likely ~~will~~ to be / it will be very green there after all this rain we've had and the lakes and rivers are sure to be full to bursting. Should be lovely. We also hope to go with you to a very picturesque village near here on the Sunday – you're bound to ~~be liking~~ like it. It's got a lovely square and ~~it's probable we~~ we'll probably eat lamb in one of the many restaurants there. I'll need to book that soon as it gets very busy.

Anyway, we're about ~~going~~ to go shopping now to get some food for your visit. I've arranged ~~meeting~~ to meet Ana outside the supermarket so I'd better go.

Bye for now and see you soon

Tomás

11A | A sight for sore eyes

What the lesson is about

Theme	Romanticism
Reading	*Daffodils*: poem by the English Romantic poet William Wordsworth
Vocabulary	Descriptive verbs
Pronunciation	Stress patterns
Did you know?	The Romanticism movement in the UK & USA

If you want a lead-in ...

Discussion starters

Methodology guidelines: Discussion starters, page xiv

- *Do you read much poetry? If so, which poets and what sort of poetry do you enjoy? Who's your favourite poet and what's your favourite poem?*
- *Who are the most famous and celebrated poets in your country? What do you know about them?*
- *What do you know about poetry in English?*

Pre-teach key words: romantic poetry

- Elicit and teach the following words connected with poetry:
  poem poet rhyme beat rhythm
  simile line verse syllable metaphor

Introducing the theme: a sight for sore eyes

- You may wish to start the lesson by explaining the unit title. *A sight for sore eyes* is used to describe something that we are pleased to see. (The reason is that seeing something beautiful should help to remedy the soreness of the eyes.)
- Elicit other expressions involving eyes and sight, for example: *We don't see eye to eye; There's more to this than meets the eye; out of sight out of mind; I'm sick of the sight of you.*

Reading & pronunciation

The reading text is the poem *Daffodils* by the English Romantic poet William Wordsworth, written in 1804. It describes a walk he went on with his wife in the Lake District (in the north of England) on a stormy day, when he suddenly came across hundreds of daffodils by a lake.

1

- Pairwork. Ask students to look at the photo and discuss the questions with a partner.

2

- Students read the poem. Tell them not to worry about the gaps at this stage.
- Ask students to read the information on the rhyme scheme for the poem. You could do the first six lines of the poem with them.
- They then choose the best alternative to complete the rest of the poem. Point out the glossary to help them.
- Don't check answers at this stage. This will be done in the next exercise.

Cultural notes: William Wordsworth

- William Wordsworth was born in 1770 and died in 1850. He lived in the Lake District, a beautiful area of northern England which influenced his poetry. The publication of Lyrical Ballads in 1798, a book of poems he wrote with Coleridge, was important in launching the Romantic Age in English literature. His greatest work was *The Prelude*, an autobiographical poem about his youth.
- Wordsworth wrote his famous poem about daffodils in 1804, published it in 1807, and revised and published it again in 1815. It was the result of a walk on a stormy day near Ullswater lake. He saw the daffodils whilst walking with his sister Dorothy. Later, Dorothy described the flowers in her diary, and William was inspired to turn her description into a poem.

Language notes: reading

- ***Vales*** are valleys.
- ***Fluttering*** is a gentle waving movement.
- To ***outdo*** someone or something is to do better than them. (In the poem, the flowers *outdo* the waves by dancing better than them.)
- When the poem was written, ***gay*** was usually used to mean happy. However, this now an old-fashioned meaning of the word. In modern English, *gay* is generally used to describe someone as homosexual.
- Wordsworth's ***inward eye*** is his imagination.
- ***Daffodils*** are tall, yellow-headed flowers that are one of the first to come out in spring.
- Note that there are a number of archaic or poetic words, most of which are explained on page 106 of the Student's Book: ***vales***, ***o'er***, ***glee***, ***gay***, ***jocund***, ***oft***, ***bliss***. There are poeticisms such as *a host/crowd of daffodils* – normally these words wouldn't go together. There is also poetic inversion: *Ten thousand saw I…*, *What wealth the show to me had brought.*
- A metaphor is a word or phrase that means one thing but is used to refer to another thing in order to emphasize their similar qualities. Examples in the poem include 'daffodils… dancing… (and)… bowing their heads' and 'the waves beside them danced'. In contrast, a simile is a phrase that describes something by comparing it to something else using *like* or *as*. An example is given in the first line of the poem, *I wandered lonely as a cloud.*
- The poem's rhyme scheme is ababcc. There are eight syllables and four beats to each line. Notice the anomalies in stress pattern created in the last line of each of the first two verses by putting the stress on the first syllable instead of the second syllable of the line: *<u>Fl</u>uttering…*, *<u>T</u>ossing their heads.*

3 3.16

- Students listen to the recording and check their answers.

1	crowd	6	gay
2	breeze	7	brought
3	twinkle	8	couch
4	bay	9	flash
5	Tossing	10	pleasure

4

- Ask students to read the information about the stress pattern of this poem and to look back at the first seven lines of the poem, which shows this pattern. Explain that the stressed syllables are marked in bold.
- Ask students to read these seven lines at the same time as you play the recording of them, so that they can hear the pattern.
- Students then underline the stressed syllables in the other lines. Tell them to say the lines out loud as they do so to help them hear the rhythm of the poem. It might help if they beat the rhythm on their desks as they say the poem.

5 3.16

- Students listen to the poem again to check their answers. They then practise reading the poem aloud with a partner.

And twinkle on the milky way,
They stretched in never-ending line
Along the margin of a bay:
Ten thousand saw I at a glance,
Tossing their heads in sprightly dance.

The waves beside them danced; but they
Out-did the sparkling waves in glee:
A poet could not but be gay,
In such a jocund company:
I gazed – and gazed – but little thought
What wealth the show to me had brought:

For oft, when on my couch I lie
In vacant or in pensive mood,
They flash upon that inward eye
Which is the bliss of solitude;
And then my heart with pleasure fills,
And dances with the daffodils.

Extra task: listening for stress

- Prepare the students for reading the poem out loud by asking students to listen, repeat and click their fingers after your model. Produce the rhythm of the first verse, replacing the syllables with 'da' and clicking your fingers on a strong stress. For example:
  da-**da**-da-**da**-da-**da**-da-**da** (lines 1 to 5)
  da-da-da-**da**-da-da-da-**da** (line 6)

VOCABULARY: descriptive verbs

1

- Tell the students that the poem includes several words to describe different ways of seeing. Ask them to read the two lines from the poem and say what way of seeing the underlined words describe.
- Point out that *glance* and *gaze*, as well as other words of seeing, can be used both as verbs and nouns. You could then ask them to look in their dictionaries for *glance* and *gaze*, and ask them what example sentences are given for the verbs and nouns for these words.

a glance – a quick look; *at a glance* means immediately, with one quick look
gaze – to look at something for a long time, especially something you find attractive or interesting

2

- Students complete the sentences with the words in the box. Point out that they need to use the same word for sentences *a* and *b* in each item, but that they may need to change the form of the word. Remind them that all these words of seeing can be either used as nouns or verbs.
- They could then compare their answers with a partner before you check with the class.

1	a) glance	b) glancing
2	a) browse	b) browse
3	a) view	b) view
4	a) stare	b) stare
5	a) gaze	b) gazed

Language notes: descriptive verbs

- To ***gaze*** is look at someone or something for a long time (because they are interesting or beautiful).
- To ***glance*** is to look quickly in passing.
- To ***browse*** is to look for information on the web or to look at things in a shop.
- To ***stare*** is to look at someone or something in a very direct way.
- To ***view*** is to look at something in detail or to look at information on the web; the view is what you can see in front of you (usually outside).

Extra task

- You could elicit and teach other verbs connected with seeing, such as, *spy, glare, glimpse, peer* or *survey.*

3

- Pairwork. Students tell a partner how true the *a* sentences are for them, i.e. the first sentences in each pair in exercise 2.

4

- Students put the verbs in the box into the correct column.

Light	Movement
shine	wander
twinkle	float
sparkle	flutter
flash	toss

5

- Students complete the list of words with the verbs in exercise 4. Point out that the verbs must collocate with all four of the nouns in the list.
- They could then compare their answers with a partner before you check with the class.

1	flutter	4	flash
2	sparkle / shine	5	toss
3	wander	6	shine

6

- Students choose five of the noun/verb collocations in exercise 5 and write a sentence for each one. Tell them to leave a gap where the verb should be.
- They then show their partner their sentences and their partner completes them. They then check their partner's answer.

Language notes: descriptive verbs

- Note, and point out to students, that these verbs have slightly different meanings depending on which noun they are matched to.
- If eyelids ***flutter*** they go up and down rapidly. If a heart ***flutters*** it beats irregularly (either because of a medical condition or because the owner of the heart has seen someone he/she is in love with). Hands ***flutter*** when they move a lot, perhaps as somebody is speaking. Flags ***flutter*** in the breeze.
- Something ***sparkles*** when light catches it and makes it bright.
- If eyes ***wander*** they look at something they shouldn't. If mind, attention or thoughts ***wander*** they move on to think about something else.
- If eyes ***flash*** they suddenly show a strong emotion such as anger. Lightning ***flashes*** in the sky. Neon signs and warning lights ***flash*** when they go on and off intermittently.
- If you ***toss*** a coin you throw it in the air to see if lands heads or tails upwards. If you ***toss*** your hair you throw it around to liven it up. If you ***toss*** a ball you throw it gently to someone else. If you ***toss*** a salad you mix it up, usually with a wooden fork or spoon.
- If you ***shine*** a light or torch you switch it on and point it. If you ***shine*** shoes or silver you polish them.

Did you know?

1

- Pairwork. Students read the information about Romanticism and discuss the questions with a partner.

Cultural notes: Romantic poets & artists

- Samuel Taylor Coleridge (1772-1834; pronounced /'kəʊlərɪdʒ/) was an English poet, critic, and philosopher who was instrumental in founding the Romantic movement in England with Wordsworth. He is probably best known for his poems *The Rime of the Ancient Mariner* and *Kubla Khan*.
- Percy Bysshe Shelley (1792-1822; pronounced /'pɜːrsiː bɪʃ 'ʃeli/) was a contemporary of Coleridge and Wordsworth. His most famous works are *Ozymandias*, *Ode to the West Wind*, *To a Skylark*, and *The Masque of Anarchy*. Shelley led an unconventional life and was very idealistic, political and critical of the status quo. He was a friend of John Keats and Lord Byron, and was married to novelist Mary Shelley.
- John Keats (1795-1821; pronounced /kiːts/) was one of the most influential of the romantic poets. A feature of his poetry is his sensual imagery. His masterpieces are his odes which remain among the most popular poems in English literature, in particular, *Ode to a Grecian Urn*, *Ode to a Nightingale* and *Ode to Melancholy*. He died at the age of 25, from tuberculosis.
- George Gordon Byron (1788-1824; pronounced /'baɪrən/) is perhaps the best known of the romantic poets today. Among Lord Byron's most celebrated works are the narrative poems *Childe Harold's Pilgrimage* and *Don Juan*. Byron was famed as much for his extravagant lifestyle as his poetry. He was, as Lady Caroline Lamb, described him, 'mad, bad, and dangerous to know'. He was also an idealist who fought with Italian revolutionaries against Austria, and on the side of the Greeks against the Turks in the Greek War of Independence, for which the Greeks consider him a national hero. He died from fever in Messolonghi in Greece.
- Sir Walter Scott (1771-1832) wrote many novels based on Scottish history which were hugely popular in his lifetime. He was one of the first best-selling novelists and he had readers all over Europe, Australia, and North America. His novels and poetry are still widely read. Famous titles include *Ivanhoe*, *Rob Roy*, *The Lady of the Lake*, *Waverley* and *The Heart of Midlothian*
- Mary Wollenscroft Shelley (1797-1851; pronounced /'meəri 'wʊlstənkrɑːft 'ʃeli/) wife of Percy Shelley was an English novelist, best known as the author of *Frankenstein*. Her parents were famous dissenters of their time. Her mother, Mary Wollstonecraft was an early feminist and her father, William Godwin was an atheist philosopher.
- American novelist James Fenimore Cooper (1789-1837) wrote adventurous historical stories known collectively as the as the *Leatherstocking Tales*. His most famous novel is *The Last of the Mohicans*
- John Constable (1776-1837) was an English Romantic painter. His most famous paintings are of the countryside in Suffolk where he was born and lived. They include *Dedham Vale* and *The Hay Wain*. In his lifetime, he sold more paintings in France than he did in England, but now his works are among the most popular in British art.
- Joseph Mallord William Turner (1775-1851) was a British artist, famous for his landscape paintings. His style of painting pioneered and influenced Impressionism. His most famous paintings often show ships and trains, including *The Fighting Temeraire*, *Rain, Steam and Speed*, and *Snow Storm – Steamboat off a Harbour's Mouth* (the painting shown on page 107 of the Student's Book).
- Washington Allston (1779-1843) was a poet and pioneer of American Romantic landscape painting. He painted dramatic subjects and experimented with light and colour.

Extra task: discussion

- Ask students to choose a literary and/or artistic movement relevant to their country and talk about:
  - the main characteristics of the movement
  - the artists, poets or writers involved
  - your feelings about the movement

Web research tasks

➲ *Methodology guidelines: Web research tasks, page xiv*

- Ask students to research a famous romantic poet or artist on the internet. This could be anyone mentioned in the *Did you know?* text. Ask students to make notes about the life, views and greatest works of the artist.
- Have students make presentations about the person they researched. Alternatively, ask them to write short biographies.

Methodology advances
Could I teach content rather than language?

- *There are researchers who believe that the best way to learn a language is to learn something through that language, and not to explicitly focus on the language (i.e. grammar, vocabulary and so on) at all. The theory goes that if the subject is interesting enough, the student will be working very hard at understanding it and enjoying it and all the language problems will quietly look after themselves 'below the surface'. After all, this is probably something like the way that babies learn their first language.*
- *This suggests that there may be some mileage in teaching them about a non-linguistic topic that is genuinely new, interesting and challenging for them without particularly focussing on any language issues that it raises, other than perhaps explaining essential unknown words they need.*
- *I think for this to be genuinely useful at a high level (or any level, for that matter) the subject content needs to be presented at a language level that is higher than where the students actually are right now – a level that provides significant but not insurmountable comprehension problems for students. Yes, that's right, you are aiming to cause your students problems!*
- *So, if you're teaching at advanced level, I think this means that you could perhaps do, for example, an uncompromising university level lecture, one that is pitched at native speaker students and which would probably be quite hard even for them to follow. But, bear in mind throughout that it isn't a test; it's (we hope) extremely interesting and inspiring! Just to give you some starting points, here are a few example content topics from my own teaching career, that I've either done myself or seen other people do: The songs of Bob Dylan (with music); How to recognize a good wine (with tasting!); Henry VIII and his wives; Bridges of the world; The soap opera (with example extracts); Shiatsu (with practice). Please remember that I'm not suggesting that you do any of these! You need to find out which topics your students are keen to learn about (and which you feel capable of teaching them).*
- *Content-based teaching such as this is known by a number of names, but perhaps most widely by a rather ungainly acronym, CLIL, which stands for Content and Language Integrated Learning. If you find it interesting, it's one of those areas that is definitely worth looking up on the internet and finding out more about. Who knows, you and your students might become so keen on the idea that next term you teach your Advanced class English purely by teaching them history! But then again, maybe not!*

IF YOU WANT SOMETHING EXTRA ...

Photocopiable activity, page 251
Teaching notes, page 207

11B | Affordable art

WHAT THE LESSON IS ABOUT

Theme	Buying works of art
Speaking	Selecting artworks for a building
Listening	An interview with Will Ramsay, the owner of a London art gallery and founder of an international art fair
Vocabulary	Prepositional phrases
Grammar	Determiners, pronouns & quantifiers

IF YOU WANT A LEAD-IN ...

Discussion starters

➋ *Methodology guidelines: Discussion starters, page xiv*

- *Do you like art? What sort of art do you admire?*
- *How often do you go to art galleries? What do you enjoy seeing?*
- *What's your favourite work of art? Who's your favourite artist/painter/photographer/sculptor?*

Pre-teach key words: art & artists

- Write *Art* on the board, and around it write *people, types of art* and *materials*. Elicit words for each category from the class. Alternatively, ask students to brainstorm words in small groups then elicit them onto the board.
- Possible answers: **people**: artist, painter, sculptor, photographer, designer, cartoonist, performance artist; **types of art**: painting, drawing, sculpture, print, modern/ traditional, installation, portrait, landscape, cityscape, still life; **materials**: oils, watercolours, paintbrush, palette, easel

SPEAKING

1

- Ask students to look at the photos of the different works of art and say what they think of them. Which one do they like best? What type of art do they like in general?
- Pairwork. Put the students into pairs and ask them to read the situation and instructions. They then decide on a work of art they think would be suitable for each of the buildings in the box. If they think none are appropriate, they should discuss what type of artwork they would commission for the building, and give reasons why they think it would be suitable.
- Go round monitoring and give help where needed.

Culture note: art & artists

- The artworks at the top of the page are, from left to right: Wading at the Shore by Edward Henry Potthaust; An untitled piece by Afro; Our Ancient Future by Robert McIntosh; Jardin Majorelle, Marrakesh, Morocco by Llana Richardson; Miss Antoinette Schulte by Charles Despiau.

2

- Students compare their ideas with the rest of the class and give reasons for their choice of artwork for the reception areas of the buildings.

3

- Groupwork. Students discuss the questions in small groups, giving as many details as they can and reasons for their choice of artwork for their school or workplace.

Extra task: presentations

- Ask each group to nominate a spokesperson to present their ideas to the class. The class listens to each spokesperson then votes on which piece of artwork they would like for the school.

LISTENING

The listening is an interview in three parts with Will Ramsey, the owner of Will's Arts Warehouse, an art gallery in London. In Part 1 he talks about his reasons for setting up his gallery, the art he sells, how he sells the work and who he sells it to. In Part 2 he talks about the Affordable Arts Fairs he set up and what happens at the fairs. In Part 3 he gives tips to people who are thinking of buying a work of art for the first time.

1 3.17

- Explain that students are going to listen to the first part of an interview with Will Ramsay, who owns an art gallery in London. Ask them to read the sentences first so that they know what information to listen out for. Tell them they need to complete the sentences with one or two words only.
- Play the recording for the student to complete the sentences.
- They could then compare their answers with a partner before you check with the class. Play the recording again if necessary.

1	accessible	5	shoe shop
2	fear (factor)	6	wills-art
3	(very) approachable	7	working atmosphere
4	fifty	8	company logo

3.17

I = **Interviewer** **WR** = **Will Ramsay**

Part 1

I: Will, you're the owner of Will's Art Warehouse, a large and very successful art gallery in London. Can you tell us a little about the gallery and what inspired you to start it all off?

WR: Sure. My aim in setting up the gallery back in 1996 was – still is – to make art more accessible, to bring contemporary art within the reach of that large sector of the general public that doesn't know very much about it, but is keen to buy. People are often just too scared to go into a gallery – many of them feel embarrassed about their lack of knowledge, they feel they might be asked something which catches them out, which gives away the fact that they know very little. I wanted to take this fear factor out of buying art, I want, I want the process of buying art to be as unintimidating and accessible as possible. Er, when I left the army I used to cycle around London visiting art galleries – I found them really intimidating places. You know, there'd often be nobody else in there, I was on my own and I could hear the echo of my own footsteps as I walked around – it made me feel really self-conscious. I didn't feel welcome, I didn't think I was being treated like a potential customer. So, my idea was to cre-... I wanted to to create a much more relaxed atmosphere for people to buy art in – my gallery's in a warehouse, we play music in the background and the staff are very approachable –

you can ask them whatever you like, they won't make you feel awkward or small.

I: Your prices are very accessible as well, aren't they Will?

WR: That's right. The art we sell is affordable art. We concentrate on relatively unknown artists, artists whose work doesn't have a premium, an extra added to the price because of their reputation. Prices start at fifty pounds and stop at around three thousand, which means we're putting original art within the grasp of average salaries – so that's oils, watercolours, photographs, prints, sculptures, whatever. Er, another important point is that we also enable buyers to choose works from a variety of artists. Traditional art galleries tend to put the work of just one artist on display at any one time. This has always seemed bizarre to me – I mean, you go into a shoe shop and find a whole range of different shoes to buy from, so why should an art gallery be any different? So, apart from the thematic exhibitions in our main gallery space – which we change every six weeks – you can also browse through our large storerooms where we keep work by up to seventy other artists.

I: That's quite a selection.

WR: Yes, it is. And if you can't actually make it in to the gallery, there's always the internet. If you click on to our website, you can search through all the work we have in stock and make your purchase via email or over the phone.

I: From abroad, too?

WR: Certainly, we send out to anywhere in the world.

I: Let me just give out that internet address, Will – I'm sure listeners will be interested in visiting the site. It's www dot wills-art dot com. And wills-art is spelt W I L L S dash A R T. I'll repeat that: W I double L S dash A R T, wills-art. Now, I noticed on your website, Will, that you have a corporate clients service. Tell us about that.

WR: Yes, it's a service we offer to organizations who are looking to buy artwork to decorate their premises – that includes offices, hotels, restaurants, hospitals, leisure centres and so on. Art on display around a building clearly helps to enhance the working atmosphere within it – and of course it represents a worthwhile investment for a business as well. As part of our service, we visit the premises and give advice on the type of art that will work for that particular company or organization and the image it wants to reflect. We discuss aesthetic concerns and consider practical issues such as budget and space – the size as well as the number of artworks.

I: And you source the artworks from your Art Warehouse, I imagine.

WR: Yes, we do, but we can also commission a specific work from an artist if necessary.

I: And I see that you offer gift vouchers to employees.

WR: That's right. Companies are often looking for new and different ways to reward loyalty and performance. Most of them want to offer incentives and bonuses to attract and retain key talent among their staff. So we will produce vouchers of any amount, which can be printed with the company logo and which the employee can use to buy a piece of art at the warehouse – something which satisfies his or her personal taste. Companies are made up of individuals and art gift vouchers are an individualized way of rewarding them for the work they do.

2 3.18

- Students listen to Part 2 of the recording and decide if the statements are true or false.
- They could then compare their answers with a partner before you check with the class. Play the recording again if necessary.

1 F 2 F 3 T 4 F 5 T 6 T

3.18

Part 2

I: Let's move on now to talk a little about the Affordable Art Fairs, which you launched in 1999. These now all take place on a regular basis in London, Bristol, Melbourne, Sydney, New York and San Francisco. Presumably, Will, the underlying ideals and principles are the same as for your Art Warehouse.

WR: That's right – the fairs are relaxed, they're fun and there's an upper limit on prices – the same philosophy but on a much bigger scale. The London fair in Battersea Park for example brings in over 100 galleries from across the UK and abroad. It's a great opportunity for them, particularly the smaller galleries, to reach a new audience, and first time buyers get the chance to see thousands of artworks in one venue.

I: And it's a great opportunity for artists as well.

WR: Of course, and we do a lot to encourage fresh, emerging talent. In Battersea we put on a Recent Graduates' Exhibition. That works as a showcase for young artists who've recently completed courses at UK art schools. It's an ideal platform for them to exhibit their work to a large number of buyers and galleries, and collectors at the beginning of their career.

I: And I see that you also offer activities for children at the different fairs.

WR: Oh, yes, we like to start them young. We usually run some kind of creative workshops or classes for children. Painting, printmaking, mask making … that kind of thing. All hands-on and all are run by experienced professionals. The kids love it and have something to show for it at the end, and if they want to, the mums and dads can leave them and go off and browse and buy at leisure.

I: Tell us about the people who buy at the fairs. Do they do so with investment in mind?

WR: Investment is largely secondary. People buy at the fairs mainly because they like the art – they want something to decorate their home, something that they'll enjoy looking at for a long time after their purchase. Certainly they may become collectors in the future – particularly as their interest and their knowledge grow. Our approach permits them to, to make that first purchase with confidence and in a relaxed environment. It's very significant that on average one visitor in every four actually buys something – that's a figure that most other fairs can only dream of.

I: And how many people actually visit your fairs?

WR: Well, if we look at the combined totals for the UK fairs last year – that's two in London, one in spring, one in autumn, and the Bristol fair – then we're talking about over 40,000 people, with a turnover of more than seven million pounds.

I: Goodness. This must all take an awful lot of organizing. You briefly mentioned earlier that you used to be in the army – has that helped?

WR: Yes, it taught me how to be well organized. That's important in any business but especially so in an event-based business such as this – there are a lot of people involved and timing is essential.

3 3.19

- Students listen to Part 3 of the recording and make notes on what Will Ramsey says about each of the items in the box.
- They could then compare their answers with a partner before you check with the class. Play the recording again if necessary.

Possible answers:
Guaranteed investment: no such thing as a 'guaranteed investment' so buy art only if you like it, not as a way of making money.
Artists' CVs: ask for CV to see stage of artist's development; attach to back of artwork so that grandchildren have information on what they've inherited.
Art fairs: go to one before you start buying to see how much things realistically cost. Also, to see which galleries you might want to visit to buy art.
Auctions: also good to go to. Can pick up bargains, but do research before buying.
Prints: buy originals – reproductions are worthless. Originals usually in editions of less than 75 – can be cheaper than paintings.

3.19

Part 3
I: Will, what tips would you give to people who are considering buying art for the first time. What do they need to think about?
WR: Well, I think the first thing to say is that you should only really buy a piece of art if you actually like it. It's got to be something you really enjoy looking at rather than just something you hope will make you a bit of money. After all, there's no such thing as a guaranteed investment. So the first question you need to ask yourself is 'Do I really like it, do I want to have it in my home?' And if the answer is yes, then don't be afraid to ask for more information about the artist – their background, their techniques and so on. Get the dealer to give you a copy of the artist's CV, so that you can see what stage they're at in their development – how much and what sort of things they've produced, where they've exhibited, whether they've had any solo shows and so on. And then attach the CV to the back of the work, along with a note about when and where you bought it and how much you paid for it. It's the kind of information your grandchildren will want to know in years to come when they inherit it from you. Erm, what else? Well, it's a good idea before you start buying to go along to an art fair.
I: Like an affordable art fair.
WR: Yes, indeed. Or any art fair, really. The point is to spend time looking around, looking at prices so you can appreciate how much things realistically cost. I mean, you'll learn for example that you won't pick up a two-metre painting for anything under about five hundred pounds. And, well, an art fair's also a good place to find out which galleries have an eye for the kind of paintings you like, galleries you might want to visit in the future when you're ready to buy. Auctions are good places to go to as well – you can often pick up some good bargains there, but make sure you do your research properly before you take the plunge and start bidding. As with any product, you owe it to yourself to find out as much as you can about a work of art before you part with your money. And when you're buying a print – a screen print or an etching for example – make sure it's an original, printed by the actual artist. Reproductions are worthless, they have no value at all. Original prints usually come in editions of less than 75 and they're great to buy – very often much cheaper than paintings.

Language notes: listening

- A ***print*** is an image created by pressing a special piece of wood, metal, etc with a raised design on it onto paper or another surface.
- An ***etching*** is a print made from an etching plate. The plate has a hard surface, into which a design has been cut, or *etched*.
- A ***reproduction*** is a copy.

4

- Pairwork. Students discuss the questions with a partner and give reasons for their answers.

Extra task: discussion

- Ask students, *What factors would you consider before buying a piece of art for your own home?* Tell them to make brief notes.
- Put students in small groups. Ask each student to tell the rest of the group what factors they thought were important. The rest of the group must then suggest an artwork for that person.

GRAMMAR: determiners, pronouns & quantifiers

Language reference, Student's Book page 114
Methodology guidelines: Grammar boxes, page xiv

1 3.20

- Students complete the sentences from the recording with the words in the box. They then listen to the recording and check their answers.

1 a little	5 Most
2 little	6 any
3 all	7 These
4 that	8 no

3.20

1 Can you tell us a little about the gallery?
2 They might be asked something which gives away the fact that they know very little.
3 You can search through all the work we have in stock.
4 Let me just give out that internet address.
5 Most of them want to offer incentives and bonuses to attract and retain key talent.
6 We will produce vouchers of any amount.
7 These now all take place on a regular basis in London, Bristol, Melbourne …
8 Reproductions are worthless, they have no value at all.

2

- Students read the information in the box and decide whether the words they wrote in exercise 1 are being used as a determiner, pronoun or quantifier.
- They could then discuss their answers with a partner before you check with the class.

1 *a little* – pronoun; quantifier
2 *little* – pronoun; quantifier
3 *all* – quantifier; determiner
4 *that* – determiner
5 *Most* – quantifier; pronoun
6 *any* – determiner; quantifier
7 *These* – pronoun
8 *no* – determiner; quantifier

Language notes: determiners, pronouns & qualifiers

- Make sure that students are clear about the grammatical distinction between a determiner (which indicates who or what you are talking about) and a pronoun (which replaces who or what you are talking about because it is already known).
- **Determiners** identify and quantify.
  Few *books* (a small amount) *were sold this year* (the year now).
- Some determiners are followed by singular verbs and nouns.
  Each *student has a book.* (*Every, neither* and *either* take singular forms, too).
- Some are followed by plural forms.
  All *children love stories.*
- Some are used exclusively with countable nouns.
  Fewer *people came this year.* (*Few, a few, many* and *several* can also be used with countable nouns).
- Some are used exclusively with uncountable nouns.
  We had ***less*** *time this week.* (Also, *little, a little* and *much*).
- Note that *few/little* have negative meanings, e.g. *Few people came – I was disappointed.* In contrast, *a few/a little* have positive meanings, e.g. *A few people came – I was pleased.*
- **Pronouns** replace nouns when the noun is known.
  Do you know that man? Oh, yes. I know ***him****!*
  Do you want any bread? I already have ***some****.*
- **Quantifiers** say how much or how many there are of who or what you are talking about. They can work as determiners or pronouns, depending on their function within the sentence.
  A lot *of people attended the meeting.* (determiner, as it expresses quantity but does not replace a noun)
  Would you like some milk? ***A little****, please?* (pronoun, as it replaces the noun.)

3

- Students choose the correct alternative to complete the sentences.
- They could then discuss their answers with a partner before you check with the class.

1	some	5	any
2	another	6	no
3	other	7	all
4	every	8	none

4

- Pairwork. Students choose five of the words and expressions in bold in exercise 3, including the words they underlined. They use these words and expressions to tell their partner about things which are true about themselves. Tell the student listening to show interest in what their partner is telling them by asking follow-up questions.

Extra task: determiners, pronouns & quantifiers

- Write the following on the board:
  both few another a little some all
- Ask students to write three sentences for each word, using each word in three different ways. Monitor and ask students whether the words are being used as pronouns, determiners or quantifiers.

VOCABULARY: prepositional phrases

1

- Look through the examples of the prepositional phrases with the students. Then students complete the phrases with the prepositions in the box.
- They could then discuss their answers with a partner before you check with the class.

1	in	5	out of
2	at	6	off
3	on	7	on
4	in	8	by

Extra task: dictionary work

- Ask students to check the meaning of any phrases from exercise 1 they don't know in their dictionaries.

2

- Students complete the sentences with the nouns from exercise 1.

1	paper; practice	4	fault; balance
2	nature; character	5	droves; person
3	work; leave		

3

- Students write five sentences, each using one of the prepositional phrases from exercise 1. Tell them to leave a gap where the noun should be, as in the sentences they completed in exercise 2.
- Go round monitoring and give help where needed.

4

- Students now give their sentences to another student to complete. They then check their partner's work when they have finished.

Language notes: prepositional phrases

- If something looks good ***on paper***, the idea is good in theory.
- If people turn up ***in droves***, they arrive in large numbers.
- If someone behaves in a way that is ***out of character***, they are not acting in the way that they normally do.
- If you see someone ***in person***, you see them face-to-face, rather than talking to them on the phone or communicating by email or, if they are famous, seeing them on TV.

Extra task: prepositional phrases

- Get students to test each other on the phrases from exercise 1. Tell each student to choose ten of the nouns and write them on a piece of paper in a random order without the prepositions. Put students in pairs. Students take it in turns to read out one of the words on their piece of paper. Their partner guesses the preposition. If they are correct, they get one point. They get a second point if they can give the meaning. Find out which person in each pair won.

IF YOU WANT SOMETHING EXTRA ...

➋ *Photocopiable activity, page 252*
➋ *Teaching notes, page 208*

11c | The sound of silence

What the lesson is about

Theme	Researching the effect of silence
Speaking	Speaking thoughts aloud
Reading	The quietest place on Earth
Vocabulary	Sounds

If you want a lead-in ...

Discussion starters

Methodology guidelines: Discussion starters, page xiv

- *What do you think is the quietest place on earth? What do you think it would feel like to be there?*
- *Where do you go when you want peace and quiet? What is the quietest place you know? What is the noisiest?*
- *Do you prefer noisy places or quiet places? Why?*

Pre-teach key words: sounds

- Ask students to write down as many words as they can think of to describe sounds. For example, *chatting, noisy, whistle, crash, knocking, bang, buzz*, etc. After one minute, put students in pairs or small groups to compare their sounds. Ask them to categorize the sounds under headings, such as *loud sounds* or *quiet sounds*, *sounds you make* or *sounds you hear*.
- Elicit some of the best words to the board.

Speaking

1

Communication activities, Student's Book pages 141, 148, 151 & 146

- Groupwork. Put students into groups of four and ask them to turn to their respective pages at the back of the book. Ask them to look at the photo and choose one of the people from it. Tell them that they are that person and to imagine what they are thinking. Allow them a few minutes to think about how the person feels in the situation they are in and what they might be thinking.

2

- Students now speak the thoughts of the person they chose aloud to their group, without showing or describing the photo.

3

- Students then discuss each others' photo, describing what they think it shows. They then check their ideas with the photos on the relevant pages at the back of the book.

Reading

The reading text is about scientific research on sound, creating a silent chamber and the effect complete silence has on people.

1

- Tell the students to sit in complete silence for one minute. Then ask them to tell their partner what sounds they heard during that minute. They should include all sounds however faint.

2

- Ask students to look at the photo and ask them what they think it is and what it might be used for. Accept any ideas, but don't confirm their answers.
- Students read the text. Tell them to ignore the gaps at this stage. They then answer the questions.

1 An anechoic chamber is a silent room, virtually free of all noise.
2 We learn that it's used for acoustic research or, in this case, for the scientific study of the human voice.
3a Whilst inside the chamber:
a <u>strange</u> experience, (quoting John Fithyan) *like being in a field in the middle of the night.*
The silence is <u>profound</u> and the room looks <u>unusual</u> too with jagged, sound-cancelling spikes ... that take on a <u>menacing</u> look in the dim light.
this <u>other-worldly</u> environment
The experience is <u>disconcerting</u>.
He also says that:
Real silence is <u>strange</u> and <u>disturbing</u>, <u>not relaxing</u>.
and that
They have a <u>profound</u> effect on the people who go into them.
b On leaving the chamber, he describes the sounds in the control room and comments:
The shock of hearing all this is as great as was the shock of hearing nothing.

3

- Students read the text again and complete the gaps in the text with the sentences. Point out that they need to read the information carefully before and after the gaps, and that they need to understand the structure of the whole paragraph in order to complete these gaps.
- They could then compare their answers with a partner before you check with the class.

1 c 2 g 3 e 4 a 5 d 6 h 7 b 8 f

Language notes: reading

- ***Anechoic*** means echoless.
- A ***decibel*** is a unit for measuring the relative loudness of sounds.
- ***Acoustics*** are the qualities of a room (or other space) that make it good or bad for carrying sounds.
- A ***laryngograph*** is an instrument for recording the larynx movements in speech – (the larynx is the throat cavity that contains the vocal cords)
- ***Ambient sounds*** are background sounds that occur naturally and accidentally in a place.
- An ***audiologist*** is someone who studies hearing.

Cultural note: John Cage

- John Cage was an American composer and pioneer of 'chance music'. He was born in 1912 and died in 1992. His famous composition 4'33' was produced in 1952. It has three movements but no notes are played. Instead, the incidental, background noises become the music.

4

- Students look back at the text again and underline all the instances of the noun *sound* that they can find, along with any accompanying verbs, adjectives or nouns. Tell the students to write down each collocation they find in their notebook and the sentence in which it appears. They can then compare their sentences with a partner.

> The quietest conditions that modern technology allow are invariably used to research sound.
> Most people cannot sleep without at least some background sound.
> It is hard to believe the unassuming walls can block out all sounds.
> [He] shows me the extensive precautions taken to keep sound pollution inside to a minimum.
> I am conscious of the sound of my breathing.
> These [fibreglass wedges] absorb virtually all the sound, meaning that measurements of sound levels typically weigh in far below zero decibels.
> He was in a room with no background sound and no echo.
> He was inspired to write his 'silent piece', 4'33", in which the 'music' is made by the ambient sounds of the concert hall alone.
>
> **Also:**
> The closest humankind can get to complete silence is the inside of a heavily soundproofed anechoic chamber.
> The room looks unusual, with jagged sound-cancelling spikes covering the walls and ceiling.

Extra task: vocabulary

- You may wish to ask students to find and underline words used in the text to describe silence (*strange, disturbing, not relaxing, profound, unpleasant, disconcerting*)
- Ask students which words they would use to describe silence.

5

- Pairwork. Students discuss the questions with a partner. When they have finished their discussion, you could go on to ask them how tolerant they are of noise in general.

VOCABULARY: sounds

1

- Students complete the sentences with one word from the text. They then say what sounds the words describe. Point out that *hum* and *whistle* can also be used both as nouns and as verbs, along with other words for sounds. Remind students of the words for seeing from the Vocabulary section in lesson 11A, which can be used either as a noun or a verb.

> *hum* – a low continuous sound
> *whistling* – a loud high sound

2

- Students choose the most appropriate words for the sentences.
- They could then compare their answers with a partner before you check with the class.

1	sizzled; rumbled	4	screech; crack
2	chiming; popping; clinking	5	rustle; rattled; banged
3	beeped; clattering	6	click; jingle; creak

Language notes: sounds

- All of the 'sound' words from exercise 2 can be used as nouns or verbs.
- ***Sizzle*** is the sound that food makes when it is being fried.
- A ***buzz*** is a continuous sound made by insects like bees or by certain types of machinery.
- To ***stutter*** is to repeat sounds in an uncontrolled way when speaking.
- A ***rumble*** is a low, deep sound made by thunder or a hungry stomach.
- To ***time*** something is to record how long something takes to do. (This is not a 'sound' word.)
- A ***chime*** is the noise made on the hour by an old-fashioned clock.
- A ***pop*** is a short, sharp, loud noise such as made by a balloon bursting (or cork being released).
- A ***plop*** is a short sound made by a small object falling into water.
- A ***clink*** is the short high sound of glass or metal objects hitting each other.
- A ***snap*** is a short, sharp noise made, for example, by breaking a pencil in half.
- A ***bleep*** is a short high sound usually made by electronic equipment.
- A ***beep*** is the sound of a car horn.
- A ***clatter*** is a series of loud short noises made when a hard object hits another hard object, (e.g. a goat's hooves running over a cattle grid).
- To ***shatter*** (not a sound word) is to break suddenly into small pieces (e.g. a dropped vase or car windscreen following a crash)
- A ***screech*** is a loud, high, unpleasant cry made when upset.
- To ***scratch*** is to pull fingernails across skin or make a mark on a metal surface (e.g. a key on a car). It can also be used to describe the sound a DJ makes by forcing a vinyl record backwards.
- A ***croak*** is a low loud rough sound that a frog makes. People may also croak when they have a sore throat.
- A ***crack*** is short sudden loud sound like a small explosion.
- A ***rustle*** is the sound of leaves in the wind.
- A ***rattle*** is a short sharp knocking noise made when something a hard object is shaken in a container.
- A ***ring*** is a continuous loud high sound.
- A ***bang*** is a sudden loud noise. It can be made by two hard objects hitting each other, or by a gun firing.
- A ***click*** is short high sound like the sound made when you press a switch.
- A ***crash*** is loud noise made, for example, by thunder.
- A ***jingle*** is the sound of metal things knocking together, e.g. keys.
- A ***creak*** is a high prolonged sound, e.g. a door opening.
- A ***shriek*** is a high, loud sound that people or animals make when scared.

Extra task: sounds

- Ask students to produce some of the sounds from exercise 2 for their partner to guess. They can use their own voices or any objects they have to hand.

3 **3.21**

- Pairwork. Students listen to the sound sequences from exercise 2. You could tell them to close their eyes as they listen. They then discuss with their partner what might be happening in each one of them.

Possible answers:
2 a New Year's Eve party
3 a girl / woman who is being picked up by her boyfriend
4 bank robbers in a getaway car confronting police at a roadblock
5 the beginning of a storm
6 parents who hear their teenage daughter come home late at night

4

Communication activities, Student's Book pages 151 & 146

- Groupwork. Divide the class into two groups: A and B. Explain that they are going to write a short story. Ask them to turn to their respective pages at the back of the book and to read the instructions. Students work in small groups (or in pairs, if they wish). Allow them plenty of time to complete their stories.
- Go round monitoring and give help where needed.

5

- Students work with a student from the other group and take it in turns to read their story out to each other.

Methodology advances
Word lists – definitions & dictations

Here are two more ideas for making effective in-class use of end-of-unit word lists.

Fast definitions

- *Make photocopies of one of the sections from the word list for each group of three to four students. Use the zoom feature to increase the size of the words. Cut the sheet up into separate words.*
- *Make groups of three or four students. In each group a student should shuffle the word slips and deal them out, face down on the table, equally to all players.*
- *Students take it in turns to pick up a word slip and attempts to convey the meaning of the word (by defining it, explaining it or giving an example of when or how you might use it) without saying the actual word itself or any form of it, and without resorting to 'cheating' (saying words it rhymes with, saying letters it starts with, etc.).*
- *The other players can look through their word list and make guesses until they find the right answer. That player wins the slip and places it in a WIN pile.*
- *The game continues with different players taking their turn until all slips have been won. The game winner is the person with the most slips in their WIN pile.*

Word list gap dictation

- *Prepare ten sentences, each containing one or more items from the word list. You can change the form of words if you wish to, e.g. putting a verb into the past tense. Underline these words in your notes.*
- *In class, dictate the sentences, but when you come to an underlined word, say 'gap' or a nonsense word of your choice. Students write down the sentences, leaving gaps where you dictate them.*
- *Students then compare sentences with a partner, to check that they have written them down correctly.*
- *Working in pairs, they should now look through the word lists and see if they can find suitable words to fill the gaps.*

If you want something extra ...

Photocopiable activity, page 253
Teaching notes, page 208

11D | The New Music Award

What the lesson is about

Theme	Entries for the New Music Award
Speaking	Discussing a device and how it works
Listening	New Music Award
Grammar	Hypothetical present & future situations
Speech feature	Dislocation

If you want a lead-in ...

Test before you teach

Methodology guidelines: Test before you teach, page xiv

- Write the following sentence starters on the board:
  I wish ...
  If only ...
  I hope ...
  It's time ...
  I'd rather ...
  I'd sooner ...
- Ask students to finish them, any way they like, to say something about their lives. Then put them in small groups to compare their ideas.
- Have a brief class feedback session, and note how accurately students use these phrases.

Introducing the theme: sounds

- Write the following on the board:
  cutlery crockery saucepans
  glasses sheets of paper
- Ask students to say what sort of sounds you could make with each.
- Ask, *How could you use these things to make music? What do you think it would sound like?*

Listening & speaking

In the listening, five people talk about their entries for the New Music Award and what they would do if they won.

1

Communication activities, Student's Book page 151

- Pairwork. Students read the information. They discuss how they think the device in the photo works and what types of sounds it produces. They then check their ideas on page 151 at the back of the book.
- You could tell students that they can find more information about this device on the following website: www.scoreforaholeintheground.org

Cultural note: Score for a Hole in the Ground

- The picture in the Student's Book shows *Score For a Hole in the Ground*, which won the New Music Award in 2005. It was designed by Jem Finer, who used to be in the punk band The Pogues. It is an installation inspired by suikinkutsu, the water chimes used in Japanese gardens to create a Zen-like ambience, and it is a sort of water instrument. Water from a pond drops water into an underground acoustic chamber filled with percussive instruments such as bells, bowls and chimes. The sounds go through pipes and are amplified by a huge metal horn. It has been described as a sonic sculpture.

2 3.22–3.26

- Students listen to the recording and make notes about each speaker and their entries for the New Music Award under the headings in the table.
- They could then compare their answers with a partner before you check with the class. Play the recording again if necessary.

Name	Sounds	Performance location or media	Title of work
Nigel	insects (e.g. flies, bees, mosquitoes)	Natural History Museum (entomology section)	The Butterfly Ball
Moira	trees (birdsong, wind, rain)	public parks, woodland (where sounds were recorded)	The Singing Ringing Tree
Damien	silence in football league stadiums / ambient sounds	CD	Deathly Silence
Annette	buildings and structures in local area (e.g. shopping centre, road bridges, tunnels)	school website	Vibrations
Mike	everyday metal objects (e.g. coins, keys, bracelets)	abandoned cinema	Metallic

3.22–3.26

1

A = Annie N = Nigel

A: This award.
N: Yeah?
A: Supposing you won it. What would you do?
N: Not much chance of that.
A: You don't know that.
N: Annie, there are professional sound artists going in for it. I haven't got a hope.
A: Alright, but just imagine you did win it. I mean, you could turn professional yourself.
N: Oh, come on. It's far too simple, my idea. I don't think the judges are going to be interested in the sounds of a few flies.
A: Don't be so negative. I think it's a great idea, composing a symphony with insects. Bees buzzing along, mosquitoes humming, and all those little rustling sounds that insects make when they're eating. Sounds really interesting – you'd get my vote.
N: Well, I'm not actually composing, really – just fusing the sounds, you know, combining them to create a symphonic whole.
A: Whatever. I think it stands a great chance. And I'm sure the Natural History Museum would be delighted to have it playing in their entomology section. Have you got a title for it, by the way?
N: 'The Butterfly Ball'.
A: Hmm. I wish I had your creativity.

2

JB = John Benton (presenter) MT = Moira Thomson

JB: … And I believe you've also submitted an entry for this year's New Music Award, Moira.
MT: That's right.
JB: Can you tell us something about it?
MT: Well, I'm calling the project 'The Singing Ringing Tree'. The name comes from a children's television programme in the 1960s.
JB: I remember it.
MT: You're showing your age now, John.
JB: I know. Terrible, isn't it? Never mind.
MT: Anyway.
JB: Yes, anyway. 'The Singing Ringing Tree'. Tell us about it.
MT: Well, my idea would be to record the sounds of nature in a number of trees around the country, then combine these sounds with music, orchestral music that would reflect the prevailing weather conditions when the recordings were made.
JB: Mmm. Sounds fascinating. Can you give us an idea of some of the sounds you'd pick up?
MT: Well, apart from birdsong, there'd be the sound of the wind – maybe a light breeze rustling the leaves in spring and summer or perhaps a howling gale rattling the branches in autumn or winter. And then of course there'd be the percussive sound of the rain either falling lightly or beating down heavily on the leaves.
JB: And on the microphones as well, I imagine.
MT: Yes, indeed, on the microphones as well.
JB: And where would you perform this piece – assuming it were chosen, that is?
MT: Well, the idea is to put on a series of concerts in the actual locations where the recordings were made – public parks and woodland, mainly. That way, I'd be giving something back to nature – returning the favour as it were.
JB: A very laudable idea. Well, thank you, Moira. Good luck with that – and with all your other projects as well, of course.
MT: Thank you, John.
JB: Unfortunately, it's time for us to go now, but *Sounds Interesting* will be back at the same time next Tuesday. Until then, it's good bye from me, John Benton, and my guest, sound artist Moira Thomson.

3

J = Jen D = Damien

J: All that money, Damien, just think what we could do with it.
D: What do you mean?
J: Well, we could pay off some of the mortgage for a start.
D: Don't be silly, Jen. It has to be invested in the project. It has to be used to pay for the recording and the performing and so on.
J: Oh. Right. It's a pity, that. Never mind. Just have to keep working, won't I? Anyway, carry on. What's this idea of yours?
D: Well, you know those one-minute silences they sometimes have at football matches – like, when an ex-player dies or something?
J: Yeah?
D: Well, I'd use the money to make a CD of those silences from football stadiums up and down the country – as many as possible.
J: That's a bit morbid, isn't it? What's the point of it?
D: Oh, for Goodness' sake, Jen, it's art. There doesn't need to be a point.
J: Oh right. Yeah. Still seems daft to me. Who's going to want to listen to a CD with silence on it?
D: It's not complete silence, is it? There's all the background sound – ambient sound, we call it. You'd be able to hear things like people coughing, mobile phones going off, maybe even the rumble of thunder in the distance.
J: Hmm. I can see them all queuing up outside the record shops to buy that one. What are you going to call it, anyway? 'The most boring CD in the world'?
D: That's the trouble with you, Jen. You just don't understand art.
J: Obviously not. Go on then, surprise me. What's the title?
D: 'Deathly silence'.
J: That's nice.

4

Annette Brown

…. Now, if your child does decide to continue with computer studies in years 12 and 13, you'll probably want to know the kind of thing they'll be getting up to. And in order to illustrate this, perhaps I could begin by talking about the school's involvement this year in the New Music Award. This has been very much a cross-curricular project involving pupils from the computer studies, technology and music departments. And what we've done is to join forces to create a piece of work which we have now submitted as an entry for the award. Some of you will have seen this on the school's website – it's called 'Vibrations', and basically, it's a collection of sounds taken from buildings and structures in the local area – the shopping centre, road bridges, tunnels and so on. The technology department collected the sounds using a device called an accelerometer, which is what engineers use to measure vibration – hence the title. And then computer studies pupils, with the help and advice of the music department, used software to convert these sounds into what we feel confident enough to call 'a piece of sound art'. Of course, the value of the project has been the process as much as the product, everyone working together in close collaboration. But if we were to go on and actually win the award – well, we can but hope – then we could use the money to buy more sophisticated equipment and software to improve the quality of the work on our website.

5
S = **Steve** **M** = **Mike**
S: What are you working on at the moment, Mike?
M: New Music Award. Don't know what I'm going to send in, though – something metallic probably. Hmm. Yeah. 'Metallic' It's a good title, that. I like it. Yep. I could use all sorts of things – just things I've got in the house, nothing special. Coins, keys, saucepans. Bracelets, maybe.
S: Mm. They make a nice jingly sound, bracelets.
M: Yeah. Jingles, jangles, clinks. Knives and forks, too – you can get a good clatter out of them.
S: Yeah. Cutlery. Good idea. Thought about the venue?
M: Ooh, no, don't know. It's early days yet.
S: Yeah, right.
M: That abandoned cinema on the edge of town, is it still there?
S: Think so.
M: Could do it there.

Language notes: listening

- ***Laudable*** means deserving praise.
- Something ***morbid*** is dark and depressing, often associated with death.

Cultural note: The Singing Ringing Tree

- *The Singing Ringing Tree* (or *Das Singende Klingende Bäumchem*) was a children's film which was made in communist East Germany in 1957. It had the look and feel of a Brothers Grimm fairy story, and it was shown in the form of a television series by the BBC in Britain in the 1960s and 1970s, with an English-language voice-over track. It was an unusual programme – and, as a result, gained a 'cult' status.

3
- Students work on their own and rank the entries in the recording in order from their favourite (1) to their least favourite (5). They then discuss their choices in small groups and decide on a winner and a runner-up to receive the music award.
- Students, working in the same groups, put together their own entry for the award. Encourage students to look back at the Vocabulary section on sounds in the previous lesson to help them with ideas. Tell them to choose one person to take notes for their entry on all the categories in the table in exercise 2, and to prepare for a presentation on their entry.
- Students choose a member from their group to present their entry to the rest of the class, using the notes they made. The class then votes for the best entry. Remind them that they cannot vote for their own entry.

GRAMMAR: hypothetic present & future situations

Language reference, Student's Book page 114
Methodology guidelines: Grammar boxes, page xiv

1
- Students correct the mistakes in the sentences by changing the underlined words. Point out that they should replace them with one or two words only. Remind them to look back at the grammar box to help them.
- They could then compare their answers with a partner before you check with the class.

1	didn't	6	walk
2	had	7	phoned
3	would get	8	bought
4	could stop	9	were to / was to
5	hope	10	would/could

2
- Pairwork. Ask students to look back at the sentences in exercise 1. Tell them to discuss the situations in which they might say these sentences and think about who or what the words in bold refer to. Point out that they can change the pronouns if necessary.

Language notes: hypothetical present & future situations

- The second conditional can be used to describe hypothetical situations in the present or future. It is formed by *if* + past simple/continuous, *would/might/could* + infinitive. Point out to students that the past simple is used to refer to hypothetical situations whether they are in the present or in the future. For example:
  If I <u>didn't have to</u> go to work, I could help you. (present)
  If we <u>were</u> to win, we would be famous. (future)
- It may help students to highlight possible errors. For example:
  It's time we left. NOT ~~*It's time we would leave*~~.
  I wish I could go. NOT ~~*I wish I would go*~~.
  I'd rather stay. NOT ~~*I'd rather I'd stay*~~.

Extra task: discussion

- Ask students to prepare ideas to answer the following questions: *What do you wish you didn't have to do this week? What do you hope will happen this week? What would you rather/sooner be doing now?*
- Have a class discussion.

SPEECH FEATURE: dislocation

1
- Read the language box with the class. Students then look back at conversation 5 in tapescript 3.26 on page 161, and underline examples of dislocation in the conversation between Mike and Steve.

Prefaces:
<u>Knives and forks</u>, too – you can get a good clatter out of <u>them</u>.
<u>That abandoned cinema on the edge of town</u>, is <u>it</u> still there?

Tags:
<u>It</u>'s a good title, <u>that</u>.
I could use all sorts of <u>things</u> – <u>just things I've got in the house</u>, nothing special.
<u>They</u> make a nice jingly sound, <u>bracelets</u>.

2 3.27
- Students complete the sentences with an appropriate word. Point out that there may be more than one possibility.
- Students then listen to the recording to check their answers.
- Note that this exercise provides models for students to use in exercise 3 and also revises collocations from the course book. Sentences 1–6 revise collocations from Units 1–6, and sentences 7 and 8 include language from this unit.

Suggested answers:

1 trousers	5 parking
2 song	6 upbringing
3 dustmen	7 newspaper
4 voice	8 window/door

3

Communication activities, Student's Book pages 140 & 153

- Groupwork. Divide the class into two groups: A and B. Ask them to turn to their respective pages at the back of the book and to read the instructions for their group. They write six sentences using the words listed which include an example of dislocation, like the ones in exercise 2. Go through the example with the class first. Explain that they need to leave gaps in their sentences where the noun in bold should go. They should then write a second sentence to clarify the meaning of the first sentence, so that another student will be able to guess the missing noun.

4

- Students pair up with a student from another group. They show their sentence to their partner for them to complete. They then check their partner's answer.

Alternative procedure: paired writing

- With stronger classes, students could do exercises 3 and 4 in pairs.

Language note: dislocation

- In sentences with dislocation, the noun is often used with the definite article *the*, possessive adjectives *my, your, her, his* etc, and determiners *this, that, these, those*. This is certainly the case with the sentences in exercise 2 in the unit. The speaker, in most cases, is clarifying the meaning of the pronoun, and is talking to someone about something which is shared knowledge.

IF YOU WANT SOMETHING EXTRA …

Photocopiable activity, page 254
Teaching notes, page 209

Answer key

11 Review

Student's Book page 174

1

1 all of ~~we~~ us; every ~~successes~~ success
2 Neither of my parents; have no ~~any~~ (*or* haven't ~~no~~ any cousins)
3 ~~is~~ has plenty of space; each of the caravans ~~are~~ is
4 most trains (*or* most of the trains); some ~~times~~ time
5 quite a few of us; see each ~~another~~ other (*or* ~~each~~ one another)
6 For all ~~that~~ his attention; many of ~~the~~ which
7 just a couple ~~of~~ now (*or* just a couple of them now); there's ~~other~~ another in the sideboard
8 ~~a~~ very little alcohol; every other ~~days~~ day

2

Suggested answers:
1 you would stop / you'd stop
2 knew how to play / could play
3 hope; they missed / they were to miss
4 were
5 would / 'd rather / sooner you
6 time you learned
7 it weren't; would be
8 there were / having; wouldn't it / don't you think it would

3

1 C 2 A 3 A 4 C 5 B 6 A 7 B 8 A 9 C
10 A 11 B 12 B

4

1 in; on; in
2 by; at
3 off; at; off
4 out of; in; by
5 out of; at; on
6 off; off

12A | Science fact

What the lesson is about

Theme	Scientific facts about everyday things
Speaking	Answering questions about why everyday things happen
Listening	Jigsaw listening giving scientific answers to questions about everyday things
Vocabulary	Words with more than one meaning
Grammar	Plurals & number
Did you know?	Science in UK schools

If you want a lead-in …

Test before you teach

Methodology guidelines: Test before you teach, page xiv

- Write the following nouns on the board and ask students to tell you which ones are plural:
  trousers children police feet fish athletics
  media fungus homework sheep
  (first row: all plural (although *fish* is also the singular form of the word); second row: *athletics*, *fungus* and *homework* are not plural; *media* is a collective noun that can take either a singular or plural verb; *sheep* (like *fish*) could be singular or plural)
- Ask students to say what the plural of these words are:
  tooth (teeth) *phenomenon* (phenomena)
  aircraft (aircraft) *knife* (knives)

Introducing the theme: science facts

- Ask students, *What's the most interesting or amazing scientific fact you know?* Tell them to write it down. Then ask volunteers to tell the class their fact. Ask other students if they believe it or would like to challenge it. Find out which facts are most interesting.

Speaking & listening

The listening is based on a popular column from the *New Scientist* weekly magazine in which people ask questions about why everyday things happen. Many of the questions appear to be quite simple but have a complex scientific answer.

1

- Groupwork. This exercise prepares students for the jigsaw listening that follows. Students work in two groups, A and B, and try to answer the questions for their group.

Alternative procedure: discussion

- If you are unable to do the paired listening with your class, follow the procedure below.
- Divide the class into groups of four. There are two As and two Bs in each group. Students read their questions and try to answer them.
- In their groups, students discuss their thoughts and their answers to each of the questions.
- Discuss the exercise together. As a class, agree on one answer for each question. Play tapescripts 3.28–3.39 for students to check their answers. How many did the class get right?

2 3.28–3.33 & 3.34–3.39

- Tell students that they are going to organize this listening activity themselves. Each group will listen to a different recording, in the same room, at the same time. Put out to students that in real life, there is usually a lot of background noise when we are listening. This exercise provides practice in blanking out that noise to focus on what is being said.
- Put the groups at different ends of the room. Give each group a CD player. Ask them to appoint one person who will be in charge of playing the CD, pausing where they feel it is necessary. Set a time limit of fifteen minutes for students to listen to the recording and make notes on what they hear.

3

- Students now work with a partner from the other group. They ask them to try and answer their questions from exercise 1 and then give them the information from their notes.
- Go round monitoring and give help where needed.
- Check the answers with the class. Ask students how they felt about taking a more active role in organization of the task.

See tapescript below for answers.

3.28–3.33

Group A
1 Why is the sea salty?
Salts and minerals such as sodium chloride, potassium and magnesium are what make the sea salty, but where do they come from? There are three main sources, the first of these being the Earth's rivers, which wash the minerals out of the ground and into the sea. Water in rivers is only very slightly salty because of their constant flow and replenishment by rainfall and springs. Sea water, on the other hand, has nowhere to go – it is held captive in the world's oceans. And when it is evaporated by the sun's heat, the minerals are left behind, making it much saltier than rivers and most lakes. The other main sources of minerals are submarine volcanism – that is, the eruption of underwater volcanoes – and hydrothermal vents, or holes in the ocean floor which pump minerals into the sea.

2 Why does our mouth dry up when we are nervous?
Speaking in public can cause us to become nervous and our mouth and throat to dry up. But what goes on in our bodies to make this occur? Basically what happens is that our body is preparing itself for a 'fight or flight' reaction, the kind of reaction which helps animals – including humans – deal with emergency situations such as attacks from enemies. What's known as the sympathetic nervous system starts working and any unnecessary functions are shut down, and that includes the digestive system: who needs to think about eating in times of danger? As a result, the production of saliva is stopped – causing the mouth to dry up – and the body's energy is used instead to prepare itself to deal with the stressful situation: blood is redirected away from the digestive system to our muscles and our heart rate and breathing rate increase. When the danger has passed and you can think once again about eating, the parasympathetic nervous system takes over and returns the body to normal. That's why it's sometimes called the 'rest and digest' system.

3 Why do clothes look darker when they're wet?
The simple answer to this question is because they reflect less light. Let's see how that works. When light from the Sun or a light bulb lands on a piece of clothing, some of it is reflected back from the clothing to the eyes of the person looking at it. That gives the observer the sensation of seeing the cloth as having a certain level of brightness. Now, as we know, cloth does not have a completely smooth, regular surface – it's made up of lots of tiny individual fibres and microfibres, thousands of them. When the cloth gets wet, water fills in the gaps between each of these fibres and as a result, much less light gets reflected back to our eyes – instead it gets refracted, bent away in a different direction, away from our eyes. And this makes the cloth look darker. The same principle applies to other porous objects like paper, concrete pavements or sand – think about that the next time you go to the beach.

4 What do seals drink?
Like other mammals seals cannot drink much sea water because of its high salt content, so where do they get their fresh water from? Well, most of it comes from the fish, squid, octopus and other things they eat, since water is a by-product of food when it is broken down. Some seals are also known to eat snow, particularly at times when they aren't catching much fish – when females, for example, are feeding their young on land and have reduced their intake of food.

5 What causes the sound of thunder?
Thunder is caused by lightning. But then what causes lightning? Well, in a storm there may be a build up of positive and negative charges in the clouds. When the build up becomes strong enough, there is an electrical discharge, a flow of electricity which we see as a bolt or flash of lightning. There's a similar effect when you walk on a synthetic carpet and then touch an electrical conductor like a doorknob or even another person and the negative charge flows away from your finger in a spark. The difference though between that spark and a bolt of lightning is that lightning heats the surrounding air to over 27,000 degrees Celsius – that's over four times hotter than the surface of the Sun. And because this heating occurs within a tiny fraction of a second, there is an explosive expansion of the air around the bolt, and, like an explosion, the rapidly expanding waves of compressed air create the noise we hear as a clap of thunder.

6 Why are eggs egg-shaped?
It's not such a silly question. They could after all be cylindrical or square-shaped, but then they would be rather uncomfortable for the bird to lay. In fact, one explanation for the egg's shape is that it is a natural consequence of the egg-laying process. At the start of its passage down the oviduct inside the bird's body, the egg is actually spherical, but its shell is soft and it transforms into the ovoid shape we are familiar with because of the way the bird's muscles contract around it. When it is laid the shell hardens and the ovoid shape remains fixed. This offers the egg certain advantages: it enables eggs to fit neatly and cosily in the nest, reducing heat loss and making the most of the available space. Also, a spherical egg could easily roll off or out of the nest, whereas a more pointed shape means the egg rolls around in a circle. Finally, and on a rather less serious note, the egg's shape enables it to fit into the egg holders in fridges.

3.34–3.39

Group B

1 Why is the sky blue?
The first thing to take into account when answering this question is that although sunlight appears to be white, it's actually made up of all the different colours of the rainbow – so that's red, orange, yellow, green, blue, indigo and violet. Another important point to recognize is that the Earth's atmosphere is composed mostly of nitrogen and oxygen – in fact, these two gases make up no less than 99% of it. Now, when the sunlight passes through the atmosphere and hits the nitrogen and oxygen gas molecules, it gets scattered in all different directions – it no longer travels in one continuous straight line to our eyes, but gets pushed out all over the place. And because the blue light has a higher frequency than most of the other colours, because it travels as shorter, smaller waves of light, more of it is scattered around the sky. So whichever direction you look in, some of this scattered blue light will reach your eyes, and it's this which causes the sky to appear blue.

2 Why can biting on aluminium foil be painful?
If you have fillings in your teeth, you may well have felt pain when accidentally biting on a piece of aluminium foil. What happens to cause this pain? Basically, you are setting up a kind of battery in your mouth. When two dissimilar metals are separated by an electrolyte – that is, a liquid which conducts electricity – an electrical current will flow between them. In this case, the current flows from the aluminium foil to the mercury filling via your saliva, the electrolyte. This current then travels to the nerve in the tooth's root, causing you to feel that awful rush of pain.

3 Why don't we laugh when we tickle ourselves?
Most of us have a ticklish spot somewhere on the body – it might be the neck, behind the knee, the armpits, the soles of our feet or any other sensitive area. Curiously, what causes us to laugh is a feeling of unease, a mild form of panic rather like that which we experience when a spider crawls over our hand. There is a certain lack of control which causes us to become tense and we start giggling or laughing uncontrollably. When we tickle ourselves there is no such tension or surprise and we are in complete control. Part of our brain – the cerebellum – tells us there's nothing to panic about, it's only us that's doing the tickling. So, no tension, no laughter.

4 Why does a whip crack?
You may have seen whips being cracked in cowboy films to make horses go faster or at the circus to makes animals perform tricks, but what causes them to make that loud explosive noise? For many years it was thought that the noise came from the tip, the very end of the whip, travelling at twice the speed of sound. But recent research from applied mathematicians at the University of Arizona has shown otherwise. According to Alain Goriely and Tyler McMillen, the crack comes not from the tip of the whip but from the loop as it accelerates along the whip's length, reaching the speed of sound and creating a sonic boom. Whether it's the tip or the loop, the fact is that whip handlers have to work at supersonic speeds!

5 Why does a chip pan fire explode if you put water on it?
Domestic chip pan fires cause around 3,000 injuries each year in the UK. So it's important to know that if the pan bursts into flames when you're frying chips, the last thing you should do is pour water on it – a fireball is created which can cause very serious scalding and burning. But why is this? What happens exactly? The main problem is that the burning oil can reach temperatures of around 300 degrees Centigrade, much hotter than the 100 degrees at which water turns to steam. So water dropped onto the oil turns into an expanding bubble of superheated steam,

which spreads rapidly upwards and outwards spraying droplets of burning fat everywhere. Exposure to the surrounding air feeds the flames and sets off the fireball. The same kind of effect is produced when hot lava from volcanoes meets water, or when water comes into contact with hot, molten metal.

6 Why do we close our eyes when we sneeze?
No, it's not to stop our eyes popping out of our head! It's unlikely that enough air from our lungs will get into the back of our eyes to shoot them out. Some scientists suggest that we close our eyes to protect them, to stop microorganisms and particles from the sneeze getting into them. But then this too seems unlikely as the substances we sneeze are shot out of our nose at great speed – up to 165 kilometres an hour – and travel some distance away from the face. No, what seems a more probable explanation is that it is simply a reflex action, and one which occurs not just in the nose and eyes – a lot of other muscles also contract when we sneeze, in the throat, the diaphragm, the abdomen, the thighs and the back. You can try and force yourself to keep your eyes open when you sneeze, but it's extremely difficult.

Language notes: listening

- ***Fight or flight*** describes the primitive mechanism that prepares animals to fight or run away in times of danger.
- A ***spark*** is a small, short electric flash of light; a ***bolt*** (of lightning) is an electric flash of light.
- ***Saliva*** is the liquid produced by glands in your mouth.
- Objects that are ***porous*** have lots of small holes that allow air or water in.
- A ***fibre*** is a thin thread.
- Light is ***refracted*** when it hits a surface and changes direction.
- ***Ovoid*** means oval-shaped.
- An ***electrolyte*** is a liquid that electricity can pass through.

Extra task: science questions

- Ask students to work in teams to prepare their own set of five interesting science fact questions. Then mix the students and have a question and answer session.
- Alternatively, get students to think of two interesting questions for homework. Tell them to research their questions on the internet. Then, in the next lesson, put students in groups to ask their questions. Websites such as Ask.com are useful resources.

GRAMMAR: plurals & number

Language reference, Student's Book page 124
Methodology guidelines: Grammar boxes, page xiv

1
- Students underline the incorrect plural form in each group of words.
- Don't check answers at this stage. This will be done in the next exercise.

2
- Ask students to look at section A of the grammar box to check their answers to exercise 1. They then justify their answers to a partner as in the example.

Correct versions of incorrect plurals with explanations:
1 *kilos* – add *s* to abbreviated words ending in *o*.
2 *monkeys* – words ending in *y* which are preceded by a vowel, do not form their plural with *ies*.
3 *shelves* – several words ending in *f* or *fe* form their plural with *ves*.
4 *geese* – an irregular plural form.
5 *sisters-in-law* – in compound nouns consisting of noun + preposition + noun, the first word is made plural.
6 *appendices* or *appendixes* – words of Latin origin ending in *ix*, retain the original Latin plural ending *ices*; most also can be used in an English plural form by simply adding *es* to the singular. For a librarian the plural is *appendices*; for the medical profession it's *appendixes*. Words of Latin origin ending in *sis* have plurals ending in *ses*.
7 *formulae* or *formulas* – some words of Latin origin ending in *a* have plural forms ending in *ae*, though an English plural form can also be used by adding *s* to the singular. The other words in the group are formed from Latin words ending in *us*.
8 *stimuli* – word of Latin origin ending in *us*. The other words are from Greek (*phenomenon*, *criterion*) and Latin (*memorandum*).

3
- Students choose the correct alternatives to complete the sentences. Point out that more than one alternative may be possible.
- Don't check answers at this stage. This will be done in the next exercise.

1 they; them
2 some; it
3 is / was
4 both alternatives are possible
5 are
6 both alternatives are possible
7 These; are
8 much; homework; is

4
- Ask students to look at section B of the grammar box to check their answers to exercise 3. They then justify their answers to a partner as in the example in exercise 2.

Language notes: plurals & number

- Most nouns in English have regular plural endings, formed in one of the following ways:
  - by adding an 's' to the end of the noun
  - by adding 'es' when the noun when the noun ends in 'ch', 'sh', 'x', 's', or 'z'.
  - by removing the final letter and adding *ies* when the noun ends in a *y*, which is preceded by a consonant.
- Some words ending in 'o' take 's' and others take 'es'. If they are abbreviations, they take 's', e.g. *kilos*.
- With words ending in 'f' or 'fe', the ending often becomes 'ves' in the plural, e.g. *knives*.
- There are, however, exceptions to these rules and some nouns have plural endings that do not follow any of these patterns (see the Language reference section in the Student's Book).
- You may also wish to point out plural forms that are confusing:

nouns that look plural but are uncountable and refer to singular forms:
aerobics *economics*
nouns that refer to single items but are plural:
jeans *scissors*
collective nouns that can be both singular and plural:
team *media*

5
- Pairwork. Students discuss the sentences in exercise 3 with a partner and say how true each one is for themselves, giving as many details as they can.

Extra task: sentence correction

- Ask students to read the Language Reference section and use it to write four correct and four incorrect sentences for their partners to look at. For example: *I haven't heard the latest news* (correct); *Three kiloes of potatos is too much to eat in one meal* (incorrect).
- Students exchange their lists and correct each other's wrong sentences.

Did you know?

1
- Pairwork. Students read the information and discuss the questions with a partner.

Extra task: discussion

- Ask students to tell you what the causes of declining interest might be, and what solutions they could suggest.

Web research tasks

➲ *Methodology guidelines: Web research tasks, page xiv*

- Ask students to research and make their own science fact quiz by thinking up interesting questions and researching the answers on the internet.
- Collect in the quizzes and use them as activities to end our lessons with. You can use the writer of the quiz as the quizmaster.

Methodology advances
Exam overview

Straightforward Advanced *is a general English course. It isn't specifically preparing your students to take any exams – though it is very possible that some of your students will need or want to take a high-level exam. For your guidance, here are some of the international exams at levels that might be appropriate for students studying this book. When looking at these descriptions, remember that* Straightforward Advanced *is at C1 level.*

University of Cambridge ESOL
- ***Certificate of Advanced English (CAE)*** *This is a general English exam at C1 level. It is accepted in many places as an appropriate level for entering higher education and for many jobs that require use of English as part of the work.*
- ***Certificate of Proficiency in English (CPE)*** *This is a very challenging exam at C2 level and tests a level of English that approaches university-educated native speaker level. Note that this exam is above the level of this Student's Book.*
- ***Business English Certificate (BEC) Higher*** *This exam tests the four skills of reading, writing, listening and speaking but focuses on business contexts, topics and language.*

British Council, IDP: IELTS Australia and University of Cambridge ESOL
- ***International English Language Testing System (IELTS)*** *The main reason for taking this multi-level exam is to get a high-enough score that will allow you take up an academic place or professional post. Many universities, colleges, training courses, companies and professional organizations recognize the qualification as proof of English language level – though the minimum score they will accept varies.*

Educational Testing Service (ETS)
- ***Test of English as a Foreign language (TOEFL)*** *This is similar to IELTS – but is more widely accepted in certain countries – and specifically in the USA. If a student wants to study in the States, this is often the qualification required.*

City and Guilds
- ***ESOL Expert level (formerly Pitman ESOL exam)*** *This is a speaking qualification at C1 level. It is unusual in being a speaking test conducted with a teacher you already know (rather than an unknown visiting examiner). The resulting recording is then sent away and marked by the exam board.*

Pearson Language Assessments
- ***London Tests of English Level 4*** *A multi-skills exam based on real-life use of language. Quite a lot shorter than the equivalent Cambridge ESOL CAE exam.*

If you want something extra …

➲ *Photocopiable activity, page 255*
➲ *Teaching notes, page 209*

12B | Wearable technology

What the lesson is about

Theme	Innovations in wearable technology
Speaking	Design and Technology competition
Reading	*Wearable electronics*: three texts about wearable technology
Vocabulary	Compound adjectives (technology)

If you want a lead-in ...

Pre-teach key words: technology

- Write the following words on the board, and ask students to check their meanings:
  sensors wires cables antenna computer chips
- Ask students to describe machines and gadgets that they have, or are in the room, using the words.

Introducing the theme: wearable technology

- Ask students, *What technology are you wearing or carrying with you?* Elicit *watch, mobile phone, iPod,* etc.
- Ask students to think about how they could describe this technology, for example, *portable, light, easy-to-use, up-to-date*. Then put the students in small groups to show each other what technological devices they have and to describe them to each other.

Vocabulary: compound adjectives (technology)

1

- Students complete the beginning of the compound adjectives in bold in the sentences with the participles in the box.
- Note that students will be able to use some of these adjectives when they do the speaking activity in lesson 12C.
- They could then compare their answers with a partner before you check with the class.

1 generated; drawn
2 saving; consuming
3 inducing
4 moving
5 conditioned; heated; guzzling; called
6 powered

2

- Pairwork. Students discuss the opinions expressed in exercise 1 with a partner.

Language notes: compound adjectives (technology)

- ***Computer-generated*** means made by a computer.
- If a piece of equipment is described as ***labour-saving***, it is something that saves people a lot of work (labour).
- If something is ***stress-inducing*** it causes stress.
- A ***gas-guzzling*** vehicle uses too much petrol (in US English, petrol is called *gas*).
- Note that *-ed* participles are abbreviated passives e.g. ***computer-generated***, whereas *-ing* participles are active e.g. ***labour-saving***.

Reading

The reading is three texts about recent innovations in 'wearable technology'. The first text is about a T-shirt that plays music when the wearer mimes playing a guitar. The second text is about an 'intelligent' bag that alerts the owner when there is something missing in it, lights up to make it easier to see inside and gives information such as the weather forecast and the latest news. The third text is about a shoe with an inbuilt computer that checks the health and improves the comfort and performance of the shoe for the wearer.

1

- Students look at the photos of wearable technological innovations. They then read the titles for the three texts about these innovations and predict what technological features each item might have.

2

- Students read the texts and check their ideas in exercise 1.

3

- Students read the texts again and complete the sentences with the letters for each of the items of wearable technology.
- They could then compare their answers with a partner before you check with the class.

1 C – *as well as exchange files with other Verb for Shoe users*
2 B – *The fabric of the bag also illuminates when there is insufficient light, making it easier for users to see inside and find what they are looking for.*
3 C – *took Hollywood by storm when it was presented at an exclusive preview there, with celebrities raving about its many features*
4 A – *even by players without significant musical or computing skills*
5 B – *make building with fabric as easy as playing with Lego™ blocks*
6 A – *there are no trailing cables for budding rock guitarists to trip over or become entangled in*
7 C – *it may one day come within the reach of the pockets of those of us that are not Hollywood celebrities*
8 B – *but what makes the BYOB so different is its versatility*
9 A – *which is adaptable to almost any kind of apparel*
10 C – *It responds to any changes in the level of activity in a matter of milliseconds.*

4

- Pairwork. Students discuss with a partner which of the items of wearable technology they would most be interested in owning, and give their reasons why.

Language notes: reading

- To ***play air guitar*** is to pretend to play a guitar by miming the action without actually holding a guitar.
- ***Lego™ bricks*** are small plastic bricks for children, with which many things can be built from houses to space stations. They are made by the Lego company.
- You could point out other compounds, for example, *left-handed*, and *easy-to-use*.

Extra task: discussion

- Ask students to consider and discuss the following questions:
  What sort of people might the three items appeal to?
  What problems might occur with the technology of these items?
  Which of these items are most likely to succeed commercially? Why?

SPEAKING

1

- Groupwork. Put students into small groups and explain that they are going to submit a project for a Design and Technology competition.
- Ask students to look at the points they need to consider before they choose one of the projects listed. They should then discuss how they are going to present their project for the competition, and choose the spokesperson to present their project.
- Go round monitoring and give help where needed.

2

- Students present their project to the rest of the class. The class then votes for the best project. Remind students that they cannot vote for their own project.

Extra task: writing descriptions

- Ask students to write a description of their item for homework. This could be a scientific description or a description in the form of a sales advertisement.

IF YOU WANT SOMETHING EXTRA ...

➋ *Photocopiable activity, page 256*
➋ *Teaching notes, page 209*

12c | Sport technology

What the lesson is about

Theme	Technology & sport
Speaking	Debate about technology in the home
Listening	A radio discussion about sport technology with one speaker who is pro-technology and the other speaker who would like technology in sport to be restricted
Vocabulary	Verb affixes
Pronunciation	Intonation (feelings)

If you want a lead-in ...

Discussion starters

Methodology guidelines: Discussion starters, page xiv

- *Do you do or watch a lot of sport? Which sports do you enjoy participating in? Which sports do you watch live or on TV?*
- *To what extent has technology become important in your favourite sports? Has technology improved the sport? Has it improved your enjoyment of the sport?*

Pre-teach key words: sport

- Write the words below on the board (they are all in the listening text):
  referee umpire spectator racket
  rally pole court vault
  footwear headgear linesman doping
- Ask students to say which sports they would connect the words with.
- (Possible answers: referee – football; umpire – tennis, cricket, etc; spectator – any sport that has an audience; racket – tennis, badminton, squash, etc; rally – tennis, badminton, etc; pole – pole vault; court – tennis, badminton, basketball, netball, etc; footwear – any sport for which shoes are worn; headgear – baseball, American football, cycling, etc; linesman – football, tennis, etc; doping – usually athletic sports in which participates can improve their performance though banned substances.)

Listening

This listening is a radio discussion in three parts about the advances in technology used in sports. Part 1 gives examples of sports which have benefited from technological developments. In Part 2 two sports experts express their feelings and put forward their arguments for and against the development of technology in sports. In Part 3 they give more details about their arguments. Note that this listening provides a model for the speaking activity which follows later in the unit.

1

- Pairwork. Students discuss the different ways in which technology may influence the sports in the box.

2 3.40

- Explain that students are going to listen to the first part of a radio discussion on technology and sport.
- Ask them to read the questions. Then play Part 1 of the recording for the students to answer the questions.
- They could then compare their answers with a partner before you check with the class. Play the recording again if necessary.

1 athletics, swimming, tennis, football
2 Athletics: Marathon runners are electronically tagged; materials' technologists are constantly working on improving footwear and clothing equipment (e.g. the pole vault, which changed from the original hardwood to bamboo, then steel and finally fibreglass).
Swimming: Swimmers now wear full-length suits.
Tennis: Tennis racket design has also changed radically.
Football: Use of microphones and earphones used by football referees.

3.40

Part 1
Hello and welcome to *For and Against*, where this week we'll be discussing the following statement: *There is too much technology in sport*. And by 'technology' we mean any human-made means, any method, machine, device or piece of clothing or equipment which is developed using scientific knowledge for practical purposes. Exactly what those purposes are in sporting terms, I'll leave for our guests to say, but it's clear that in recent times technology has revolutionized the world of sport.

In athletics, for example, marathon runners are now electronically tagged and their progress during a race can be followed online; materials technologists are constantly working on improving footwear and clothing for the different athletics events; and their work extends to equipment, such as the pole in the pole vault – we've seen there a progression from hard wood to bamboo in the early 1900s, followed by steel in the 1950s and the more flexible fibreglass in the 60s.

Many swimmers now wear full-length swimsuits which are made from material designed to reduce friction in the water. These made their first appearance as recently as the year 2000, in Sydney, Australia. And tennis rackets – both their material and their design – now bear little resemblance to those used in the 1970s when personalities like Bjorn Borg or John McEnroe graced the tennis courts. It would be strange, unthinkable even, for players of the calibre of Rafa Nadal to appear on court now with a racket made of wood.

And then of course there is the use of microphones and earphones by football referees, who are now able to communicate more easily with their linesmen and the fourth official.

Now, our two studio guests today will be debating the extent to which these developments and others like them are beneficial to sport; whether technology should continue in the same way to help us achieve our sport-related goals or whether it is having too much influence and should be kept out of sport, or at least be subject to more restrictions.

Cultural notes: tennis players

- Bjorn Borg (born 1956) is a former Swedish tennis champion of the 1970s and 1980s. He won eleven Grand Slam titles: six French Open titles and five consecutive Wimbledon titles. John McEnroe (born 1959) is form New York and was a contemporary of Borg, who won seven Grand Slam titles: four US Open titles and three Wimbledon titles. Borg was cool and showed no emotion on court, whereas McEnroe was fiery and confrontational, and regularly argued with the umpire.
- Rafael 'Rafa' Nadal Parera, (born 1986 in Mallorca) is a Spanish tennis player, ranked number two in the world in 2007. He is a three-time Grand Slam champion, having won three consecutive French Open singles titles (2005-07), and has twice been a runner-up at Wimbledon (2006-07). Nadal is undefeated in his career at the French Open, having won all 21 matches he has played en route to his three championships.

3 **3.41**

- Ask students to read the question. Then play Part 2 of the recording. Students write notes on the three arguments in favour of technology and three arguments against them.
- They could then compare their answers with a partner before you check with the class. Play the recording again if necessary.

Geoff Winning's three arguments in favour of technology:

- Technology enables athletes to improve their performance.
- Technology helps maximize safety in sport.
- Technology ensures a greater degree of fairness in sport.

Sally Plumtree's three arguments against technology:

- Technology has come to dominate sport and as a result overshadows human achievement.
- Technology reduces the human touch in sport, making it more mechanical and less entertaining.
- Sports people can use technologies which endanger health, such as blood and gene doping.

3.41

Part 2
P = Presenter GW = Geoff Winning
SP = Sally Plumtree

P: Let me introduce our guests. Firstly, we have Geoff Winning, who's a sports scientist and regular columnist for the magazine *Technosport*. Good morning, Geoff.

GW: Good morning.

P: And we also have with us Sally Plumtree, the successful former athlete and now an equally successful freelance sports journalist. Good morning, Sally.

SP: Hello, Peter.

P: Right, let's begin. For listeners who are new to our programme, both Geoff and Sally now have approximately one minute each to put forward their main arguments. Geoff, let's begin with you – you're very much pro-technology. Tell us why.

GW: Well, the effects of technology in sport cannot be understated. And there are basically three areas where its application is of tremendous benefit. The first of these, of course, is the fact that it enables athletes to improve their performance, to surpass their own limits. Some of the examples of developments you mentioned just now have led to humans running or swimming faster, jumping higher or in the case of tennis, hitting harder. Technology helps us to push out the boundaries of human achievement, to see just what the human body is capable of. Secondly, it helps to maximize safety in sport. Helmet design in cycling and hockey is an example of this, and so is the headgear used in amateur boxing, those heavily padded hats that protect boxers from soft tissue damage. And then finally, technology ensures a greater degree of fairness in sport. Now, you mentioned the use of microphones in football, but there is also the use of video evidence to help the referee in his job, and now in tennis, the Hawkeye system which creates virtual 3D images to help the umpire in disputed line calls. Performance, safety and justice – the three reasons why technology should continue to be used in sport.

P: Thank you, Geoff. Now, Sally, over to you. Why are you in favour of more restrictions in the use of technology?

SP: Well, like Geoff I, too, have three main arguments to support my case. Firstly, technology has come to dominate sport, so much so that I believe it overshadows human achievement and we are losing the raw physical challenge that is central to sporting competitions. When I was competing we depended much more on ourselves, on our own abilities and efforts, not on the work of scientists and engineers. It really was human achievement and not technological achievement that was on show. Secondly, I-I think that spectators realize this and their enjoyment of sporting events has been diminished as a result. This is particularly true with the video and computer technology used in the control of football and tennis matches. It reduces the human touch of sport, makes it more mechanical, less entertaining. Human error in refereeing decisions has always added that extra excitement to sport, particularly when there are fiery characters around like Wayne Rooney or John McEnroe, who you mentioned earlier. And finally, the prevailing climate of using technology to run that extra thousandth of a second faster encourages sportsmen and women to bend the rules, or to put it another way, to cheat. We see them using technologies which endanger health, such as blood doping, gene doping and all manner of drugs. So …

P: Thank you, Sally, have to stop you there. Time's up, but I think you made your points.

Cultural notes: technology in sport

- ***Hawkeye*** is the technology that permits umpires to review a 3D image of a shot being played in tennis in order to judge whether a ball was in or out.
- Wayne Rooney is an England international footballer, currently playing for Manchester United. As well as being very talented, he is a fiery and aggressive player, and was sent off in the quarter final of the World Cup in 2006.

4 **3.42**

- Students listen to Part 3 of the recording and decide if the statements are true or false.
- They could then compare their answers with a partner before you check with the class. Play the recording again if necessary.
- Ask students to work in pairs and discuss the following question: *Which of the two guests do you agree with most and why?*

1 T 2 F 3 F 4 T

3.42

Part 3
P = Presenter GW = Geoff Winning
SP = Sally Plumtree

P: Now, let's pick up on one or two of those points you made there. Interestingly, you both mentioned the role of technology in decision-making during football and tennis matches. Sally said it reduces the spectator's enjoyment. Would you agree with that, Geoff?
GW: Not at all, no. I'm absolutely certain that the cameras will only serve to heighten interest, to intensify the drama and the tension. And we'll still see the same displays of passion and anger from competitors – but they'll be directed more at themselves rather than at the referee or the umpire.
SP: Hmm, they'll certainly be good for match officials, but I really cannot see that they'll make a game more exciting. Anyway, I think there are other reasons why tennis in particular no longer captivates spectators like it used to. And it's all down to technology.
P: In what way?
SP: Well, it was always such an exciting sport before, with long rallies that had everyone on the edge of their seats. Then in the late 1970s, early 80s, players began using the oversize racket – the one with the very large head. And sure, tennis became a much faster sport, but there aren't so many of those rallies now, and there's a lot more dead time without any action, time when nothing's happening. And as a spectator, I find that dull.
GW: Maybe, but the oversize racket makes it easier to hit the ball, and that can only be a good thing for amateur players – let's not forget them.
P: OK. Some interesting points there. Geoff, let's go back to what you said about technology helping us to push out the boundaries of human achievement. Are all forms of technology acceptable in your book?
GW: Yes, I think if everyone has access to the same equipment, then virtually any technological innovation is acceptable.
SP: Oh right. So presumably then, doping is acceptable, as long as everyone has access to it. That's brilliant.
GW: I'm not suggesting that at all. That should be obvious. There is no way we can justify the use of performance-enhancing drugs or any kind of interference with our blood or genetic make-up. These practices are not permitted by sporting authorities, and for good reason. There are moral issues involved here, quite apart from the legal aspects and the potential dangers to our health.
P: Yes, you did use the word equipment, perhaps we should emphasize that.
GW: That's right. And its use has to be standardized by the relevant sporting authority. A good example of this is in the sport of cycling. Radical new designs in the 1980s and 90s meant that previous records were being smashed beyond recognition. The International Cycling Federation felt these so-called 'superbikes' were having too much influence on the sport and their huge cost gave richer countries an unfair advantage. So consequently they were banned from certain competitions such as the Olympics or the world hour record. It just shows that there are controls on the use of technology and we should feel safe in that knowledge.
P: Anything to say on that, Sally?
SP: Well, I'm pleased the Federation saw sense in the end, but I just think the whole episode highlights the uneasy relationship that exists …

Language notes: listening

- To ***pick up on*** something (in conversation) is to talk about it in more detail.
- ***It's down to…*** means *it's because of…*
- The question *Are all forms of technology acceptable **in your book**?* means 'Are all forms of technology acceptable to you?'

5
- Students check their answers in tapescripts 3.40–3.42 on pages 162 and 163.

Extra task: discussion

- Write the main points of the discussion on the recording on the board: the use of cameras, the use of helmets in boxing, improved racket technology
- Put students in groups of three or four to give their opinions about these three issues and debate them.
- Have a class feedback session.

Pronunciation: intonation (feelings)

1 3.43
- Pairwork. Students read out their exchange in the manner indicated in the brackets. Tell them to exaggerate their intonation as much as they can. Tell them to swap roles so that each of them has the chance to say both sentences in the manner indicated.
- Ask students to listen to the recording and pay particular attention to the intonation of the speakers. Then ask them to read out the exchange again. Ask them if they felt there was any improvement with their intonation.

2 3.44
- Make sure students understand all the terms to express feelings in the box. Play the recording. Students read the exchanges as they listen and match the feelings in the box with those of the speakers. Point out that more than one answer may be possible.

Suggested answers:

1	A worry	B reassurance
2	A admiration	B sarcasm
3	A curiosity	B irritation
4	A surprise / enthusiasm	B indifference
5	A enthusiasm	B suspicion

3.44

1
A: Oh, I wonder what that noise is.
B: Oh, that always happens when you turn it on.

2
A: Oh, isn't he a talented cyclist?
B: Oh, yeah. I mean, no one else could pedal like that, could they?

3
A: Oh, I wonder if he works with computers for a living.
B: Oh, I don't know. Ask him if you want to.

4
A: Oh, are you coming with us as well?
B: Oh, yeah, I thought I'd tag along – see what was going on.

5
A: Oh, yeah, John's going to be there, too.
B: Oh, yes, I heard that, too. That's interesting.

3
- Students now practice reading out the exchanges with their partner, using the same intonation as they heard the speakers use in the recording.
- You could play each part of the recording again, for the students to listen to and then practise the exchange.

Language notes: intonation (feelings)
- Ask students how we express feeling through intonation. Point out that the stronger the feeling, the wider the intonation pattern. The intonation is flat when expressing indifference but very wide when expressing enthusiasm. Point out too that the intonation tends to fall when the speaker is certain or confident about what they are saying, and tends to rise when the speaker is unsure and tentative. The intonation rises to express surprise or worry but falls when expressing admiration or irritation.
- Encourage students to start with their intonation very 'high' when expressing the strong feelings, and to think of their 'pattern' swooping up and down.
- Point out the role of stress when saying these phrases. When using sarcasm, for example, certain words are over-stressed (e.g. the word *pre**su**mably* in the example sentence).
- In more general terms, you may wish to remind students that English has a very wide intonation pattern, and that exaggerating the pattern is a good idea (especially for speakers of languages – Latin languages for example – with a narrower pattern).

4
- Students read the exchanges again, expressing a different feeling from the one in the box.
- You could then ask them to join up with another pair and repeat their exchanges for the other pair to guess what feelings are being expressed.

Extra task: dialogues
- Ask students to work in pairs to write an expressive three line dialogue (person A says something, person B says something, person A responds). Tell them that they are going to act out their dialogue expressing a different feeling in each line.
- When students are ready, ask a few pairs to act out their dialogues. The rest of the class must say which feelings are being expressed.
- A way of adding context to this activity is to cut out some pictures of people talking from magazines (e.g. two shoppers in the street, two people on a TV programme). Hand out the pictures to pairs, and ask them to improvize their dialogues around the pictures.

SPEAKING

1
- Groupwork. Put students into two groups, A and B. (For larger classes, divide the class into four groups – two Group As and two Group Bs).
- Ask the students to read the statement. Tell Group A that they should agree with the statement, and to brainstorm and note down as many different arguments to support it. Tell Group B that they disagree with the statement, and to brainstorm and note down as many arguments to show why they disagree with it.

2
- The groups decide on the three most convincing arguments from exercise 1 and choose a representative from the group to present their case to the rest of the class. Tell them that they have just one minute to put forward their argument.
- Give them a few minutes so that the group can make final preparations for the presentation. Refer them to the *Useful language* box at the bottom of the page. Then they present their case to the class.
- Go round monitoring and give help where needed.

3
- The discussion now opens up to the whole class. (For larger classes, the groups join up with another group, so that a Group A is working with a Group B.) Tell students that they can expand on the points their representative made, adding further arguments and examples to the ones that were made. They should also make counter arguments and try to discredit the views of the other group. Remind students to look at the Useful language box at the bottom of the page to help them.

VOCABULARY: verb affixes

1
- Students complete the sentences from the recording with the correct form of the word in brackets.
- They could then compare their answers with a partner before you check with the class.

1	enables	6	heighten; intensify
2	maximize / ise	7	captivates
3	ensures	8	justify
4	dominate	9	emphasize / ise
5	endanger	10	standardized / ised

2
- Ask students to underline the affixes used in exercise 1. They then use these same affixes to form verbs from the groups of words listed. Point out that some of the words will require further spelling changes.
- They could then compare their answers with a partner before you check with the class.

1	categorize / ise	summarize / ise	stabilize / ise
2	classify	identify	exemplify
3	enlarge	encourage	enrage
4	assassinate	differentiate	evaluate
5	threaten	flatten	lengthen

3
- Students choose the correct alternative to complete the sentences.
- Note that you could refer the students back to the Vocabulary section in lesson 3C where there are several examples of *over-* used to form verbs.

- They could then compare their answers with a partner before you check with the class.

1	download	5	outlived
2	overstretch	6	overcome
3	outclassed	7	undergo
4	undercharged	8	outweigh

Language note: verb affixes

- You may wish to point out the stress rules (or tendencies) with the verb affixes in this lesson.
  Prefixes tend not be stressed in English, e.g *en**able**, en**sure**, en**dan**ger*.
  Some suffixes cause the syllable before the suffix to be stressed, e.g. *-ify*: *in**tens**ify*.
  Other suffixes cause the syllable next but one to the suffix to be stressed, e.g. *-ate* and *-ize*: ***cap**tivate, **dom**inate, revo**lu**tionize, **stan**dardize*.
  With verbs formed using particles, the particles tend not to be stressed: *under**state**, over**sha**dow*.
  Note, however, these are tendencies with plenty of exceptions.

4

- Pairwork. Students tell their partner how true the statements and opinions in exercise 3 are for themselves. The students listening can show interest in what their partner is saying if relevant by asking follow-up questions.

Extra task: verb affixes

- Ask students in pairs to write five similar either/or sentences using other words with verb affixes from the lesson. Tell them to exchange their sentences with a different pair. Can they guess the correct word in the sentence?

IF YOU WANT SOMETHING EXTRA ...

➲ *Photocopiable activity, page 257*
➲ *Teaching notes, page 209*

12D | The end?

What the lesson is about

Theme	Revision of the topics, grammar & vocabulary covered in the Student's Book
Speaking	Ranking & selecting photographs *Did you know?* revision quiz
Vocabulary	Revision of vocabulary covered in Units 1–3
Grammar	Revision of grammar covered in Units 1–3
Did you know?	Revision of topics covered in Units 1–3

If you want a lead-in ...

Discussion starters

Methodology guidelines: Discussion starters, page xiv

- *What do you feel you have learnt from the course? What is the most interesting topic covered in the Student's Book? What would you like to learn more about?*
- *What was your favourite speaking activity? Which grammar activity did you find most difficult? Which vocabulary exercise did you find most useful?*

Introducing the theme: revision

- Ask students to choose one topic from the Student's Book which particularly interested them.
- Students turn to the appropriate page of their books. They read about the topic and make notes about it.
- Put students into groups of three or four. Using their notes, they tell each other about their favourite topics.
- Ask some of the students to tell the class about their chosen topics.

Methodology advances
Is promoting autonomy the key?

- *The term* learner autonomy *refers to ways in which the student takes more control over their own learning, taking more of the decisions and responsibility. The idea of encouraging it is based on a belief that it is empowering, that the more personal involvement and investment a student has in their work, the more motivated they are likely to be and the more likely to succeed. At all levels of language learning there are good arguments for promoting more learner autonomy, but perhaps it is at Advanced level where it becomes an absolute necessity.*
- *At lower levels, a teacher could make a reasonable case for always keeping the class working on the same things at the same pace, for always deciding things on behalf of students and for allowing the students to remain fairly dependent on the teacher's advice and feedback. At Advanced level the reasons that support such an argument no longer hold any water. Students are able to clearly express their own views, they know a lot about language learning and teaching (having likely been a 'subject' for some years), are probably studying for quite varied reasons, like different things, have very different, perhaps fossilized problems, and so on.*
- *While it is certainly valuable to study a single Student's Book together to give shape and coherence to the course programme, it is important to also allow, encourage and even require a good degree of autonomy so that the course can actually respond to their individual characters, needs, tastes, working styles, strengths and weaknesses.*

Revision Units 1–3

Vocabulary

1
- Students choose the correct alternative to complete the sentences.
- Don't check answers at this stage. This will be done in the next exercise.

2
- Students check their answers to exercise 1 in Units 1–3.

1 D 2 A 3 C 4 A 5 B 6 B 7 D 8 C

Word building

1
- Students complete the sentences with the correct form of the word in brackets.
- Don't check answers at this stage. This will be done in the next exercise.

2
- Students check their answers on pages 13 and 33.

1 fluency; accuracy
2 sadness; disappointment
3 procedures
4 imaginative
5 harmful
6 unexpected

3
- Pairwork. Students read the statements in exercise 1 again and discuss with their partner how true they are for themselves.

Grammar

1
- Students choose the correct alternative to complete the sentences.
- Students then check their answers on pages 9, 17 and 23.

1 finished; 're working
2 so; not
3 finding; being; looking
4 to inform
5 like
6 older; less
7 that
8 play

Did you know?

1

- This exercise tests students on how much they can remember about the *Did you know?* sections from Units 1–3.
- Students work on their own and answer the questions. They can then discuss their answers with a partner but don't check answers at this stage. This will be done in the next exercise.

2

- Students check their answers on pages 13, 23 and 29.

1 Help the Aged
2 (Admiral Lord) Nelson
3 The first statue to occupy the fourth plinth in Trafalgar Square. It depicts a pregnant disabled artist.
4 the Republic of Ireland
5 PlasTax or The Plastic Bag Environmental Levy

Revision Units 4–12

1

- Groupwork. Put students into three groups: A, B and C. Explain that each group is going to devise a revision test, writing similar types of questions as those used in the Revision questions for Units 1–3. Tell them to note what units they are writing questions for. They should write twelve questions in total for the test – between two and four questions for each of the sections: *Vocabulary*, *Word building*, *Grammar* and *Did you know?*

2

- Students now form new groups, comprising of one student from each of the groups A, B and C. Ask them to read the instructions. They then ask their questions to the other students in turn and then add up their score to find the winner.

Speaking

1

- Groupwork. Put students into small groups. Explain that they are all photo editors. Their job is to choose two photos to illustrate the final page of this Student's Book. Ask them to look at the photos on the page. They must decide which ones they think are suitable for the Student's Book. Tell them that they must choose at least one of the photos, but if they cannot decide on a second photo, they can write a brief description for another photo, outlining their requirement for the photo (e.g. whether it should show people, objects, nature), keeping in mind that these images should be relevant for this Student's Book.
- Students then tell the class what photos they have chosen, and if they wrote a new description for a photo, they tell the class about it. They should also explain why they have chosen these photos and why they are suitable for the Student's Book.
- The class can then have a vote on the photos and select a final two for the page.

2

- Students discuss the questions in their groups, and give reasons for their answers and any further details.

Web research tasks

Methodology guidelines: Web research tasks, page xiv

- Ask students to choose a topic or grammar point covered in the Student's Book that they would like to know more about.
- Students research the topic on the internet.
- Students make a presentation to the class, using the information they have found on the web.

If you want something extra ...

Photocopiable activity, page 258
Teaching notes, page 210

Answer key

12 Review

Student's Book page 175

1

Suggested answers:
1 c 2 g 3 e 4 f (or g) 5 h 6 a (or e)
7 d 8 b

2

1 identified
2 threatened
3 categorizes / ises
4 differentiating
5 Endangered
6 Endangered
7 evaluated
8 classified / classed
9 summarizing / ising
10 enables

3

1 download
2 undergo
3 overcome
4 outnumber
5 undercharge
6 overtake
7 outweigh
8 downplay

4

1 three ~~kiloes~~ kilos; of ~~tomatos~~ tomatoes
2 two young ~~ladys~~ ladies; sells ~~work of arts~~ works of art
3 make ~~yourselfs~~ yourselves; get some ~~knifes~~ knives
4 different ~~country's~~ countries; and in some ~~easies~~ cases
5 different chemical ~~formula~~ formulae / formulas; on pages two ~~hundreds~~ hundred

5

1 are; their
2 are; them
3 is; it
4 are; was
5 is; it (*or* are; they)

1 | Writing An autobiography

Speaking

1
- Model this activity first by drawing your own lifeline on the board with details of significant events in your life, your future plans, hopes and predictions, using the events and turning points listed.
- Students then draw their own lifelines to represent their life. Remind them to use the events and turning points listed as a guide.

2
- Pairwork. Students compare their lifelines with a partner and ask each other questions to find out some of the significant events in their partner's life.

Reading

1
- Students read Murat's autobiography and compare it with their own life.

2
- Ask students to look at Murat's lifeline at the bottom of the page. They complete the lifeline with the events listed.
- Students can compare their answers with a partner and then discuss what have been the happiest and unhappiest times in Murat's life.

Pre-school years
1 looked after by maternal grandmother

Schooldays
2 sent away to attend secondary school
3 won the school prize for English

After school
4 did military service
5 studied English at university

After university
6 worked as a tour guide
7 met his wife
8 got married
9 moved to Scotland
10 re-trained as a plumber

Present
11 working as a plumber

Future
12 set up travel agency

3
- Students look back at the autobiography and find and underline the time expressions.

Time expressions

on March 31st 19__	in the evenings
up to the age of five	On my graduation
at the age of twelve	While I was working
At first	Afterwards
As time went on	two years later
during this period	Since my arrival
in my final year	currently
After leaving school	in five years' time
then	

Language focus

Using time expressions

1
- Students put the time expressions in the appropriate columns to describe their life.
- They could then compare their answers with a partner before you check with the class.

Suggested answer:

past
in those days
during my adolescence
three years later
as a child
at the age of ten

present perfect
for the last five years
to date
so far
ever since

present
at present
currently
at the moment

future
next year
in six months' time
some day

2
- Students choose one expression from each of the columns and write a true sentence about their life.

Describing your family

3

- Students read the sentences and decide whether both the alternatives in italics are possible or only one. If they decide that both alternatives are possible, they must explain the difference in meaning between the two.

1 an only child
2 people
3 'Eldest' would usually be used when referring to a person, but 'oldest' would not be incorrect.
4 older
5 three brothers (when they're only boys) / siblings (normally, you'd say *brothers and sisters* rather than *siblings*)
6 brought up (looked after by my grandmother) / educated (taught by my grandmother)
7 step-sisters (the children of the new mother and her former partner)
8 lenient (few rules) / strict (lots of rules)
9 close-knit
10 had

Verb-noun collocations

4

- Students match the verbs with the nouns to make collocations.
- They could then compare their answers with a partner before you check with the class.

take a gap year
train as a nurse
get a place at university
go to school
do research

graduate from university
leave school
do a degree
qualify as a solicitor
apply for a scholarship

5

- Students write four sentences about their life using a verb-noun collocation and a suitable time expression.

Methodology advances
Writing at C1 level

- *Here are some of the descriptors of writing abilities at C1 level as set out in the Common European Framework and its associated portfolios:*
  - Can write clear, well-structured texts of complex subjects, underlining the relevant salient issues, expanding and supporting points of view at some length with subsidiary points, reasons and relevant examples, and rounding off with an appropriate conclusion.
  - Can write clear, detailed, well-structured and developed descriptions and imaginative texts in an assured, personal, natural style appropriate to the reader in mind.

material from Council of Europe

- *In other words, the writer has to be very stylish, clear and effective – even on complex and sophisticated subjects! We're talking about more than just writing about your last holiday!*
- *In my experience of Advanced classes, students who may be fine in terms of listening, speaking and reading are often significantly below this level on writing, which seems to be the skill that trails behind all the others, possibly reflecting the modern belief that the most important skills for most students will be speaking and listening.*

Some ways of helping Advanced students with writing

- *Make sure your students get writing experience in a range of genres. At Advanced level they need to move well beyond the familiar, to explore challenging genres such as academic argument, persuasive articles, autobiography, critical essay and so on. Writing lessons 1–6 provide practice with these and other important genres.*
- *As well as longer pieces, also set short real-world writing tasks such as memos, diary entries, notes, phone call messages, meeting agendas, brief transactional emails, and so on. Such writing is short and condensed but still needs to be organized and clear. It can provide particular problems even for high level students. Because they are short, they are also ideal for intensive study and redrafting work in class to improve them, something that is harder to do consistently with very long texts.*
- *In every writing task, remind students that they are not just seeking to write clearly and accurately, but to write with a distinct style that reflects who they are.*
- *When you read their work and give feedback, make sure that you comment on a range of areas and don't just focus on the 'traditional' areas of overall meaning, grammar, vocabulary, punctuation and spelling. Bear in mind the CEF descriptors. If appropriate for specific writing tasks, give comments on areas such as: the depth of an argument, how well it is supported, how aware the writer seems to be of the needs of a potential reader, how much there is a clear personal style to the writing, how natural the text sounds, and so on.*

Writing

1

- Ask students to decide on three or four different events or periods from their lifeline and arrange them into paragraphs. Point out that they should include their current situation and future plans or hopes.

2

- Pairwork. Students tell their partner about the events in their autobiography.

3

- Students write their own autobiography, using the notes they made in exercise 1.
- Refer students to the *Useful language* and *Remember to …* boxes at the bottom of the page to help them with their autobiography.
- Students could write the autobiography in class or for homework.

Extra task: guess who

- If possible, ask students to write their autobiography on a computer or word processor so that their handwriting cannot be identified. Tell them not to include their name or any very obvious personal details in the autobiography. When the texts are complete, collect them in and distribute them to different students. Students read out the autobiographies they have been given. The rest of the class tries to guess who the autobiography belongs to. This activity can work particularly well with students who do not know each other well.

Extra task: peer correction

- Put students in pairs. Tell students that they are to play the role of editor, reading and criticizing each other's autobiographies. The editors should make a photocopy of the original text and then make suggestions as to how the autobiography could be improved, both in terms of its content and structure as well as the language that is used.

Extra task: celebrity biographies

- In the *Straightforward* Advanced Workbook, students are asked to choose a famous person (alive or dead) whose life they would like to know a bit more about and to write a biography of that person. You should allow them a few days to research and write about the person's life, using the internet or books from the library.
- In class, ask students to present their biographies without naming the famous person they have written about. The rest of the class tries to guess who the famous person is.
- You could tell the students to illustrate their autobiographies with pictures of the famous people they are writing about downloaded from the internet. The finished biographies could then be made into an attractive wall display for the classroom.

2 | Writing An article

SPEAKING

1

- Students choose the statements that best describe their attitude to sending text messages, and explain why they chose the statements.
- Pairwork. Students discuss the question with a partner.

2

- Students read the situation and try to decipher the text message.
- Find out if they know any other examples of text language in English.

> My summer holidays were a complete waste of time. Before, we used to go to New York to see my brother, his girlfriend and their three screaming kids face to face. I love New York. It's a great place.

Cultural note: text messages

- The Short Message Service (SMS) enables people to send text messages to each other via mobile phones. The first ever text message is thought to have been sent to Richard Jarvis, director of Vodafone from Neil Papworth of Sema Group in 1992.
  Text messaging was slow to catch on initially, with the average customer texting 0.4 messages a month in 1995. By 2000, this figure had risen to 35. At the time of publishing, a billion text messages are sent each week in Britain. That is as many as were sent in the whole of 1999. In 2004, a study from the University of Leuven in Belgium found text messaging to be addictive. Further research by the Australia's Queensland University likened the level of addiction to that of cigarette smoking.

Language notes: text language

- Many people use abbreviations and symbols in their text messages. This 'text language' is also known as *rebus*. See the example below.
  How r u? = How are you?
- The developing language of the SMS text is phonetic. That is to say, it represents the sound of words and not the dictionary spelling, as the example illustrates. This language seems to have evolved naturally as SMS messaging has grown in popularity. While some abbreviations are relatively simple to decipher, others are less immediately obvious. Here are a few common examples:

  AFAIK = As far as I know
  ATB = All the best
  BTW = By the way
  CID = Consider it done
  CUL8R = See you later
  EZ = Easy
  LOL = Lots of luck / Laughed out loud
  LUV = Love
  OTOH = On the other hand
  2MORO = Tomorrow
  CU 2MORO = See you tomorrow
  THX or TX = Thanks
  WUSIWYG = What you see is what you get
  YBS = You'll be sorry
  YKWYKD = You know what you could do?

Extra task: SMS abbreviations

- Write the abbreviations from the language notes on the board. Ask students to work in pairs or small groups to try to guess what the abbreviations mean. You could do this as a competition to see which pair or group can be the first to correctly identify all the abbreviations.
- Challenge the students to come up with their own SMS text language. Brainstorm some possible phrases for them to abbreviate (e.g. 'Bye for now' = BFN). Set aside ten minutes of class time for students to finish developing their text language or ask them to do this for homework.

Language note: emoticons

- Emoticons are also commonly used in text messages. They are symbols that you type in an email or text message to show how you feel. There is an example of an emoticon in the girl's text message in exercise 2. : - means 'screaming'. Below are some other common emoticons and their meanings.
  : -) = *happy*
  : -)) = *very happy*
  : - D = *grinning*
  :'- D = *crying with laughter*
  xxx = *kisses*
  : - (= *sad*
  : - ((= *very sad*
  > : - (= *angry and sad*
  > : - | = *angry*

Extra task: text message challenge

- If your students have mobile phones, set them a text message challenge. Their challenge is to text each other using as many abbreviations and emoticons as they can, naturally and appropriately, in a text message of no more than 50 words. This could be done in class, or could be set for homework.
- If your students commonly send text messages to each other, encourage them to do this in English.

READING

1

- Students read the texts quickly. They then match the headings with the correct paragraph.
- They could then compare their answers with a partner before you check with the class.

> 1 c   2 a   3 b

2

- Ask students to read the facts listed about textaholics.
- They could then work with a partner and decide whether the facts were given in the text. They mark them G (for given) or NG (for not given). They then check their answers in the text.

> 1 G   2 G   3 NG   4 G   5 NG   6 G   7 NG   8 G

3

- Students discuss the questions.

Language focus

Writing definitions

1

- Students read the definitions for *textaholic*. They then write definitions for the four addictive types. Point out the language in the box which they should use in their definitions.
- You could then ask a few students to read out their definitions to the class.

Possible answers:
1 A shopaholic is obsessed with buying new things.
2 A coffee addict suffers from withdrawal symptoms if they can't have a cup of coffee.
3 A chocoholic has constant cravings for chocolate.
4 An email addict can't live without checking their inbox for emails.

Making a deduction

2

- Students complete the descriptions of addictive behaviour (a–d) with the correct noun for the addictive types (1–4) in exercise 1.

a) 4 – an email addict
b) 1 – a shopaholic
c) 2 – a coffee addict
d) 3 – a chocaholic

Possible answers:
e) If so, then the chances are you that you are a lottery addict.
f) If the answer is yes, you're certainly addicted to your dictionary.
g) If it is, you could be addicted to junk food.

Describing cause & effect

3

- Students read the sentences and underline the expressions used to describe cause and effect. Point out that they should label them C (for cause) and E (for effect) as in the example.

1 Poor education (C) <u>is at the root of</u> many social problems (E).
2 Overwork (C) <u>can lead to</u> stress (E).
3 Severe stress (C) <u>can result in</u> high blood pressure (E).
4 High blood pressure (C) <u>is a risk factor in</u> heart disease (E).
5 <u>The underlying causes</u> of most addictions (E) are psychological (C).
6 Many emotional difficulties in adults (E) <u>stem from</u> childhood insecurities (C).

4

- Students write four sentences describing either the cause or effect of each of the topics listed.
- They can then compare their sentences with a partner. Elicit a few examples from the class.

Possible answers:
1 Air pollution can lead to respiratory diseases.
2 Childhood obesity is often due to poor diet.
3 Symptoms of road rage include speeding and aggressive driving.
4 Sitting for too long at a computer can result in poor posture.

Writing

1

- Pairwork. In pairs, students decide on one of the titles to write a website article. They list the characteristics that type of person has, the problems that may have resulted from the addiction and advice to help them.

2

- Students write their website article, using the notes they made in exercise 1. Point out that they should follow the structure for the three paragraphs as given.
- Refer students to the *Useful language* and *Remember to …* boxes at the bottom of the page to help them with their article.

Extra task: text message headlines

- Write the following news headlines on the board:
  Text messages aid disaster recovery
  Text messages help smokers quit
  Text message voting to be trialled
  Text message bullies face expulsion
  Killer text message found
  Casino gambles on text messaging
  Text message saved hiker
- Ask students to choose one of the headlines and to write a short news story about it, allowing 10–15 minutes for this. On completion, students could swap texts and check and edit each other's work. You could ask students to type their headlines into an internet search engine to see if they get any matches. If they do get a match, they could then compare their story with the real life versions and report back to the class.

Methodology advances
Writing ideas

Here are two ideas for helping students improve aspects of their writing.

Intensive writing focus

- *When students have done a writing task, we usually concentrate mostly on the whole text, its structure and its message. This means that the small details and problems can get overlooked. An interesting activity at a high level is to really focus in on a small part of what students have written and look very closely at it.*
- *Ask students to select three consecutive sentences from anywhere in the piece they have just written, totalling at least 50 words. (If students can't find any, they aren't writing long enough sentences!) Once selected they should be copied out neatly in the middle of a new piece of paper, leaving lots of space between lines.*

- *Every student should pass their piece of paper on to another student. When they receive a new text, students should read it and add comments of their own to the paper, e.g. about the whole text, words, grammar, spelling, misunderstandings, style, and so on, or offering rewordings, suggestions, alternative ideas, etc. They could, for example, underline a phrase and draw a line to link it to a comment written in the page borders.*
- *After a few minutes, the papers are passed on again to new readers who make new comments, and then again a few more times. When five or six people have added their thoughts, the papers can be returned to the original writers to read. Encourage students to meet up with comment writers and ask questions about anything that isn't clear.*
- *The writer can then redraft their sentences (if they want to) and add back into the original text.*

Ditch the plan?

- *Students often find it hard to successfully structure and paragraph their texts. Although it is good practice to make careful plans before starting to write, some students prefer the content of their writing to emerge when they are engaged in the act of writing. In effect, doing the writing creates the writing.*
- *For these students, starting a writing task by writing rather than planning – a quick ten-minute speed-write, aiming to get a concentrated version of the whole task down in a short time – might work best. And only after they have some content can they then take a step back and consider how best to structure it for a second draft.*
- *One good way to obtain useful feedback on writing is to get students to read what they have written aloud to another student, who can ask questions or make suggestions. Or try this:*
- *When students have finished a first draft of their text, they pass it on to a partner.*
- *The partner should now read this and, without talking to the writer at all, make a diagrammatic representation (e.g. a flow-chart or a mind map) of the structure of the text as they find it, i.e. make short notes that show the flow of the contents and arguments through the writing.*
- *When the diagram is ready they hand it back to the writer who checks if that is actually what they intended. Students can discuss misunderstandings or suggestions, before going on to start work on the next draft.*

3 | Writing A work email

Speaking

1

- Ask students to imagine they could work for a short time in an English-speaking country. They discuss the questions with a partner.

2

- Pairwork. Students discuss the questions with a partner.
- Students then read the statements and decide if they are true or false.

1 True
2 False
3 True (even in formal emails)
4 True
5 True
6 True (Commas are often omitted, or used to join sentences. Exclamation marks are common in informal emails.)
7 True and false (People tend to disagree on this point.)
8 True (However, even 'formal' emails are often more informal than formal letters.)

Note that the language of emails is constantly changing and students may have different opinions.

Language note: emails abbreviations

- You may want to point out that abbreviations are also commonly used in informal emails. Here are a few of the most common. You could write these on the board and ask the class to explain them.

ASAP = *as soon as possible*	FYI = *for your information*
pls = *please*	Weds = *Wednesday*
mtg = *meeting*	eve = *evening*
rgds = *regards*	BW = *best wishes*
BTW = *by the way*	re = *regarding*
TBC = *to be confirmed*	ATB = *All the best*

Reading

1

- Students read the four emails and match them with their answers a–d.
- They then discuss what they think happened to Halina from the information they read about her in the emails.

1 d 2 b 3 a 4 c

Halina came to the UK and applied for a work placement with someone who knew her university tutor. She had an interview and was offered the placement. She arranged to see her friend Beth in London, but had to reschedule the meeting as it clashed with her interview.

2

- Students look back at all the emails in exercise 1 and say what function 1–8 each of them performs.
- Students then underline the expressions in the emails the writers use to perform the functions 1–8.

1 1 – *Can you make lunch?*
2 d – *Sounds great*
3 a – *Good news about the interview*
4 4 – *We will be able to offer you a three-month placement*
5 c – *I would be delighted to accept your offer*
6 a – *Hope it goes well – I'll keep my fingers crossed for you*
7 3 – *I'm really sorry but I can't make lunch after all*
8 b – *Would you be able to drop by for lunch?*; 4 – *Could you contact me asap?*

Language focus

Formal & informal style

1

- Students read the expressions and mark them a) formal, b) neutral or c) informal.
- They could then compare their answers with a partner before you check with the class.

Formal: 2; 10; 13
Neutral: 3; 5; 6; 8; 11; 12; 14
Informal: 1; 4; 7; 9

Making arrangements & requests in emails

2

- Tell students that each of the exchanges contains a formal or informal alternative. They should choose the best alternative to complete the excerpts from email exchanges. Point out that in one case, two alternatives are possible.

1

Beth:	Can you make
Halina:	Sounds great
Beth:	Sorry about this.
Halina:	How about Thursday?
Beth:	See you then.

2

Mr Rogers:	Could you send me details of
Ms Brown:	Let me know if this is difficult.
Mr Rogers:	I'm afraid I'm busy; Could we possibly reschedule this?
Ms Brown:	Any time next week would be good.
Mr Rogers:	Unfortunately, I'll be out of the office next week.

3

- Students match each of the statements 1–5 with the correct request a–e in response to it.
- They could then compare their answers with a partner before you check with the class.

1 e 2 d 3 c 4 a 5 b

Writing

1

- Pairwork. Put students into A and B pairs.
- They each write an email for some of the situations listed. Remind them to look back at the language they have studied in the lesson to help them.
- Refer students to the *Useful language* box at the bottom of the page, but not the *Remember to …* box. Ask them to cover this, as they will be checking their work against this in the following exercise.
- They then 'send' the email to their partner, who must 'write' a reply to that email.
- Remember, emails are a very computer based concept. The task may not work as well if students do their writing using pen and paper. If facilities allow, get students to use computers to write their emails to each other.

Extra task: work emails

- If you have a class with students who are in work, you could ask them to bring in examples of similar work emails that they have sent or received. Of course, remind students that they will be looked at by others, so ask them to ensure that there is nothing that is confidential in the emails. In class, get students to work together with one or two others and share their emails. Ask students to see if there are any things they have learnt in this lesson that would lead them to change any of their emails.

2

- Pairwork. Students look back at the emails that they have written. Ask them to look at the *Remember to …* box and to check how much of the advice in it they followed and to amend their copy if necessary.

4 | Writing A narrative

Speaking

1

- Pairwork. Students discuss the questions with a partner.

2

- Students read the opinions and say whether they agree or disagree with them and give their reasons.

Reading

1

- Students read the short story and choose the best meaning to explain the final sentence in the story.
- They could discuss their choice with a partner before you check with the class.

3 Violence breeds violence. (Referring back to Joey's earlier comment). Students may also argue for 2.

2

- Students to read the story again and put the events in the order in which they happened.
- Students could then work in small groups and discuss what they think happens next in the story. Then they tell the rest of the class their version.

Correct order: 3, 9, 4, 1, 5, 10, 7, 2, 8, 6

Language focus

Using narrative tenses

1

- Students find and underline examples of the four tenses in the story.

1 *past continuous – the sun was just beginning to appear / Al and Joey … were making their way home*
2 *past perfect simple – they had broken into a car / they had set off on foot / a fight he had had earlier that day / Brad had attacked Al's brother / Al had managed to grab Brad's gun / no sooner had they turned into the main street*
3 *past perfect continuous – They had been walking for over an hour*
4 *past simple – neither of them knew how to drive / they found an all-night café / they went in and ordered a coffee / Al started boasting / Al stroked it proudly / 'Don't be crazy, man' said Joey / the two friends arrived back at the estate / they suddenly found themselves / Brad … started running towards them / Al pulled out the gun and pointed it at Brad / the other members of Brad's gang fled / Joey gazed at the scene in horror / Al realized / he handed his gun over / 'It's a dead end' he said to Brad*

2

- Students say which tenses are used to do the functions listed. They then find and underline examples from the story.

1 Past simple: *they found an all-night café / they went in and ordered a coffee / Al started boasting / Al stroked it proudly / 'Don't be crazy, man' said Joey / the two friends arrived back at the estate / they suddenly found themselves / Brad … started running towards them / Al pulled out the gun and pointed it at Brad / the other members of Brad's gang fled / Joey gazed at the scene in horror / Al realized / he handed his gun over / 'It's a dead end' he said to Brad*
2 Past continuous: *the sun was just beginning to appear / Al and Joey … were making their way home*
3 Past perfect simple: *they had broken into a car / they had set off on foot / a fight he had had earlier that day / Brad had attacked Al's brother / Al had managed to grab Brad's gun*
4 Past perfect simple: *no sooner had they turned into the main street*
5 Past perfect continuous: *They had been walking for over an hour*

Linking events

3

- Students can work with a partner and discuss how the two events were linked in the story. You could do the first one with the students as an example.
- After students have finished the exercise, they look back at the story to check their answers.

1 Having missed their last train home, they had broken into a car …
2 … they had broken into a car, only to find … that neither of them knew how to drive.
3 They had been walking for over an hour when they found an all-night café.
4 Taking the gun out of his pocket, Al started stroking it.
5 No sooner had they turned into the main street than they found themselves face to face with Brad.
6 Al pointed his gun at Brad while the other gang members fled.

Language notes: participle clauses

- You may want to use this opportunity to revisit and reinforce the grammar work done in lesson 7C on participle clauses. Go through the following explanation with the class:

  We use a present participle clause
  a) to describe the first of two actions happening in close sequence. For example:
  They found an all-night café, so they went in and ordered a coffee could also be written as *Finding an all-night café, they went in and ordered a coffee.*
  b) with stative verbs, to describe the reason for an action
  Fearing for his life, Al pulled out the gun.
- We use a past participle clause to stress that the first action has completely finished before the second one starts. For example:
  Having missed their last train home, they had broken into a car parked in an alleyway.

Extra task: participle clauses

Ask students which sentences from exercise 3 use participle clauses (1 and 4). Ask students to rewrite sentences 2, 3 and 5 using participle clauses.
(Answers: 2 Having broken into a car, they found… that neither of them knew how to drive. 3 Having walked / After walking for over an hour, they found an all night café. 5 (After) turning into Main Street, they found themselves face-to-face with Brad.)

4

- Students match the beginnings of the sentences with their endings.
- They could then compare their answers with a partner before you check with the class.

1 d 2 e 3 b 4 a 5 c

Describing emotion

5

- Students choose the most appropriate word to complete the sentences.
- They could then compare their answers with a partner before you check with the class.

1 horror
2 disappointment
3 embarrassment
4 annoyance
5 bemusement
6 astonishment
7 consternation

WRITING

1

- Ask students to look at the list 1–4 and to give examples of the type of bad behaviour these people possess.
- Pairwork. In pairs, students choose one of the people from the list to write a story in which this person changes their bad behaviour.

2

- In their pairs, the students plan their story, using the paragraph stages a, b and c.

3

- Students write their story, using their notes in exercise 2.
- Refer students to the *Remember to …* box at the bottom of the page to help them with their story.

5 | Writing A letter of complaint

Speaking

1
- Ask students to look at the picture and to imagine that they have rented this flat. Tell them that there are lots of things wrong with it. Ask them to say what they are.
- Students then look at the list of problems with the flat and decide what they would do in each case, e.g. fix it themselves, ask the landlord to fix it, ignore it or move out.

2
- Pairwork. Students read the questions and compare their ideas with a partner.

Cultural note: tenants & landlords in the UK

- **Council houses**
  UK citizens are entitled to a place in a house owned by the local council. Priority is given to people living in crowded or unsanitary conditions, people whose health is affected by poor housing and families who are forced to live apart due to inadequate housing.
  Council houses are owned by the local government authority, and rent is paid to the council by the tenant. Tenants in council properties enjoy certain rights. For example, they can ask the council to repair anything which is likely to affect their health, safety or security. Here are a few examples:
  unsafe power or lighting sockets or electrical fittings
  a blocked flue to an open fire or boiler
  a leaking roof
  a toilet which doesn't flush
  a blocked sink, bath or basin
  leaks from a water or heating pipe, tank or cistern
  loose or broken handrails or banisters
- **Private rented housing**
  This is a growing part of the UK housing market. Almost 12 per cent of all UK households lived in private rented accommodation in 2007. It accounts for 12 per cent of all housing stock in England and 10 per cent of housing stock in the UK as a whole.
  Although the private rented sector has been growing in the UK, it is still relatively small compared to some other European countries. Private renting has advantages over owner-occupation for many people because of its flexibility and accessibility. It is particularly important for young people without dependents, who cannot, or do not want to buy a home of their own.
  Getting a private landlord to carry out and pay for repairs on a rented property is notoriously difficult – however they are bound by law to make certain repairs and to maintain the property.

Reading

1
- Students read the letter from a tenant to their landlord about the problems she is experiencing with her flat and put the paragraphs in the correct order. Ask them what made them decide that order.

Correct order: 2, 4, 1, 3

2
- Students say what the problems the tenant is experiencing with the flat are, and they explain the consequences of these problems.

The central heating is erratic and at times does not come on at all – she had to borrow a fan heater from a friend; the temperature in the flat is frequently freezing.
The windows in the living room do not shut properly – the room is extremely draughty.
Several of the sockets in the bedroom are loose – a safely hazard.
The lift in this block is frequently out of order – she has to use the stairs.

3
- Students read the expressions 1–9. They then find and underline their formal equivalents in the letter.
- They could then compare their answers with a partner before you check with the class.

1 I have discovered a number of problems …
2 As you will appreciate, these problems are causing a great deal of inconvenience and distress …
3 I am writing to you to express my concerns.
4 … let me know how you propose to resolve these problems.
5 A further source of irritation is …
6 … as a matter of urgency …
7 I would like to draw your attention to the fact …
8 I would therefore be grateful if you could contact me … / I look forward to hearing from you.
9 I am writing with regard to the flat …

Language focus

Article use

1
- Students match the rules 1–6 in the grammar box with extracts a–i which explains the use of *the* in the extract.
- They could then compare their answers with a partner before you check with the class.

a 5; 6 b 1 c 4; 2 d 3; 3 e 5; 4 f 5
g 2; 1 h 6 i 5

Language note: articles

- Articles pose the single greatest grammar problem for many students, particularly those from many Eastern European and Asian countries. This is because these students do not have an equivalent in their own language.
  The indefinite article (*a/an*) is used to introduce a new item or to talk about an item which is not specific, e.g. *I bought a new computer yesterday. / He's a nice man.*
  The definite article (*the*) is used when we already know what is being referred to. This may be because:
  - it has been mentioned before, e.g. *I saw a film last night on TV last night. The film was really strange.*
  - there is only one of them, e.g. *The Earth is the third planet from the Sun.*
  - we have specified which one we are talking about, e.g. *I love the dress that you wore last night.*
  There is a substantial focus on article use in *Straightforward* Upper Intermediate (lessons 11A and 11C). This is a good opportunity to revisit this area with the reading text generating some nice examples.

Writing about results of problems

2

- Students match the problems to their consequences.
- They could then compare their answers with a partner before you check with the class.

1 c 2 d 3 b 4 e 5 a

3

- Students write the consequence for each of the problems, using some of the expressions underlined in exercise 2.

Possible answers:
1 ... so that I've had to live off convenience foods.
2 ... which constitutes a safety hazard.
3 ... which means that I'm having trouble sleeping at night.
4 ... which means it is extremely uncomfortable.
5 ... and as a result the room is extremely stuffy.

Writing

1

- Pairwork. Put students into pairs and ask them to read the instructions for the task. They make a list of the problems they encountered on their holiday and notes on their consequences. They then make notes on what action they think should be taken.
- Finally, they write a letter of complaint. They should start the letter with the phrase given and the guide for structuring their letter of complaint into three paragraphs.
- Refer students to the *Useful language* and *Remember to ...* boxes at the bottom of the page to help them with their letter.

6 | Writing An essay

Speaking

1

- Ask students to look at the list of activities and say which of them they have done recently and if they enjoyed doing them.
- They also say which of the activities they have never done and why, and if they would ever consider doing them in the future or not.

2

- Students look back at the list and classify the ones that they would call 'the arts'. Ask them to suggest other activities which they would include in a list of the arts.

Extra task: art definitions & discussion

- Ask students to write a definition for 'the arts'. Students then look up 'the arts' in their dictionary and compare the definitions. You may want to draw their attention to the difference between the definitions for 'art' (paintings, drawings, sculptures etc), 'arts' (subjects of study that are not scientific, such as history etc) and 'the arts' (activities such as art, music, film etc considered together).
- Ask students to say what they consider the value of art to be.
- Ask students to discuss the following question as a pre-reading activity:
  'Do you think that the arts should be publicly funded? Work with a partner to make a list of reasons for and against.'

Reading

1

- Students read the essay about public funding of the arts and decide which of the statements best reflect the writer's opinion.

3 (Public money should be used to fund the arts because art is an important human activity.)

2

- Students complete the writer's plan. To do this, they look back at the essay and make notes for each of the points as in the example for paragraph 1.

Paragraph 1
Introductory statement: Value of the arts in civilized society
Supporting statement: Enriches people's lives
Controversial question: Should the arts be publicly funded?

Paragraph 2
Main opinion: The government should subsidize the arts
Arguments: a) Artists couldn't survive without subsidies; b) The arts contribute to our cultural heritage; c) The arts play a social role; d) The arts are important for their own sake

Paragraph 3
Counter-argument: Money would be better spent on the poor, healthcare, education and social welfare schemes
Refuting counter-argument: a) A healthy society is one that values arts; b) The arts should be accessible to everyone

Paragraph 4
Conclusion: A spectrum of activities should be funded
Supporting statement: Enjoyment of the arts is part of being human

3

- Students look back at the essay again and underline the discourse markers or expressions that are used to introduce each of the points from the essay plan in exercise 2.

Paragraph 1
Few people would contest …
However, it is also true …
The question is …

Paragraph 2
It is my view that …
First of all, …
Secondly, …
However, the main argument for …

Paragraph 3
There are those who argue that …
However, I believe that …
Indeed, …

Paragraph 4
In conclusion, …
This is not purely … but because …

4

- Students say whether they agree or disagree with the writer's opinion and why.

Language focus

Expressing a viewpoint

1

- Students complete the expressions in the table with the words in the box.
- Write the following statements on the board:
  Much contemporary art does not deserve to be called art.
  Most artists are not appreciated in their own lifetime.
  Most Hollywood blockbusters have no artistic value.
- Nominate individual students to express their own opinions about the statements by modifying them with an expression from the table. Use this as an opportunity to focus on natural stress, rhythm and intonation patterns for the modifying expressions.
- Allow students a couple of minutes to read and think about the statements. They then express their own opinions about the statements by modifying them with an expression from the table.

1 claimed
2 widely
3 say
4 agreed
5 view
6 personally
7 would
8 whether
9 evidence
10 case
11 doubt
12 dispute

Arguing against a viewpoint

2

- Students complete the sentences to argue against the view being expressed.

Possible answers:

1 There are those who argue that anyone can learn to play a musical instrument. However, many of those who have been forced to take music lessons as children would argue that this is not the case.
2 Of course, not everyone has an innate talent for art. But surely everyone can take pleasure in drawing and painting?
3 It is true that pop music has a wider popular appeal than classical music. But it could also be argued that most pop music does not have lasting value.
4 Opponents of modern art argue that it has no aesthetic value. But surely beauty is in the eye of the beholder?
5 Advocates of free speech claim that censorship stifles debate. However, it is also the case that complete freedom of speech could result in slander and libel.

3

- Ask students to look back at the opinions in exercise 2. They choose two of them and write similar statements using the underlined expressions.

Methodology advances
Beyond the plateau

You've probably heard of the plateau effect in language learning. This refers to the way that many students reach a level of English (often around Intermediate or Upper Intermediate level) at which they can do most of the things they want to do with their language with a 'good-enough' level of success – after which their motivation to keep improving may slacken off dramatically. They don't perceive that any further investment of time and energy is likely to make a worthwhile or substantial-enough improvement over where they have already reached.

Another cause of the plateau effect arises from the learner's sense of diminishing returns gained from studying increasingly complex but less obviously useful language items.

When a beginner starts studying English, every day in class brings along useful new grammar and vocabulary, virtually every piece of which is undeniably important and clearly usable in everyday situations. As the learner climbs up the long ladder of learning English, they keep meeting new tenses, important structures, key lexical sets and so on. They may get a sense that English learning means collecting new item after new item.

However, around Upper Intermediate level, the student-collector starts to notice that the nature of their collecting is changing. There aren't any big new tenses to learn. The new vocabulary they are learning seems less immediately useful or even obscure – often used for understanding reading texts rather than for active everyday use. Whereas progress as a Beginner could be easily measured with new grammar and lexical items ticked off minute by minute, at higher levels the steps forward may come much more slowly. The learning might therefore feel less interesting, less purposeful and less rewarding. It can take quite a degree of motivation to keep putting the effort in.

And for a teacher, the challenge of motivating a class may also seem more challenging; you might wish to be able to offer an exciting new tense every week, but the reality is that there is a finite number of tenses and grammatical items. The grammar that students study in an Advanced lesson will be often be fine-tuning items first studied long ago or finding out about variations or exceptions to rules. It's all useful – but it doesn't necessarily have the same impact as, say the first time you taught a whole class to use 'going to'.

It's important that a teacher keeps the plateau effect in mind, not least because high-level students aren't always aware of it – and it may be helpful to explain it to them, for example, when your students become a little disgruntled at what seems to be increasingly slow progress in high-level classes. Go through some of the reasons mentioned above. Agree that 'yes, progress will feel slower – but that's normal'. Then, go on to discuss why it's worth persevering!

WRITING

Writing an essay expressing an opinion

Extra task: opinion tennis

- Writing a long piece of text can be a daunting prospect, even for Advanced students. You could try this short, fun activity as a warm-up for the main writing task.
- Ask the students to work in pairs. They will each need a blank piece of paper. Ask each student to write a sentence at the top of their piece of paper expressing an opinion. Their sentence should be about some aspect of art (e.g. *good art is too expensive for any but the most wealthy to buy*). Students in each pair should then exchange their pieces of paper, and write one sentence to respond to the first sentence written by their partner. Do not allow more than 60 seconds for students to write their sentences. One of the aims of this activity is to show that writing does not have to be a long and laborious activity.
- Students then hand back their papers to their partners and the activity continues in the same way, with opinions being written and responded to. Stop the activity after five minutes, or when students have reached the bottom of their piece of paper.

1

- Pairwork. Put the students into pairs and ask them to read the instructions.
- Students decide with their partner on one of the statements in *Language focus* exercise 2 to write about.
- They write a list arguing for and against the statement.
- They then write sentences saying why they think the topic is controversial and giving their own opinion about it.
- They then plan their essay. Tell them to follow the structure of the writer's plan for the text in the Reading section on page 136.
- Students then write their essays individually, using their plan. Refer them also to the *Useful language* and *Remember to …* boxes at the bottom of the page to help them with their essay.
- Students could write the essay in class or for homework.

2

- Students swap their essay with someone who chose a different topic. They read the essay and then say if they thought the arguments expressed were convincing.

Resource materials

Resource materials

Worksheet	Interaction	Activity	Focus
1A Survey on change	Whole class	Survey	Theme: change.
1B Approximations	Groupwork	Speaking game	Speech feature: approximation.
1C Two lives	Pairwork	Storytelling	Theme: life stories at different ages. Vocabulary: age.
1D Four in a row	Groupwork	Board game	Vocabulary: noun suffixes.
2A Quick sorting	Pairwork	Game	Verbs that take gerunds, infinitives with *to* or bare infinitives.
2B Can you train your brain?	Pairwork	Reading out loud	Pronunciation: chunking.
2C My bicycle & me	Pairwork	Song	Listening. Theme: bicycles and cycling.
2D The museum of ourselves	Individual & groupwork	Simulation	Comparisons.
3A Money expressions	Groupwork	Definition game	Vocabulary: expressions about money.
3B Really nice it was!	Pairwork	Matching game	Speech feature: fronting.
3C It's all over!	Groupwork	Matching game	Vocabulary: words starting with *over*.
3D Newly-found wealth	Individual & groupwork	Making speeches	Vocabulary: adjectives with suffixes.
4A Complaints	Pair & groupwork	Roleplay	Vocabulary: expressions connected with complaining.
4B Mobile phone spies	Groupwork	Simulation	Reported speech.
4C The *Straightforward* awards	Groupwork & whole class	Simulation	Theme: awards ceremonies.
4D What on earth is going on?	Pairwork	Speaking game	Modal verbs: *must*, *might*, *may* and *could* for speculating and deducing.
5A A flatpack text	Pairwork	Reading puzzle	Reading. Relative clauses.
5B Tag talk	Groupwork	Speaking game	Speech feature: question tags.
5C Housework	Pairwork	Song	Listening. Theme: housework. Verb & noun phrase collocations.
5D Regrets	Individual & groupwork	Speaking game	Hypothetical past situations.
6A Runaways & breakdowns	Pairwork	Storytelling	Writing. Vocabulary: nouns from phrasal verbs.
6B Pierced ears & bloodshot eyes	Pairwork	Speaking game	Vocabulary: body collocations.
6C Natasha at 21	Individual & groupwork	Discussion	Reading.
6D Babysitting blues	Individual & whole class	Storytelling	Vocabulary: babies and babysitting.

Worksheet	Interaction	Activity	Focus
7A School issues	Individual & groupwork	Simulation	Theme: schools and behaviour.
7B Time to do something about it	Individual & groupwork	Internet forum	Writing. Theme: rude behaviour.
7C Clare Francis	Individual & pairwork	Rewriting	Participle clauses.
7D A criminal's own story	Pairwork	Storytelling	Writing. Vocabulary: crime and legal matters.
8A Lost property	Individual & pairwork	Guessing game	Reading. Literary descriptions.
8B Word stress game	Pairwork	Board game	Pronunciation: changing word stress.
8C You've got to have friends	Groupwork	Discussion	Vocabulary: relationships. Attitude adverbials.
8D To be perfectly honest	Groupwork	Speaking game	Discourse markers.
9A Three new cities	Individual & groupwork	Researching & presenting	Theme: new cities.
9B Home!	Groupwork	Game	Vocabulary: describing homes and properties.
9C Jamaica farewell	Pairwork	Song	Listening. Theme: tropical islands.
9D Experimental travel	Groupwork	Speaking game	Speech feature: vague language.
10A Endurance event	Pairwork	Roleplay	Theme: achievements and difficulties.
10B It's not this! It's that!	Pairwork	Pronunciation game	Futures. Pronunciation: contrastive stress.
10C Television quiz	Individual	Quiz	Vocabulary: television.
10D Getting to the top	Groupwork	Board game	Vocabulary: success and failure.
11A Instant poem	Individual	Guided writing	Vocabulary: descriptive verbs.
11B Search & replace	Individual & pairwork	Rewriting	Vocabulary: prepositional phrases.
11C Sounds peculiar	Groupwork	Storytelling	Listening. Vocabulary: sounds.
11D Counselling	Groupwork	Board game	Theme: counselling. Hypothetical present and future situations.
12A Octopuses or octopi?	Groupwork	Quiz	Plurals.
12B Hi-tech reviews	Pairwork	Writing	Theme: technology.
12C What a beautiful dress!	Pairwork	Roleplay	Pronunciation: intonation (feelings).
12D These foolish things	Pairwork	Song	Listening. Theme: memories.

Teacher's notes

1A Survey on change

Activity
Whole class. Students survey each other's opinions and ideas about different kinds of change.

Focus
Theme: change.

Preparation
Photocopy one worksheet for every twelve students. Cut the worksheet up into separate cards.

Procedure
- Explain that students are going to carry out a survey about their opinions to different types of change.
- Hand out one question card to each student.
- Students mingle asking each other their question. Tell students to make brief notes about the answers they hear. This will help ensure that they have something useful to say in the feedback stage.
- Encourage students to ask follow-on questions and have short discussions rather than give one word answers.
- Finish with a whole class discussion in which students share the most interesting answers they heard.

Extension
Ask students to write a paragraph about the answers they heard and any conclusions they can draw about the class's opinion to their question.

Note

As this task involves meeting different people and speaking to them about their ideas and opinions, it might work well as an icebreaker and 'getting to know you' task with a new class, or a class where students don't know each other very well.

1B Approximations

Activity
Groupwork. Students answer each other's questions with imprecise answers.

Focus
Speech feature: approximation.

Preparation
Photocopy one worksheet for each group of three students. Cut the worksheet up into separate cards.

Procedure
- Divide the class into groups of three. Distribute the cards equally (nine to each student).
- Explain how to play the game. A student chooses one of their questions and asks it to either of the other students in the group. This student must respond without using any precise numbers, dates, measurements, ages, times, etc. or any exact information of any kind. They must also use at least one approximation.
- After the student has replied to the question, the other two students decide if it was an acceptable answer (i.e. it followed the rule above).
- If the answer is acceptable, the question card is put in a discard pile and not used again in the game. The person who just answered the question asks the next question.
- If the answer isn't acceptable (i.e. the student used precise information of some kind), then the questioner hands that student the card to keep. They must try to get rid of it by asking it again to someone else later on in the game. The questioner can then ask a new question to the other player (not the same person who just received a card).
- The winner is the player who gets rid of all their cards first (or who has the fewest when the game is stopped).

1C Two lives

Activity
Pairwork. Students narrate life stories.

Focus
Theme: life stories at different ages. Vocabulary: age.

Preparation
Photocopy one worksheet for each pair of students. Cut the worksheet in half.

Procedure
- Divide the class into pairs. Hand out worksheet A to one student and worksheet B to the other student in each pair. Tell students not to look at each other's worksheets.
- Explain that each worksheet shows pictures of a person's life at various ages. Explain that this person is now 80 years old.
- Ask students to work on their own to prepare the story of their character's life, using as many of the words and expressions in the box as possible. Tell them to think about the person's whole life and not just what they see in the pictures, i.e. including what came before or after the pictures. The last picture is blank and represents *now* – so students should invent what the picture shows and what has happened to the person over recent years.
- When they are ready, students should meet up with their partner and tell their story.
- After both stories have been told, the pair should agree at least one way in which the two separate life stories might have connected at some point (e.g. the two people worked together).

1D Four in a row

Activity
Groupwork. Students try to win a line of four squares in a game board about noun suffixes.

Focus
Vocabulary: noun suffixes.

Preparation
Photocopy one worksheet for each group of three to four students. (You may like to have extra photocopies for each student to note down the correct answers after the game is over.) Photocopy one set of answers (on this page) for each group. Each student will need ten to fifteen counters of one kind, e.g. coloured sweets, to place on the game board.

Procedure
- Divide the class into groups of three or four students. Ask each group to appoint one student as game master. The game master is a judge and doesn't play the game.
- Hand out one worksheet to each group and give the answer sheet to the game master. Tell the game master not to show the answers to anyone.
- Explain that the aim of the game is to get four counters in a line (horizontal, vertical or diagonal).
- Ask students to take it in turns to choose one of the squares where they think they can make a noun from the adjective or verb by adding a suffix. They write the word.
- The game master then checks the answer sheet and says if the word is correct or not. (N.B. The word must be spelt correctly.)
- If the word is correct, the student places their counter on the square. If the word is wrong, the next student can try to do it (then the next, and so on).
- The game continues with the next student choosing a square. The first student to win a line of four squares is the winner.
- At the end of the game, make sure students are sure of all the correct answers. You might want to distribute extra worksheets for them to use to write down the correct answers.

Answers
1 goodness 2 infancy 3 scarcity 4 silence
5 quietness 6 efficiency 7 reluctance 8 frequency
9 cruelty 10 happiness 11 patience 12 tidiness
13 intelligence 14 urgency 15 similarity
16 complexity 17 technicality 18 eccentricity
19 unemployment 20 certainty 21 privacy
22 peculiarity 23 weakness 24 probability
25 entertainment 26 denial 27 acknowledgement
28 judgement 29 advancement 30 management
31 difference 32 disappointment 33 dismissal
34 pleasure 35 achievement 36 exposure
37 proposal 38 coincidence 39 amazement
40 dependence 41 failure 42 demonstration
43 acceptance 44 punishment 45 refusal
46 departure 47 involvement 48 procedure
49 interference 50 settlement 51 forgiveness
52 government 53 attendance 54 commitment
55 infection 56 concentration 57 invention
58 supervision 59 occurence 60 investment

Note

Although this exercise uses suffixes focussed on in the Student's Book lesson, there are also words on the game board which are not in the lesson, though students will probably know them. Students are encouraged to try and apply the rules learnt in the lesson to the other words.

2A Quick sorting

Activity
Pairwork. Students make quick decisions about grammar.

Focus
Verbs that take gerunds, infinitives with *to* or bare infinitives.

Preparation
Photocopy one worksheet for each pair of students. Cut the worksheet up into separate verb cards and the game board. Each pair will need a watch with a second hand.

Procedure
- Explain that students are going to sort verbs depending on whether they take gerunds, infinitives with *to* or bare infinitives.
- Divide the class into pairs. Hand out one set of cards to each pair, placed face down on the table, and the game board.
- Explain how to play the game. Student A times ten seconds. During this time, Student B takes three verb cards and quickly places each card into one of the three locations on the game board (*gerund*, *bare infinitive* or *infinitive with* to). There isn't much thinking time! After the ten seconds has finished, the cards may not be moved.
- Student B then checks that his/her quick decisions were correct. For each verb, he/she should try to make a good English sentence containing the verb followed the correct verb form (according to its location on the game board).
- Student B keeps the card for each sentence that is grammatically correct. If the sentence is not correct, the card is returned to the main pack of cards.
- Student A then plays three cards in the same way, and so on until the cards are finished, or you stop the game. The winner is the student with the most cards.

Answers
(N.B. Verbs in italics can go in more than one category.)

gerund: admit, adore, avoid, *begin*, *continue*, deny, *dislike*, finish, *forget*, give up, *hate*, imagine, keep, look forward to, postpone, recommend, *regret*, *remember*, resist, risk, *try*

bare infinitive: make, must, should, would rather

infinitive with *to*: agree, allow, ask, *begin*, *continue*, *dislike*, expect, *forget*, *hate*, hope, hurry, manage, need, promise, qualify, *regret*, *remember*, vote, *try*

2B Can you train your brain?

Activity
Pairwork. Students prepare a text for reading aloud.

Focus
Pronunciation: chunking.

Preparation
Photocopy one worksheet for each student.

Procedure
- Explain that students are going to prepare a text for reading aloud by marking the pauses between chunks of text.
- Divide the class into pairs. Hand out one worksheet to each student.
- Ask students to read through the whole text.
- Tell Students A they will work on the sections of the text labelled A, and Students B will work on the sections of the text labelled B.
- Students should now work individually and go through their sections marking / to divide the text into chunks for reading aloud (as in *Pronunciation* exercise 3 in the Student's Book lesson). They should also mark words that will be strongly stressed with an underline.
- When students are ready, they should join up with their partner and try reading their different sections aloud, reviewing how successful their chunking is. If there is time, pairs can compare with other pairs and see if they had similar answers.

Variation
The reading aloud could be done as a whole class workshop, with different students reading short sections and getting feedback from you and other students before re-trying to see if they can improve their delivery.

Answers
There are many possible ways to divide the text into chunks, and stress can also be varied according to personal choice. This is just one possible way of doing it. / marks divisions between chunks. Underline marks strongly stressed words.

Until recently, / a person's IQ / (a measure of all kinds of mental problem-solving abilities, / including spatial skills, / memory / and verbal reasoning) / was thought to be / a fixed commodity / largely determined by genetics. /

But recent research / suggests that a very basic brain function / called working memory / might underlie our general intelligence, / opening up the intriguing possibility / that if you improve your working memory, / you could boost your IQ too. /

Working memory / is the brain's short-term information storage system. / It's a workbench / for solving mental problems. /

For example, / if you calculate 73 / – 6 / + 7, / your working memory will store the intermediate steps / necessary to work out the answer. / And the amount of information / that the working memory can hold / is strongly related / to general intelligence. /

A research team in Stockholm, Sweden, / has found signs / that the neural systems that underlie working memory / may grow / in response to training. / Using brain scans, / they measured the brain activity of adults / before and after / a working-memory training programme, / which involved tasks / such as memorizing the positions / of a series of dots on a grid. /

After five weeks of training, / their brain activity had increased / in the regions associated with this type of memory. /

Perhaps more significantly, / when the group studied children / who had completed these types of mental workouts, / they saw improvement / in a range of cognitive abilities / not related to the training, / and a leap in IQ test scores / of eight per cent. /

It's early days yet, / but the research team leader / thinks working-memory training / could be a key / to unlocking brain power. / 'Genetics determines a lot / and so does the early gestation period,' / he says. / 'On top of that, / there is a small percentage / – we don't know how many / – that can be improved by training.'

2C My bicycle & me

Activity
Pairwork. Students listen to the song *Bicycle* by Livingston Taylor.

Focus
Listening. Theme: bicycles and cycling.

Preparation
Photocopy one worksheet for each student. Fold the worksheet along the dotted line so that the lyrics are not visible. CD player.

[1]

Procedure
- Divide the class into pairs. Hand out one worksheet to each student.
- In pairs, students look at the cartoon and the words. They discuss and predict which words they will hear in the song. Use the discussion to check that students understand some terms related to cycling.
- Don't play the song yet. Ask pairs to match the verbs and noun phrases.
- Play the song. Students listen and check their answers to parts 1 and 2. Check the answers with the whole class.
- Ask students to unfold the worksheet so that the lyrics are now visible and play the song again.
- Discuss the questions in part 4 as a class. Students can listen again and sing along with the song.

Answers

1 All the items are in the song.
2 wear a helmet, downshift my Shimano gears, ride light bikes, cost big bucks, curse smelly trucks, pad my butt, feel my heart
3 a) (fixed expression) I'm pleased that the road ahead is safe.
  b) I hope she doesn't open her car door and knock me off, sending me 'flying' through the air.
  c) I'm forty years old. I'm having a wonderful time riding my bike.

Language notes

- *Guillaume* is a French man's name. The English equivalent is William.
- *Lycra* is a famous brand name for spandex (a lightweight, very flexible material).
- *Wrap-around sunglasses* are sunglasses whose arms cover the side of your face.
- *Shimano* is a famous Japanese manufacturer of cycling equipment.
- *Styrofoam* is an insulating material made from polystyrene.
- *Ruts* are places in a path or road where cars or other vehicles have cut a deep mark into the surface (which makes it more difficult for cyclists to ride there).
- A *Dodge Diplomat* is an old make of car, last made in the 1980s.
- *Butt* is US slang for your bottom. When a cyclist *pads his butt*, he adds soft items to his clothing that will make it more comfortable to ride a bike.

2D The museum of ourselves

Activity
Individual & groupwork. Students introduce their personal possessions as if they were museum exhibits.

Focus
Comparisons.

Preparation
You will need to set up this activity at least one day before actually doing it in class (see Set-up notes below). Photocopy one worksheet for each group of three students. Students will need scissors.

Set-up
At least one day before the activity, explain the task to students. They will need to bring in three (portable) personal possessions from home to the next lesson. They should choose old, unusual or curious items as they will be introducing them to the class.

Procedure
- Check that students have brought in their items as requested. (It may be an idea to have a bag ready with some emergency substitute items for the inevitable students who have forgotten!)
- Divide the class into groups of three. Explain that each group runs a museum. Assign each group a section of the room for their 'museum'. Make use of space at the front, sides and back of the room (and perhaps space outside the room if you have any).
- The students' task is to select three exhibits, arrange them into a display, write the labels for the exhibits and prepare the speeches that they will give as guides when showing visitors around.
- First, each group should select the most interesting exhibit from each person. (N.B. It is the other two students who should make the selection, after discussion with the owner.)
- Hand out the worksheet to each group. Ask students to now arrange the exhibits (i.e. deciding where to place them), write the labels (there is an example below), cut them out to place by the items and write descriptions for the guides to give (using structures from the language box).
- When students have finished their preparations, ask half of the groups to be 'visitors' to the other half's museums while the other half 'guide' them. Each student guide introduces one item in the museum. After a while, reverse the roles.

Example exhibit label

Rare souvenir plate from Malta
Manufactured circa 1989
The unusual bus design has been carefully hand-painted with the distinctive use of green and blue.
Owned by the Bogart family since a holiday in 1990 when it rained every day.

3A Money expressions

Activity
Groupwork. Students guess definitions of money expressions.

Focus
Vocabulary: expressions about money.

Preparation
Photocopy one worksheet for each group of three students. Cut the worksheet up into the Expressions list and the three cards (A, B and C).

Procedure
- Divide the class into groups of three students. Hand out an expressions list to each group and a different card (A, B or C) to each student in the group. Tell students not to look at each other's cards.
- Tell students that they each have five example sentences that have a similar meaning to five of the expressions in the expressions list.
- Allow some time for students to look at their examples and the expressions they go with.
- Explain how to play the game. In their groups, students take it in turns to read out one of their example sentences. The other two students look at the list of expressions and each make a guess as to which expression matches the example sentence. If they get it right, they get a point.

- Play continues with an example sentence from the next student, and so on until all fifteen sentences have been matched.
- The winner is the student with the most points at the end.

3B Really nice it was!

Activity
Pairwork. Students match sentences to contexts.

Focus
Speech feature: fronting.

Preparation
Photocopy one worksheet for each pair of students. Cut the worksheet up into the three sections.

Procedure
- Divide the class into pairs. Hand out one picture sheet to each pair, worksheet A to one student and worksheet B to the other. Tell students not to show each other their worksheets.
- Explain that students are going to take it in turns to read out one of their sentences. (N.B. Warn them not to read out the answer in brackets at the end!) The other student decides which picture shows the location where the sentence was spoken.
- If they are correct, they get a point. If they are wrong, they can have a second guess for half a point. If their second guess is wrong, the reader tells their partner the answer.
- If students are not sure why an answer is correct, they should read the sentence again and work together to decide why it is correct.

Extension
- When students have finished, ask them to prepare a new game. Each student writes four new sentences using fronting about the pictures on the sheet.
- When both students in a pair are ready, they play the game again using their own clues.

3C It's all over!

Activity
Groupwork. Students match words and definitions.

Focus
Vocabulary: words starting with *over*.

Preparation
Photocopy one worksheet for each group of three to four students. Cut the worksheet up into separate cards.

Procedure
- Divide the class into groups of three or four students. Hand out one set of cards to each group and place face down on the table.
- Explain that the small cards are words and the long ones are definitions.
- Students take it in turns to turn over a card (short or long). The card they turn over is left visible on the desk for the rest of the game (so gradually there are more and more cards).
- When a student sees two cards (a word and a definition) that they believe match, they can take them and place them in front of them. Once they have taken the cards, they belong to them and can't be put back!
- The game continues until all the cards have been revealed and students have made all the matches they want to.
- At the end of the game, go through the answers with the class. Students get two points for each correct match. An incorrect match costs them minus one point!
- The group winner is the student with the most points in a group. The class winner is the student with most points in the whole class.

Note
N.B. Although many of these items are not presented in the Student's Book lesson, most should be straightforward enough to work out. A few items (e.g. *overbearing*) may prove tricky, but this will make the game more interesting and will help students to learn new items.

3D Newly-found wealth

Activity
Individual & groupwork. Students make short speeches.

Focus
Vocabulary: adjectives with suffixes.

Preparation
Photocopy one worksheet for each group of five students. Cut the worksheet up into separate cards. (You may want to make extra copies of the top part of the worksheet for each group.)

Procedure
- Divide the class into groups of five students. Hand out one text about Sylvanu (an imaginary island very similar to Naura in the Student's Book lesson) to each group. Hand out one word card to each student. Tell students not to show each other their cards.
- Ask groups to read the text about Sylvanu and the topics A, B and C for discussion.
- Allow students about ten minutes to individually think of arguments agreeing or disagreeing with each of the three topics. Encourage them to make notes. Students should also think of natural ways that they could use as many adjectives as possible from their word card when giving their views.
- When they are ready, students should formally discuss the three topics, attempting to make use of all their adjectives. Each student should offer a short speech on each topic after which others can ask questions, disagree, expand on the argument, etc.
- At the end, review who successfully used the most adjectives during their three speeches. Discuss which ones were most difficult to include naturally.

4A Complaints

Activity
Pair & groupwork. Students do short roleplays.

Focus
Vocabulary: expressions connected with complaining.

Preparation
Photocopy one worksheet for every twelve students. Cut the worksheet up into the topic cards and individual expression cards.

Procedure
- Divide the class into groups of six students. Hand out one topic card to each group.
- With the whole class, take a few minutes to brainstorm the most unusual or unreasonable complaints someone might have for each of the topics. For example, on budget airlines, students might suggest ideas such as 'I only arrived two hours late but the plane hadn't waited for me' or 'They wouldn't let me take my pets with me on board.'
- Divide each group into three pairs of students.
- Explain that each pair of students will have to prepare either a one-person monologue or a two-person dialogue containing a short complaint connected to one of the topics. This does not need to be a real complaint – it can be an invented and unusual problem (such as those brainstormed).
- Tell students that in their complaint, they must include three expressions that you will (secretly) give them. All the expressions have exactly four words. Students should try to include all of these expressions naturally in their speech so that no one else notices them being used.
- Hand out three expressions cards to each pair. Remind them to keep these secret. Allow at least 10–15 minutes preparation time so that students can prepare a good, strong complaint.
- When students are ready, ask the three pairs to come back together in their group. Each pair says their complaint (encourage them to use stress and intonation to make their point strongly). The other students should keep a note of any expressions they think were on the secret cards. At the end of the speech they should say their guesses. They win one point for every word they correctly spotted or five points if they correctly spotted the whole four-word expression from the card.
- The winning pair in each group is the one with most points at the end.

Variation
With stronger and more confident classes, make groups of three and ask each student to individually prepare their complaint.

4B Mobile phone spies

Activity
Groupwork. Students listen to a speech and report back on its content.

Focus
Reported speech.

Preparation
Photocopy one worksheet for each student. Cut the worksheet in half.

Procedure
- Divide the class into groups of three to five students. Explain that they work for Mobon, a large mobile phone telecommunications company.
- Hand out one role card (but not the speech) to each student and ask them to read it.
- Explain that you are the Director of *TTC9,* one of Mobon's main rivals. They are going to listen to you make a speech. Students should imagine that they are doing some 'industrial spying' and make notes about the speech to bring back to Mobon.
- Read the Director's speech (as printed on the bottom of the worksheet) aloud at normal speed. (You could pause a little between sentences to allow time for note taking.)
- When you have finished, ask students in each group to talk together and agree what they heard. Remind them to practise using reported speech and point out the list of verbs on their role card, many of which can be used.
- Finish with a whole class feedback of what the Director said.
- (Optional written consolidation) Ask students to work together in their groups to prepare their own written report of what they heard, using as many different reporting verbs from the worksheet as they can.
- Hand out copies of the printed Director's speech so that students can check if they reported well or not.

4C The *Straightforward* awards

Activity
Groupwork & whole class. Students take part in a mock Oscars-style Awards ceremony.

Focus
Theme: awards ceremonies.

Preparation
Photocopy one worksheet for each pair or group of three students.

Procedure
- Explain that students are going to hold an awards ceremony in class.
- There are twelve awards. Divide the class into pairs or groups of three so that each pair/group can prepare at least one nomination.
- Hand out one worksheet to each pair/group. Inform each pair/group of the award(s) from the list that they will make nominations for.
- Students now prepare a list of three candidates for the award and three short speeches to explain why each candidate is suitable. (N.B. With some classes you may need to monitor during this stage to make sure that no cruel or unkind nominations are being planned.)

- At the end of preparation time, hold the awards ceremony. In turn, invite pairs/groups to announce their nominations.
- Each award will now need a winner. You can decide the winner in any way of your choosing, e.g.
  1 You could allow the nominating team to also announce the winner.
  2 You could appoint a winner yourself.
  3 You could have a whole class vote.
- When the winner is announced, invite him/her to the front to make a spontaneous, short acceptance speech.
- Continue with the other awards. Manipulate things if necessary to make sure a number of different people receive awards and get to make speeches.

4D What on earth is going on?

Activity
Pairwork. Students read dialogues and speculate about what is going on.

Focus
Modal verbs: *must*, *might*, *may* and *could* for speculating and deducing.

Preparation
Photocopy one worksheet for every eight students. Cut the worksheet up into four separate dialogue cards.

Procedure
- Divide the class into pairs. Hand out one dialogue card to each pair.
- Ask pairs to look at their dialogue and quietly discuss what they think it might be about. They should think about possible answers to the five questions.
- Allow pairs a few minutes to practice reading the dialogue in as interesting a way as possible. Monitor and give advice on how to make the performances sound better.
- When students are ready, make groups of eight who have prepared different dialogues (i.e. each group has students who have prepared dialogues 1, 2, 3 and 4). Pairs take it in turns to perform their dialogues.
- When each pair has performed their dialogue, the audience should discuss the questions and agree on the most interesting answers. Were they the same answers as the actors had imagined?
- At the end, bring the whole class together and compare ideas. Which is most unusual or imaginative?

5A A flatpack text

Activity
Pairwork. Students reassemble a jumbled text.

Focus
Reading. Relative clauses.

Preparation
Photocopy one worksheet for each pair of students. Cut the worksheet up into separate cards.

Procedure
- Remind students that Ingvar Kamprad made a fortune by selling flatpack furniture for people to build themselves at home. Explain that students are going to assemble a flatpack text about Steve Jobs of Apple computers.
- Divide the class into pairs. Hand out one jumbled set of cards to each pair.
- In pairs, students match the sentence beginnings with the sentence endings. Point out that white cards match with white cards and black match with black. Monitor while students are working to check that they are matching correctly.
- Students then try and reassemble the text. Point out that the text is striped (white, black, white, and so on). Also that the first and last sentence in the text is shown by the thick grey horizontal line at the top of the cards (for the first sentence) and bottom (for the last sentence).
- When they have finished, let students compare their texts with other pairs. There is no need to go through the complete text as a whole class unless students have problems or questions.

Extension
When students have finished the activity, ask them to turn over all the sentence endings cards. How many sentences can they now complete with a meaning that is close to the original?

5B Tag talk

Activity
Groupwork. Students have a conversation using question tags.

Focus
Speech feature: question tags.

Preparation
Photocopy one worksheet for each group of three to four students. Cut the worksheet up into cards.

Procedure
- Divide the class into groups of three or four students. Hand out one set of cards, placed face down on the table.
- Ask students to randomly pick up five. (The other cards won't be used in this round of the game.)
- Explain that you will call out a topic title (see list below). Any student in the group can start a conversation about the topic, and others can join in whenever they like. The aim is for students to include all five of their question tags in the conversation, as naturally as possible.
- After a few minutes, ask students to stop talking and for each group to review which student has managed to naturally use the most tags. After this, they should collect in all the cards and shuffle them.
- Call out a new topic for discussion. Students pick up five new cards and the game restarts. You could play it two or three times in total.

Possible topics (continued on next page)

Choose two or three most suitable for your own class:
- Things people can't live without
- Doing dangerous things

- Video games are better than books
- How to bring up a young child
- What are the best investments?
- How to become a better driver
- Films that change your life
- Staying healthy
- Will we still be in touch with each other in ten years' time?

5C Housework

Activity
Pairwork. Students listen to the song *Housework* by Robert Palmer.

Focus
Listening. Theme: housework. Verb & noun phrase collocations.

Preparation
Photocopy one worksheet for each student. Fold the worksheet along the dotted line so that the lyrics are not visible. CD player.

[2]

Procedure
- Divide the class into pairs. Hand out one worksheet to each student.
- In pairs, students complete the table in part 1. With stronger classes, encourage them to think of less common verbs (e.g. instead of the fairly obvious *wash the plates*, they could choose *stack the plates* or *dry the plates*).
- Play the song. Students listen and note the verbs the singer uses. Check the answers with the whole class.
- Discuss the questions in part 3 as a class. There may be some very different opinions. Encourage students to refer to the lyrics to support their views. Students can listen again and sing along with the song.

Answers
1 Possible verbs (N.B. Many others are possible.) shout goodbye from out of the window; stack the plates; dry the dishes; strip the bed; pick up the pillows; straighten the rug; shut the windows; organize the drawers; check the closet; shove the dirty clothes in the hamper; push the vacuum round the carpets; tidy the shelves; clean the glassware; heat up some lunch; sort the garbage; file the bills; collect the dry-cleaning; withdraw some cash out of the dispenser; fill up the freezer; chill some wine for later this evening; cook the dinner; put the roast into the oven; prepare the veg; lay the table; play some music; find the candles

3 These are opinion questions with no correct answers. As to whether the man is happy or not, this is a little ambiguous. Although he keeps repeating 'The housework makes you happy' and 'The housework keeps you feeling alive', students might argue that his comments are not entirely convincing. It almost sounds as if he is trying to convince and persuade himself that his life of endless domestic routines is satisfying. Is he only trying to make the time pass quickly until his wife comes home?

5D Regrets

Activity
Individual & groupwork. Students imagine various regrets and thoughts about the past that various characters might have.

Focus
Hypothetical past situations.

Preparation
Photocopy one worksheet for every eight students. Cut the worksheet into separate role cards.

Procedure
- Explain that students are going to think about regrets and thoughts about the past that various characters might have.
- Hand out one role card to each student. Tell students not to show each other their cards.
- Students work individually to write notes for points 1–3, imagining what their character's life is like and thinking about what they regret and don't regret. Tell them to use all three of the structures listed on their card.
- When students are ready, divide the class into groups of three or more students.
- Students take it in turns to read out their answers to points 2 and 3 (i.e. not the description in point 1 or the role card itself).
- When they have heard the regrets and non-regrets, the other students should discuss together to see if they can guess as accurately as possible who the person is that is being described. When they have said their guess, the original student can read the role card aloud. How close were they?

6A Runaways & breakdowns

Activity
Pairwork. Students invent a story.

Focus
Writing. Vocabulary: nouns from phrasal verbs.

Preparation
Photocopy one worksheet for every four students. Cut the worksheet in half.

Procedure
- Explain that students are going to invent a story. Ask the whole class to agree two numbers between one and twenty-one.
- Divide the class into pairs. Ask each pair to write down five further numbers between one and twenty-one (not including the two already chosen).
- Hand out one worksheet to each pair. Pairs look at the words corresponding to the seven numbers chosen (the two chosen by the class and the five they chose).
- They then create a written story that must include these seven words. Allow about 20–30 minutes for this.

- When they have finished, pairs can compare stories, e.g. swapping with another pair, listening to them read aloud, displaying them on the classroom wall, etc.

6B Pierced ears & bloodshot eyes

Activity
Pairwork. Students guess what medical problems a cartoon patient has.

Focus
Vocabulary: body collocations.

Preparation
Photocopy one worksheet for each student.

Procedure
- Divide the class into pairs. Hand out one worksheet to each student.
- Ask students, on their own, to look at the two boxes of words and make five features and/or health problems using one word from each box, e.g. *pierced ears, bloodshot eyes*.
- Warn students that many Box A / Box B collocations are not possible. If students are not sure whether the collocation is possible, they should check in a dictionary or ask you. (N.B. Some of the possible collocations in the task, e.g. *cauliflower ear*, are not featured in the Student's Book lesson.)
- When students have decided on their five features or problems, they should draw these on their character (but not write the name of the feature or problem). Tell students not to show each other their worksheets.
- Explain how to play the game. In their pairs, and keeping their pictures secret, students take it in turns to try and find out what features and problems their partner's character has. One student says a part of the body, e.g. *ears*, and the other student guesses by asking up to three *Does he have …?* questions, e.g. *Does he have pierced ears?*
- If students have not found the answer after three guesses, their partner should show them that part of the picture (covering up the other parts) and the other student can try to guess based on what they see.
- (Optional) When students have finished the activity, bring the whole class back together. Use the board to collect all the collocations that have been used. Point out which ones are common and if any are unusual or sound wrong.

Language notes
- With some Box A words only one Box B collocation is likely, e.g. flyaway hair, rosy cheeks, cauliflower ear, bloodshot eyes, double chin, black eye, rotten teeth, runny nose, bushy eyebrows, wrinkled forehead.
- Other Box A words can be followed by a number of possible Box B words. Here are some common collocations: pierced ears/nose/lip/tongue/belly button/eyebrow; blocked nose/ears; bruised arm/leg/ankle/knee/forehead; swollen arm/leg/ankle/wrist/finger/toe/hand/foot/knee/lips; broken arm/leg/wrist/finger/toe/nose/foot; long arms/nose/fingers/legs/hair/eyelashes; bare feet/chest; false teeth/eyelashes/arm/leg; scarred stomach/cheek/chest.

6C Natasha at 21

Activity
Individual & groupwork. Students read more about the Natasha story from the Student's Book lesson.

Focus
Reading.

Preparation
Photocopy one worksheet for every student.

Procedure
- Divide the class into groups of three or four students. Hand out one worksheet to each student.
- Allow groups enough time to discuss the questions in part 1 and compare ideas. At the end, collect some ideas in the whole class.
- Ask students to read the newspaper article and check their predictions. Allow enough reading time for them to understand the text.
- When students are ready, they go back into groups to discuss their reactions and compare them with their predictions. Bring everyone together again for a whole class discussion.
- After the discussion, students look at the questions in part 2 and read the text again to find the answers. Discuss the answers as a class.
- Ask students to find the adjectives in part 3 in the text and check they understand what they mean. Check the answers with the whole class.

Answers
2 a) There are no bombs now. Children don't get injured. It isn't damp. Children don't cry all the time. It smells of laundry now. The orphanage atmosphere is 'warm' not 'cold'. The staff spend time with the children now.

b) She didn't meet her mother. She was afraid that her mother wanted to meet her for the wrong reasons – perhaps looking for money.

3 *pitch dark* (line 8): If something is pitch dark it is totally dark.

personal odyssey (line 18): An odyssey is a long journey of discovery. Natasha is on a personal odyssey – which means that she is finding out things about herself.

chaotic flight (line 25): A flight is a journey of escape from something. It was chaotic because so much was difficult and improvized.

special needs (line 31): If a child has special needs, it requires extra help because it is mentally or physically disabled.

warm atmosphere (line 35): If something has a warm atmosphere, it feels pleasant and welcoming.

Notes
- Students may be curious to find out what happened to Natasha, the orphan featured in the texts in lesson 6C of the Student's Book. This text reveals how she grew up and what happened when she returned to Sarajevo.
- Do this activity after students have read the story of Natasha in the Student's Book lesson. If this activity isn't done immediately after the reading of that text, start by getting students to recall what happened in that story.

6D Babysitting blues

Activity
Individual & whole class. Students reconstruct and narrate a picture story.

Focus
Vocabulary: babies & babysitting.

Preparation
Photocopy one worksheet for each student. Also photocopy one worksheet and cut it up into separate pictures.
- If you have fewer than twelve students, cut up the worksheet into fewer pieces (i.e. some students will have pieces with two or three pictures). N.B. Between them, the students should have the entire picture story.
- If you have more than twelve students, you will need to photocopy and cut up extra worksheets so that everyone has one picture each (and some will have the same picture).

Procedure
- Explain that students are going to reconstruct a picture story.
- Hand out one piece of the picture story to each student. Tell them to look at their pictures but not to show them to anyone else.
- Explain the aim of the activity is for students to find out what the whole story is, by describing their pictures to each other but without looking at each other's pictures.
- Students now mingle, meeting different students and describing what they have in their picture.
- When some time has passed and students have heard a number of different people's descriptions, encourage them to try and work out the story. (N.B. This may take up to half an hour.)
- When students have worked out a version of the story, let them sit down again. Hand out the worksheets with the full story.

Extension
Extend the activity by asking students, in pairs, to think of an interesting way to narrate this story. Encourage them to find lively, varied ways to make the story come alive. When they are ready, students can tell the story to the whole class or other pairs.

Variation
For weaker classes, rather than a class mingle, divide the class into groups of three to four students to reconstruct the story from the pictures.

7A School issues

Activity
Individual & groupwork. Students discuss issues to do with running a school.

Focus
Theme: schools and behaviour.

Preparation
Photocopy one worksheet for every two students. Cut the worksheet up into separate role cards.

Procedure
- Explain that students are going to meet to discuss several issues to do with running a school.
- Hand out one worksheet to each student. Ask students to work individually. They should read the introduction and then make notes about their views on each of the problems. Allow at least ten minutes for this preparation stage.
- When students are well-prepared, divide the class into groups of at least five students. Appoint one person in each group as Head Teacher, who will lead the meeting.
- Allow students fifteen minutes (or whatever time you choose) to reach an agreement on as many issues as they can.
- At the end you can have a short discussion in the whole class, comparing decisions made in the different meetings.

Note
In order to make the task as accessible as possible, the task is set in your own school (i.e. where your students are currently studying). However, if the problems do not seem realistic or appropriate for your school, tell the students that they should imagine that they work for a school called Hedgerow College, which is very similar to St George's school described in the Student's Book lesson.

7B Time to do something about it

Activity
Individual & groupwork. Students write replies to an internet forum.

Focus
Writing. Theme: rude behaviour.

Preparation
Photocopy one worksheet for each student.

Procedure
- Hand out one worksheet to each student. Students read the forum entries.
- Divide the class into groups of three or four students to discuss their initial response to the entries.
- Students now work individually to imagine and write the next three replies to William (or the other posters) in the boxes. One of the replies should reflect their own views. The other two should be completely imaginary.
- When students have written their responses, let them read each other's. (They could guess which answer represents the writer's own views – though that may be obvious!)

7C Clare Francis

Activity
Individual & pairwork. Students rewrite a text about the author Clare Francis.

Focus
Participle clauses.

Preparation
Photocopy one worksheet for each student. Cut the worksheet in half.

Procedure
- Explain that students are going to read a text about Clare Francis, the author of *A Dark Devotion*, from the Student's Book lesson.
- Hand out the top half of the worksheet to each student. Ask students to work individually to read the text.
- Ask students to find a way of rewriting part or all of each numbered section so that it includes at least one participle clause. (You could do the first section as a worked example with the whole class.)
- When students have reworked the sections of text, divide the class into pairs to compare their answers.
- When they have finished, hand out the bottom half of the worksheet to each student. Ask them to compare their answers with this text. (Make sure they understand that this is only one possible answer, and a number of other solutions will be possible.)

7D A criminal's own story

Activity
Pairwork. Students write a story about a criminal using ten verbs.

Focus
Writing. Vocabulary: crime & legal matters.

Preparation
Photocopy one worksheet for each student.

Procedure
- Explain that students are going to invent a story about a criminal.
- Hand out one worksheet to each student.
- Dictate the list of verbs (see below) to the class. Ask students to write them all down in Box 1.
- Divide the class into pairs. Ask students to compare lists to check they have spelt the verbs correctly.
- Ask pairs to choose just ten of the verbs – those they think are most suitable for telling a story about a criminal. They should then agree the best sequence for the verbs, i.e. the order they might come in the story. Tell both students in each pair to write down the list in Box 2. (N.B. Don't warn students at this stage that they are preparing a list for another pair rather than for themselves.)
- Each pair should now hand their worksheets to another pair (and receive another pair's list of verbs in return).
- Now pairs have to invent a story using the other pair's choice of verbs and choice of order! Ask students to write the full text of their story in Box 3.
- Students then meet up with another pair – not the pair that originally gave them the verbs list – and listen to each other's stories. The listening pair should write down the ten verbs in sequence in Box 4 as they hear them.

Verbs
1 convicted 2 caught 3 broke 4 sentenced 5 stole 6 served 7 arrested 8 held 9 charged 10 ran 11 forgot 12 advised 13 planned 14 pleaded 15 crept 16 found 17 denied 18 put 19 entered 20 learnt

Variation
- Instead of the final stage above, do this: When the stories are ready, ask students to underline the ten verbs in their text.
- Students should meet up with another pair – not the pair that originally gave them the verbs list. One pair reads their story aloud – but whenever they come to an underlined verb they say 'beep' instead of the verb. The pair listening to the story should write down the verb they think is missing in each gap. At the end, they can check if they got all ten correctly or not.

8A Lost property

Activity
Individual & pairwork. Students read four short literary descriptions and guess who they are describing.

Focus
Reading. Literary descriptions.

Preparation
Photocopy one worksheet for each student. Students will need access to the internet for this task.

Procedure
- Hand out one worksheet to each student. Students can work individually or in pairs as you prefer.
- Students look at the list of people and do a quick internet search to find out about any that are unknown to them.
- Explain to the class that four of the people in the list are guests staying in the hotel at the moment. The staff have found four pieces of lost property (listed at the bottom of the worksheet).
- Students read the texts and try to work out (a) who the guests are and (b) which item they have lost. (N.B. Each guest has lost one distinctively personal item.)
- Allow students some time to see if they can complete the task without any further clues. Pairs can compare and discuss answers when they think they have them.
- Check the answers with the whole class.

Answers
Room 101: Sherlock Holmes
(text from *A Study in Scarlet* by A. Conan-Doyle)
Lost property: a violin

Room 102: Mr Darcy
(text from *Pride and Prejudice* by Jane Austen)
Lost property: an invitation to a dance

Room 201: Cleopatra
(text from *Roman History* by Cassius Dio)
Lost property: a snake

Room 202: Alice
(text from *Alice in Wonderland* by Lewis Carrol)
Lost property: a flamingo and a ball (for playing croquet)

8B Word stress game

Activity
Pairwork. Students play a word stress board game.

Focus
Pronunciation: changing word stress.

Preparation
Photocopy one worksheet for each pair of students. Each student will need about ten counters of one kind, e.g. coloured sweets, to place on the game board.

Procedure
- Divide the class into pairs. Hand out one worksheet to each pair.
- Explain how to play the game. Player A aims to make a continuous chain of their counters connecting any hexagon on the left of the board to any one on the right. Player B must do the same but from top to bottom of the grid. The winner is the first person to complete their chain. (N.B. Players should try to block the other player by placing their counter in the way.) In the example game below, the player using triangles has won because he/she has made an unbroken line from top to bottom.

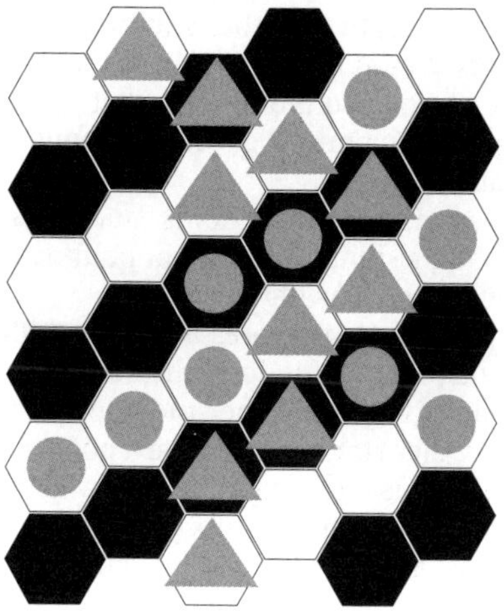

- Players take it in turns to choose any hexagon that doesn't have a counter on it yet. They must then make a good sentence using the word from that hexagon with the correct word stress. The word can have grammatical changes (e.g. the verb *insult* could be *insulted* or *insulting*) but must remain a noun or a verb (as indicated by the shading of the hexagon). Sentences must be a minimum of five words long.
- If their partner agrees that the sentence is good, the player leaves their counter on this hexagon. If the partner points out a mistake (e.g. with meaning, grammar or stress), the player can't place a counter on the hexagon. (They can try again next turn if it is still free.)

Note
It's probably a good idea to allow the use of dictionaries in this activity so that students can check meaning and pronunciation.

8C You've got to have friends

Activity
Groupwork. Students ask and answer questions about attitudes to friendship.

Focus
Vocabulary: relationships. Attitude adverbials.

Preparation
Photocopy one worksheet for every four students. Cut the worksheet up into separate question cards.

Procedure
- Hand out one worksheet (A, B, C or D) randomly to each student.
- Explain that students have been commissioned to research people's attitudes to friendship by an internet site that specializes in reuniting old friends.
- Ask students to stand up and mingle, meeting different people. They should get answers to the three questions on their card from a variety of different people and make notes of responses they get in order to write a report later on. Encourage students to ask follow-on questions and have short discussions rather than give one-word answers.
- Allow enough time for students to meet and talk to at least three or four different people.
- Ask students with different letters to work together in pairs, pooling their results in order to write a short report on 'What contemporary people think about friendship'. Encourage them to use the attitude adverbials from page 81 of the Student's Book, e.g. *Interestingly, not many people thought …, Predictable enough, most people didn't agree that … .*

8D To be perfectly honest

Activity
Groupwork. Students have short conversations on a range of topics.

Focus
Discourse markers.

Preparation
Photocopy one worksheet for every three students. Cut the worksheet up into separate cards.

Procedure
- Ask students to work individually and write a list of four topics that would be interesting to discuss. Encourage them to think of a range of current, local, national and international topics that are lively, controversial or interesting.
- Divide the class into groups of three students. Hand out a set of cards to each group, placed face down on the table.
- Each student should randomly draw five cards from the pile. Their task is to try and use all the discourse markers on their cards naturally in a conversation.
- One student in each group names one of their topics. In their groups, students take part in a free-for-all discussion about that topic. Students can join in, interrupt naturally, change the subject, etc. whenever they want to. Every time they use one of the items on their cards naturally and appropriately, they can place the card face-up on the table in front of them.
- The first person to place all their cards is the winner (and the game can start again with a new topic).

9A Three new cities

Activity
Individual & groupwork. Students research a city. They then make a short presentation.

Focus
Theme: new cities.

Preparation
Photocopy one worksheet for each student. Students will need access to the internet for this task.

Procedure
- Divide the class into three groups, A, B and C. Hand out one worksheet to each student.
- Explain that students are going to search for information about a city on the internet and then make a presentation about the city. Tell students that the cities are all 'new' created and designed cities, not just 'evolved' ones.
- Allocate a time of your choosing (15–30 minutes) for students to use the internet and research answers to the worksheet questions about their city. Make sure students are clear that they will all need to prepare a presentation, so they should aim to collect lots of useful data. Pairs of students from each group could work together in this research phase, but remind them that they will all need their own notes. Point out that not all the questions on the worksheet may be relevant to their city.
- At the end of the research time, ask students to take some time (15–45 minutes) to work on their own and prepare a short presentation (to last about 3–5 minutes) about their city. Warn them that the presentation must not simply be a reading aloud of the facts or answers to questions on their worksheet. They should shape and organize what they have learnt into an interesting presentation.
- When students have finished preparing, make groups of three (with one student from each original group). Students take it in turns to make their presentation.

Variation
- When students make their presentations in groups, monitor and see which ones sound particularly interesting. If there is time and interest, at the end ask one student for each city to present to the whole class.
- If your class does not have easy simultaneous internet access, set the preparation stage for homework.

9B Home!

Activity
Groupwork. Students play a snap-type game to describe different properties.

Focus
Vocabulary: describing homes & properties.

Preparation
Photocopy one worksheet for each group of three students. Cut the worksheet up into separate picture cards and vocabulary cards.

Procedure
- Divide the class into groups of three students. Hand out one set of picture cards and one set of vocabulary cards to each group, both sets placed face down on the table.
- A student in each group should deal out ten vocabulary cards to each student.
- Explain how to play the game. One student turns over the top picture card and shows it to the other two players.
- The other two students should look at their vocabulary cards to see if they can find a word or phrase that describes something in the picture, e.g. *run-down* with the picture of the old mansion.
- If they find a suitable card, they shout *Home!* and show their card. If both students shout, the student holding the picture card determines who was the quickest.
- The picture-holding student also decides if the vocabulary card really matches the picture. If it does, the card is placed in a discard pile. If it doesn't, the student must take back the card and the other student can have a go.
- After this, the picture card is replaced in the pile and the pack of pictures should be shuffled to mix them up.
- The next student picks a picture card and the game continues.
- The winner is the first student to get rid of all their cards.

9C Jamaica farewell

Activity
Pairwork. Students listen to the song *Jamaica farewell* by Harry Belafonte.

Focus
Listening. Theme: tropical islands.

Preparation
Photocopy one worksheet for each student. CD player.

[3]

Procedure
- Ask students what other famous islands they know about (apart from Tobago in the Student's Book lesson). Encourage a whole class discussion by asking questions about the islands they mention, e.g. *Do you have a romantic image of the island? Would you like a holiday there? Do you think you would like to live there?*
- Write *Jamaica* on the board and find out if students know anything about this island. Tell them a little, if they don't (see *Notes* below).
- Explain that students are going to listen to a famous romantic song about Jamaica.
- Hand out one worksheet to each student. Explain that the ending of each line of the song has been mixed up at the bottom of the page.
- In pairs, ask students to fill in the line endings, making their best guess at the complete song. Point out:
  (1) that it may not be possible to guess the correct answer as several endings may be possible.
  (2) that they have information about the rhyme pattern to help them. If students are not familiar with this, point out the letters at the end of each line and tell them that answers with the same letter have the same ending sound, e.g. *stop* rhymes with *top*.
- When students have finished, first let them compare with other pairs, then play the song for them to check.
- Students can listen again and sing along with the song.

Answers
13; 9; 7; 4 12; 6; 1; 8 2; 16; 5; 3 10; 14; 15; 11

Notes
- Jamaica is an English-speaking tropical island nation in the Caribbean Sea, about 150 miles south of Cuba. Many world-famous musical styles originated in Jamaica, including reggae and ska. The singer Bob Marley came from Jamaica. The religion Rastafarianism began there.
- Akey (or Ackee) is the national fruit of Jamaica. It is related to the lychee. Ackee and saltfish is a traditional Jamaican dish. Salt cod is sautéed with ackee (boiled), onions, peppers, tomatoes and herbs.

9D Experimental travel

Activity
Groupwork. Students talk about an imaginary trip.

Focus
Speech feature: vague language.

Preparation
Photocopy one worksheet for each group of three students. Cut the worksheet up into separate picture cards and the phrases card.

Procedure
- Divide the class into groups of three students. Hand out one set of picture cards to each group, placed face down on the table, and the phrases card.
- Explain that each group is on holiday together in an unusual place. They should imagine that they are going on a walk and will see a number of interesting things.
- Students take it in turns to turn over a random picture card and draw their friends' attention to it, by saying one of the phrases from the card, e.g. *Oh, look over there!* All three students should now discuss what they can see.
- Students can speculate about what the things are used for, how they work, who the people are, and so on. They should use as much vague language from the phrases card (or similar expressions) as possible.
- After a short time, the next student turns over the next picture, and so on, until the 'walk' is over.

10A Endurance event

Activity
Pairwork. Students invent a new endurance event. They then act out an interview with someone who participated in the event.

Focus
Theme: achievements & difficulties.

Preparation
Photocopy one worksheet for each pair of students. Fold the worksheet along the dotted line.

Procedure
- Divide the class into pairs. Hand out one worksheet to each pair, with only the top half visible.
- Explain that students are going to use the questions to invent a new endurance event. You could brainstorm some unusual ideas together if the class is low on inspiration, e.g. walking across a desert, swimming up a local river, playing underwater football for 24 hours, running a marathon on the Moon, etc.
- When pairs have completed the invention task, ask them to unfold the worksheet. Explain that they should now imagine that their event has just happened and someone has just finished successfully taking part in it. They now write a role card for this character, using the prompts to help them.

- When pairs have completed both tasks, they should swap their worksheet with another pair.
- Explain that students are now going to act out an interview with a participant of this event. Pairs should read about the event and study the role card. One student now takes on the role of a TV interviewer who has just caught the participant as they finish the event. The other student plays the participant. Encourage students to be creative and go beyond the basic information on the cards. Allow the interviews to run for at least four or five minutes.

Extension

- When students have finished the first roleplay, mix the pairs. Ask all the students who played the role of a participant to move to a new partner (but not one of the students who wrote their role card). The student who played the interviewer now takes the role of the participant.
- The new interviewer will now be someone who doesn't know anything about the event, so will need to ask some questions about what exactly was involved, and the participant will need to explain more details about the event itself.

Answers

1i No – not the **Sales** Department. The Director is due to visit **Marketing**.
2f Mika's collecting the **reports**. Could you bring along the **files**?
3k It says on the box that it's **indestructible**. It's **bound** to break.
4a I'm hopeful about **my** chances in the election. But I think **you're** about to lose in a big way.
5b The original plan was to get just **two**. Right now, she's thinking of buying a whole **set**.
6j How stupid I am! Why did I turn the **computer** on? I wanted to listen to the **radio** news.
7h They're on the point of deciding to **sell** all their shares. But surely now's the time to **buy** more.
8e Wasn't the package due to arrive by **9**am? Ah no – it says here 'before **midday**'.
9c Six **fifteen**? No! The meeting's to start on the **hour**.
10l Kenneth believes they'll be **late** for the deadline. I'm sure they **won't**.
11d I'm supposed to arrive there next **Thursday**. But I'm only leaving here on **Friday**.
12g **Everyone** has agreed to the new measures. Now, what about **you**?

10B It's not this! It's that!

Activity

Pairwork. Students complete and match pairs of sentences. They then read them aloud using contrastive stress.

Focus

Futures. Pronunciation: contrastive stress.

Preparation

Photocopy one worksheet for each student.

Procedure

- Divide the class into pairs. Hand out one worksheet to each student.
- Ask pairs to complete the sentences with the words in the box and then get them to go straight on to matching the pairs of sentences without checking the answers as a whole class. (This is because a number of words may grammatically fit some of the gaps in the sentences – but students will also need to think about the meaning in task two to decide whether their chosen word is the best one.)
- Check the answers with the whole class.
- Ask pairs to decide where the contrastive stresses are in the sentences. Check the answers before students go on to practise saying the sentences. Monitor while students are practising the sentences to check that they are using the correct stress.

10C Television quiz

Activity

Individual. Students find the correct definitions for words related to television.

Focus

Vocabulary: television.

Preparation

Photocopy one worksheet for each student.

Procedure

- Hand out one worksheet to each student. Point out that students have a lot of definitions but no words. Allow students enough time to read carefully through the definitions.
- Explain that you are going to read out a list of words and students have to choose the best definition for each word.
- Do an example with the class to make sure that everyone understands what to do. Read out *the anchor* and ask students to find the best definition of this word. Confirm that the answer is definition 3. Explain that students now have to do this for all the words you read out. Point out that you will include three items that are not in the list of definitions!
- Read the words on the next page (without the numbers, which are the answers). N.B. The underlined items are the ones that are not in the list.
- At the end, let students check with each other, then go through all the answers together.
- Optional follow-on: Students could write definitions for the three extra words.

Teacher script and answers

the anchor (3)	an episode
a documentary (7)	a reality show (15)
a sitcom (6)	out-takes or bloopers (10)
a couch potato (22)	live coverage (8)
a TV guide (16)	extras (4)
a spin-off (13)	the lead (5)
a remote control (20)	prime time (17)
a commercial break	a TV licence (26)
the watershed (19)	pay-per-view (14)
a soap opera (11)	product placement (25)
breaking news (9)	a ratings war (24)
a cliff-hanger (12)	channel-hopping (21)
an EPG – Electronic Programme Guide (18)	a studio (1)
	the host
the box (23)	dressing rooms (2)

a commercial break – the time between programmes when advertisements are shown
an episode – a programme that is one part of a story that has, for example, six parts
the host – the person who chats with the celebrity guests in a talk show

Note

The quiz expands on vocabulary introduced and worked on in the Student's Book lesson and there will be some items that students will not have met before. Encourage them to make their 'best guess' at the time you read words out (rather than just collect them all in a list to do later).

10D Getting to the top

Activity

Groupwork. Students play a board game where they talk about success and failure.

Focus

Vocabulary: success & failure.

Preparation

Photocopy one worksheet for each group of three to four students. You will need a dice for each group and a counter for each student.

Procedure

- Divide the class into groups of three or four students. Hand out a game board, a dice and counters to each group.
- Explain that the aim of the game is to be the first person to get to the top of the mountain. However, like all things in life, there are ups and downs.
- To start, all students place their counters at the base camp. Students take it in turns to throw the dice.
- Depending on the number on the dice, they look at the first sentence in the list for that number and decide what the missing word is, using a word from the box. They then say the complete sentence to the others in the group, e.g. if the student throws 3, they read 3a): *I think I have a bright future ahead of me.*
- If the other students agree that the missing word is correct and the sentence has a success meaning, the student moves their counter two steps up the mountain.
- If the other students agree that the missing word is correct but the sentence has a failure meaning, the student stays where they are on the mountain.
- If the other students agree that the missing word is not correct, the student must move their counter one step down the mountain. (N.B. These rules are summarized on the game board.)
- The next player to throw a number that has already been thrown should complete the next sentence in the list, e.g. 3b. N.B. Words from the box can be used repeatedly throughout the game.
- The winner is the first player to reach the summit.
- Check the answers for the gapped sentences with the whole class at the end.

Answers

1 a) aim/goal b) mess c) chance d) make
2 a) fallen b) blank c) overnight d) high
3 a) ahead b) doing c) came d) bankrupt
4 a) pay b) turned c) make d) lost
5 a) make b) further c) achievement d) mess/shambles
6 a) flop b) shambles c) thriving d) success

Language note

In the feedback stage, students may argue that some answers are grammatically possible, e.g. *My new recording only sold twelve copies. A complete success!* You will need to point out that although the collocation *complete success* is possible, it doesn't fit in with the meaning of the previous sentence which is negative not positive.

11A Instant poem

Activity

Individual. Students do a guided-writing exercise to write a poem.

Focus

Vocabulary: descriptive verbs.

Preparation

Photocopy one worksheet for each student.

Procedure

- Ask students how they feel about writing poems. (Don't worry if you get a number of negative or uninterested responses.) Explain that writing poetry can be very enjoyable and that you can help them to write one.
- Hand out one worksheet to each student. Take some time to make sure they are clear how it works, i.e. each instruction guides them to write a part of the poem. You could do an example first line together. Make use of the example poem at the bottom of the page to show what a completed poem might look like.
- While students work, monitor and help with language questions. Aim to be encouraging about their work. If possible, also write a poem yourself using the framework. (Students are likely to find this reassuring.)
- When students have finished, allow them to share poems with others (if they want to). Some students will probably be keen to read theirs aloud to the class. (N.B. Some people may be embarrassed about others reading their 'creative writing'.)

11B Search & replace

Activity
Individual & pairwork. Students look for sections of text that can be replaced with prepositional phrases.

Focus
Vocabulary: prepositional phrases.

Preparation
Photocopy one worksheet for each pair of students. Cut it up into three sections.

Procedure
- Divide the class into pairs. Hand out worksheet A to one student in each pair, and worksheet B to the other.
- Ask students to read their text and see if they can find any parts of the text that could be replaced with one of the prepositional phrases listed at the bottom of their worksheet. The places where words can be replaced are not underlined or indicated in any way.
- Point out that students have different texts but the same list of possible prepositional phrases – so each student will only need some of the items. Don't tell students how many items can be used in each text.
- When they have finished, each pair should look at each other's texts and check them together. Tell them that all of the prepositional phrases except one are used only once, either in text A or B. The students should try to find out which one is used twice (*out of sight*).
- Hand out the answers section of the worksheet to each pair. Allow time for students to check it against their versions. Alternatively, check the answers as a class.

11C Sounds peculiar

Activity
Groupwork. Students listen to sound sequences and tell the stories.

Focus
Listening. Vocabulary: sounds.

Preparation
Photocopy one worksheet for each group of three students. Cut up the sound words at the bottom of the worksheet into separate cards. CD player.

[4] [5]

Procedure
- Divide the class into groups of three students. Hand out one set of pictures and the word cards to each group.
- Ask students to match the words to the pictures, placing the words on top of the pictures. Point out that it isn't a one-to-one match. Some words could go with more than one picture – and some pictures could have more than one word. Some will be a matter of opinion as well!
- When they have finished, groups can compare with others to see if they have the same answers.
- Explain that students are going to listen to a recording of some of the sounds (see below). They should decide what sounds they hear and the order the sounds come in.
- Play the first sound sequence recording. Compare answers with the class at the end.
- Ask students to work together and see if they can agree what the story told by the sounds is.
- When they are ready, invite volunteers to narrate their story while you play the recording, providing sound effects.
- Repeat this for the second sound sequence.

Sound sequences
For reference, here are the lists of sounds. There is also a possible story for each sequence which you may want to tell your class. (N.B. These are not right answers, just one possible interpretation of the sounds.)

First sound sequence
Person humming and whistling; sizzling; buzzing; 'Oh'; footsteps; creaking; muttering; 'No'; door slamming; footsteps; sizzling; humming and whistling; knocking and buzzing; 'Oh'; footsteps; creaking; 'Ah'; laughter; pop; clink; beep beep beep beep; 'Agggh'; running footsteps.

Possible story
Joanna was cooking a special meal for her friend. The doorbell rang at a difficult moment forcing her to stop cooking to answer the door. It was a double-glazing salesman. She quickly got rid of him and went back to her cooking, only to be interrupted again a few seconds later. She was ready to give the salesman a piece of her mind, but when she opened the door it was her friend. She'd brought some champagne which they opened and started drinking. Suddenly the smoke alarm went off. They ran back to the kitchen, but the dinner was on fire!

Second sound sequence
Whistling; rustling; chiming; shattering; footsteps; click click; creak; beep; rumbling; rustling; laughter; footsteps; bang; buzzing and sirens; 'Oh dear'; screech; footsteps running; whistle; clatter; cough; 'Ahhhh'.

Possible story
The wind whistled through the alleyway. Dan carefully broke the glass in the office window then climbed in. He crept along the corridor and found the safe which he skilfully opened. Dan excitedly took out all the necklaces, feeling very happy. Unfortunately, on his way out he accidentally slammed a door, setting off the alarms. Within a short time the police were on the scene. Dan dropped the necklaces and tried to hide – but they quickly found him.

11D Counselling

Activity
Groupwork. Students suggest help they could give to various characters.

Focus
Theme: counselling. Hypothetical present & future situations.

Preparation
Photocopy one worksheet for each group of three students. You will need a dice and one counter (used by all players) for each group.

Procedure
- Check or pre-teach *counselling* (helping someone by encouraging them to talk about their situation).
- Divide the class into groups of three. Hand out one worksheet, a dice and a counter to each group. Students place the counter on the start square.
- Explain how to play the game and make sure that everyone understands what to do. The first player throws the dice and moves around the game board.
- The player now looks at two things: (a) the key for the number thrown by the dice at the top of the worksheet, and (b) the square the counter landed on. For example, if the player threw 2 the key shows that 2 means 'You are counselling' and the counter has landed on 'a bored shop assistant' so the whole task is 'You are counselling a bored shop assistant.'
- The player must say two sentences using language from the lesson (printed at the bottom of the worksheet) and following the task instruction, e.g. *Supposing you took a vacation?* or *If you were to work shorter hours, would that help?*
- If the player throws a 1, 3 or 5, they must talk about their *own* situation (as if they were a bored shop assistant themselves), e.g. *I wish I had a more interesting job* or *If only I could afford to walk out right now!*
- Players get one point for each good sentence they make. Advice to a person cannot be repeated during the game.
- The winner is the student with the most points at the end.

12A Octopuses or octopi?

Activity
Groupwork. Students do a team quiz on irregular plurals.

Focus
Plurals.

Preparation
Photocopy one worksheet for each group of three to four students.

Procedure
- Explain that students are going to do a quiz on plurals.
- Divide the class into groups of three or four students. Hand out one worksheet to each group.
- Allow ten minutes for students to work together and decide their answers for the twenty questions. They mustn't use printed dictionaries, electronic dictionaries or any other reference material. Tell them to write their answers on the worksheet.
- When the time is up, ask groups to hand their worksheets to another group for checking.
- Go through the questions one by one with the class. The winning team is the one with the most correct answers.

Answers
1A 2B (criteria) 3C (singular: datum) 4A 5A 6B (loaves) 7C (singular: medium) 8A (for a computer peripheral, some dictionaries now list both *mouses* and *mice* – but there is still a lot of disagreement over this one!) 9A 10C (singular: phenomenon) 11 shelf 12 nucleus 13 appendix 14 formula 15 diploma 16 erratum 17 analysis 18 moose 19 brother 20 index

12B Hi-tech reviews

Activity
Pairwork. Students write a review of a new invention.

Focus
Theme: technology.

Preparation
Photocopy one worksheet for each pair of students.

Procedure
- Explain that students are reviewers for *Hi-tech* magazine – a publication that aims to keep readers up-to-date on all the latest equipment and new gadgets.
- Divide the class into pairs. Hand out one worksheet to each pair.
- Explain that manufacturers have sent samples of four brand new products to the magazine. Ask each pair to choose one of the items on the worksheet that they would like to review.
- Ask pairs to look at the guidance notes on the worksheet and write a review of the product.
- At the end, display the reviews around the classroom and allow time for students to read each other's work.
- Have a class feedback session to find out which items students thought were the most interesting, bizarre and/or inventive, and which they would actually consider buying themselves.

12C What a beautiful dress!

Activity
Pairwork. Students write and act out dialogues.

Focus
Pronunciation: intonation (feelings).

Preparation
Photocopy one worksheet for each student.

Procedure
- Divide the class into pairs. Hand out the worksheet to each student.
- In pairs, students practise reading dialogue one using the intonation written on the right of each line. Students can also write one extra final line to conclude the dialogue if they wish. When students are ready, listen to some different performances in the whole class.
- Change pairs. Ask students to now look at dialogue two. They do this in the same way, but before they can practise reading it, they should first go through the text deciding what kind of intonation they can use for each line.
- Repeat for dialogues three and four. In dialogue three, students must think of lines that match the intonation given. In dialogue four, students can create their own short dialogue from scratch. As before, listen to some different performances in the whole class.

12D These foolish things

Activity
Pairwork. Students listen to the song *These foolish things* sung by Bryan Ferry and recall their own memories from the course.

Focus
Listening. Theme: memories.

Preparation
Photocopy one worksheet for each student. Fold the worksheet along the dotted line so that the lyrics are not visible. CD player.

[6]

Procedure
- Hand out one worksheet to each student.
- In pairs, students discuss the questions in part 1.
- Compare answers as a whole class, then play the recording for students to check their answers to part 1 and to do part 2.
- Play the song again for students to do part 3. Check the answers with the whole class.
- Ask students to unfold the worksheet so that the lyrics are now visible and play the song again.
- Allow thinking time for part 4 before leading this into a class discussion.

Answers
1 Everything is mentioned in the song except for (h) New York / The Statue of Liberty and (l) visiting an art gallery.
2 Correct order: i, a, c, d, j, k, g, e, m, f, b
3 These lines refer to other things that remind him of her: Those stumbling words that told you what my heart meant; The winds of March that make my heart a dancer; Gardenia perfume lingering on a pillow; Silk stockings thrown aside; Dance invitations; The scent of roses; The waiters whistling as the last bar closes; The song that Crosby sings (= Bing Crosby, famous singer of romantic songs).

Note
You could use this worksheet as a way of concluding the course, allowing students to think about and celebrate things they have enjoyed about other people during their time together.

1A | Survey on change

1

What one change would make the biggest positive difference to your life?

2

What, in your opinion, has been the most dramatic change in the world over the last ten years?

3

Have you ever significantly changed your appearance?

4

What do you think will be the most dramatic change in the world in the next 30 years?

5

Has your attitude to anything or anyone in the news changed in any way over the last few years?

6

How has your home town changed in your lifetime?

7

Has your attitude to anything in the field of entertainment (e.g. music, film, TV) changed in any way over the last few years?

8

Do you think the world is changing for the better or for the worse? In what way?

9

Do you think you would ever completely change your whole way of life? How?

10

How do you feel about change in general?

11

Tell me one thing you have done in your lifetime to help change the world (even in a very small way).

12

If you could change your studies or career to something totally different, what would you do?

1B | Approximations

When did you get up this morning?	How many students around the world do you think have studied with this book?	When did we start doing this activity?
How many books have you read in your life?	What's the longest walk you've ever done?	What's the furthest you have ever been away from home?
What's the heaviest thing you've ever had to carry?	What's the time?	How much money do you have in your bag?
How many hours did you study English at home last week?	How many people are in your family?	Where would you like to go on holiday?
What would you like to do next year?	How good is your English?	How much money do you think a doctor makes in a year?
Where's the nearest post office to here?	Is there an easy way to get to the town centre from here?	What do you know about Ancient Egypt?
How long have you been using that pen?	How long does the summer last here?	How many people come to this school?
What was the largest crowd you've ever been in?	What time did you go to bed last night?	How many people have you talked to today?
How many meals have you eaten in the last seven days?	How many bones do you have in your body?	How much money would you like to win?

1c | Two lives

A

a toddler　a pre-teen　a teenager　a middle-aged woman　a …-year-old　a senior citizen
came of age　just turned …　wrong side of …　mid-life crisis　coming up to …　getting on for …

B

a toddler　a pre-teen　a teenager　a middle-aged man　a …-year-old　a senior citizen
came of age　just turned …　wrong side of …　mid-life crisis　coming up to …　getting on for …

1D | Four in a row

Adjectives	Adjectives	Verbs	Verbs	Verbs
good 1	intelligent 13	entertain 25	propose 37	interfere 49
infant 2	urgent 14	deny 26	coincide 38	settle 50
scarce 3	similar 15	acknowledge 27	amaze 39	forgive 51
silent 4	complex 16	judge 28	depend 40	govern 52
quiet 5	technical 17	advance 29	fail 41	attend 53
efficient 6	eccentric 18	manage 30	demonstrate 42	commit 54
reluctant 7	unemployed 19	differ 31	accept 43	infect 55
frequent 8	certain 20	disappoint 32	punish 44	concentrate 56
cruel 9	private 21	dismiss 33	refuse 45	invent 57
happy 10	peculiar 22	please 34	depart 46	supervise 58
patient 11	weak 23	achieve 35	involve 47	occur 59
tidy 12	probable 24	expose 36	proceed 48	invest 60

2A | Quick sorting

keep	imagine	resist	should
hope	vote	hate	regret
ask	qualify	remember	give up
promise	admit	hurry	continue
deny	begin	finish	recommend
must	expect	make	risk
avoid	allow	would rather	forget
postpone	dislike	try	need
look forward to	adore	agree	manage

gerund	bare infinitive	infinitive with *to*

2B | Can you train your brain?

Use **/** to mark divisions between chunks and underline to mark strongly stressed words.

A Until recently, a person's IQ (a measure of all kinds of mental problem-solving abilities, including spatial skills, memory and verbal reasoning) was thought to be a fixed commodity largely determined by genetics.

B But recent research suggests that a very basic brain function called working memory might underlie our general intelligence, opening up the intriguing possibility that if you improve your working memory, you could boost your IQ too.

A Working memory is the brain's short-term information storage system. It's a workbench for solving mental problems.

B For example, if you calculate 73 – 6 + 7, your working memory will store the intermediate steps necessary to work out the answer. And the amount of information that the working memory can hold is strongly related to general intelligence.

A A research team in Stockholm, Sweden, has found signs that the neural systems that underlie working memory may grow in response to training. Using brain scans, they measured the brain activity of adults before and after a working-memory training programme, which involved tasks such as memorizing the positions of a series of dots on a grid.

B After five weeks of training, their brain activity had increased in the regions associated with this type of memory.

A Perhaps more significantly, when the group studied children who had completed these types of mental workouts, they saw improvement in a range of cognitive abilities not related to the training, and a leap in IQ test scores of eight per cent.

B It's early days yet, but the research team leader thinks working-memory training could be a key to unlocking brain power. 'Genetics determines a lot and so does the early gestation period,' he says. 'On top of that, there is a small percentage – we don't know how many – that can be improved by training.'

2c | My bicycle & me

1 You're going to listen to a song called *Bicycle* about a man who loves cycling. Which of these words do you think will be in the song?

purple
wrap-around sunglasses
a little old lady
Lycra
an alien
ruts
a French guy named Guillaume
Styrofoam
big hill
fat

2 The following words are all in the song. Match each verb with a possible noun phrase.

wear	my heart
downshift	my butt
ride	light bikes
cost	a helmet
curse	big bucks
pad	my Shimano gears
feel	smelly trucks

3 Listen to the song and check your answers to parts 1 and 2.

4 What do you think these lines from the song mean?

a) Glad I am that the coast is clear.
b) I hope she doesn't teach me how to fly.
c) A forty-something spree is my bicycle and me.

FOLD

Bicycle

I ride my bicycle to work each day
It's not so far
It's better for me than my car
I wear a helmet that is made of
Rigid Styrofoam
Inspected by a French guy named Guillaume
I downshift my Shimano gears
I pedal hard and I'm out of here
Glad I am that the coast is clear
Glad I am to be
My bicycle and me

Some Saturdays at six a.m. I get up
With Bill and Flo
In the parking lot of Ho Jo's west of town
We ride light bikes that cost big bucks
We curse at smelly trucks
Mile after mile 'til the sun is almost down
What a ride, what a life
Maybe I'm crazy, don't ask my wife
I've been in love with these spinning wheels
Since I was maybe three
My bicycle and me

Now, pedal that bike, pedal that bike
Don't open that door 'til I go by
Pedal that bike, pedal that bike
That little old lady in the Dodge Diplomat
I don't think she sees me
I hope she doesn't teach me how to fly

I wear Lycra, it fits really closely to my skin
White to purple is the place where it begins
I pad my butt and I'm careful
To stay out of ruts
Wrap-around sunglasses, I'm an alien
Feel my heart go pit-a-pat
Hello big hill, goodbye fat
Life goes by just like that
A forty-something spree is
My bicycle and me

2D | The museum of ourselves

Museum labels

Write the museum labels for the exhibits.
The labels should include the item's name and a little factual information.

Information for the museum guides

Prepare what the guides can say to the visitors. (N.B. Your information can be truthful and factual, or entirely fictitious.) Include at least six structures from the language box below in your descriptions.

Exhibit 1 – Name: ____________________

What it is:

History of the item ✦ Story about the artist/manufacturer ✦ Curious story about the item, etc.

Exhibit 2 – Name: ____________________

What it is:

History of the item ✦ Story about the artist/manufacturer ✦ Curious story about the item, etc.

Exhibit 3 – Name: ____________________

What it is:

History of the item ✦ Story about the artist/manufacturer ✦ Curious story about the item, etc.

like	the more … the …	as … as
not such a … as …	slightly	a great deal
by far the …	nowhere near as … as	

3A | Money expressions

Expressions list

I lived beyond my means.	I have a nest egg.	We went Dutch.
I paid an arm and a leg for it.	I bet my bottom dollar on it.	I bought him off.
I decided to foot the bill.	I cut my losses.	I offered a penny for his thoughts.
I got it at face value.	I broke even.	I cooked the books.
I'll probably have to grease her palm.	I bought it for a song.	I was strapped for cash.

A	B	C
I really believed it would be OK so I risked all my money. ANSWER = I bet my bottom dollar on it.	The price I paid was far too expensive. ANSWER = I paid an arm and a leg for it.	I didn't make any profit (but I didn't lose any money either). ANSWER = I broke even.
I have some money saved in case I need it in the future. ANSWER = I have a nest egg.	I gave money to stop the threats. ANSWER = I bought him off.	I had already lost some money and decided not to waste any more. ANSWER = I cut my losses.
When the money didn't add up properly, I dishonestly changed the figures. ANSWER = I cooked the books.	It was much cheaper than it should have been. ANSWER = I bought it for a song.	I was almost penniless. ANSWER = I was strapped for cash.
When I went out with her, both of us paid our own part of the bill. ANSWER = We went Dutch.	I paid exactly the amount of money printed on the item. ANSWER = I got it at face value.	I paid for everything. ANSWER = I decided to foot the bill.
I spent far more money than I was earning. ANSWER = I lived beyond my means.	I asked him what was on his mind. ANSWER = I offered a penny for his thoughts.	I think a bribe may be necessary. ANSWER = I'll probably have to grease her palm.

3B | Really nice it was!

A

Really nice it was! Friendly service. Super food. Such a lovely break we had. They even served breakfast in bed. (ABOUT A HOTEL)

Such a dull time we had! Really boring people they were and hardly any food. (ABOUT A PARTY)

Why on earth they put up such a monstrosity here I couldn't begin to imagine! (ABOUT AN UGLY BUILDING)

Gorgeous he was! No choice. Asking him out was the only thing I could do! (ABOUT AN ATTRACTIVE MAN)

Hilarious she is! You must go and see her before the season ends! (ABOUT A COMEDIAN)

How frightening it was! We had to watch from between our fingers. (ABOUT A HORROR FILM)

B

What a superb panorama we saw from the top. Really beautiful. (ABOUT THE COUNTRYSIDE)

All night we watched it. Complete waste of time it was. Wish we'd seen the football on the other side. (ABOUT A DULL TV PROGRAMME)

Why people light up when there are children nearby is one thing I'll never understand. (ABOUT SMOKING)

How cold it was that year! We had to break the ice on the surface before we could start! (ABOUT SWIMMING IN WINTER)

Two hundred dollars surcharge she added! I couldn't believe it! (ABOUT A TRAVEL AGENT'S)

Right at the start I asked her – and she still hasn't told me what to do! (ABOUT A CLASSROOM)

3c It's all over!

overact	If you ____, you perform (on stage or film) in an exaggerated way.
overactive	If you have an ____ imagination, you tend to imagine things that aren't true.
overbearing	If you are ____, your behaviour is unpleasant – too loud and dominant.
overcharge	If a shop takes too much money from you for a product, they ____ you.
overconfident	If you are ____, you are too sure and certain of yourself.
overdo	If you ____ things, you work too hard and for long hours.
overdraft	If you have an ____, you are in debt to the bank.
overdress	If you ____, you wear clothes that are too formal for the occasion.
overdue	If something is ____, it is late.
overemotional	If you are ____, you get upset and cry very easily.
overenthusiastic	If you are ____, you become very excited about things.
overestimate	If you ____ something, you predict a quantity or amount that is too high.
overflow	If your bath starts to ____, the water comes over the side.
overgrown	If your garden is ____, it is untidy and full of weeds.
overindulge	If you ____, you eat and drink too much and possibly feel ill as a result.
overpower	If you ____ someone, you take control of them because you are stronger.
overpriced	If something is ____, it costs more than it is worth.
overrated	If something is ____, people think it is much better than it really is.
overstay	If you ____, you spend longer in a place than you are welcome.
overtime	If you work ____, you earn extra money by staying longer at work.

3D | Newly-found wealth

Sylvanu

You live on the beautiful, but remote tropical island of Sylvanu where some valuable mineral resources have just been discovered. The quantity is however far less than found on Nauru and will run out in just a few years.

Discuss how the newly-found wealth should best be spent in order to satisfy both the immediate and long-term needs of the islanders and their descendants.

A

The country should invest in building new hotels and also start a big advertising campaign overseas. By attracting tourists, the country can create work and sustain its income even after the mineral resources have run out.

B

At the moment 20% of the population live in below-standard housing and have limited access to health care. The immediate need is to provide a better standard of living for these people. The money should all be used to build good housing and to improve health services.

C

Why should the government get the money? It belongs to the people of the island and should be distributed equally to every individual on Sylvanu for them to spend as they wish.

1	2	3	4	5
harmful	original	advisable	advantageous	stressful
cautious	personal	forgettable	sensible	substantial
humorous	informative	applicable	successful	homeless
numerous	representative	environmental	global	financial
responsible	voluntary	predictable	powerful	persuasive
imaginative	comparative	imaginary	worthless	knowledgeable

4A | Complaints

Expressions

driving me to distraction	completely freak me out
gets on my nerves	gets up my nose
a good old moan	is it just me
drives me absolutely mad	a commonly-held opinion
muttering under their breath	kick up a fuss
not nice at all	sick to death of
moaning about nothing again	annoys me to think
vent all my anger	piece of my mind
what I object to	I am fed up

Topic card

Budget airlines
Multi-national companies
Public transport
Mis-advertising

Red tape
Noise
Rude people
Modern TV

Topic card

Budget airlines
Multi-national companies
Public transport
Mis-advertising

Red tape
Noise
Rude people
Modern TV

4B | Mobile phone spies

Role card

You work for **Mobon**, a large telecommunications company that provides mobile phone services. Your company has one major rival – **TTC9** and the two are in constant competition.

You believe that **TTC9** is about to launch an important new product. It is essential that you find out about your rival's plans … even if you have to do some spying!

1 The Managing Director of **TTC9** is to give a major speech today to his/her marketing team. Your team of spies will go and (secretly) listen. Make very careful notes.

2 Go back to **Mobon** and compare notes on everything you heard.

mobon
mobile telecommunications

SOME REPORTING VERBS
stressed estimated suggested
predicted invited regretted
warned announced reminded
thanked claimed apologized
accused wondered blamed
remarked advised
recommended

The Director's Speech to the TTC9 Marketing Team

"

Shall we start? Right. Thank you very much for coming. I have a number of important announcements to make today, but please remember that everything you hear is top secret. It is absolutely vital that our competitors don't get to hear of our plans. And, I should warn you that we suspect that one of our rivals is actively trying to spy on our activities. So please be on your guard!

As you know, subscriptions have been falling sharply over the last two years and we need to find something dramatic to attract customers back. If we don't do something soon, TTC9 will be dead in the water in less than three years.

So, what is the reason for this dramatic decline? Well, ladies and gentlemen, it is simply that our company has failed to keep up with technological advances. Our rivals, and I'm thinking especially of Mobon here, have been very creative. Mobon already has seven phone models fitted with the fantastic *FaceTrace* system that marks all your friends' locations on handy maps. How many of our phones have this? I'll tell you – exactly none. This is extremely disappointing.

I won't continue with this catalogue of failures. It's time to look forward. And I have our exciting new product to tell you about. It's called *Spring!* and it's much more than a phone. This is a key to social networking. With *Spring!* you can see a photo profile of any other *Spring!* user within 500 metres of you plus free phone access to them. Just imagine how that will transform the dating scene! We confidently believe that this will be the club phenomenon of next year.

"

4c | The *Straightforward* awards

1

Greatest contribution to general happiness and well-being

for the person who has made a really positive difference to other people

2

Cappuccino or drinks king/queen of the year award

so … who drinks the most coffee? soft drinks? mineral water?

3

Wearer of the outstanding fashion item of the year award

for the person who wore that unforgettable piece of clothing

4

Most surprising or memorable thing said all year award

for the person who said the thing everyone remembers

5

The Elvis Presley award

for that invisible person who doesn't seem to be in class very often – but people keep reporting that they saw him/her at the mall or in a café

6

Class entertainer award

for the person who keeps us all laughing

7

Best bad excuse of the year award

for the person who gave the most memorable bad excuse (for being late, not doing homework, etc.)

8

The mad scientist award for untidiness and disorganization

for the person who always has their papers everywhere

9

Soap Opera Star award

for the person who would make the best subject for a soap opera

10

News services award

for the person who tells everyone the latest news

11

Snack monster of the year award

for the person who manages to get through the most chocolate, crisps or other snacks

12

Most memorable event of the year award

for the person who started or was at the centre of an event nobody can forget

4D | What on earth is going on?

1

A: *(nervously)* Is he here yet?

B: I'll have a look out of the window. No. I can't see anyone.

A: What have we forgotten?

B: I don't know. I'm sure we've got something wrong.

A: How do you feel?

B: Awful.

(knocking sound at the door)

A: Oh dear.

What on earth is going on?
Who are the people?
Where are they?
What's happening?
How do they feel?
What do you think will happen in the end?

2

A: *(shouting)* No! Not there!

B: Sorry.

A: Too late. That's ruined it.

B: I didn't know. I thought that was the way it worked. Can anyone help?

A: I don't think anyone could get here until the morning.

B: Well. Let's hope there are no accidents.

What on earth is going on?
Who are the people?
Where are they?
What's happening?
How do they feel?
What do you think will happen in the end?

3

A: What should we do?

B: I think we have to open it.

A: But if we do that it will ...

B: Well, we aren't certain, are we?

A: I think it's starting to make a noise.

B: We've got no choice. I'm going to ...

A: Be careful ... Oh no!

What on earth is going on?
Who are the people?
Where are they?
What's happening?
How do they feel?
What do you think will happen in the end?

4

A: I can't find him anywhere.

B: Don't be silly! That's not possible.

A: We've got to find him. It's vital.

B: When did you last check?

A: About an hour ago. Everything was fine.

B: Right. You look there. I'll check over here.

What on earth is going on?
Who are the people?
Where are they?
What's happening?
How do they feel?
What do you think will happen in the end?

5A | A flatpack text

Steve Jobs is one of America's most successful entrepreneurs, despite the fact that for many years he has been the Chief Executive who	received the smallest pay cheque in the world – just $1 a year!
So who is this low-paid man? Well, he's someone who	has frequently led the way in both computing and entertainment.
In fact, it was Jobs, together with co-founder Steve Wozniak, who	kick-started the personal computer revolution in the 1970s with the release of the revolutionary Apple II computer.
The Apple II was one of the first home computers which	really took off.
He was also largely responsible for the way we interact with computers using a mouse. Even in the early days, design was a factor that	was taken very seriously at Apple.
The Apple Macintosh which	was first introduced in 1984 was beautiful.
It was the first home machine that	had any elegance to its look and the first to use a purely graphical interface.
In fact, Apple computers are still the machines which	art and design professionals choose for their work.
More recently Steve Jobs has been involved in the successful launch of the iMac, which	is yet another successful good-looking computer.
However, the product that Jobs is best known for is that little white box that	sits in your pocket – the iPod™ music player.
With an eye to the future Jobs must hope that the iPhone and a long line of other iCreations will continue being the things that	everyone wants.
And if his machines don't take over – maybe his films will! Jobs has had a long connection with Pixar, the animation studio which	makes blockbuster films such as *Finding Nemo* and *Toy Story*.

5B | Tag talk

isn't it?	is it?	could we?	couldn't he?
won't they?	will you?	don't you?	do you?
will she?	won't they?	does it?	doesn't it?
can't you?	can I?	wasn't I?	was I?
aren't you?	are you?	should she?	shouldn't they?
can you?	can't you?	didn't he?	did she?
were you?	weren't you?	don't you?	do they?
would you?	wouldn't they?	doesn't it?	does it?

5c | Housework

1 Think of a possible housework verb to go with each item. You cannot repeat any verbs.

	goodbye from out of the window
	the plates
	the dishes
	the bed
	the pillows
	the rug
	the windows
	the drawers
	the closet
	the dirty clothes in the hamper
	the vacuum round the carpets
	the shelves
	the glassware

	some lunch
	the garbage
	the bills
	the dry-cleaning
	some cash out of the dispenser
	up the freezer
	some wine for later this evening
	the dinner
	the roast into the oven
	the veg
	the table
	some music
	the candles

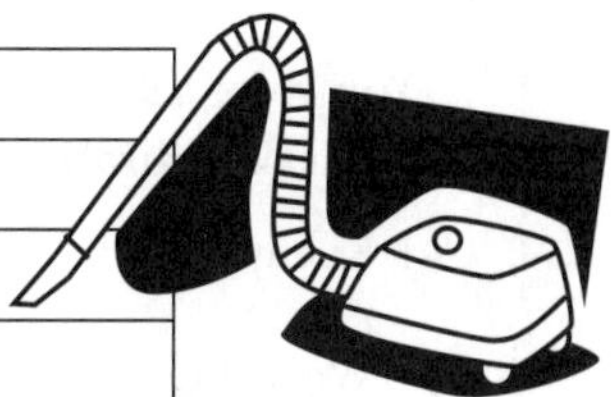

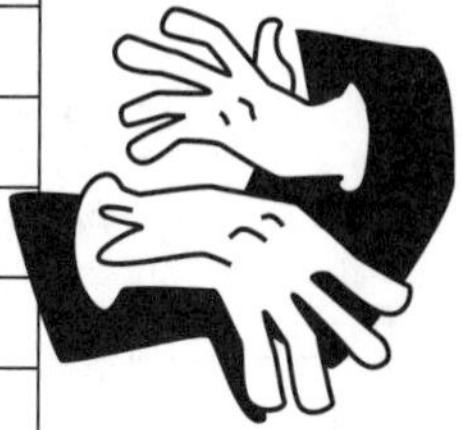

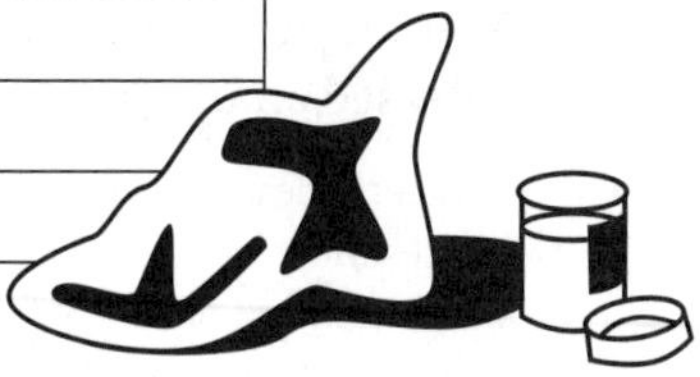

2 Listen to the song. What verbs does the singer use?

3 This song is about a husband who stays at home doing the housework while his wife goes out to work. How common is this in your country? Do you know any relationships like this? Do you think the singer is happy or not?

FOLD

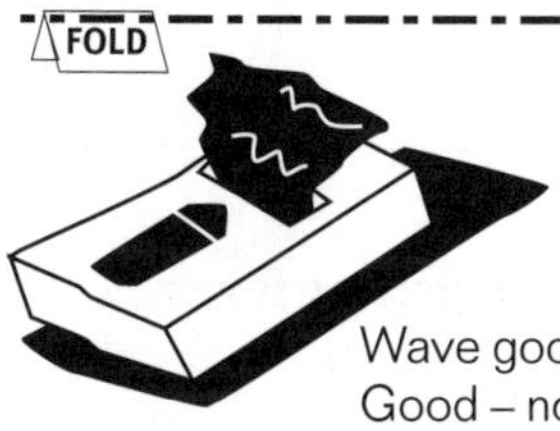

HOUSEWORK

Wave goodbye from out of the window.
Good – no trouble starting the car.
Time for just one more cup of coffee.
You know the housework won't wait.

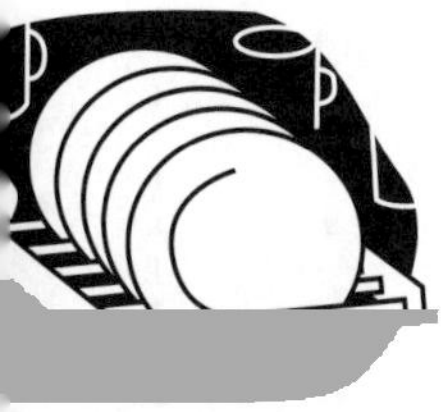

Where to start now? Time to get going.
The housework keeps you feeling alive.
Clear the plates and wash up the dishes.
Rrr! Let's go – now the bedroom.

Make the bed and fluff up the pillows.
The housework makes you happy.
Shake the rug and open the windows.
The housework keeps you feeling alive.
Close the drawers and tidy the closet.
The housework keeps you going.
Throw the dirty clothes in the hamper.
Rrr! Let's go – looking better.

Rrr! Let's go – get the vacuum.
Round the carpets, under the table.
The housework makes you happy.
Dust the shelves and polish the glassware.
The housework keeps you feeling alive.
Make some lunch and take out the garbage.
The housework keeps you going.
Pay the bills and get the dry-cleaning.
Rrr! Let's go – time for shopping.

Bread and milk and plenty of groceries.
The housework makes you happy.
Get some cash out of the dispenser.
The housework keeps you feeling alive.
Don't forget to stock up the freezer.
The housework keeps you going.
Get some wine for later this evening.
Home by five! Now the kitchen.

Rrr! Let's go – make the dinner.
Get the roast into the oven.
The housework makes you happy.
Peel the veg and then set the table.
The housework keeps you feeling alive.
Freshen up and put on some music.
The housework's got you dancing.
Light the candles. There goes the doorbell.
Rrr! She's home – perfect timing!

Welcome back, dear. How did your day go?
The housework's nearly over.
How about an aperitif, dear?
I'll get the dinner. You open the wine.
Pass the salt. You want more potatoes?
No more housework.
Leave the dishes until tomorrow.
Rrr! Let's play.

5D | Regrets

A

You were a successful business person until you went on a disastrous skiing holiday last year.

1 Briefly describe your life and what you are doing at present.
2 Write three regrets you have (e.g. about something you have done or about your life).
3 Write one thing you don't regret.

- *I wish* + subject + *'d / hadn't*
- *If* + subject + *'d / hadn't*
- *had* + subject + (*not*) past participle

B

You are a politician and the next election is in a week's time.

1 Briefly describe your life and what you are doing at present.
2 Write three regrets you have (e.g. about something you have done or about your life).
3 Write one thing you don't regret.

- *I wish* + subject + *'d / hadn't*
- *If* + subject + *'d / hadn't*
- *had* + subject + (*not*) past participle

C

You are the CEO of a large software company which released an important new program last week.

1 Briefly describe your life and what you are doing at present.
2 Write three regrets you have (e.g. about something you have done or about your life).
3 Write one thing you don't regret.

- *I wish* + subject + *'d / hadn't*
- *If* + subject + *'d / hadn't*
- *had* + subject + (*not*) past participle

D

You are a mountain climber at the top of a high peak but there are some problems.

1 Briefly describe your life and what you are doing at present.
2 Write three regrets you have (e.g. about something you have done or about your life).
3 Write one thing you don't regret.

- *I wish* + subject + *'d / hadn't*
- *If* + subject + *'d / hadn't*
- *had* + subject + (*not*) past participle

E

You are a parent with three young children. You haven't had a chance to work for more than eight years.

1 Briefly describe your life and what you are doing at present.
2 Write three regrets you have (e.g. about something you have done or about your life).
3 Write one thing you don't regret.

- *I wish* + subject + *'d / hadn't*
- *If* + subject + *'d / hadn't*
- *had* + subject + (*not*) past participle

F

You are a 45-year-old actor who is getting fewer and fewer good roles.

1 Briefly describe your life and what you are doing at present.
2 Write three regrets you have (e.g. about something you have done or about your life).
3 Write one thing you don't regret.

- *I wish* + subject + *'d / hadn't*
- *If* + subject + *'d / hadn't*
- *had* + subject + (*not*) past participle

G

You will retire next year after a lifetime in a very dull job.

1 Briefly describe your life and what you are doing at present.
2 Write three regrets you have (e.g. about something you have done or about your life).
3 Write one thing you don't regret.

- *I wish* + subject + *'d / hadn't*
- *If* + subject + *'d / hadn't*
- *had* + subject + (*not*) past participle

H

You are a novelist. All your books are out of print.

1 Briefly describe your life and what you are doing at present.
2 Write three regrets you have (e.g. about something you have done or about your life).
3 Write one thing you don't regret.

- *I wish* + subject + *'d / hadn't*
- *If* + subject + *'d / hadn't*
- *had* + subject + (*not*) past participle

6A | Runaways & breakdowns

1 upbringing	8 takeaway	15 outburst
2 checkout	9 outlook	16 outcome
3 breakout	10 outset	17 getaway
4 handout	11 outfit	18 payout
5 turnout	12 runaway	19 breakdown
6 downturn	13 workout	20 downpour
7 breakthrough	14 uprising	21 outbreak

1 upbringing	8 takeaway	15 outburst
2 checkout	9 outlook	16 outcome
3 breakout	10 outset	17 getaway
4 handout	11 outfit	18 payout
5 turnout	12 runaway	19 breakdown
6 downturn	13 workout	20 downpour
7 breakthrough	14 uprising	21 outbreak

6B | Pierced ears & bloodshot eyes

A

pierced
blocked
rotten
bruised
swollen
broken
black
bushy
runny
long
bloodshot
cauliflower
rosy
flyaway
bare
wrinkled
double
false
scarred

B

hair
ear(s)
forehead
eyebrow(s)
eye(s)
eyelashes
nose
lip(s)
teeth
tongue
cheek(s)
chin
chest
stomach
belly button
arm(s)
wrist(s)
hand(s)
finger(s)
leg(s)
knee(s)
ankle(s)
foot/feet
toe(s)

6c | Natasha at 21

'Abandoned by mother. Father unknown. Instead I have a wonderful life in England.'

The last time she was in this narrow cellar, Natasha Nicholson was a frightened child of nine, sheltering from the Serbian bombing of Sarajevo. It was dark and damp. Candles were lit to relieve the gloom. 'I was scared,' she recalls. 'There was the constant sound of babies crying in their cots. When the shelling started, you just went down in your nightie and sometimes you would be in the pitch dark for hours.'

Today, in a basement far smaller than she remembers, there is a pleasant fug of drying laundry and Natasha, now aged 21, is being swallowed up in the pillowy embrace of Fazila, the white-overalled laundress. Fazila worked in the orphanage kitchen at the time Natasha was spirited away to England from war-torn Sarajevo twelve years ago.

Natasha is just back home in Surrey after spending five weeks on a personal odyssey to the place of her birth, her first return visit to Sarajevo. Every day, she worked with children at the orphanage where she was abandoned by her mother at the age of five months.

'This is like travelling back in time,' she said as she saw the orphanage for the first time since the chaotic day of her flight. 'So much is exactly as I remember it. This cellar, and the playground bring back images of war and blood. I remember shrapnel falling in the play area. One friend was shot through the shoulder and two children were hit in the leg.'

Natasha's rapport with the orphanage children, many with special needs, was remarkable. Everyone expected her suddenly to remember Bosnian, but she never managed more than two or three words and wonders how she ever spoke it. She was struck by the warm 'playgroup' atmosphere of Bjeleve orphanage compared with its austerity when she was a child. 'Then it was a cold place and we were left to our own devices.'

Through contacting a Sarajevan lawyer who had helped her father with the adoption process, Natasha discovered that her mother – formerly a factory cook and now apparently a cleaning lady – had tried to contact her only eighteen months ago. 'It was a shock to find out she had been making inquiries. She would want me to help her. She would want money. I knew her intentions were all wrong. I was afraid of what might come up. She might one day decide to turn up and I don't think I could cope. Deep down, I would really like to have met her,' she says, 'but realistically I have to admit I was not ready for it.

'I am very lucky and privileged to have been given a second chance. And sometimes, after I've been grumpy, I'll say to my dad, "Look, what you did for me was absolutely fantastic."'

1 Imagine that you are Natasha. The war was over long ago. You have grown up in England with your new family and you are now 21 years old. You have decided to return to Sarajevo for the first time since you left, all those years ago. What do you hope to see, do or find there? Do you think it will be the same or completely different from your memories? Will you go to the orphanage? Will you try to trace your family? Do you think going back will make you regret having been taken away from Sarajevo as a child?

2 Discuss these questions.

a) What are some of the differences between then and now in the orphanage?

b) Did she meet her mother? Why or why not?

3 Find these adjectives in the text. What do they describe? What do they mean?

pitch	personal	chaotic	special	warm

6D | Babysitting blues

7A | School issues

You are a senior teacher at your school. Today you're going to attend a meeting where you and other staff members will discuss and make decisions on the issues listed below. Before the meeting, read through and decide what your ideas are on each one.

1 The school recently spent €1,500 buying new books for the library. However, just three months later you have found that many of those new books are missing. You're not sure whether they have been stolen or simply mislaid. What should the school do about it?

2 Should the school invest in a set of new electronic signs and message boards? What would be the advantages and disadvantages?

3 A small group of students have been asking for more student involvement in school decision making. Is this a good idea or will it make school management more difficult? What could be done?

4 Your school has a small budget of €200 to decorate the school environment (e.g. adding posters, painting walls, buying plants, etc.) and make it more attractive. How should this be spent?

5 Small arguments keep breaking out in the lunch queue. You believe that this happens when people think that others have pushed into the line (maybe when students 'save' places for friends). You are worried that these arguments could become more violent one day. What can be done?

You are a senior teacher at your school. Today you're going to attend a meeting where you and other staff members will discuss and make decisions on the issues listed below. Before the meeting, read through and decide what your ideas are on each one.

1 The school recently spent €1,500 buying new books for the library. However, just three months later you have found that many of those new books are missing. You're not sure whether they have been stolen or simply mislaid. What should the school do about it?

2 Should the school invest in a set of new electronic signs and message boards? What would be the advantages and disadvantages?

3 A small group of students have been asking for more student involvement in school decision making. Is this a good idea or will it make school management more difficult? What could be done?

4 Your school has a small budget of €200 to decorate the school environment (e.g. adding posters, painting walls, buying plants, etc.) and make it more attractive. How should this be spent?

5 Small arguments keep breaking out in the lunch queue. You believe that this happens when people think that others have pushed into the line (maybe when students 'save' places for friends). You are worried that these arguments could become more violent one day. What can be done?

7B | Time to do something about it

William07 — Mar 23 2008, 09:19 PM — Post #1

regular
Posts: 17 ☆
Joined: 11 May 02
From: Germany
Member No.: 659

Time to do something about rude behaviour
I'm so tired of seeing rude behaviour all around me that I've decided to start doing something about it. Instead of just keeping quiet and pretending that nothing has happened, I've started making a fuss. For example, when someone on the train is talking very loudly on their mobile phone I go over, sit right next to them, take out my own phone and start talking into it even more loudly than them! Or when I see people pushing into the front of a queue, I walk up to them and then make a loud announcement that this person has just pushed into a queue. What do you think of my approach?

Susiesusie — Mar 23 2008, 10:38 PM — Post #2

regular
Posts: 21 ☆
Joined: 3 February 07
From: Ferney-Voltaire, France
Member No.: 1131

What an interesting idea! I wish I had the courage to copy you – but it takes a lot of nerve. And surely there are some things that you can't easily do anything about – like when a person doesn't hold the door open for a mother with a pushchair. By the time you see what has happened, it's too late, isn't it?

PeterC — Mar 23 2008, 11:12 PM — Post #3

regular
Posts: 921 ☆☆☆☆☆
Joined: 26 July 04
From: Bratislava, Slovakia
Member No.: 147

You're mad! I'm surprised you haven't been beaten up. I think your behaviour is ruder than the behaviour you are criticizing! If someone behaved like that to me, I'd be very angry. Why can't you just politely tell them what is annoying you?

Post #4

regular
Posts:
Joined:
From:
Member No.:

Post #5

regular
Posts:
Joined:
From:
Member No.:

Post #6

regular
Posts:
Joined:
From:
Member No.:

7c | Clare Francis

Read this text about the author of *A Dark Devotion*. For each numbered section, rewrite part (or all) of the text so that it includes at least one participle clause.

Clare Francis

Clare Francis, the author of *A Dark Devotion*, was born in Thames Ditton, England, the younger of two sisters.
(1) She obtained a degree in Economics at University College London, after which she went on to work in marketing for three years.

(2) She didn't want to stay in the business world and so began an 'unplanned' five-year career in sailing.

(3) Clare learnt to sail at the age of nine during childhood summer holidays on the Isle of Wight and was already an accomplished yachtswoman.

(4) She made a solo voyage across the Atlantic – just the beginning of her adult sailing adventures.

(5) After she had completed many other challenging events, she set off with a crew of eleven on the *Whitbread Round the World Race*.

(6) She wrote three works of non-fiction about her adventures and then took the leap into fiction. Her first novel *Night Sky*, which was published in 1983, was an international success, going on to reach number one in the *Sunday Times* bestseller list.

Clare Francis, the author of *A Dark Devotion*, was born in Thames Ditton, England, the younger of two sisters.
(1) After obtaining a degree in Economics at University College London, she went on to work in marketing for three years. (2) Not wanting to stay in the business world, she began an 'unplanned' five-year career in sailing.

(3) Having learnt to sail at the age of nine during childhood summer holidays on the Isle of Wight, Clare was already an accomplished yachtswoman. (4) Making a solo voyage across the Atlantic was just the beginning of her adult sailing adventures. (5) After completing many other challenging events, she set off with a crew of eleven on the *Whitbread Round the World Race*.

(6) After writing three works of non-fiction about her adventures, Clare then took the leap into fiction. Her first novel *Night Sky*, published in 1983, was an international success, going on to reach number one in the *Sunday Times* bestseller list.

7D | A criminal's own story

Box 1

Write down the verbs your teacher dictates.

Box 2

Choose ten of the verbs suitable for telling a criminal's story and arrange them into the best sequence for the story.

1	2	3	4	5
6	7	8	9	10

Box 3

Using the verbs exactly in the same order as in Box 2 above, prepare your story, as told by the criminal himself/herself.

Box 4

Catch the ten verbs.

1	2	3	4	5
6	7	8	9	10

8A | Lost property

Marie Curie (famous scientist)	John Lennon (one of the Beatles)	Alice (*Alice in Wonderland*)
Beethoven (classical composer)	Mary Poppins (nursery nurse)	Princess Leia (*Star Wars*)
William Shakespeare (playwright)	Cleopatra (ruler of Egypt)	Wonder Woman (superhero)
Mr Darcy (romantic hero of *Pride and Prejudice*)	Sherlock Holmes (detective)	James Bond (secret agent 007)

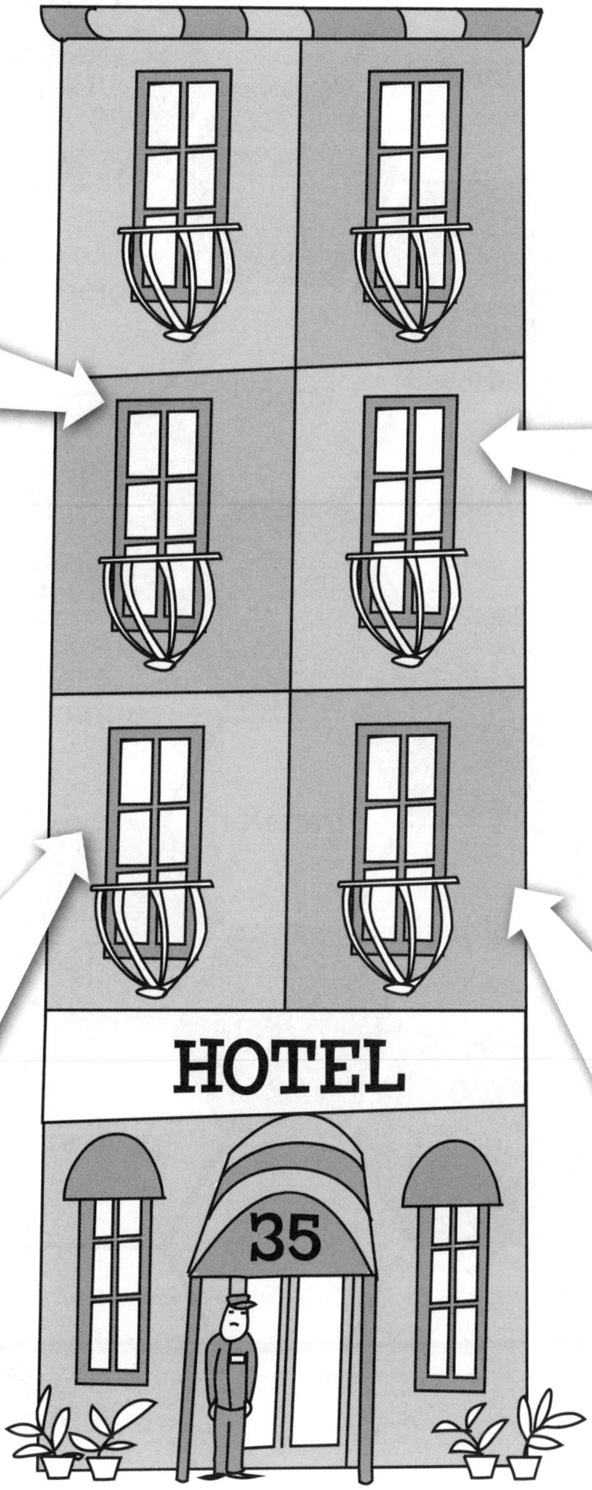

Room 201
For she was a woman of surpassing beauty, and at that time, when she was in the prime of her youth, she was most striking; she also possessed a most charming voice and a knowledge of how to make herself agreeable to everyone. Being brilliant to look upon and to listen to, with the power to subjugate everyone, even a love-sated man already past his prime, she adorned and beautified herself so as to appear in the most majestic and at the same time pity-inspiring guise.

Room 101
His very person and appearance were such as to strike the most casual observer. In height he was rather over six feet, and so excessively lean that he seemed to be considerably taller. His eyes were sharp and piercing, save during intervals of torpor; and his thin, hawk-like nose gave his whole expression an air of alertness and decision. His chin, too, had the prominence and squareness which mark the man of determination. His hands were invariably blotted with ink and stained with chemicals, yet he was possessed of extraordinary delicacy of touch, as I frequently had occasion to observe when I watched him manipulating the fragile philosophical instruments.

Room 202
She took up the fan and gloves, and, as the hall was very hot, she kept fanning herself all the time she went on talking: 'Dear, dear! How queer everything is today! And yesterday things went on just as usual. I wonder if I've been changed in the night? Let me think: was I the same when I got up this morning? I almost think I can remember feeling a little different. But if I'm not the same, the next question is, Who in the world am I? Ah, that's the great puzzle! I'm sure I'm not Ada,' she said, 'for her hair goes in such long ringlets, and mine doesn't go in ringlets at all; and I'm sure I can't be Mabel, for I know all sorts of things, and she, oh! she knows such a very little! Besides, she's she, and I'm I, and – oh dear, how puzzling it all is! I'll try if I know all the things I used to know. ... Let's try Geography. London is the capital of Paris, and Paris is the capital of Rome, and Rome – no, that's all wrong, I'm certain! I must have been changed for Mabel!'

Room 102
He soon drew the attention of the room by his fine, tall person, handsome features, noble mien; and the report which was in general circulation within five minutes after his entrance, of his having ten thousand a year. The gentlemen pronounced him to be a fine figure of a man, the ladies declared he was handsome and he was looked at with great admiration for about half the evening, till his manners gave a disgust which turned the tide of his popularity; for he was discovered to be proud, to be above his company and not all his large estate in Derbyshire could then save him.

Lost property: a snake   a flamingo upside down with a croquet ball near it's head   a violin   an invitation to a dance

8B | Word stress game

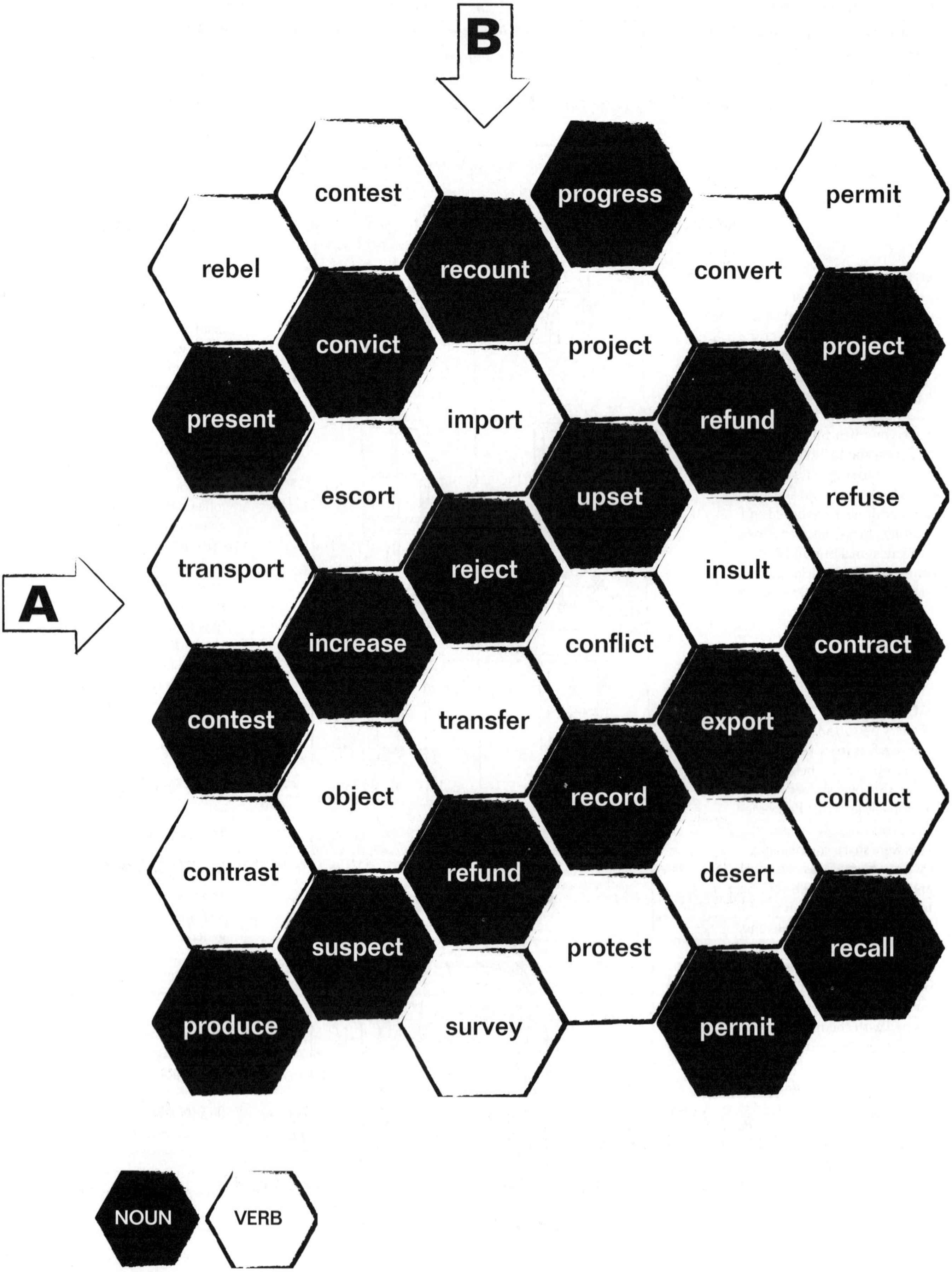
B
A
contest
progress
permit
rebel
recount
convert
convict
project
project
present
import
refund
escort
upset
refuse
transport
reject
insult
increase
conflict
contract
contest
transfer
export
object
record
conduct
contrast
refund
desert
suspect
protest
recall
produce
survey
permit
NOUN
VERB

8c | You've got to have friends

A

Do you think you could live happily without any friends?

Can you make close friends with someone you only know on the internet?

How quickly can you establish a good rapport with someone you have just met?

B

What are the key essentials to establishing a good rapport with someone?

How many close friends have you had for more than ten years?

Is it better to be very close friends with your neighbours or just to be nodding acquaintances?

C

Have you ever had a massive argument with a best friend?

Who would you turn to when you really got into deep trouble – family or friends?

Have you ever asked a friend to lie for you in order to help with a problem you have?

D

How much are you truly 'yourself' in front of your friends?

Have you ever become close friends with someone after half-knowing them for years?

Do you think it's possible to have a close friend of the opposite sex without there being any hint of romance?

8D | To be perfectly honest

for one thing	I mean	let's be honest
for another thing	to put it another way	to be honest
plus	after all	to be perfectly honest
as well as that	at least	admittedly
as a rule	anyway	still
on balance	actually	all the same
generally speaking	in fact	even so
ultimately	in actual fact	mind you
let's be honest	for one thing	I mean
to be honest	for another thing	to put it another way
to be perfectly honest	plus	after all
admittedly	as well as that	at least
still	as a rule	anyway
all the same	on balance	actually
even so	generally speaking	in fact
mind you	ultimately	in actual fact

9A | Three new cities

Research one of the following new cities. Use this worksheet to help you search and make notes.
(N.B. Not all these questions may be relevant for your city.)

Student A: Brasilia (in Brazil) **Student B:** Shenzhen (in China) **Student C:** Islamabad (in Pakistan)

City name ______

When was the city founded? ______

How long did it take to build? ______

Why was it built? ______

Why was it built in this location? ______

What was the basic shape, structure or design of the city? ______

Is the city distinctly different from others in the same country? ______

How? ______

What are some of the famous buildings, monuments and locations? ______

Is it generally a successful city? ______

What problems does the city have? ______

How is the city likely to change in the future? ______

Will any major new buildings be built in the future? ______

Is it a popular tourist location? Would you recommend people to visit? ______

What do you think is the most interesting museum? ______

How could the city be improved? ______

Other notes / anecdotes / personalities, etc. ______

9B | Home!

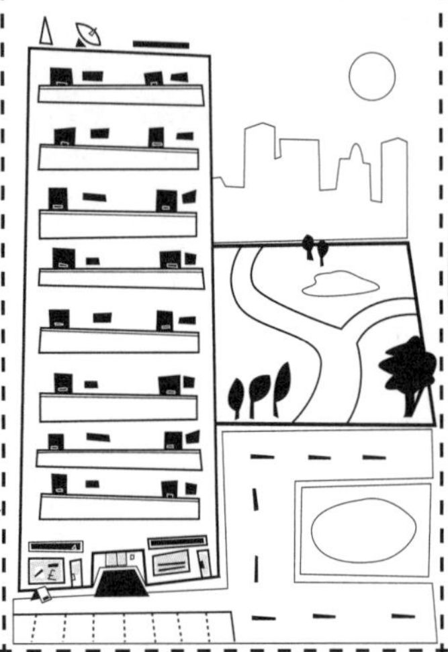

newly built	in a poor decorative state	high-rise
conveniently located	desirable	well-furnished
in a poor condition	would suit a DIY enthusiast	scruffy
thatched	cramped	semi-detached
in need of repair	gloomy	detached
cosy	brightly-lit	commands great views
run-down	poorly furnished	period
overgrown	derelict	in need of renovation
draughty	overlooking a park	rickety
tastefully decorated	has wonderful views	infested

9c | Jamaica farewell

Down the way	______________________	A
And the sun shines daily	______________________	B
I took a trip	______________________	C
And when I reached Jamaica	______________________	B
But I'm sad to say	______________________	A
Won't be back	______________________	A
My heart is down,	______________________	D
I had to leave a little girl	______________________	D (nearly!)
Down at the market	______________________	E
Ladies cry out while	______________________	F
'Akey' rice,	______________________	G
And the rum is fine	______________________	E
Sounds of laughter	______________________	F
And the dancing girls	______________________	H
I must declare	______________________	F
Though I've been	______________________	H

1 my head is turning around
2 you can hear
3 any time of year
4 I made a stop
5 salt fish are nice
6 for many a day
7 on a sailing ship
8 in Kingston town
9 on the mountain top
10 everywhere
11 from Maine to Mexico
12 I'm on my way
13 where the nights are gay
14 sway to and fro
15 my heart is there
16 on their heads they bear

9D | Experimental travel

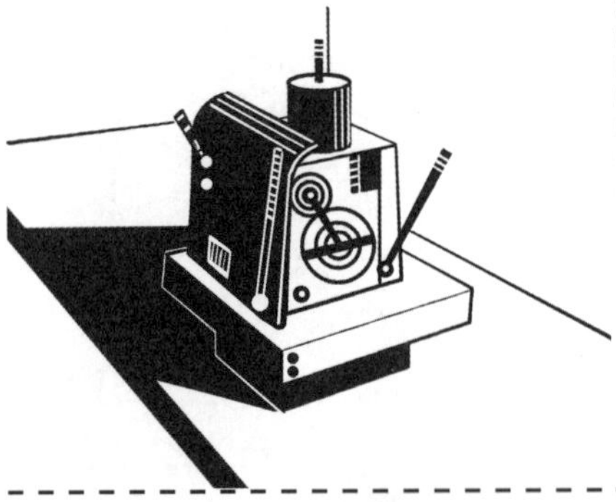

Noticing things

Have you seen that / those?
My goodness! What on earth is that / are they?
Oh, look over there!
What's that?
What are they?
I've never seen one of those before!

Vague language

I think it's a sort of …
It's probably used for … and stuff like that.
It's made from … and that sort of thing.
I don't really … things like that.
I think it's a … or something.
It's kind of …
… and so on.
I sort of feel …
Don't they do … and all that?

10A | Endurance event

Create a new headline-grabbing endurance event – something that will capture the imagination of the world and really test participants in a variety of ways.

DESIGN THE EVENT

Name your new event.

Where will it happen?

Will it happen at a particular time of year and/ or time of day?

Will participants take part as individuals or as teams?

What kind of people will take part? What sort of skills will they need?

Describe the event itself. What will participants do? What will be the difficulties? How long will it take? What will be the biggest physical and mental challenges participants will face?

FOLD

Now write a role card for a participant who has just successfully completed the endurance event.

Participant role card

You have just successfully completed the

________________________________ event.

You found the event extremely …

Your biggest problems were …

The moment when you felt happiest was when …

You almost gave up when …

Two unexpected and surprising incidents happened to you during the event. This is a description of what happened and your response to these incidents.

It's all over now! You feel …

The first thing you are going to do now is …

10B It's not this! It's that!

1 Find possible words from the box to fill the gaps in these sentences.

A

1 No – not the Sales Department.
2 Mika's collecting the reports.
3 It says on the box that it's indestructible.
4 I'm ________ about my chances in the election.
5 The original plan was ________ get just two.
6 How stupid I am! Why did I turn the computer on?
7 They're on the ________ of deciding to sell all their shares.
8 Wasn't the package ________ to arrive by 9am?
9 Six fifteen? No!
10 Kenneth ________ they'll be late for the deadline.
11 I'm ________ to arrive there next Thursday.
12 Everyone has agreed to the new measures.

B

a) But I think you're ________ to lose in a big way.
b) Right now, she's thinking of buying a whole set.
c) The meeting's to start on the hour.
d) But I'm only leaving here on Friday.
e) Ah no – it says here 'before midday'.
f) Could you bring along the files?
g) Now, what ________ you?
h) But surely now's the ________ to buy more.
i) The Director is due to visit Marketing.
j) I wanted to listen to the radio news.
k) It's ________ to break.
l) I'm sure they ________.

due	won't	supposed	to point	bound	believes	about	hopeful	time	about

2 Match each A with a continuation from B. (If you have problems, see if changing any of the gapped words helps.)

3 Decide where the contrastive stresses are. Then practise saying the comments with your partner, using contrastive stress.

10c | Television quiz

Places

1 where many TV programmes are filmed
2 where the actors put on their costumes

People

3 the person who introduces the news programme (US)
4 the actors who play characters in the crowd and rarely speak
5 the most important actor in a TV film

Programmes

6 a funny series of programmes, usually involving the same characters and locations
7 a factual programme
8 reports about an event, broadcast as it happens
9 an announcement about something that's just happened (or is still happening)
10 recordings of mistakes made by actors and other well-known figures
11 a TV story about many people that usually lasts for years
12 an exciting ending to a TV episode (to encourage you to watch next week)
13 a new series that is based on an earlier successful series
14 TV programmes that cost money to watch (e.g. a major football match)
15 an unscripted programme in which people are filmed as they live or try to do things

The schedule

16 a magazine where you can find out what is on TV
17 the time in the evening when most people watch TV
18 an on-screen listing of what is on TV
19 a time (9.00pm in the UK) after which programmes unsuitable for children can be shown

Watching TV

20 a small hand-held device that lets you change channels
21 when you keep changing TV channels
22 a lazy person who watches TV for hours every day
23 a colloquial name for a TV (UK)

The TV business

24 when different TV companies compete to win the biggest audience
25 when companies advertise by having their items visible in the programme itself
26 the way that BBC TV is funded in the UK

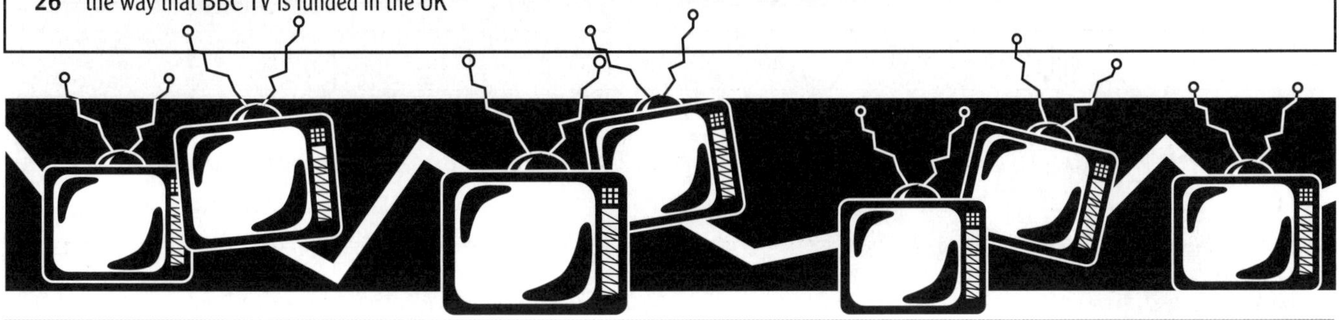

10D | Getting to the top

⚀

a) I hope I'll achieve my ________ of winning the race.
b) This is terrible. I'm making a real ________ of this report.
c) I think I stand a reasonable ________ of getting a promotion.
d) I don't think I'll even ________ it into the B team.

⚁

a) Oh no! All my brilliant plans have ________ through!
b) I think I'm drawing a complete ________ with this question.
c) I think I'm going to be an ________ success!
d) Wow! People think I'm a real ________-flier

⚂

a) I think I have a bright future ________ of me.
b) I'm ________ very well, thank you!
c) Oh no! All my hard work ________ to nothing.
d) Oh no! I've lost all my money. I'm completely ________.

⚃

a) All my hard work is beginning to ________ off.
b) It started badly but it ________ out well in the end.
c) I know I can ________ it to the top.
d) I thought I could win – but it's a ________ cause.

⚄

a) Look at me. I can't even ________ it to the next level.
b) Doing this night class might help ________ my career.
c) I get an enormous sense of ________ from doing this job.
d) Help. I'm making a complete ________ of this meal.

⚅

a) My new recording only sold twelve copies. A complete ________.
b) This task is so disorganized. It's a total ________.
c) I'm really ________ with these new responsibilities.
d) I'm an all-round ________ at everything I do!

achievement ahead aim bankrupt blank
came chance doing fallen flop further
high goal lost make mess overnight pay
shambles success thriving turned

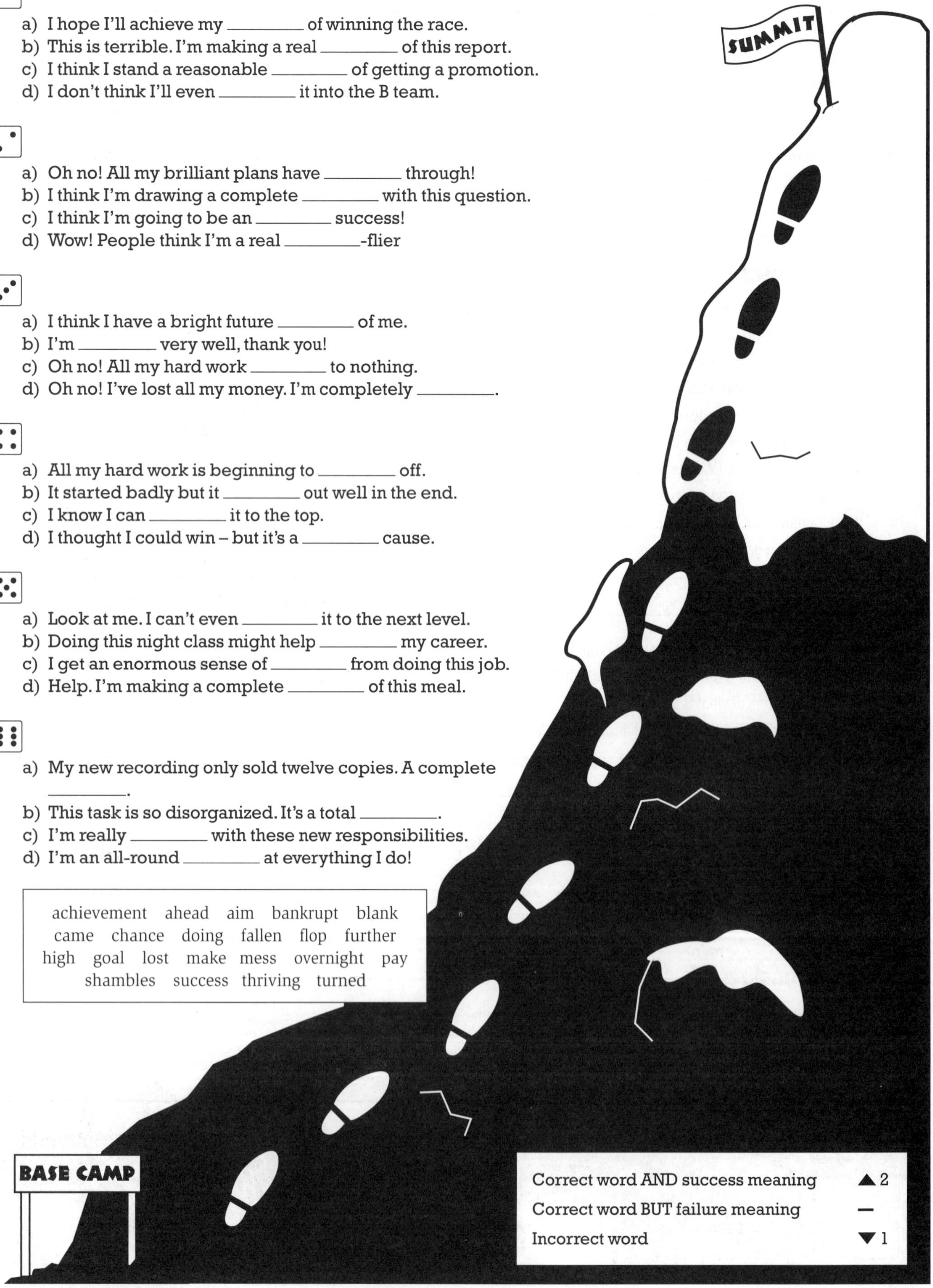

Correct word AND success meaning	▲2
Correct word BUT failure meaning	—
Incorrect word	▼1

11A | Instant poem

______________________ (Write how you moved or travelled, e.g. *walked hurriedly, wandered slowly, flew like a bird.*)

______________________ (Say where you went, e.g. *down by the river, into class.*)

______________________ (Use the gerund form of a verb of seeing, e.g. *glancing at, noticing, gazing at.*)

______________________ (Describe what you saw. Include at least one adjective and noun, e.g. *scraps of old newspaper, some smartly-dressed teenagers.*)

______________________ (Use a gerund form to say more about what you saw, e.g. *floating on the water, arguing loudly.*)

______________________ (Use a comparison to say what this looked or sounded like, e.g. *It looked like the sky at night. Their voices echoed like an explosion.*)

______________________ (Say what you thought or how this made you feel, e.g. *This made me think of my home town. I felt happy.*)

______________________ (Choose your own closing line.)

(Now go back and give your poem a name.)

Here is an example of a poem following this structure.

At the zoo

I wandered around the boating pool at the park
Noticing
the young children
Queuing by the ice cream stall.
They sounded like small birds fighting for food.
Suddenly I thought of my own children far away.
I ran to a bench and searched eagerly for my phone.

11B | Search & replace

A

As I was on a break from work for a few days, I was looking forward to catching up on my reading in an unhurried way. But first, I went to my local supermarket to see if they had any packets of my favourite fruit drink in the shop. They didn't seem to be visible so I found an assistant. He said he was actually not still in his work time but he could still help me. He told me that the drink was not in the store at the moment. I became quite angry, which was not normal behaviour for me. I apologized – I mean it wasn't as if my life was threatened! In fact I did find one packet later – it was somewhere where it was not visible on the wrong shelf – but it was too old.

in practice in tears off duty in person at fault
on trial on leave at my leisure in stock
out of date on display out of character
at stake on loan out of stock in ruins
in custody out of sight out of breath off limits

B

I ran down the corridor until I was not able to run any more. The thief was so far away that he was not visible. How had he got in? The office was officially 'no entry' to all visitors – though, of course, the reality was that people still wandered in. I had lost my laptop and was almost crying. All my work for the project was completely destroyed. And what was worse, the machine was only being borrowed from the boss. I knew that I would have to explain to her directly myself. In retrospect, I could see that it was me who made the mistake. Though at that moment the only thing I wanted to see was the thief being held by the police or prosecuted in a court!

in practice in tears off duty in person at fault
on trial on leave at my leisure in stock
out of date on display out of character
at stake on loan out of stock in ruins in custody
out of sight out of breath off limits

Answers

A

As I was **on leave** for a few days, I was looking forward to catching up on my reading **at my leisure**. But first, I went to my local supermarket to see if they had any packets of my favourite fruit drink **in stock**. They didn't seem to be **on display** so I found an assistant. He said that he was actually **off duty** but could still help me. He told me that the drink was **out of stock**. I became quite angry, which was **out of character**. I apologized – I mean it wasn't as if my life was **at stake**. In fact I did find one packet later – it was **out of sight** on the wrong shelf – but it was **out of date**.

B

I ran down the corridor until I was **out of breath.** The thief was **out of sight**. How had he got in? The office was officially **off limits** to all visitors – though, of course, **in practice** people still wandered in. I had lost my laptop and was almost **in tears**. All my work for the project was **in ruins**. And what was worse, the machine was only **on loan** from the boss. I knew that I would have to explain to her **in person**. In retrospect I could see that it was me who was **at fault**. Though at that moment the only thing I wanted to see was the thief **in custody** or **on trial**!

11c | Sounds peculiar

shatter	buzz	click	chime	ring
rumble	clatter	creak	beep	screech
mutter	whisper	whistle	sizzle	hum
pop	clink	bleep	rustle	bang

11D | Counselling

You are ... | You are counselling ... | You are ... | You are counselling ... | You are ... | You are counselling ...

START

an honest politician

a bored shop assistant

a tired teacher

a celebrity that the public has got bored with

a time traveller from the future who has got trapped in our time

a dishonest politician

a Formula 1 driver who is starting to feel nervous about driving

an office manager who all the staff think is rude and unhelpful

a reality-show contestant who wants to make money after the series finishes

an ant who hates being just one of the crowd

an artist who has run out of inspiration

an exhausted mother of a one-year-old baby

a robot who desperately wants to be human

Supposing   Assuming   Imagine that   Suppose   If ... were to
I'd sooner   I wish   If only   I hope   I'd rather

12A | Octopuses or octopi?

Singulars and plurals quiz

Part one

Are these underlined words correct or not? Choose A, B or C for each question.

A This is correct.
B This is incorrect and sounds wrong to most users of English.
C This is incorrect but is commonly misused in this way and is considered an acceptable error.

Questions	Answers
1 The university college has two main campuses.	**1** ______
2 There are three important criterias to bear in mind when choosing the next Director.	**2** ______
3 Don't lose it! The data in this file is very important.	**3** ______
4 There were three small octopuses in the pool.	**4** ______
5 Staying on an old farm was great but unfortunately I had to look after the geese.	**5** ______
6 Could you bring in the fresh loafs of bread from the larder?	**6** ______
7 The most effective media for local advertising is radio.	**7** ______
8 I need to get two new computer mouses for our office PCs.	**8** ______
9 I thought the dwarves were brilliant in *The Lord of the Rings*.	**9** ______
10 This is an amazing phenomena and we are privileged to witness it.	**10** ______

Part two

What is the singular of these words?

Questions	Answers
11 shelves	**11** ______
12 nuclei	**12** ______
13 appendices	**13** ______
14 formulae	**14** ______
15 diplomas	**15** ______
16 errata	**16** ______
17 analyses	**17** ______
18 moose	**18** ______
19 brethren	**19** ______
20 indices	**20** ______

REVIEW

Write a review of the new invention using this structure.

Paragraph 1: Facts about the product
Paragraph 2: What happened when you tested it
Paragraph 3: What you think about it and your recommendations

Try to cover some of the following areas. Make sure you include both facts and opinions.

- What is the name of the invention?
- How much does it cost?
- How widely available is it?
- What does it aim to do?
- Did it do that when you tested it?
- What happened when you tested it?
- Who is it suitable for?
- How easy is it to use?
- Would the ordinary man or woman in the street have problems using it?
- How long did it take to set up?
- Does it serve a useful purpose?
- Do you think it is well-made?
- What are the most impressive things about it?
- What doesn't seem so good?
- Are there any serious design flaws?
- Is there anything actually dangerous about it?
- Is it good value?
- Would you recommend it?
- Do you want one yourself?

Budget personal flying saucer

Three-dimensional printer

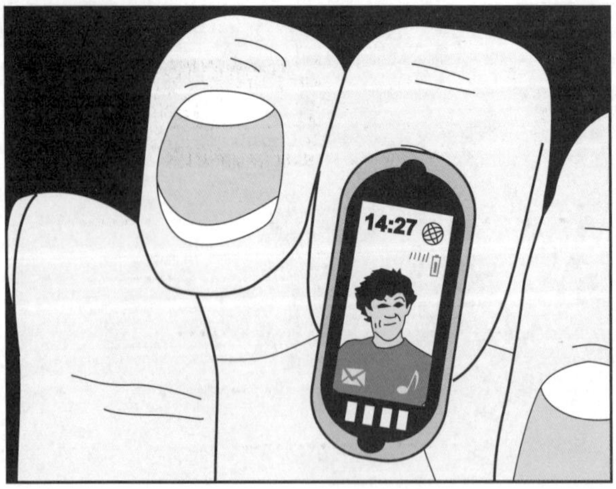

Fingernail mobile internet

Whole-house fully-independent robot cleaner and tidier

12c What a beautiful dress!

Dialogue one

Good morning, Jack!	ENTHUSIASM
Hello.	INDIFFERENCE
You played really well in the football game last night.	ADMIRATION
And so did you. That own goal was brilliant.	SARCASM
That's very unkind. I did my best.	IRRITATION
Sorry – I didn't mean it. It wasn't your fault.	REASSURANCE

Dialogue two

What a beautiful dress!	
Why are you flattering me? Do you want something?	
Well, no. I was just being friendly!	
Come on. Let's go to the clubroom.	
But I think Harry might be there. I really don't want to meet him today.	
No problem. I saw him leave an hour ago.	
Really? Who was he with?	

Dialogue three

	CURIOSITY
	REASSURANCE
	SARCASM
	WORRY
	SURPRISE
	ENTHUSIASM

Dialogue four

12D | These foolish things

1 You're going to hear a song in which a man remembers a woman who used to be very important to him.

a) Which of these things do you think are most likely to remind him of her and their relationship?

b) Think of a reason why each one might carry a memory, e.g. plane ticket because they flew to Paris for a holiday.

2 Listen and number the pictures in the order you hear them.

3 What other things are mentioned that 'remind me of you'?

4 This course is coming to an end. What will remind you of your studies? Look around the room at the other students and your teacher. For each person choose some positive things that you are most likely to remember about them.

These foolish things

Oh, will you never let me be?
Oh, will you never set me free?
The ties that bound us are still around us
There's no escape that I can see
And still those little things remain
That bring me happiness or pain
A cigarette that bears a lipstick's traces
An airline ticket to romantic places
And still my heart has wings
These foolish things
Remind me of you

A tinkling piano in the next apartment
Those stumbling words that told you what my heart meant
A fairground's painted swings
These foolish things
Remind me of you

You came, you saw, you conquered me
When you did that to me, I somehow knew that this had to be
The winds of March that make my heart a dancer
A telephone that rings, but who's to answer?
Oh, how the ghost of you clings
These foolish things
Remind me of you

Gardenia perfume lingering on a pillow
Wild strawberries only seven francs a kilo
And still my heart has wings
These foolish things
Remind me of you

The sigh of midnight trains in empty stations
Silk stockings thrown aside, dance invitations
Oh, how the ghost of you clings
These foolish things
Remind me of you

The smile of Garbo and the scent of roses
The waiters whistling as the last bar closes
The song that Crosby sings
These foolish things
Remind me of you

How strange, how sweet to find you still
These things are dear to me
That seem to bring you so near to me
The scent of smouldering leaves, the wail of steamers
Two lovers on the street who walk like dreamers
Oh, how the ghost of you clings
These foolish things
Remind me of you, just you